St. Pauls Cathedrall

Pauls Wharfe

1700

Scenes from London Life

Maureen Waller

Hodder & Stoughton

For my parents,
Margaret Mary and John Gamble Waller,
with love and gratitude

Copyright © 2000 by Maureen Waller
First published in Great Britain in 2000 by Hodder and Stoughton
A division of Hodder Headline

The right of Maureen Waller to be identified as the Author of the Work
has been asserted by her in accordance with the Copyright, Designs
and Patents Act 1988.

10 9 8 7 6 5 4 3 2

British Library Cataloguing in Publication Data.
A CIP catalogue record for this title is available from
the British Library

ISBN 0 340 73966 5

Printed and bound in Great Britain by
Mackays of Chatham PLC, Chatham, Kent

Hodder and Stoughton
A division of Hodder Headline
338 Euston Road
London NW1 3BH

Acknowledgements

I SHOULD LIKE TO thank my good friend Tim Hely Hutchinson, who has shown interest in this project from the start. I owe a debt of gratitude to my editor, Roland Philipps, for his belief in me and for giving me this opportunity to publish my first book. He has been kind and supportive throughout. I am grateful to the other members of the Hodder & Stoughton team for their enthusiasm and professionalism.

My thanks are due to my agent, Maggie Pearlstine, and to Matthew Bayliss and Toby Green, who have all been unstinting in their efforts on my behalf. I am grateful to Professor Lisa Jardine for steering me towards London in the eighteenth century. Thanks also to my friend Jane Ashelford for lending me her expertise on the dress of the period and on the picture research. As ever, she made it fun. Thanks to Jerome Boyd-Maunsell for his assiduous research at a couple of crucial moments.

This book would not have been possible without the help of the staff and superb collections in the London Library, Guildhall Library, the British Library and its Newspaper Library at Colindale, Senate House Library in the University of London, the Greater London Record Office at Clerkenwell and Lambeth Palace Library. Special thanks go to Mr Jeremy Smith and Mr John Fisher in the Prints and Maps Section at Guildhall Library. Mr Ian Murray at the Worshipful Company of Barbers kindly showed me their account books for the period, and Mr S. W. Massil at the Huguenot Society Library at University College London was most helpful in providing me with material.

I am most grateful to Dr Thomas Stuttaford for his advice on disease, and to my father, Dr John Waller, for his lengthy explanations of the same. Any howlers there are my own. I wish to thank Barry Turner and Tony Rennell for giving their valuable time to read the script and for their helpful comments and criticism.

Above all, I owe an enormous debt of gratitude to Brian MacArthur for his endless patience, encouragement, good humour, emotional and practical support, and advice on how to write. He has listened to hours of what Daniel Defoe thought, and what Londoners before us said and did. It may now be possible for him to venture out with me without being treated to a description of the contents of the Fleet Ditch or the whereabouts of plague pits on an innocent expedition to dinner.

Contents

A New Mapp of the CITTY of LONDON much Inlarged since the Great Fire in which hath been Added since aney other Mapps of LONDON before this hath been Publ[...]

THE RIVER

St Georges Fielde

A Scale of half A Mile

Printed & Sold By Henry Overton at the white Horse without Newgate London

Foreword

'... the chiefest emporium, or town of trade in the world; the largest and most populous, the fairest and most opulent city at this day in all Europe, perhaps the whole world'

LONDON IN 1700 WAS the most magnificent city in Europe. It took its beauty from Wren's skyline of churches, especially as viewed from the river. Dominating the city, the new St Paul's rested on its hilltop nearing completion. Only the dome was outstanding, prompting the wag Ned Ward's analogy, 'As slow as a Paul's workman with a bucket of mortar'. The River Thames was the artery of the metropolis, the wide thoroughfare dotted with thousands of pleasure craft and red and green passenger boats plying their trade. London Bridge with its density of houses and souvenir shops was the only bridge linking the north and south banks. And below it at the Port of London the ships lined up like a floating forest to unload their cargoes from the furthest corners of the world. Only a few miles away the hills of Hampstead and Highgate provided a reassuring rural backdrop to the thriving metropolis at their feet.

The capital dominated the kingdom to an extent that it has never done before or since. It was home to at least 530,000 people – one in nine of the entire population – while the second city, Norwich, had a population of 30,000. Not only did so many of William III's subjects live in London, but the city impinged on the lives of many more. It was a magnet to all classes. Aristocracy and gentry flocked to London to be seen at court, to attend parliament, to settle their legal affairs, to enjoy the season and arrange marriages for their children, and to shop. London was a shopper's paradise, a great emporium of goods for its hungry consumers. The booming newspaper industry in Grub Street found a ready market in London's coffee-houses where everything was up for discussion. London was the centre of a lively publishing trade, the

1

The Thames was London's main highway, dotted with thousands of passenger boats and pleasure craft. Below London Bridge ships queued up like a floating forest to unload their cargoes (*Guildhall Library, Corporation of London*)

theatre and music. Visitors absorbed its ideas and culture and disseminated them to all parts of the kingdom.

But this great city could not sustain itself. The mortality rate was higher than it had been a century previously. In any year there were more burials than christenings. One in three babies died before the age of two. Only one in two of the survivors passed the age of fifteen. Adults in their twenties and thirties, often family breadwinners, were particularly vulnerable. The streets were open sewers, the drinking water was contaminated, the stink of decaying refuse and overflowing graveyards was pervasive, houses did not have the conveniences of running water or flush lavatories – and anyway, there was no understanding of basic hygiene. The atmosphere was thick with sulphurous coal smoke belching out of thousands of domestic and industrial fires, begriming the inhabitants and stultifying the gardens.

Tuberculosis was widespread and a particularly virulent strain of smallpox cut a swathe through the densely packed population. Medicine was largely helpless in the face of disease and a broken limb could be the harbinger of infection and death. It is not surprising, therefore, that native-born Londoners were chronically sick and of poor constitution, and the metropolis needed a constant influx of more robust migrants from the provinces. About 8,000 young people from all parts of the kingdom and as far away as Ireland poured in every year, attracted by the promise of wages 50 per cent higher than anywhere else.

The Great Fire of 1666 gave London its opportunity for expansion. It had already burst from the confines of the City's square mile – the area roughly encompassed by the Roman walls from Ludgate in the west to London Wall in the north to the Tower in the south and along the bank of the Thames as far as Blackfriars – to such outlying parishes as Bishopsgate Without and Aldgate to the north and east. To the east, the intermittent urban sprawl stretched along the routes of Ratcliffe Highway and Whitechapel out as far as Mile End. The squalid housing of the seamen and port workers lay in dank alleys along the river from Wapping to Rotherhithe.

On the south bank, Southwark, with its metal-working industry and breweries, lay close to open fields. Beyond the northern fringes of the City lay the open spaces of Moorfields, the Artillery Ground and the nonconformist burial ground at Bunhill Fields. To the north-west, Clerkenwell housed artisans employed in the clock-making industry, while further east from Spitalfields to Whitechapel hamlets of weavers' cottages were rapidly encroaching on the brick fields and becoming a massive conurbation. Across the fields north of the City lay Islington Spa with its cow pastures and the village of Hackney with its fine suburban villas.

To the west there were two main thoroughfares linking the City through a stream of continuous housing to Westminster. That to the north skirted Smithfield Market and stretched the length of Holborn, past the decaying tenements of St Giles to Tottenham Court and the Oxford Road. Open fields stretched north of the Oxford Road to the New Road, which linked the village of Marylebone in the west with St Pancras in the east. To the south of the Oxford Road lay Soho with its fashionable square and myriad busy streets, largely inhabited by Huguenot craftsmen and traders in luxury goods, running down as far as Leicester Fields. Between Holborn and the Strand lay the Bedford estate at Covent Garden with its gracious architecture and increasingly licentious reputation.

The more southerly route from the City stretched along Fleet Street into the Strand and on past Charles I's statue at Charing Cross down to Whitehall. The sprawling palace itself had been burned down in 1698 and now only the Banqueting House remained. After the Restoration, the presence of the court at Whitehall and St James provided the impetus for that snappy dresser Henry Jermyn, Earl of St Albans, to develop housing for the rich in St James's Square and its vicinity. At the north-east corner of St James, Pickadilly (named after the pickadillies, borders to ruffs and collars, sold by the original inhabitant of the site) ran into Portugal Street (named in honour of Charles II's queen) which continued towards Hyde Park.

The buildings largely petered out at the junction of St James's and Hyde Park and deer were free to roam between the two. Mayfair had yet to be developed and was still the site of a fair that had become so raunchy the authorities were about to close it down. Visitors to William and Mary's new palace in the village of Kensington could travel through Hyde Park along the Route du Roi – which became Rotten Row in popular parlance – unmolested by footpads because it was torchlit all the way. From Whitehall the road carried on in a westerly direction to Westminster Abbey and on to the site of the Horse Ferry – where a coach and horses could be transported across the river – and beyond into open fields where the milkmaids frolicked on May Day. The distant village of Chelsea with its Physick Garden and boarding schools for young ladies lay further west along the riverbank.

At no other time in the nation's history was such a high proportion of its trade, manufacturing and industry concentrated in the capital. Daniel Defoe likened London to the heart of the nation, pulling in goods from the provinces and the wider world, manufacturing them, and either consuming them or dispersing them. London's needs stimulated the growth of other towns. Ships plied the east coast from the Tyne to the Thames bearing coal from Newcastle – a tax on coal had financed the rebuilding of London after the fire. But other towns were poised to compete with the capital in specific areas of trade or manufacture as the eighteenth century got under way.

In her *Through England on a Side Saddle in the Time of William and Mary*, Celia Fiennes was complimentary about Liverpool, once 'a few fishermen's houses and now grown to a large fine town and but a parish and one church ... the streetes are faire and long, its London in miniature'. She was also impressed by Leeds, 'a large town, severall large streets cleane and well pitch'd and good houses all built of stone ... this is esteemed the wealthyest town of its bigness in the country, its manufacture is the woollen cloth the Yorkshire cloth in which they are all employ'd and are esteemed very rich and very proud'. By the time Daniel Defoe published *A Tour through the Whole Island of Great Britain* in 1724, he described Manchester as 'one of the greatest, if not really the greatest mere village in England' and acknowledged that the increase in

A bucolic scene in St James's Park - the haunt of milkmaids, deer and courtiers out for a pleasant stroll (*Guildhall Library, Corporation of London*)

population over the last thirty years had led to a manufacturing boom. Bristol, of course, was a potential rival to London in the Atlantic slave trade, which was on the brink of massive expansion. And over the border the pretty town of Glasgow on the Clyde would inherit the tobacco trade.

The Glorious Revolution of 1688, which saw the triumph of parliamentary government, was a watershed in England's history. Londoners had witnessed the key events of the turbulent seventeenth century. They had watched awestruck as the axe swung down on the neck of their anointed sovereign, Charles I, at his public execution outside the Banqueting House at Whitehall on a freezing day in January 1649. In May 1660 they had cheered the return of the merry monarch Charles II and his court from exile. In December 1688 the Catholic James II had slipped out of Whitehall Palace in disguise and taken ship for France, throwing the Great Seal into the Thames in a typical act of Stuart impetuosity. As it seemed he had left the throne vacant, James's elder daughter Mary and his Protestant nephew and son-in-law, William, Prince of Orange, were invited to take his place. In February 1689 they sat in the Banqueting House – where forty years before their grandfather Charles I had gone to his death to uphold the royal prerogatives – and by favour of both Houses of Parliament accepted the offer of joint crowns with conditions attached in the Declaration of Rights.

As William III and Mary II they reigned as the first constitutional monarchs. It was a price William was prepared to pay to harness England's wealth and manpower in his life-long struggle to curb the overweening power and territorial ambitions of Louis XIV of France. For the first time since Henry VIII's foray into France in the early sixteenth century, England was involved in a land war in Europe and would remain so intermittently all the way up to Waterloo. The reluctance of his new subjects to play a part in European affairs exasperated William, who despaired that 'people here are so little sensible of what goes on outside the island, although it behoves us to have as much interest and concern as the people on the Continent'.

William's war, which lasted from 1690 to 1697, when the two combatants paused in order to gather their strength before resuming in 1702, required vast, unprecedented sums of money on a scale that had never been imagined in previous wars. Clearly the war could not be financed out of the royal revenue, and existing taxes were onerous enough. Various expedients, such as national lotteries that tapped into the craze for gambling, were used to raise money. Fortuitously, the political stability and maturity inherent in the new constitutional regime meant that at last plans of the Scot William Paterson and prominent men in the City of London to establish a national bank could come to fruition. Whereas in the past the royal word of honour had proved unreliable when it came to monetary matters – as when Charles I had raided the Mint in 1640 and Charles II had put a Stop on the Exchequer in 1672, ruining some of London's top goldsmith-bankers – the new scheme meant that loans would be raised against the wealth of the nation and guaranteed by parliament.

In 1694 the first £1,200,000 was raised from the public within a fortnight to be lent to the government at 8 per cent interest on condition that the subscribers were incorporated as a joint stock company with the title 'Bank of England', although in practice it was considered a London bank. In the first instance, repayment of the loan

William III and Mary II were sworn in as constitutional monarchs in the Banqueting House, where their grandfather Charles I lost his head for upholding the divine right of kings (*Guildhall Library, Corporation of London*)

was secured by an 'Act for granting to their Majesties several rates and duties upon tunnage of ships and vessels, and upon beer, ale and other liquors'. A particular novelty was that there was no fixed time period in which the loan would be repaid while interest would be paid in perpetuity. This meant the creation of a permanent national debt, which stood as high as £12 million by 1700.

But while William came in for a great deal of criticism from the traditional landed interest for getting the nation head over heels in debt, the new borrowing arrangements financed a war that was really about the capture of empire – which would bring its own rewards. It was the desire to share those rewards that brought Scotland into the Union of 1707. Although the bank played a major role in extending credit facilities to big merchants so that the latent strengths of the economy could be exploited, it hardly impinged on the lives of ordinary people at this early stage. Comparisons in the value of money between then and now are meaningless, but it is noteworthy that the value of the lowest bank note was £10 at a time when a London shopkeeper earned about £45 a year and a housemaid £5 a year.

Against this backdrop of public events, this book holds up a mirror to catch a reflection of the daily life of Londoners at the turn of the century. Buoyant, ebullient, optimistic, audacious, violent, brutal, gutsy – they thrust themselves forward demanding to be heard. Their voices well up from letters and court documents, at first a series of muffled whispers, then an insistent clamour, as if for three centuries they have been waiting for an audience. And these personal revelations are buttressed by the commentaries of their contemporaries, not least by the author Daniel Defoe, born in the parish of St Giles, Cripplegate and an observer of the London scene all his life.

A note about the calendar:

In Edward Chamberlayne's edition of *Angliae Notitia, or the Present State of England* for the year 1700, he tells us: 'The year in England, according to the cycles of the sun and moon, and according to almanacks, begins on the first day of January; but the English state begins the year from the day of Christ's incarnation on the 25th of March.'

For the purposes of this book, I have adhered to the modern calendar.

CHAPTER ONE

Marriage

*Thousands of Londoners had no idea whether they were legally
married, nor even what might constitute a legal marriage*

THIRTY-FOUR YEARS after the Great Fire, the worshippers at St Paul's still gaze up at an open sky. Within a decade, Wren's completed dome will cast a shadow over the grim Fleet Prison, the ominous building where debtors count out their days. At the foot of Ludgate Hill lies the Fleet Ditch, wide enough for a coal barge to sail north to Holborn, if it can tackle the stinking sewage, discarded guts and offal, drowned puppies and dead cats sliding down its muddy channel towards the Thames. Passing the brawling concert of fishwives and stall-holders gathered around the Fleet Bridge, we come to a warren of alleyways known as the Rules of the Fleet. Here, forty marriage-houses do a busy trade.

Now and again, a clergyman's anxious face peers out through the grimy panes, cracked and warped, under a sign depicting a man's hand joined with a woman's advertising 'Marriages Perform'd Within'. Working as brothers in business, clergy and tavern keepers send out the 'plyers', urchins and street people, to tout for their strange trade. The women are particularly persistent, tugging and pulling at the sleeves of those who pass. 'Sir, will you be pleased to walk in and be married?'

What fairer request could there be? A couple eager to accede is invited with due courtesy to step inside. Perhaps they will be in the most famous marriage-house of all, the Hand and Pen by the Fleet Bridge. Ushered through the ubiquitous fug of beer fumes and pipe smoke, they are chaperoned by a blowsy landlady clutching a register through to a private room set up as a chapel to await the parson. It is late in the afternoon and darkness already permeates the smoky sky. A glance at the hands of the chapel clock, though, and each partner sees that they are stuck permanently at nine o'clock, for weddings are legal only if performed within the canonical hours of 8 a.m. to noon.

The couple waits patiently for the parson to appear. Perhaps this will be James Colton, deprived of his living by the Bishop of London for ill practices, but carrying out his illicit marriage trade with impunity. Or it could be Nehemiah Rogers, a Fleet prisoner who 'goes at large ... a very wicked man, as lives for drinking, whoring, swearing, he has struck and boxed ye bridegroom in ye chapple, and damned like any com'on souldier'.

Whoever the parson, he will come armed with fake certificates, properly carrying the royal arms, but lacking an official stamp, with blank spaces where the names should already have been written. The certificates are kindly supplied by Bartholomew Bassett, clerk to Robert Elborrow, elderly incumbent at the Fleet Prison's own chapel; indeed, for a small consideration Bassett will also enter the marriages in the Fleet register, so that they may be deemed thoroughly official.

Bassett's business acumen is hardly out of place. The Fleet, after all, is a commercial concern, and ideally placed to take advantage of that handy piece of legislation of 1694–6 which taxed marriages at a specific rate, imposing a stamp duty on every licence and certificate issued. In the last few years, the Fleet has gained the lion's share of the clandestine marriage trade, undermining the competition which traditionally claimed exemption from ecclesiastical jurisdiction: the so-called 'peculiars', the churches of St James' Duke's Place, St Pancras and Holy Trinity Minories. Bassett is raking in well over £200 a year at the Fleet, subletting the prison cellar to unbeneficed clergymen to perform marriages without banns or licence, unfazed by the 1696 Act which imposed a £100 fine for such an offence. Since some of these clergymen are confined to the Fleet for debt anyway, they have nothing to lose. Certainly, Bassett is happy to supply them with whatever they require.

Clandestine marriages flout the basic requirements of the Church of England as laid down in the canons of 1604. These assert that a marriage must be performed publicly in the parish of one of the parties, after due publicity has been given to it by the reading of banns on three successive Sundays. Alternatively the couple can procure a licence from a reputable ecclesiastical authority bearing a fully paid government stamp. Yet for all its shadiness, clandestine marriage is the preferred option of thousands of Londoners. In this year of 1700, 2,251 marriages – perhaps a third of all marriages – will be celebrated in the sordid surroundings of the Fleet. The eager participants pour in from the populous and impoverished outlying parishes of Stepney, Whitechapel, Cripplegate Without, Aldgate and St

Giles-in-the-Fields. A few even arrive from as far afield as Hertfordshire and Essex. Some of these spouses-to-be will describe themselves as gentlemen, professional and clerical people; but the vast majority are craftsmen, labourers, coachmen, boatmen, tradesmen, innkeepers and itinerants, attracted by the Fleet's promise of marriage on the cheap.

Some harbour darker motives. An uncle wishes to wed his niece, so he goes to the Fleet; a woman has succumbed to the charms of her brother-in-law, so they go to the Fleet. They are joined by servants and apprentices, forbidden to marry by the terms of their employment; by widows unwilling to surrender their jointure or trading privileges on remarriage; by defiant or desperate couples judged by parish authorities to be too poor to marry; and by sailors disembarking at the port of London for a hasty marriage – or marriages. In fact, almost every walk of life comes to rub shoulders at the Fleet, to partake in the growing business of clandestine marriage.

Once the parson appears, some minutes are spent haggling over his fee, before the coins are placed on the open prayer book: 2s 6d is the norm, out of which the parson will tip the plyer 6d and pay the landlord a small fee for the use of the room. A certificate and register entry will bump the cost up to 7s 6d. This is a week's wages for a working man, but at a third of the cost of a regular marriage is still deemed to be good value. The landlord's apparent generosity in the room-hire is disingenuous. He stands to profit from the rowdy celebration of drinking and dancing that follows, the sale of bride cakes at 6d each, and from the charge of a shilling or so for the hire of a bed for those unable to delay consummating their union.

Since clergy and tavern-keepers have such a thriving business here, some are even going into partnership, with the parson on the payroll at £20–£30 a year and the landlord pocketing the fees extracted from the bridegroom. Sometimes the bridal party fails to reach agreement on the price, an argument ensues and blows are struck. Some unfortunate couples underestimate the cost and have to leave unmarried. Mostly a compromise is reached. The wedding ring may be pawned to clinch the bargain, or perhaps the couple will forgo the certificate and leave 'half-married'. Cheapness is as much an imperative as speed and secrecy in a Fleet marriage: 'without loss of time, hindrance of business, and the knowledge of friends'.

With drink on his breath, his shabbiness emphasised by a soiled surplice, and the Book of Common Prayer in hand, the parson skips through an abridged version of the marriage service. The canons demand it in full, but this is no time to be a jobsworth. The formalities dispensed with, he makes a note of the details in his pocket book, later to be transcribed into a register; unless, of course, he is being paid to keep the marriage a secret and the surnames out of the register. Entries may be inserted or removed by the unscrupulous, or totally falsified so that a marriage may be pre-dated and a pregnancy legitimised. There are many omissions from the register, and the parson's pocket book is highly revelatory: 'N.B. they had liv'd together four years as man and wife; they were so vile as to ask for a certifycate antidated' and, 'N.B. the woman was big with child, and they wanted a certifycate antidated; and because it was not comply'd with, they were abusive with a witness.'

Tampering with entries in the registers for births, marriages and deaths is an offence carrying a £100 penalty under an Act of 1689, but it is carried on with impunity, especially by the obliging Bassett who 'antidates as he pleases'. Under a pretext of legality, the marriage-house also keeps a register, which is open to even greater abuse. Such registers have no legal status but can do a powerful amount of damage. One such landlady 'offered … a marriage certifycate for a young woman that happened to be with child, and was hunted by the parish offices, and she said, for half-a-guinea it might be enter'd backwards in the book, and would skreen her from the anger of her friends'. Anybody, so it seems, may have a certificate at her house for half-a-crown, and have their names entered in her book, for as long time past as they please. Should a clandestine marriage founder, the lack of reliable evidence and the eagerness of witnesses to perjure themselves for a few pence will prove a headache for the courts.

In 1700 the laws and customs relating to marriage were so chaotic and contradictory that thousands of Londoners had no idea whether they were legally married, nor even what might constitute a legal marriage. There was a hazy notion that vows taken before witnesses, such as 'I, John, do take thee, Hannah, to be my wife' followed by consummation, meant that the couple was 'married in the eyes of God'. For many this, together with the acceptance and approval of their neighbours, was more than enough. In ecclesiastical law these 'spousals' were regarded as binding and irrevocable. The common law, however, conferred property rights only on those who had gone through a public ceremony. In practice, this meant a husband could not claim any of his wife's property, she could not claim her rights as a widow, nor could the children of the union claim inheritance as legal heirs.

To complicate matters further, since canon law and common law were not marching in step, a ruling made in a common law court could be overturned in the ecclesiastical court of appeal. To the general public, this was an incomprehensible legal quibble – and of little concern to those who had no property. A conditional promise made *'per verba in futuro'* to the effect that 'I, Hannah, will marry thee, John, if my father gives his consent' was not a binding contract, unless the words were followed by immediate consummation, which was taken to mean consent in the present.

For most ordinary people, what was significant was the giving of tokens to their intended, especially a ring or a coin split in two, the acceptance of which was popularly believed to imply a formal contract. 'We're contracted,' exclaims one of Farquhar's characters in *The Inconstant.* 'Contracted! Alack a day, poor thing. What, you have changed rings or broken an old broad piece between you!' But the Church did not recognise such gifts as relevant and a verbal contract without witnesses was unlikely to be upheld, as one disappointed young man discovered after his beloved had married someone else:

> the said Stephen told how the said Mary Russell, that she was the first woman he had ever courted, that he had settled his affections upon her, and hoped she would not deceive him, to which she answered that she would not deceive him or to that effect; then the said Stephen Wilson put a ring upon the said Mary Russels finger … said I give you this ring as a contract of marriage between ye and me, and that you'l have no other man, to which the said Mary Russel replied I promise to marry you Mr Wilson and no other man.

Some of the confusion could be traced back to the Middle Ages. A church wedding for the performance of the sacrament of marriage was a fifteenth-century innovation. At the Reformation marriage ceased to be a sacrament, although it remained a spiritual act and therefore indissoluble. It was generally assumed that the presence of a priest made a marriage official. The Anglican Church had neglected to update the old medieval marriage laws in England when Catholic Europe had done

14

These scenes of married life perfectly illustrate the costume of the period, although the warring couple seem to have torn off each other's head-dress and wig

(Witt Library, Courtauld Institute, London)

so at the Council of Trent in 1563. The Republic had confused the issue in the 1650s by introducing the concept of civil marriage, so making the Church's involvement seem dispensable in the popular mind. The Restoration had swiftly ended that experiment and the Anglican Church had regained its ascendancy, but this left the vast body of nonconformists to make their own arrangements. They married in their own chapels or meeting-houses. The marriage legislation of 1694–6 added a new dimension. For the first time the state had a vested interest in the formal performance of marriage because of the taxes it accrued from it. Resentment at state interference and a natural inclination to defy authority and beat the system, especially in the avoidance of the standard 5s tax on licences and certificates, encouraged an increasing number of Londoners to marry behind the state's back, in the vicinity of the Fleet.

Despite the state's official disapproval, a clandestine marriage was still regarded by the Church as valid and indissoluble as long as it fulfilled certain basic requirements. The couple must not be too closely related through blood or marriage. The male must be over the age of fourteen, the female over twelve, and both had to be over twenty-one if the consent of a parent or guardian was not forthcoming. Given the ease with which clandestine marriage was carried out and the dubious nature of the paperwork, the whole system was inevitably open to abuse. It was common for a woman seeking to legitimise her bastard child and avoid the shame of a public whipping to make a hasty marriage to a stranger at the Fleet. Wife-swapping certainly took place, some of it quite brazen:

> On Tuesday last two persons, one of Skinner Street, and the other of Webb's Square, Spittle Fields, exchang'd wives, to whom they had been married upwards of twelve years; and the same day, to the content of all parties, the marriages were consummated at the Fleet. Each husband gave his wife away to the other, and in the evening had an entertainment together.

One clergyman confided in his pocket book his suspicion that a couple he had just married had both been women – and indeed there is evidence of such unions. A foreign visitor to London, César de Saussure, noted in amazement another form of abuse:

> A woman when she marries is freed from her debts. And in order to

benefit by this law cases have been known of women up to their ears in debt, and on the point of being thrown into prison, going to the Fleet, and there finding some bachelor prisoner who, in return, for a payment of three guineas or so, will agree to marry her, that is to say, to go through a marriage ceremony. A priest is called, who marries the couple forthwith, neither licence nor publication of banns being necessary for a marriage in the Fleet. A bottle of beer or wine is drunk, the priest gives a marriage certificate, and the newly married bride departs and never sees her husband again. When the creditors come to be paid, she produces her marriage certificate, and she cannot be arrested, having a husband; neither can they make him responsible for his wife's debt, he being a prisoner already. This extraordinary abuse is permitted by the laws.

Many still believed that if a woman married in her shift her husband could not incur her debts; sadly, this did not stand up in law. The law courts were full of suits involving clandestine marriages, but the secrecy of the proceedings made it difficult to prove a clandestine marriage had taken place if it ran into trouble and one of the partners was trying to repudiate it. Bigamy posed a particular problem. 'Hence, too, happen polygamies, easily conceal'd, and too much practised,' wrote the Frenchman Henri Misson, a keen observer of English customs. The law eventually caught up with one such offender and dealt with her severely:

Mary Stokes, alias Edwards, was tried for marrying two husbands; the first named Thomas Adams, to whom she was married on the 15th of July, five years ago at St James' Dukes Place, the second was one Sebastian Judges, to whom she was married 5th of November last, at the same place; The evidence to prove both the marriages, swore it plainly against her, that she had married one William Brown besides, and that she stay'd with Judges but one night, and ran away in the morning; and she stayed 8 days with Adams; afterwards she was married to one William Carter, which made 4 in all; after that she was taken at the Red-Lyon in Bishopsgate Street; She said that she was advised that she might safely marry another husband, having been convicted before for marrying two husbands about half a year ago. Upon the whole it appeared, that she was an idle kind of a slut, for she would get what money she could of them, and then run away from them; she was found guilty of felony.

Mary Stokes was condemned to death.

But despite the complications and pitfalls, clandestine marriage remained immensely popular. One of its more sinister sides was that it provided a golden opportunity for the enticement or abduction of heiresses. 'Hence comes the matches between footmen and young ladies of quality, who you may be sure live no very easy life together afterward,' Misson comments. Drink and drugs were useful tools in a kidnapping, and several young heiresses and wealthy widows woke up to find themselves in bed with some stranger, having been subjected to a forced marriage and raped while unconscious.

Daniel Defoe deplored 'the arts and tricks made use of to trepan and as it were kidnap young women away into the hands of brutes and sharpers [which] were very scandalous, and it became almost dangerous for any one to leave a fortune to the disposal of the person that was to enjoy it and when it was so left, the young lady went always in danger of her life'. Although young women in London were given an extraordinary amount of freedom to go out and about in the town, an heiress, he wrote, 'was watched, laid wait for and as it were besieged by a continual gang of rogues, cheats, gamesters and such like starving crew, so that she was obliged to confine herself like a prisoner to her chamber'. If she ventured outside, she might be 'snatched up, seized, hurried up into a coach and six; a fellow dressed up in a clergyman's habit performing the ceremony and a pistol clapt to her breast to make her consent to be marry'd'.

One such unlucky heiress, worth £200 a year and £600 ready cash, was 'decoyed away from her friends ... and married at the Fleet chapel against her consent'. The search was on for the perpetrators 'who have used the young lady so barbarously, that she now lyes speechless'. As long as Bassett and his friends were in business, such marriages could be accomplished. It was only the 1753 Marriage Act that finally put an end to their devious work.

Even within what might be seen as 'regular marriage', people often tried to get around the law. All classes of society resented the reading of banns prior to a wedding, seeing this as an unwarranted interference in their private business. 'To proclaim banns is a thing nobody now cares to have done; very few are willing to have their affairs declar'd to all the world in a public place, when for a guinea they may do it snug, and without noise,' wrote Misson, 'and my good friends the clergy ... are not very zealous to prevent it. Thus, then, they buy what they call a licence, and are marry'd in their closets, in the presence of a couple of friends, that serve for witnesses; and this ties them for ever.'

An increasing number of Londoners felt uncomfortable at the public nature of a wedding by banns. These weddings had to take place in the full glare of publicity during divine service, between the hours of 8 a.m. and noon on a Sunday, this being the day when the whole population was supposed to attend church. It was often public knowledge that the bride or groom had enjoyed sex – 'bundling', or heavy petting, being a widespread custom – with more than one partner before marriage. Such couples wanted to avoid the nudges and guffaws of those in the congregation who knew of past indiscretions. Those entering into a blatantly mercenary match might have wished to avoid the embarrassment of public comment.

Parish fees were posted on tables displayed in the churches, and those for marriage were to be laid on the prayer book with the ring during the ceremony. A licence, which required a sworn statement from parties under twenty-one that they had the consent of parents or guardians, was considerably more expensive. In the Archdiocese of Canterbury, into which many of the London parishes fell, it cost 10s for a licence to marry without banns outside one's parish of residence, and 20s to do so outside the canonical hours. Dean Humphrey Prideaux deplored the venality of the diocesan administrators who encouraged the practice of ignoring the canons in order to extract fees from the sale of licences. However, it suited the new fashion for 'persons of quality, and many others who imitate them ... of being marry'd very late at night in their chamber'.

Of course, as Misson observed, there were some who enjoyed the ostentation of a big public wedding:

> When those of a middling condition have a mind to be so extravagant as to marry in publick (which very rarely happens) they invite a number of friends and relations; everyone puts on new cloaths, and dresses finer than ordinary; the men lead the women, they get into coaches, and so go in procession, and are marry'd in full day at church. After feasting and dancing, and

having made merry that day and the next, they take a trip into the country, and there divert themselves very pleasantly.

The bride of 1700 never wore white. If she could afford them, brightly coloured silks were preferred. Her garters, which played an important part in the bedding ceremony, would be elegant silk sashes tied below the knee. Blue was popular, perhaps because of its residual associations with the Virgin Mary, but red or white garters were also worn. Bridesmaids and guests sported gilded rosemary and bay. Rosemary, carried to weddings as well as funerals, was dipped in scented water. The bridal path would be strewn with rushes.

In *The Ten Pleasures of Marriage*, Aphra Behn pokes fun at a fashionable couple and the enormous expense of their wedding. The wife enjoys such a lavish shopping spree that 'it is no wonder that all womankind are so desirous of marriage, and no sooner lose their first husbands, but they think immediately of a second'. She continues:

> because it was impossible to invite every one to the wedding, this sweet Venus must be led abroad, and shewed to all her husbands friends and acquaintance; yea, all the world must see what a pretty couple they are, and how handsomely they agree together. To which end they trick and prick themselves up daily in their best apparel; garnishing both the whole city and streets with tatling and pratling; and staring into the houses of all their acquaintance to see whether they are looked at.

The notion of the 'honeymoon' – the month a newly married couple might spend alone together – was becoming established.

For the majority of 'middling' Londoners, whom Misson liked to observe, their weddings were much more low-key, thereby avoiding much expense and trouble:

> The bridegroom, that is to say, the husband that is to be, and the bride, who is the wife that is to be, conducted by their father and mother, or by those that serve them in their room, and accompany'd by two bride men and two bride maids, go early in the morning with the licence in their pocket and call up Mr Curate and his clerk, tell him their business; are marry'd with a

low voice, and the doors shut; tip the minister with a guinea, and the clerk a crown; steal softly out, one one way, and t'other another, either on foot or in coaches; go different ways to some tavern at a distance from their own lodgings, or to the house of some trusty friend, there have a good dinner, and return home at night as quietly as lambs.

One of the reasons for all the secrecy was to avoid a 'charivari', the raucous noise and obscene suggestions that 'vulgar' people of the town would make in a street demonstration beneath the couple's window. Only bribes of money and drink would get rid of them. 'If the drums and fiddles have notice of it they will be sure to be with them by daybreak,' Misson commented wryly, 'making a horrible racket, till they have got the pence.' In private, though, there was plenty of ceremony:

and when bed time is come the bride men pull off the bride's garters, which she had before unty'd that they might hang down, and so prevent a curious hand coming too near her knee. This done, and the garters being fastened to the hats of the gallants, the bride maids carry the bride into the bed chamber, where they undress her, and lay her in bed. The bridegroom, who by the help of his friends is undress'd in some other room, comes in his night-gown as soon as possible to his spouse, who is surrounded by mother, aunt, sisters, and friends, and without any further ceremony gets into bed... The bridemen take the bride's stockings, and the bride maids the bridegroom's; both sit down at the bed's feet and fling the stockings over their heads, endeavouring to direct them so as that they may fall upon the marry'd couple. If the man's stockings, thrown by the maids, fall upon the bridegroom's head, it is a sign she will quickly be marry'd herself; and the same prognostick holds good of the woman's stockings thrown by the man.

When undressing the bride, the bridesmaids had to be sure to remove every pin and dispose of it. To keep one was very bad luck and meant that the culprit would not be married before Whitsuntide. Bride lace (ribbons) and knots (ribbon bows) were distributed as favours among the guests and worn on hats for several weeks. Gloves and scarves were also distributed as favours. Some brides wore gloves to bed, their removal symbolising the loss of virginity. Finally, the bridal couple was given a posset: a potion made of milk, wine, yolk of eggs, sugar, cinnamon, nutmeg. They would try to swallow this as quickly as possible so as to 'get rid of the troublesome company'.

By 1700 London had established itself as a national marriage market for all sections of society. The élite flocked to town in the spring for the season, which afforded the opportunity for eligible bachelors to meet potential mates from outside their limited rural circles. At a more mundane level, London was a magnet for thousands of migrants, those young people who left home between the ages of ten and seventeen to become apprentices, live-in domestic servants and labourers – they in due course would find their marriage partners in the capital.

And marriage *was* a market, like any other. Politica in Daniel Defoe's *The Levellers* and other cynics likened it to a 'Smithfield bargain', referring to the famous London horse-traders' haunt: 'Matrimony is, indeed, become a mere trade; they carry their daughters to Smithfield, as they do horses, and sell to the highest bidder.'

Spurred on by their ambitious mothers, young women were fiercely competitive in their bid to catch a husband, and with good reason: at a ratio of ten men to thirteen women, the women were placed at a distinct disadvantage. In vain Defoe urged them not to throw themselves at men, yet had to recognise that money was the driving force. His heroine Moll Flanders took a realistic view: 'The market is against our sex just now; and if a young woman have beauty, birth, breeding, wit, sense, manners, modesty, and all these to extreme, yet if she have not money, she's nobody, she had as good want them all, for nothing but money recommends a woman.'

Defoe condemned marriage for money as the equivalent of violent rape, and no basis for happiness: 'Ask the ladies why they marry, they tell you 'tis for a good settlement... Ask the men why they marry, it is for the money ... How little is regarded of that one essential and absolutely necessary part of the composition, called love, without which the matrimonial state ... can never be happy.'

Again and again his characters express the mercenary nature of contemporary marriage in the capital. Moll Flanders found 'that the state of things was altered as to matrimony, and that I was not to expect at

London what I had found in the country, that marriages were here the consequences of politic schemes for forming interests, and carrying on business, and that love had no show, or but very little, in the matter'.

Marriage was an expensive business and the timing of a man's marriage was largely governed by his economic circumstances. Among the aristocracy and gentry governed by primogeniture a younger son stood to inherit little or nothing, so that he needed some time to establish himself in a profession or business before he could think of marriage. If and when he did marry, it would be to a woman with a good portion that would permit him to live in the style to which his upbringing had accustomed him. Typically, he would marry as he approached thirty a woman ten years younger.

It was just as important for a tradesman to establish some 'bottom' before taking a wife. Defoe argued in *The Complete Tradesman* the improvidence of early marriage. He noted that 'as the custom now is, generally speaking, the wife and the shop make their first show together; but how few of these early marriages succeed'. He warned that early marriage led to ruin because a young man 'cripples his fortune, stock-starves his business, and brings a great expense'. Wisely, the bookseller John Dunton deferred marriage until he had discovered 'whether my trade wou'd carry two'.

The age difference between husband and wife was proportionate to the wealth of the man. The higher the social group, the younger the bride, since a girl from a wealthy family would receive a portion from her father and had no need to delay marriage. Those of middling and lower status needed to save up for marriage and so married later. Most London men of middling status married in their mid to late twenties; London-born women tended to wed at twenty-one or less, a few years younger than women who had migrated to the city, who waited until their mid twenties. Among the poor, the woman could bring little to the marriage except her own labour, and since the couple would always be impecunious, there was little point in prevaricating.

With romance an ideal and little else, and marriage for the majority of Londoners delayed until their twenties, St Valentine's Day took on a special significance. It was obviously a novelty for César de Saussure: 'The 14th of February, or St Valentine's Day, is a festival day for young people. Sometimes young men will draw lots for a favourite valentine. What I think most amusing is that a young man may on that day meet a maiden, and though he has never seen her before, he may if he will it ask her to be his valentine, and she cannot refuse him unless she already has one. This custom is the cause of many marriages.'

For the upper classes, where marriages were arranged between parents of the couple and their lawyers, there was little wooing. In Henry Fielding's satirical *Love in Several Masques*, Sir Positive Trap sees no need for courtship: 'I never saw my lady ... till an hour before our marriage. I made my addresses to her father, her father to his lawyer, the lawyer to my estate ... the bargain was struck. What need have young people of addressing, or anything, till they come to undressing?'

Where property was concerned, the virginity of the bride-to-be was an essential part of the marriage transaction. A man needed to know that the heir to his estate was legitimate. Some considered pre-marital sex to be the most heinous of crimes: 'For a man to make a whore of the very woman who he intends and really designs to make his wife,' wrote Defoe in *Conjugal Lewdness: Or, Matrimonial Whoredom*, 'defiles his own bed, pollutes his own seed, spreads bastardy in his own race, and shows a most vitiated appetite.' However, most young men and women were given a surprising degree of licence to experiment with pre-marital sex. Knickers had not been invented, women were naked beneath their skirts and there were no barriers to men's lust.

Bundling, or sexual play between a couple, usually stopped short of full intercourse. As a precaution against pregnancy it often took place in the presence of other women, a mother, sisters or friends. In some instances, a board was placed down the middle of the bed between the couple, although they were free to lie together and indulge as best they could all night. Bundling did not necessarily lead to marriage, and indeed a girl could 'bundle' with more than one man before marriage.

But bundling was a dangerous game, open to misinterpretation and abuse. A case heard in the consistory court reveals the unfortunate consequences in a London family 'of the middling sort'. Ostensibly the sisters Abigail and Clarissa Harris shared a bed for mutual protection and warmth, as was common practice among unmarried people. In the course of the night, however, Abigail would often move into the bed of a male guest – in the full knowledge of her mother. Mrs Harris evidently hoped to use her daughter's sexual favours to lure this or some other hapless young man into marriage. She failed and Abigail was left pregnant and abandoned. As twenty-four-year-old William Barlow told the court:

I first met Abigail Harris when her father asked me and a friend to dine with him in June 1699, whither I used to goe often afterwards to see her, her mother and sister ... I have had free access to Abigail at her father's house where I have been free and familiar with her, and often in the presence of her sister or some other person in the family kiss and imbrace her, squeeze her by the hand, sit in her lap, feel her naked breasts and take up her coats and see her legs. She has permitted me to feel her belly and thighs, and I have attempted to feel her privy parts but she has resisted and not suffered me.

The Harris case indicates that mothers of the middling class seemed to play a far more active role than fathers in arranging marriages for their daughters. Moll Flanders sums up the typical situation: 'And as to the father, he was a man in a hurry of public affairs and getting money, seldom at home, thoughtful of the main chance, but left all those things to his wife.' In the end, of course, the father had the final say because he held the purse strings.

As the new century dawned, an emerging trend was soon to rise to alarming proportions: pre-marital pregnancy and its companion, bastardy. Very often a couple intending to marry did so once the woman became pregnant. A man failing to do his duty in this respect would be hounded by the parish authorities and served with a maintenance order. One in ten English brides was pregnant on her wedding day. Fear of pregnancy, disgrace and ruin, the disapproval of 'friends' and neighbours, kept promiscuity in check. Contraception was limited to condoms fashioned from sheep's intestines, measuring as much as nine and half inches long and three inches wide and tied with a ribbon. Since they were imported from France, they were expensive and beyond the reach of most ordinary people. They were used almost exclusively as a protection against venereal disease rather than to prevent pregnancy. Married women sometimes resorted to abortion once they felt their families were complete. Many recipes to 'bring on the courses' secreted in household and medical books could be tried to abort an unwanted child. Savin, a concoction made from rue, was known to promote uterine contractions.

The degree to which parental approval and consent was involved in the marriage decision corresponded to the amount of property involved, so that aristocratic marriages were the most circumscribed. Of course, by their mid twenties, there was a good chance that many Londoners would have lost one or both of their parents, and women in this category would be described as being 'at their own disposal'. By the time many migrants married in their twenties, they had been living away from home for several years, and their parents had little say in their choice of a marriage partner, if indeed they ever had the chance to meet them. Even in marriages of men and women over the age of twenty-one who did not need parental consent, however, parents were usually consulted. The four daughters of the Essex clergyman Ralph Josselin brought their prospective suitors home for parental inspection before marriage, even though they had been earning their own livings in London households for some years. It was not the done thing to marry without consulting a parent. In her diary, Elizabeth Freke frequently alludes to her guilt at being married privately without her father's knowledge or consent. She blames her own impetuosity for her subsequent unhappiness:

> Thus was three of my unhappy years spent in London, where I twice miscarryed and where I lost two thousand and five hundred and sixty pounds outt of my six thousand seven hundred sixty foure pounds. And I never had to my remembrance, fife pounds of itt and very little of my husbands company, which was noe small griefe to me I being governed in this marriage wholly by my affections, withoutt the consentt or knowledge of any of my friends.

At this period, 'friends' denoted people of influence – employers and others who dispensed patronage – whose approval was sought and considered desirable in the choice of a marriage partner or a career. Friends could also be called on to intercede with parents on young people's behalf.

There were widely divergent views on the merits of allowing young adults freedom in their choice of a spouse. Nonconformists such as Defoe were all in favour of liberty, believing the best recipe for marital success to be companionship, affection and friendship. John Dunton, who honed in on the new phenomenon of 'affective individualism' and gave an eager public its first agony column in the *Athenian Mercury*, advised children to 'endeavour as much as possible to submit to their parents' choice; unless where 'tis a plain case that t'would make 'em miserable'.

Even if they were allowed a measure of freedom, girls could not afford to be too choosy in the highly competitive marriage market of 1700. They took a risk if they turned away more than one or two suitors. The early feminist Mary Astell, who was not married herself, recognised their dilemma: 'A woman indeed can't properly be said to choose, all that is allow'd her, is to refuse or accept what is offer'd.' Girls were seen as silly creatures who needed guidance. It was no accident that Lord Halifax's *Advice to a Daughter*, which advocated the importance of the input of friends and relatives in the choice of a young lady's marriage partner, became a huge bestseller among the upper classes whose rather patronising view of female judgement it expostulated.

Whatever the parental pressures, a marriage could not take place without a 'full, free and mutual consent' between the parties. *The New Whole Duty of Man* was unequivocal about children's rights and duties. When a parent 'will enjoin a child, upon mere motives of advantage, to marry, where there is no foundation of love, nor prospect of content; it is hardly to be thought, that such instances are to be complied with'. Thus, if 'parents offer to their children what they cannot possible like, and what all considerate people cannot but disapprove, there is no doubt to be made, but that, in such a case, children may refuse; and if their refusal be made with decency and humility, that it will not fall under the head of sinful disobedience'.

In the last resort, parents could use money as a leverage to persuade errant children to obey their wishes. It was the custom that if 'the daughter of a citizen of London marries in his life-time, against his consent, unless the father be reconciled to her before his death, she shall not have her orphanage share of his personal estate'. In the event, few Londoners excluded children from their wills because they had married without their consent, and the Common Sergeant took a lenient view when it was his duty to decide such cases.

The mercenary nature of marriage was symptomatic of the age. Foreigners such as César de Saussure remarked on the English obsession with money. 'A sign that they are very fond of wealth is that as soon as you mention anyone to them that they do not know, their first inquiry will be, "Is he rich?"' Marriage was a major means of transferring property and one of the surest ways to make money. Inevitably there was a temptation to marry for financial advantage. The higher the couple's social status, the more mercenary the marriage. In *Some Reflections upon*

Marriage, Mary Astell describes the upper-class marriage. 'What will she bring is the first enquiry? How many acres? Or how much ready coin?'

It was hard to withstand pressure to marry for money. One young man wrote in despair to the *Athenian Mercury*:

> Q. Gentlemen, I desire your help, if you have any pity. There's a very old-old-woman, that says, she's mightily in love with me. She has an estate of an hundred pounds a year, but is a confounded toper, and drinks brandy eternally. My father is very earnest I should have her, but I can't endure the sight of her. I'm very young, but for all that am in love with a young woman, much of my own age, who has but little money, but she's a special good housewife, can get her living herself, and is willing to have me but my father is vehemently against it, because this old aqua-vitae-bottle carrier has got so much money. Pray give your advice what a poor young fellow ought to do in this miserable case ...

He is advised to 'tarry till you're older'. The columnist muses that the father should marry the woman himself, but inevitably 'she knows a young bedfellow is good for a consumption, and therefore, ten to one, would prefer you before him'. However, 'your duty is to refuse what your father requires of you, as handsomely and dutifully as you can' and to 'get your friends to intercede for you'.

Despite all the financial manoeuvring, romantic love was not completely absent. It was still seen as the ideal, and letters, diaries and epitaphs show that many couples – even when their marriages were arranged – came to love each other. Sexual passion had no place in this ideal. Defoe thought him 'an ill husband that uses his wife as a man treats a harlot' and that lust 'brings madness, desperation, ruin of families, disgrace, self-murders, killing of bastards'. The passions were thought to be notoriously capricious and liable to lead people astray. People tended to marry within their own social circle, to absorb the standards and aspirations of their parents. It was quite sufficient for partners to have 'a kindness' for each other. Love was all very well and good, but character and religious compatibility and financial interest were the important considerations when it came to marriage.

Londoners have always had a reputation for pragmatism, so that it is no surprise that the financial often took precedence over the romantic.

Defoe describes men literally shopping for a bride, setting themselves up as meriting a wealthy spouse even if they had no estate of their own. Men might visit a scrivener or a matchmaker to seek out a woman of fortune on their books:

> Elizabeth Wildey is generally accounted and reputed among her friends and acquaintances to bee a matchmaker or a person who getts her livelyhood by match makeing and pretending to help persons of both sexes to fortunes for money and reward ... During the time of her lodging at my house she told me that shee was promised a thousand pounds by Mr Spencer for making a marriage up between him and Sir John St Alban's widow.

Men of the middling sort needed the money that came as their wife's portion (sometimes paid in instalments) to set up independently in business or for a further injection of capital into an existing business. Defoe himself received a dowry of £3,700 when he married Mary Tuffley in 1684, money that he bitterly regretted losing on failed business ventures.

The cost of marriage was spiralling. The steep rise in portions was directly linked to the inverse ratio of men to women. It was necessary to buy into marriage and the terms were drawn up as in any other business transaction. First each party investigated the other's credentials. A man's claims of character, fortune and expectations needed careful scrutiny. Then came the haggling. The two main elements of a marriage contract were the portion brought by the woman and the settlement to provide for her maintenance if her husband should predecease her. A bride's portion was usually equivalent to three years' income from her husband's estate, or three times his income. In turn there was a correlation between the size of the portion a woman brought to the marriage and the settlement she would receive on widowhood. The divorce case of a wealthy London couple, Ann and Charles Norvos, illustrates a typical arrangement. She brought a portion of £7,000 and her corresponding settlement was to be £700. In such an overheated market, however, settlements were growing smaller.

Once settled, the woman's portion was paid to the bridegroom's father. 'To London, to receive £3000 of my daughter-in-law's portion, which was paid in gold', John Evelyn recorded in his diary. The daughters of Ralph Josselin received portions ranging from £240 to

£500, he and his wife being rather better off by the time their youngest daughter came to be married. Of course some girls were disappointed in the size of the portions available to them, and were unable to find a suitable husband as a result. Politica in *The Levellers* was a case in point:

> You know my father was a tradesman, and lived very well by his traffick; and, I being beautiful, he thought nature had already given me part of my portion, and therefore would add a liberal education, that I might be a compleat gentlewoman; away he sent me to the boarding-school, there I learned to dance and sing, to play on the bass-viol, virginals, spinnet and guitar. I learned to make wax work, japan, paint upon glass, to raise paste, make sweet-meats, sauces, and everything that was genteel and fashionable. My father died, and left me accomplish'd, as you find me, with three hundred pounds portion; and, with all this, I am not able to buy a husband. A man that has an estate answerable to my breeding, wants a portion answerable to his estate; an honest tradesman, that wants a portion of three hundred pounds, has more occasion of a wife that understands cookery and housewifery, than one that understands dancing, and singing, and making of sweet-meats. The portion, which nature gave me, proves now my detriment; my beauty is an obstacle to my marriage; an honest shop-keeper cannot keep a wife to look upon.

Equally as complex as the portion was the settlement. While the landed classes generally took care of the settlement through a jointure – by which lands to a certain value would be allocated for the widow's annual maintenance – land was of less relevance in the London business community. There was little attraction in tying up capital in land with a return of only 4 per cent or 5 per cent when it could be used in more lucrative – if more dicey – trading ventures. A London merchant might pledge to bequeath his widow a certain sum agreed in the contract to trustees 'to place out at interest upon security'. By the custom of London, a widow was anyway entitled to one-third of her husband's estate – half if he had no children – which could amount to more or less than she would have received under a jointure arrangement.

Sometimes provision would be made for the wife's separate estate if she had property of her own and had put it under the management of trustees prior to her marriage. She might also be allowed to bequeath a fixed sum from her portion as she wished – Ann Norvos had the power to dispose of £500 in her will. Like many of the better off, she also received pin money of £100, an annual sum that a husband had to provide for his wife's personal expenditure. There was a certain amount of grumbling about pin money. It was seen as a worrying new trend towards a wife's independence. 'Separate purses between man and wife,' thundered the *Spectator*, 'are in my opinion as unnatural as separate beds.'

The degree to which money was at the heart of courtship is symptomatic of the degree to which finance and commerce were underpinning the heart of London at the turn of the eighteenth century. Only when the vexed question of the marriage contract was settled could any vestiges of romantic love be displayed. Now was the moment for the spousals, when the couple exchanged vows and the woman received an engagement ring containing a posy. Descriptions of missing rings and those snatched by highwaymen advertised in the newspapers recall many such couplets: 'Two made one By God alone' and 'Vertuous love Will never remove'. The actual wedding ring, which could be jewelled, would be placed on the third finger of the left hand at the marriage ceremony. Only then would the spiritual, romantic and financial bond be complete.

It may have been the English custom for people of the opposite sex to greet each other with a kiss on the mouth, but married couples resisted the new fashion of addressing each other by their first names. This apparently innocuous innovation was the subject of intense debate in a hierarchical society where a wife was expected to show her husband deference. Theirs was an unequal partnership in law. If a man murdered his wife, he would be hanged for felony. A woman who murdered her husband committed treason and was burned alive.

On her wedding day a woman surrendered her rights as a *feme sole*, a single woman, which were generally the same as those enjoyed by men. Until then, she could own property, which she could bequeath by will. She could make contracts. She sued and was sued. But a married woman was a *feme covert* and subject to a whole series of legal handicaps which placed her in the same category as wards, lunatics, idiots and outlaws. Although she might assume a position of superiority over her unmarried sisters, she was most definitely inferior to her husband. The legal commentator Blackstone summed up her position: 'By marriage, the husband and wife are one person in law: that is, the very being or legal existence of the woman is suspended during the marriage, or at least incorporated and consolidated into that of her husband; under whose wing, protection, and *cover*, she performs everything.'

A husband owned his wife. If she had an affair with someone, her lover was technically encroaching on her husband's property: 'The corrupting of a man's wife, enticing her to a strange bed is by all acknowledged to be the worst sort of theft, infinitely beyond that of goods.' But given the mercenary nature of the age, the wronged husband was less likely to fight a duel than to sue for damages in a case of criminal conversation. Damages could be set so high that his wife's seducer would be confined to prison indefinitely for debt. If the wife was injured, the husband was injured too and could bring an action against the perpetrator.

The legal impotence of the married woman outraged the reformers of the age. Defoe's heroine Roxana was cynical about the whole business: 'The very nature of the marriage contract was, in short, nothing but giving up liberty, estate, authority, and everything to the man, and the woman was indeed a mere woman ever after, that is to say, a slave.'

After the Glorious Revolution of 1688 it was recognised that the king had a breakable contract with the people, as outlined in Locke's groundbreaking *Two Treatises on Government*. So it was logical for some to ask, did not the husband have a similar contract with the wife? As Lady Brute in Vanbrugh's *The Provoked Wife* quips: 'The argument's good between the King and the people, why not between the husband and wife?' Mary Astell echoed the question: 'If all men are born free, how is it that all women are born slaves?' And yet she advised resignation on the part of married women:

> She then who marrys ought to lay it down for an indisputable maxim, that her husband must govern absolutely and intirely, and that she has nothing else to do but to please and obey. She must not attempt to divide his authority, or so much as dispute it, to struggle with her yoke will only make it gall the more, but she must believe him wise and good and in all respects the best, at least he must be so to her. She who can't do this is in no way fit to be a wife.

Perhaps what was most galling was that the personal property a woman brought to her marriage became her husband's absolutely. He could dissipate her fortune, use it to pay his gambling debts, lose it on failed business ventures, and withhold from her and her children the money for subsistence. When Elizabeth Freke married without her father's consent, he was still kind enough to give her a portion, a mortgage on an estate. Her husband promptly sold it to Sir Josiah Child. 'This was not kind done,' she exclaimed, 'for by itt I were turned outt of doors, and nott a place to putt my unfortunate head in.' A wife could be thrown out of her husband's house – a house that might have been purchased with her own money – on to the streets.

Everything about the marriage system seemed to conspire against the women of the age. Yet there were some glimmers of hope. By 1700 some moves towards women's financial independence were under way. Pin money represented a small advance. A woman's marriage contract could allot her certain goods and lands 'to her own separate use and enjoyment' which had been agreed by her husband. Or she might, before marriage, convey property to trustees who would pay her a separate income.

Those marital disputes that reached the courts more often than not boiled down to the contentious issue of money, specifically when a wife withheld access to her personal wealth. Husbands bitterly resented this trend. Elizabeth Freke's husband subjected her to threats and physical abuse and abandoned her and their child for years at a time without maintenance because she would not yield control of a trust put aside for her son to him. A woman might be subjected to life-threatening violence in an effort to persuade her to yield to a husband's demands. He might threaten to commit her to Bridewell, a house of correction, or incarcerate her in a madhouse, an increasingly common practice that Defoe thought scandalous. The barber and wig-maker Thomas Hall beat his wife Mary until she miscarried, threw her clothes in the fire and tried to burn her, encouraged his children by a previous marriage to abuse her, and was going to confine her to the madhouse, until she handed over the records of her personal estate.

Even when a woman allowed herself to be exploited, she could not expect gratitude and loyalty from her husband. Ann Ferrers complained that her husband William had taken several hundred pounds and pawned her jewels, while she 'out of her own estate did maintain the whole family and he never contributed towards the same two shillings ... and notwithstanding all the said obligations the said William Ferrers hath abused her in a base and scandalous manner and when he had impoverished her as aforesaid left her and betooke himself to lewd women and whores'.

Violence against women was also used to persuade their families into paying their portion or standing surety for loans. The divorce for cruelty case of Chambers v. Chambers illustrates another dimension. Apparently John Chambers resented the children of his wife Elizabeth's former marriage. They were forbidden access to his house in Lombard Street to visit their mother. On discovering that her daughter Ann was admitted secretly, Chambers 'fell into a great passion with his wife ... and did then in a violent and cruel manner throw his wife who was big with child against the bedside and kick't her severall times ... and leaving her on the floor, went to strike the said Ann ... who made herself away out of the house'. The nub of the problem was that Elizabeth 'would not give him an account of the estate of her former husband', which involved her children's inheritance.

Everyone was used to the spectacle of violence. The authorities put wrongdoers in the pillory or whipped them at the cart's tail through the streets. Criminals were hanged and their bodies sequestered by the state. Parents flogged children, masters their apprentices and mistresses their servants. So it was not considered out of order for a husband to beat his wife. As her superior, it was assumed that he had a right to chastise her. Yet attitudes were changing, and, as between king and people, marriage was construed as a contract with mutual rights and obligations. Although he was the senior partner, a husband should not abuse his authority. His obligations were affection, fidelity and care, while his wife's were to be submissive and obedient. The behaviour of the violent or flagrantly unfaithful husband was not condoned.

Domestic strife was increasingly the pattern of the day. Defoe remarked that London neighbourhoods rang to the increased pitch of marital discord. But at least the neighbours were not afraid to come to the defence of the hapless victim, and women frequently turned to the support of female neighbours, relatives and friends as a counter-balance to male dominance. In the last resort they could call in the law, as Elizabeth Powell did when her husband beat her up so badly she miscarried. Fleeing her house in Aldgate, she called on a friend to 'go along with her to gett a constable to serve a warrant on him to bind him over to the peace'.

Their position might be inferior to men, but in general London women gave as good as they got and were well able to take care of themselves. As ever, it was largely the characters themselves who determined the distribution of power in a marriage. Ravenscroft's play *The London Cuckolds* hilariously portrays City wives getting the better of their husbands. The knack is to let the men *think* they are in control. Edward Chamberlayne in his *Angliae Notitia* went so far as to assert of Englishwomen that 'their condition *de facto* is the best in the world; for such is the good nature of Englishmen towards their wives, such is the tenderness and respect, giving them the uppermost place at table, and elsewhere, the right-hand everywhere, and putting them upon no drudgery and hardship; that they are, generally speaking, the most happy women in the world'.

Certainly the fashionable readers of *The English Lady's Catechism* recognised that their situation was quite a good one, as one of its characters conceded: 'I hate everything that Old England brings forth, except it be the temper of an English husband, and the liberty of an English wife.'

Like many foreign visitors, César de Saussure was struck by English chauvinism in both senses of the word. He was pleased to discover that Englishwomen did not share their husbands' contempt for foreigners, even preferring them to their own men. This was hardly surprising, he speculated, as 'Englishmen do not spoil their women by flattery and attentions, generally preferring drinking and gambling to female company'. He was intrigued by the sanguine attitude of the more sophisticated towards infidelity: 'If Englishmen are not jealous of their wives, neither are the wives jealous of their husbands. A wife is not generally unhappy when she discovers her husband has a mistress; on the contrary, it sometimes happens that if her husband so desires it she will be polite towards her rival, but at the same time she will probably console herself with a friend, and thus both husband and wife are happy.'

Another foreign visitor, Beat Louis de Muralt, went further: 'Most of the husbands keep mistresses. Some have carry'd them home, and made them eat at the same table with their wives, and yet no mischief happen'd. I believe, if they had a mind they would make them lie in the same bed, and I don't know whether there have not been some that thought it. After this, the English may, no doubt, boast to have the best wives in the world.'

A newly married couple in 1700 would almost certainly have a copy of _Aristotle's Masterpiece_, the bestselling sex manual. Epitomising the attitude of the day, sex was presented without any tag of sin or guilt, and without the psychological baggage it later acquired. For fear of encouraging the overindulgence it warns against, the book sets out neither to titillate nor to illustrate coital positions. Aretine's _Postures_ had already done that. _Aristotle's Masterpiece_ assumes that every married couple wants to have children, and that barrenness is a terrible thing (attributable to the wife). It presents itself as a straightforward guide to 'the business of generation':

> When a married couple, from a desire of having children, are about to make use of those means that nature ordained to that purpose, it would be very proper to cherish the body with generous restoratives, so that it may be brisk and vigorous and if their imaginations were charmed with sweet and melodious airs, and care and thought of business in a glass of racy wine, that their spirits may be raised to the highest pitch of ardour and joy, it would not be amiss; for any thing of sadness, trouble, and sorrow, are enemies to the delights of Venus. And if, at any such times of coition, there should be conception, it would have a malevolent effect upon the child.

The male and female genitalia, it argues, are not dissimilar. 'There is no vast difference between the members of the sexes' for 'the use and action of the clitoris in women is like that of the penis or yard in men, that is, erection.' Like other popular manuals of the time, _Aristotle's Masterpiece_ recognised that the woman was capable of multiple orgasms and that such pleasure was to be encouraged. In her midwifery book Mrs Jane Sharp ventured so far as to advise that the 'clitoris will stand and fall as the yard doth, and makes women lustfull and take delight in copulation, and were it not for this they would have no desire nor delight, nor would they ever conceive'.

None of the manuals offers advice as to how to become more sexually attractive. Given that bad breath from rotting teeth and the pungent odours of unwashed bodies and clothes rarely taken off were the norm, presumably these were no deterrent to sexual attraction or enjoyment. It was noticed, however, that even upper-class Englishwomen, who had better facilities to attend to intimate personal hygiene, neglected 'care in the cleanliness and sweetness of their persons'. Sexual activity was prone to be interrupted by chronic gynaecological problems, infections and venereal disease. Couples were warned against excess. The octogenarian Evelyn wrote that 'too much frequency of embraces dulls the sight, decays the memory, induces gout, palsies, enervates and renders effeminate the body, and shortens life', while Defoe completed this dire list of consequences with 'rottenness and other filthy and loathsome distempers'.

The multiple factors of high mortality, late marriage, and comparatively early death meant that a prolonged union was unlikely. Many relationships were transient and temporary. In the event of each partner surviving what was then considered a normal lifespan, a man and a woman might enjoy between seventeen and twenty years of marriage until parted by death. Only 50 per cent of marriages achieved this. Few parents lived long enough as a couple to see their children grown up, married and living in a home of their own. One quarter of all marriages were second marriages of either one or both of the parties. As the widows of London and Westminster put it in a petition to the House of Commons: 'We that have had good husbands, are encouraged to try once more, out of hopes of meeting the same success; and we that have had bad ones, are not for all that deterr'd from matrimony, but hope to mend our hands in a second bargain.'

Officially, the only end to a marriage was death. The Protestant Reformation may have been prompted by a king's divorce but it failed to provide divorce for anybody else. The new degree of freedom to choose one's spouse meant that there were greater emotional expectations from marriage and disappointment if they were unfulfilled. Inevitably, marital separation became more frequent, and women were becoming less shy of crying foul when they had been wronged.

Nevertheless, a legal separation was difficult for a woman to achieve, however deplorable her husband's behaviour. Contemporaries called it divorce, but *divortium a mensa et thoro* meant simply separation from bed and board without permission to remarry. Many of the cases heard in the ecclesiastical courts involved adultery or adultery with cruelty. For a woman to bring such an action against her husband, she not only had to be desperate, but also to have a real sense that wrong had been done her. In a society in which women were brought up to defer to men, to be resigned and submissive, this was not always so. All the sordid details of the marriage would be revealed in court and for public consumption. Each side marshalled the case to look like good pitted against evil – but the onus was on the woman to convince a male court. Here, as anywhere else, she had to act the passive victim, since signs of assertiveness could easily lead the court to conclude that she had provoked or deserved her husband's behaviour.

Witnesses were vital in these cases, particularly household servants who seemed to spend an inordinate amount of time squinting through keyholes and listening at doors. Thanks to household structures, no man could conduct an affair or beat his wife without their knowledge. Even the sheets they had to wash (however infrequently) could provide evidence enough of adultery. Servants could be called on to intervene if physical abuse got out of hand. In the Summers household where Elizabeth was frequently being beaten and kicked by husband John, Samuel Pickard 'was in bed and asleep and the said John's apprentice boy William Winter came up and waked him and desired [him] to make hast down following him, that his master was killing his mistress'.

Once a case was in court, men sometimes tried to offer the servants bribes, as John Chambers did when he 'ordered them to be silent and not to speake of his abuses to his said wife'. Unfortunately, witnesses were usually all too willing to perjure themselves for financial reward: 'the said Margaret is of a notorious scandalous life and conversation and a very wicked person, and frequently committed to prison for stealing, whoreing and cheating ... she will swear an untruth at any time for any small reward.' Apparently she 'swore she was going to gett three guineas and was to have a new gown and petticoats to swear that one Mrs Smith was married to one Mr Smith'.

Apart from the bias of the legal system in favour of men, there were many other conditions that made divorce an ordeal for women. Women had little or no money of their own and litigation was prohibitively expensive. Costing at least £20 – the equivalent of one or two years' income of a London labourer and ten times the annual earnings of a working woman – it was inevitably confined to the upper and well-heeled middling classes. If she was able to meet the necessary expenses, a woman was able to sue for maintenance – forthcoming only if she were proved to be the innocent party. Alternatively, a private deed of separation negotiated between the two parties and drawn up by a 'conveyancer' would provide maintenance for the woman. Maintenance could and did often peter out, and it might not be adequate:

> Whereas ... it is affirmed by the said Christian that the said
> Elizabeth is able to gain a livelihood by working att his trade,
> the said Elizabeth is so infirm and disabled in her body limbs
> and sight by the blows bruises and knocks that she hath received
> from the said Christian, that she ... cannot use any bodily labour
> or work with her needle by reason of the weakness of her eyes
> occasioned by blows on her head in so much that it is feared that
> without good maintenance her life cannot continue long.

The laws on adultery were also heavily weighed against the woman.
Although men's adultery was never penalised, there were dire
consequences for women who found lovers either within marriage or
after separation. Maintenance would be stopped abruptly if there were
even a whiff of another relationship. The separated woman was
condemned to a life of loneliness and isolation. Worst of all, she lost her
children. A father had exclusive control of the children in any marriage.
He owned them as he did his wife, at least until their maturity. In a
divorce he retained custody of them even if he were the guilty party. She
might never see them again. There can be no doubt that a woman
would have had to have been sorely mistreated to be willing to undergo
all of these trials, but it is also a sign of the growing sense of women's
rights that so many of them did not shrink from this step.

Some women simply walked out on their husbands. The newspapers
are peppered with announcements of elopements and husbands hurriedly
disclaiming their wife's debts:

> Whereas Elizabeth Stephenson, wife of George Stephenson, late of
> Falken Court, near the King's Bench, in Southwark, hath eloped
> from her said husband, and since hath contracted several debts with
> a design to ruin her husband. These are therefore to give notice to
> the publick, that the said George Stephenson will not on any
> account whatever pay or allow of any debt so contracted by the said
> Elizabeth Stephenson, either before or since her elopement.

On marriage even a wife's 'chattels', or household goods, became the
property of her husband. She could retain only her 'paraphernalia', or
personal clothing. So Isabella Goodyear acted with some audacity when
she absconded with her husband's property:

Whereas Isabella Goodyear, the daughter of Rich. Cliffe of Brixholme in the County of Devon, and wife of Aaron Goodyear of London, merchant, about 18 months since abandon'd and forsook the bed and since the board of Aaron her said husband, carrying with her in goods, plate, and other goods to the value of £200 and upwards, and whereas the said Isabella hath as well been sollicited by the said Aaron her husband, as also by several of his acquaintances, to return to and cohabit with him, under all assurances of being civilly receiv'd and maintain'd according to his quality and circumstances, which the said Isabella hath, and still doth obstinately refuse. These are therefore to give notice to all traders, and all other persons whatsoever, that from and after this present notice they do not maintain, sustain, or detain the said Isabella from the said Aaron her husband, or any of his goods or plate carryed off by the said Isabella, either by lending her money or selling her goods, or by any other ways whatsoever, under penalty of the law, and forfeiture of the credit, if any, given to the said Isabella from the notice hereof.

The righteous-sounding Aaron was doubly injured, because his wife was his property too. A woman who eloped was to all intents and purposes an outlaw. Her husband could compel her to return, or bring an action against anyone harbouring her. He could abduct her and confine her to a madhouse or keep her locked up at home. She was still under her husband's 'cover' and suffered from the same legal disabilities – she was unable to enter a legal contract, use credit to borrow money, buy or sell property. If she did manage to earn her own living, there was nothing to stop her husband seizing her goods or wages. Her property had already become her husband's on marriage, yet by eloping she lost all right to dower.

For the poor, unencumbered by property, it was easy just to walk out of a marriage and set up home with someone else: 'The said John Combs had left the cohabitation of his wife for some years and did live with one Elizabeth Gwyn as his wife near Spittlefields markett.' So well ensconced were these two that some of John's pals at the Two Brewers alehouse nearby thought they were married: 'They continued drinking till about two of the clock in the morning and then the said John went to bed to a woman whose Christian name is Elizabeth who he acknowledged to be his wife.'

It was easy to disappear and never be heard of again. Press gangs could take husbands willing or otherwise, but the eager response to the call to arms on the brink of renewed war with France suggests that the army or navy presented attractive alternatives to marriage for some men. If a man failed to return within seven years, the woman was free to marry again. But there were financial implications to this easy flight. With bigamy easy and common, there were many deserted wives among the poor and others claiming parish relief. The overpopulated London parishes were feeling the financial strain, and efforts were made to track down errant husbands and make them fulfil their financial obligations. Women who had been married clandestinely and were subsequently finding it difficult to prove, had trouble getting maintenance. Phyllis Chamblott complained of the 'unkindness of her husband in leaving her and her child and not taking any care for their maintenance'. When she appealed to her husband's mother for help, she was turned away.

As a last resort the poor might resort to wife-sale, a sort of public self-divorce usually agreed amicably between the parties. Just as in the sale of cattle at Smithfield, the husband 'puts a halter about her neck and thereby leads her to the next market place, and there puts her up to auction to be sold to the best bidder, as if she were a brood mare or a milch-cow'. In practice the deal would have been made beforehand between the husband, keen to exonerate himself from any future obligations towards his wife, and the man who wished to take her. She might cost anything from a few pence to a few guineas. A fee would be payable to the clerk of the market as in any other transaction. In the popular mind this allowed both parties to marry again. Needless to say, it was illegal in the eyes of both the secular and ecclesiastical courts and increasingly condemned in the press.

There was an interesting alternative to *divortium a mensa et thoro*. By some anomaly in a state where divorce was prohibited, *divortium a vincula* could be obtained by private Act of Parliament. This granted full legal severance with permission to remarry. Such an option was confined to the rich and powerful whose wives had committed adultery before fulfilling their duty by providing an heir for a great estate. When Charles II had attended the Roos divorce hearings in the House of Lords in the 1670s, he thought they were as good as a play. Such cases were rare and their success was not assured.

In 1700 the guardians of Sir George Downing, fourteen, were arranging a match for him with a twelve-year-old girl. When it took place the following year the couple were 'put to bed ... and continu'd there a little while, but in the presence of the company, who all testify they touched not one the other; and after that, they came together no more; the young gentleman going immediately abroad, the young woman continuing with her parents'. The Downings never did consummate the marriage, and in due course 'each party having …contracted an incurable aversion to each the other, is very desirous to be set at liberty'. The court ruled against them on the grounds that they were 'man and wife both by the laws of God and the land; and since nothing but adultery can dissolve a marriage, and no adultery is pretended here, the marriage continues indissoluble'.

Even for the more privileged sections of society, a marriage once entered into was a difficult bond to break. And so young men grasped an alternative: bachelorhood.

Not only were young men in short supply, but they showed a marked reluctance to marry. While the political economist Sir William Petty uttered dire warnings of population decline, women worried that they would be left on the shelf. Spinsterhood was an unwanted new social phenomenon attracting opprobrium. Women were supposed to submit themselves to male authority. Marriage was a market, virginity was a valuable commodity, spinsters were withholding their assets.

Things had become so desperate that a petition was got up – *The Ladies of London and Westminster to the Honourable House for Husbands* – subscribed by 'threescore thousand hands, and never a cracked maidenhead amongst 'em'. 'You need not be reminded with what scorn and contempt the holy state of matrimony has of late years been treated,' it began. 'Every nasty scribbler of the town has pelted it in his wretched lampoons; it has been persecuted in sonnet, ridicul'd in Court, exposed in the theatre, and that so often, that the whole subject is now exhausted and barren.'

Younger sons of the upper and middling classes balked at the expense of marriage and its commitments. They showed an 'aversion to the squalling of children, and rocking of cradles, though the sot can sit a whole day at Wills [coffee-house], amidst the eternal quarrels of the no-wits, and the endless disputes of the no-politicians'. The petition continues: 'the graver sort exclaim at the caudles, the pins, the midwives, the nurses, and other concomitants of wedlock; they pretend the taxes run high, and that a spouse is an expensive animal; little considering that they throw away more upon their dearly beloved vanities than would maintain a wife, and half a dozen children.'

The marriage market had become so overheated that some fathers deliberately kept their daughters out of it, unable or unwilling to pay the escalating portions. On the other hand, an unmarried girl was a long-term burden on her family. She might well end up as an upper servant in the household of a relative – as did Samuel Pepys' rather plain sister Pauline. The increasing frivolity of women's education was designed to catch them a husband rather than to earn them a living.

But, ultimately, only money could buy a girl a husband, and this had never been more the case than in 1700, especially since London women did not have the field to themselves. They recognised that they had two rivals in the marriage stakes – liquor and loose women:

> 'Tis a burning shame ... that the young fellows of the town should so scandalously abandon themselves to the bottle. They ply their glasses too warmly to think of anything else; and if the liquor happens to inspire them with any kind of inclinations, the next street furnishes them with a store of conveniences to relieve their appetites. And this leads us to the second block in our way, which is the intolerable multitude of mistresses, who ... divert the course of those streams which would otherwise run in the regular channel of matrimony. As long as these contraband commodities are encouraged or connived at, it cannot be expected that vertuous women should hear a good market price, or that marriage should flourish.

Quick to seize its opportunity, the government imposed a standard tax of 1s a year on bachelors and widowers over twenty-five. Hot on its heels, co-operative societies and insurance associations were formed with the object of providing money to their subscribers for the expenses of matrimony. And there were some interesting side-effects in the English language and sexual practice: the novel term 'old maid' entered common parlance, and masturbation was seen as a dangerous new vice with its own bestselling tract, *Onania*; *or, The Heinous Sin of Self-Pollution,* coming in 1710.

For the plain fact was that, with women developing some latent sense of independence, the costs of marriage spiralling, prostitution flourishing, marriage was not such an attractive option any more. Unless, of course, it was a clandestine affair, in the shadow of St Paul's.

CHAPTER TWO

Childbirth

*A woman who married in her twenties endured almost twenty
years of repeated pregnancy and lactation*

I N THE STILLNESS of the night a church bell struck the hour. 'Past one
o'clock and all's well!' cried the watch. There was a cough in the
house above and someone muttered and rolled over in his sleep.
Keeping close to the wall, two dark hooded figures hurried along, their
shoes slipping on wet paving stones as they tried to keep up with the
link-boy ahead. Suddenly he paused and in the smoky light of his torch
warned them of a mound of filth left by the night-soil men. Shielding
their faces from the stink of the kennel, they pressed close to the boy as
they entered the uneasy darkness of Lincoln's Inn Fields. Two streets
beyond, a left turn at the sign of the Globe & Sun, over against the south
side opposite the church, three houses down. A slither of light beckoned
them on, a man hovered anxiously, then opened the door wide in
welcome.

The highly respected midwife Madame X – so called because of the
anonymous account book she left – and her apprentice have arrived at
the home of one of her women in labour. The father-to-be ushers them
upstairs, although there is no longer any need of his services. The onset
of his wife's labour pains had earlier propelled him out of the house to
summon the gossips invited to witness the birth. Madame X need only
follow the buzz of their chatter to find the lying-in chamber. The
shutters are closed against the outside world and the shadows of the
women dance on the walls in the flickering light thrown by fire and
candles.

The gossips are female friends, relatives and neighbours whose
favourite occupation has lent a whole new meaning to a word originally
used to describe a sponsor at a baptism. As the popular saying goes: 'for
gossips to meet at a lying-in, and not to talk, you may as well dam up

Gossips invited to witness the birth of a baby whiled away the hours in a buzz of
chatter, giving a whole new meaning to the word gossip (*British Library*)

the arches of London Bridge, as stop their mouths at such a time.' The women's testimony will protect the mother from suspicion if the baby should die, although of course everyone looks forward to celebrating a safe delivery. The woman now moaning with pain would have been a gossip herself on many such occasions, so that she was no stranger to the mysteries of childbirth.

Aphra Behn captured the frenetic atmosphere in *The Ten Pleasures of Marriage*:

> For the midwife is not able alone to govern and take care of all things that must be fetcht, brought and carried to and again; therefore of necessity the friends must be fetcht with all the speed imaginable, viz, sisters, wives, aunts, cousins, and several familiar good acquaintances must have notice of it, and ... come to her quickly, quickly, quickly, without any delay; and if you do not invite them very ceremonially, every one according to their degrees and qualities, it is taken to be no small affront.

Childbirth was cloaked in darkness and superstition. The gossips would have ensured that the woman in labour was wearing some garment of her husband's, so that a portion of her sufferings would be transferred to him. Her mother, a Londoner herself or up from the country for the occasion, might have given her an eaglestone for luck. There was no anaesthetic to relieve the pains of childbirth. All the labouring woman could do was sip a caudle of wine warmed with sugar and spices to keep up her spirits through the long ordeal. Just as from the moment she realised she was pregnant she had dutifully taken the advice offered by the renowned London midwife Mrs Jane Sharp in her childbirth manual and drunk a glass of sage ale every morning to strengthen the womb.

She was not totally ignorant of what lay ahead. A plethora of popular manuals, including Jane Sharp's *The Midwives Book, or, the Whole Art of Midwifery Discovered*, Dr William Sermon's *Ladies Companion, or, The English Midwife*, John Pechey's *A General Treatise of the Diseases of Maids, Big-bellied Women, Child-bed Women, and Widows, Together with the Best Methods of Preventing or Curing the Same* and *The Compleat Midewife's Practice Enlarged* and Dr Hugh Chamberlen's translation of *Des Maladies des Femmes Grosses et Accouchées* by the leading French man-midwife François Mauriceau, might through a haphazard combination of wisdom and nonsense have given her a few tips on how to look after herself during pregnancy and some idea what to expect in labour. She could hardly have derived much encouragement from John Pechey's description:

> All the time their being with child, which is a nine months sickness, they are inclined to nauseousness, vomiting, to pains in the back, reins, and hips, violent coughs, swelling of the legs and thighs, piles, and many other diseases, and upon some indispositions of the body to miscarriage, which is the worst and most dangerous of all. When they are in labour, and when they lie in, they are encompassed with many difficulties and dangers ...

The mother's state of mind at the moment of conception was thought to leave its imprint on the child. Birth defects were blamed on something that happened to the mother during pregnancy. For instance, a harelip would be attributed to a hare crossing her path. It was considered taboo to have sex during menstruation, in case a resulting child would be deformed. A woman should avoid sex during pregnancy. In the first four months it was considered dangerous in case she dislodged the baby, similarly in the sixth and eighth months, but in the ninth it was thought to facilitate the delivery.

Her movements about the town were curtailed:

> She must not ride on horse-back, or in a coach, or waggon, all the time she is with child, especially when she is near her time ... But she may be carried in a chair, or litter, or walk gently ... She ought to avoid great noises, as the noise of guns, or great bells ... And it must be carefully noted, that when she walks she must walk in low heeled shoes; for big bellied women are apt to stumble, because they cannot see their feet, by reason of the bigness of their bellies.

Every woman feared and dreaded giving birth and prayed fervently for a safe delivery. The bills of mortality of the London parishes bear witness to the high incidence of women dying in childbirth, and of those who succumbed to other infectious diseases after being laid low by it. Maternal mortality varied from parish to parish. It was not necessarily the rich who survived. Many poor women fared better simply because they dispensed with the sometimes disastrous interference of a midwife. But in general there were 23.5 deaths per 1,000 baptisms. Over her whole childbearing span, a woman had a 6 to 7 per cent chance of dying in childbirth. It was not inappropriate to prepare for death. Elizabeth Joceline, who bequeathed a work of advice for the upbringing of her motherless daughter, may have been unnaturally morbid, however, for 'when she first felt her self quick with child (as then travailing with death itself) she secretly took order for the buying of a new winding sheet'.

A London midwife such as Madame X had to buy a licence to practise after being examined by the diocesan bishop at Doctors' Commons. Testimonies to her suitability had to be provided by six honest women. The bishop was more concerned with a midwife's moral character than her medical skills. After all, there was always a lurking suspicion that a woman healer was synonymous with a witch. The umbilical cord, caul, afterbirth and stillborn foetus played their parts in witchcraft rites. The Church forbade its licensees to perform any act of destruction against a child or to conceal a birth. Throughout the ordeal of childbirth, a midwife had to do her best to make the mother of a bastard name the father, so that he could be made to pay maintenance, if not punished for fornication by being whipped at the cart's tail. Although some begrudged her the power, she was obliged to baptise any child dying before a clergyman could reach it. In keeping with her oath of office, she had to draw no distinction between rich or poor women in need of her services. While she received fees commensurate with her clients' means and so could expect to be well rewarded by the rich, she had to be prepared to deliver a 'parish' baby for a nominal sum or indeed help the woman giving birth in the gutter for free.

Although male medical practitioners had little practical experience of childbirth, they had a university education and so felt equipped to list the qualities a midwife should possess. According to Dr William Sermon:

> As concerning their persons, they must be neither too young, nor too old, but of an indifferent age between both; well composed, not being subject to diseases, nor deformed in any part of their body; comely and neat in their apparell, their hands

small, and fingers long, not thick, but clean, their nails pared very close; they ought to be very chearfull, pleasant, and of good discourse, strong, not idle, but accustomed to exercise ... Touching their deportment: they must be mild, gentle, courteous, sober, chaste, and patient, not quarrelsome, nor chollerick; neither must they be covetous, nor report anything whatsoever they hear or see in secret, in the person or house of whom they deliver; for, as one saith, it is not fit to commit her into the hands of rash and drunken women, that is in travel of her first child. As concerning their minds; they must be wise and discreet; able to flatter, and speak many fair words, to no other end, but only to deceive the apprehensive women, which is a commendable deceit, and allowed, when it is done for the good of the person in distress.

In the lying-in chamber nature was barely allowed time to take its course. Even such a successful midwife as Madame X might be guilty of over-interference in the birth process. After coating her hand with duck fat as a lubricant, her first task according to Jane Sharp was 'to thrust it up into the womb to feel how the child lyeth'. It was common practice to stretch the neck of the womb, literally pulling and tearing the sides apart to forge a passage for the baby. If the foetal membranes were ruptured in the process, labour would be slower and more difficult. Infection from the midwife's hands was easily transmitted through the internal abrasions and lacerations caused by the scratching of her fingernails against tender flesh. The patient might well die of puerperal fever as a result, although this had yet to reach the epidemic proportions it did in the lying-in hospitals later in the century.

Some London midwives were adept at manual manipulation if the child was lying in an abnormal position. The less scrupulous might resort to rolling or shaking the long-suffering patient in a blanket, which along with other childbed abuse meant she would probably suffer from incontinence, painful intercourse and embarrassing discomforts for the rest of her life. There was no remedy for a prolapsed womb. Many midwives were helpless in the face of any complication. This was the moment to call in the man-midwife who might be able to overcome the problem by using surgical instruments, but some midwives left it too late and lost mother and child as a result. The famous man-midwife

Hugh Chamberlen argued, if a little smugly, that it was far better for a midwife to have a woman and child saved 'by a man's assistance, as to suffer either to die under her own hand'. It is hard to see how the man-midwives could be as helpful as he claimed since, in deference to their patients' modesty, they tended to work with their hands buried under the sheet, averting their sight from their patient's nether regions.

After various failed attempts on the part of Elizabeth Cellier, midwife to Queen Mary of Modena, and other London midwives to form their own professional body for training, monitoring and the founding of lying-in hospitals, midwives were in retreat. Because they were not part of a professional body, they were not permitted to use surgical instruments. The College of Physicians was too snooty to acknowledge the 'cunt-doctors' but a man-midwife might well belong to the Worshipful Company of Barber-Surgeons. The Chamberlen family had already invented the forceps, although for some inexplicable reason they were hugging the secret to themselves. They would not be patented for another twenty years by the last of their line. But as others gradually introduced forceps of various designs, more and more women were turning to man-midwives in the belief that they could save their lives. The entrance of the better-educated male into midwifery would drive up the cost of delivery and lower the status of midwives as they were edged out into the poorer reaches of the market. It would no longer be an attractive career for the widows, sisters and daughters of apothecaries, surgeons and other professional men.

Whatever their ability to wield instruments, even man-midwives acknowledged that caesarean sections were too risky to be attempted except on dead women. In lieu of the forceps to bring the child out alive, there was the crochet hook to remove a dead child piece by piece. Jane Sharp explains:

> If the head come forward, fasten a hook to one eye ... or under the chin, or to the roof of the mouth, or upon one of the shoulders, which of these you find best, and then draw the child out gently that you do the woman no hurt ... If but one arm comes forth you cannot well put it back again, the passage being too narrow ... then cut it off with a sharp knife from the body, do so also if both hands appear together, or one leg, or both, if you cannot easily put them back or take them forth with the

body; as you cut the arms from the shoulders, so you must cut the legs from the thighs, your instruments being very sharp for quick dispatch; when some parts are cut off from the body, then turn the rest to draw it out the better.

Almost inevitably such a procedure tore the womb, and in some instances killed the mother. Her recipe for 'bringing away a dead child' sounds infinitely preferable, although one doubts its efficacy:

> Any of these herbs half a dram in powder drunk in white wine will do much, viz of bettony, or sage, or penny-royal, fetherfew or centory, ivy-berries and leaves, or drink a strong decoction of master-wort, or of hysop in hot water, it soon will bring the dead child forth; because the afterbirth is corrupted in such cases and comes forth in pieces, it is fit to drink of the same drink till all be come away, or the roots of polipody stamped and warm'd laid to the soles of her feet presently works the effect.

Assuming that Madame X's patient was safely delivered, she would cut the cord using her traditional knife of office. She might intervene again to tear the placenta from the lining of the womb before natural separation had time to take place. The darkened room would be pungent with the smells of childbirth. The heat emanating from the banked-up fire and the fug of closely packed, unwashed bodies would be oppressive. Even so, *Aristotle's Masterpiece* advised that 'if a woman has had a very hard labour, then after delivery it is convenient to wrap her in the skin of a sheep taken off before it is cold, putting the fleshy side to her rein and belly ... and in so doing the dilation made in the birth will be closed up, and the melancholy blood expelled from those parts'. When it was all over, Jane Sharp recommended a nourishing broth, but on no account was a patient to be allowed to fall asleep for at least four hours after delivery.

The lying-in chamber would be the woman's sanctuary for a month following the birth. The gossips remained to police it, warding off an importunate husband feeling deprived of her services. Even a poor household managed an approximation of this. Since it was believed that a woman was defiled by childbirth, sex was forbidden until after her purification in church. So strictly was this observed that some men recorded in their diaries the first time they resumed sexual relations: 'My wife's month being now out we lay together.'

A dry nurse was hired for the month to attend to the woman's needs. She was to be treated as an invalid, in bed for the first fortnight, her 'privities' kept clean by poultices and soothed with herbal washes. After a fortnight she was allowed to sit up. The 'upsitting' must have been especially welcome because the soiled bed linen that she had had to lie in since the birth was changed at last. The shutters or curtains were thrown open and she saw daylight for the first time since her pains began. Now she could receive a steady stream of visitors of both sexes.

Her husband was well advised 'to store your cellar well'. In this respect, Sir Thomas Cave was in a happy position, as he confided in a letter to Lord Fermanagh: 'I am provided for caudle better than expected, for his Grace the Duke of Montague has sent his gentn. with nine doz. of fine French white wine, as a present against my wife's lying in.' Above all, the gossips had to have their feast, a bibulous occasion which inevitably involved the swapping of childbirth stories.

While she was confined to her lying-in chamber and unable to attend church prior to her purification ceremony, a mother missed her baby's christening ceremony. This usually took place within three to five days of the birth. In the Anglican Church a boy had one female and two male godparents, while a girl had one male and two female godparents. When a relative of Ned Ward, author of *The London Spy*, invited him to stand godfather he was reluctant: 'The first fruits of their marriage having lately crept into this world of affliction, the joyful father very closely solicited me to do the penance of a godfather that the little epitome of the lad might be craftily cleansed from the sin of his birth. I submitted to his request, and engaged myself, for once, to stand as a Tom-Doodle for an hour or two, to be bantered by a tittle-tattle assembly of female gossips.'

He was dreading running the gauntlet of the gossips, whom he was obliged to kiss in greeting. 'At last I came to the door, which I passed three or four times, as a bashful lover does by his mistress's lodgings, before I had courage enough to enter, fancying every time I went up to the door, that I heard a confusion of women's tongues come through the keyhole.'

No sooner was the religious part of the ceremony over and the parson had toasted the new mother in 'a bumper of Canary' and left with 'a

It was advisable to lay in a good cellar for the gossips' feast, where the baby in his tight swaddling clothes was naturally the centre of attention (*British Library*)

paper of sweetmeats for his wife or his children', than the company settled down to a good supper and prodigious drinking, while the inebriated women chewed over the latest scandal, commiserated with each other about their servants and swapped indiscretions about their husbands.

It was customary for the guests to tip the midwife, who was a guest of honour. The baby, too, would receive christening gifts. Silver items such as spoons, porringers and caudle cups were supposed to bring luck. Coral was believed to have magical properties: 'Some children grow lean and pine away,' Jane Sharp wrote, 'some believe in amber and coral about the child's neck as a sovereign remedy.' Ned Ward does not record his gift to his new godson. He was certainly relieved when the whole episode drew to a close. 'What now remained for me to do was to go upstairs to bid my bedridden relation much joy of her new Christian, and to receive thanks for the trouble she had put me to.'

The new mother's lying-in month ended with her churching. Sniffed at by the Puritans as Catholic superstition, the purification ceremony remained popular despite its penitential overtones. Wearing a veil as a symbol of her continuing enclosure, she ventured into the outside world for the first time since giving birth, accompanied by her midwife and gossips. Kneeling in church in a pew reserved for the purpose, she gave thanks to God for delivering her from 'the great danger of childbirth', allusions to the 'snares of death' and 'the pains of hell' being all too appropriate but thankfully behind her until the next time.

In *The Ten Pleasures of Marriage*, Aphra Behn describes a fashionable young wife making the most of her lying-in month, which has cost her indulgent husband a small fortune in childbed linen and alcoholic refreshment for gossips and visitors. Above all, 'you won't be troubled with the pains of sucking, or disturbed of your natural rest; now you must let the wet-nurse take care of everything, and look after or meddle with nothing yourself'. It was common practice for anyone who could afford it to hire a wet-nurse to feed the child, although this was deplored by the majority of medical practitioners. François Mauriceau stated that 'the first and principal of all the qualities in a good nurse is that she be the own mother of a child'. Jane Sharp advocated maternal breast-feeding 'because it agrees better with the child's temper; for the milk of the mother is the same with that nutriment the child drew in in the womb'.

The clergyman Henry Newcome was especially critical of women of luxury who considered their own beauty and comfort to be more important than safeguarding their children's health by breast-feeding. 'A lady that will condescend to be a nurse,' he complained, 'though to her own child, is become as unfashionable and ungenteel, as a gentleman that will not drink, swear and be profane, but dares be out of fashion in leading an exactly vertuous and sober life.' Newcome noted there was a greater bond between a mother and a child who had been breast-fed by her. Whereas in fashionable society 'it is too common an observation, that some ladies shew a greater fondness toward their dogs than their children'. Certainly the wet-nurse would be well into lactation before taking on the other woman's child, who would miss the breast milk secreted immediately after delivery when it is richest in immune factors.

There was a theory that a child absorbed more than a stranger's milk when being fed by her. A child might well absorb her temperament too. Great care was to be exercised in choosing a wet-nurse. François Mauriceau described some of the qualities to look for: 'In general, she must be very healthful, and of a good habit, not subject to any distemper; that she come of parents that never had stone in the reins or bladder, not subject to gout, King's-evil, falling-sickness, or any hereditary disease; that she hath no spot, nor the least suspicion of any venereal distemper; that she have no scab, itch, scald, or other filth of the like nature; that she be strong ...'

Perhaps the main reason that parents who could afford it put their children out to nurse was that sex during lactation was frowned upon. It was thought to curdle the mother's milk. Husbands who had been deprived too long during the months leading up to the birth now reasserted their rights. Crying babies were to be out of sight and hearing. Certainly not in the marital bed. Babies were fed on demand until they were weaned at about two years old. Breast-feeding was seen to constrict the mother from carrying out her other duties, while for London's many traders there were financial considerations: it was more economical to pay a nurse to feed the child than to lose a wife's services in household and shop. A baby put out to a wet-nurse tended to be breast-fed too long, and because human milk is short of iron, the child would suffer from an iron deficiency anaemia.

The first concern of such a mother was to stop her milk. *The Queen's Closet Open'd* contains this recipe 'to dry up milk in women's breasts':

'Take a quantity of aquavite, and a quantity of sweet butter, melt and temper them together, and anoint the breast therewith, laying a brown paper betwixt them, and so do as often as the paper drieth, till the milk be dried up; this is also good to keep the ague out of the breast.'

From the onset of menstruation at the relatively late age of sixteen or seventeen to the menopause in her early forties, a woman who married in her twenties endured almost twenty years of repeated pregnancy and lactation. She had fewer periods than her modern counterpart. Lactation was known to act as a contraceptive, but if the woman was under pressure to produce an heir or put her child out to nurse, repeated pregnancies at short-spaced intervals were inevitable. From her many pregnancies a woman of wealthy or middling status might bear only four live children, of whom only one or two might survive childhood. So much effort with so little result. For the poor with inferior living conditions and diet, sexual drive and fertility were lower. The fact that poor women breast-fed their children until they were weaned at up to two years of age, however, meant that their births were spaced at more sensible intervals.

In between live births there was a high proportion of foetal wastage through miscarriages, stillbirths and induced abortions. Miscarriages were described as 'moles', lumps of dead flesh believed to result from weakness of the womb or in the male seed. Women of all classes seem to have been more prone to miscarriage, suffering from nutritional deficiencies, weak muscles and pelvic deformities. This may be why married women were able to induce abortion with comparative ease once they felt their families were complete. Household medicinal books were full of recipes purporting to prevent miscarriage or 'bring on the flowers', which conveniently served an alternative purpose. Elizabeth Freke swore by a mixture of nutmeg, cinnamon, cloves, mace, ginger, aniseed and liquorice in water, sweetened with sugar, drunk often: 'This hypocrass soe taken will strengthen the body and preserve conception iff it be true; iff not itt will bring itt away with ease and safety and has done many women good to my knowledge and is a very good medycyne.'

A human cargo of newborn babies was carried by wagon and horseback along the busy trails between London and the country parishes which provided the capital's grain and other foods. Here London's babies were farmed out to wet-nurses. While wet-nursing provided employment for many respectable country wives and poor women hired by the parish, Henry Newcome felt that the whole business was cynical and mercenary. He suspected that wet-nurses were not above sub-stituting children who died in their care with others.

A picture emerges of ignorance and neglect, of small babies in tight swaddling clothes left like parcels hanging on a hook or in a corner of the room for hours. Swaddling slowed down the heartbeat and diminished a baby's crying. It is unlikely that a baby was washed and changed as often as necessary. 'Nurses generally are so negligent, that nastiness oft breeds diseases, and the keeping of the child dirty, is a sure preludium of its funeral,' Newcome warned. He recalls a fellow minister's experience in such a country parish:

> That a worthy divine, the rector of Hayes, about twelve miles from London, with great grief told him, that his parish (being large and populous, and situate in a very wholsome air) at his first coming thither was replenished with infants sent abroad to be nursed; yet in the compass of one year he had buried them all except two: And that the same numbers of nurseries being again twice supplied (through the mercenary diligence of those women) out of London, he had again this same year laid them all in their graves before their time. So that by this account, the citizens seem to put out their children, not so properly to be nursed as to be murdered.

For babies of poorer parents left behind in the disease-ridden capital with its smoke-choked skies and contaminated water, life was just as perilous. Many died from neglect, the unsanitary conditions, and from being smothered in bed by their mothers – whether by accident or intent it was never easy to determine.

Some babies were unwanted, born to unmarried women who were desperate to conceal their shame. These births took place in secrecy, the woman struggling to manage alone and trying not to cry out and alert others to her plight. Without witnesses, there would always be a suspicion that a mother giving birth alone had killed her baby. The Old Bailey Sessions Papers record hundreds of such incidents:

> Jane Watson, late of London, spinster, was indicted for murdering her female bastard child, in feloniously choaking and strangling the same: The evidence, being her landlord and

landlady, deposed that they knew of the prisoner's being with child; and perceiving a drop of blood on the stairs, they entered her room; and enquiring what she had done with her child, she told them it was still-born, and that it was delivered two days before; and upon searching the room, found the child put into a box at the bed's foot; and the prisoner told them she imputed the child's death to a fright she had by a horse. The evidence further deposed, that they could see no marks of violence on the child. The prisoner in her defence said, she had made provision for her child, and call'd for help. Which could not be heard below stairs because of the great noise there, her landlord keeping a tin-shop; That she had several days before bespoke a midwife to assist her. The midwife being call'd into the court, declared she had engaged her, and by other circumstances really believed the prisoner had no ill design, but only was unwilling to expose herself to the scandal.

Jane Watson was extremely lucky that the midwife came to her defence, so that she was found not guilty. The law naïvely assumed that if the woman had made preparations for childbirth there could be no premeditated intention to murder the child. Defoe was extremely sceptical: ' 'Tis but too common a thing to provide child-bed linnen before-hand for a poor innocent babe they are determin'd to murder.'
Servants who became pregnant were likely to lose their place, although the mistress of Phebe Ward, a twenty-five-year-old migrant from Yorkshire, was more solicitous than most. It appears that Phebe was already pregnant by one of any number of men by the time she arrived in London:

and got into good service in a worthy family, where being suspected to be with child, and ask'd the question, she positively deny'd it several times: And tho' she was kindly and charitably offer'd by her mistress (with whom she had not liv'd above a month) to be taken care of, and well provided for, in her lying-in, if she would own (as it greatly appear'd) that she was with child; Yet this miserable wretch did then make great protestations that she never had knowledge of any man, and therefore could not be with child. She confess'd ... that the child (as far as she could perceive) was born alive; and that she smother'd it and then threw it into the vault where it was found.

Once an illicit birth had taken place, the problem loomed as to how to dispose of the baby. Some might be smothered or strangled at birth. Others, like the bastard child of widow Mary Goodenough, 'perish'd for want of suitable help and due attendance'. 'Being in great poverty and straits, even to the want of bread for her and hers', she had sold her sexual favours to a married man. Neighbours discovered her with the dead child wrapped up in the bed at her feet. She was duly found guilty and executed, leaving a son of seven and a daughter of eleven alone in the world.

The authorities sought to tackle the problem by imposing the severest penalty:

> Whereas many lewd women that have been delivered of bastard children, to avoid their shame and to escape punishment, do secretly bury or conceal the death of their children; and after, if the child be found dead, the said women do alledge that the said child was born dead, whereas it falleth out sometimes ... that the said child or children were murthered by the said women their lewd mothers... Be it enacted that if any women ... be delivered of any issue of her body, male or female, which being born alive, should by the laws of this realm be a bastard; and that she endeavour privately either by drowning or secret burying thereof, or any other way, either by herself or the procuring of others, so to conceal the death thereof, as that it may not come to lighter, whether it were born alive or not, but be concealed; In every such case, the said mother so offending shall suffer death, as in the case of murther, except such mother can make proof of one witness at least, that the child was born dead.

Despite the law, desperate women continued to resort to desperate measures to conceal their shame. The Old Bailey Sessions Papers record:

> Christine Russell, of the parish of St Paul's Covent Garden, was indicted for the murther of her male infant bastard ... by throwing the same into the house of office. The first evidence was

her mistress, who deposed, that the prisoner was a servant in the house, and in the morning, it being the fast-day she came down and sat by the kitchen-fire, and told her mistress she was not well, upon which, she bid her go up stairs, which she did; ... she askt her to hire a char-woman for that day ... that she did hope to be better the next day to do her work her self; a while after she did mistrust that she had had a child, and askt her if she was married, and she answered No, then she said, What have you done with the child; and she confest that it was in the house of office... The next evidence was the char-woman, who said, that she took the child out of the vault, and when she found it, there was two pieces of brickbars lay upon the breast of it. The midwife deposed that it was very likely that the child was alive born, by reason it was a very large child, and come to its full time; and said, she found no marks about it, only that the arm was broke ... The prisoner said, that she had a great fall about a fortnight before, which hurt her very much, and that she never felt the child to stir afterwards, but she could not prove that ever she had made any one acquainted with her condition. The jury found her guilty.

She was sentenced to death.

In *The Fable of the Bees* Bernard de Mandeville pleaded the cause of such desperate women:

It is commonly imagined, that she who can destroy her child, her own flesh and blood, must have a vast stock of barbarity, and be a savage monster, different from other women; but this is likewise a mistake, which we commit for not understanding nature and the force of passions. The same woman that murders her bastard in the most execrable manner, if she is married afterwards, may take care of, cherish and feel all tenderness for her infant that the fondest mother can be capable of.

There was an alarming rise in foundling babies, the majority being only one or two months old. Their numbers fluctuated according to the seasons of conception. The harsh winter months saw the highest casualties. Those mothers who placed their babies in churches or hospitals and at the door of the new workhouse in Bishopsgate clearly wanted them to be rescued. Many had notes attached to their clothing stating their name, age, whether they had been baptised. Illegitimacy, widowhood during pregnancy or soon after, desertion by the husband, leading to impoverishment and inability to support the child were the common causes of abandonment. 'I am not able to subsist any longer by reason of my husband being dead and the times is severe hard and having much sickness this half year,' wrote one desperate mother.

Many mothers saw abandonment as a temporary expedient until such time as their fortunes improved:

> This child was borne of unhappy parents wich is not abell to provide for it; therefore I humbelly beg of you gentellman whoever hands this unfortunat child shall fall into that you will take that care that will become a feallow crattear and if God makes me abell I will repaye the charge and reclame the child with thanks to you for the care: her name is Jahn Bennett; she is baptised ... pray belivef that it is extrame neseassty that makes me do this; and shall be your humbell thankfull sarvnt to my livess end.

Defoe was critical of such women, writing in *Augusta Triumphans*: 'Those who cannot be so hard-hearted to murder their own offspring themselves, take a slower, tho' as sure a way, and get it done by others, by dropping their children, and leaving them to be starved by parish nurses.' Every effort would be made to trace the mother of a foundling, so that she might be punished in the pillory or in a house of correction. The parish officers would go so far as to advertise in the newspapers to identify the mother and her parish. They had an incentive to do so, since if the child could not be returned to its own parish they had the responsibility for its upkeep.

Poor, abandoned children shared the same fate as their wealthier contemporaries. They were sent into the country to be nursed at the expense of the parish that reluctantly claimed them. Parish children were supposed to be inspected once a year. Their chances of survival in the negligent care of 'the wet-nurse mercenaries' must have been slim. Defoe pleaded for a foundling hospital to care for such children, but it was not until the 1740s that Sir Thomas Coram realised this dream.

CHAPTER THREE

Childhood

*'Children, when little, should look upon their parents as their
lords, their absolute masters, and stand in awe of them'*

IN LONDON, BETWEEN one-quarter and one-third of babies died before
their first birthday. Only half of all children passed the age of fifteen.
Newborn babies might inherit the name of a dead sibling, or two
living children might be given the same name in the certainty that they
would not both survive. This was not callousness on the part of their
parents. Nor did parents love their children less because they were likely
to be short-lived. There was resignation in the face of death, which was
seen as God's will. When John Evelyn's son of a few weeks suffered the
common fate of being 'overlaid' by his nurse – smothered as she rolled
too close to him in bed – it was 'to our extreme sorrow, being now
againe reduced to one: but God's will be done'.

Parents grieved for their dead children, the more acutely the longer
they were with them. When Ralph Josselin's baby son died, 'it was ye
youngest and our affections not so wonted onto it', while on the death of
a five-year-old son Evelyn wrote of 'our inexpressible grief and affliction'.
While only her brothers and sisters lived long enough to come to
London as migrant workers, Mary Josselin received one of the most
heartfelt tributes ever to a dead child in her grieving father's diary:

> This day a quarter past two in the afternoone my Mary fell asleep
> in the Lord, her soule past into that rest where the body of Jesus
> and the soules of the saints are, shee was: 8 yeares and 45 dayes
> old when shee dyed, my soule had aboundant cause to bless God
> for her, who was our first fruites … it was a pretious child, a
> bundle of myrrhe, a bundle of sweetnes; shee was a child of ten
> thousand, full of wisedome, woman-like gravity, knowledge,
> sweet expressions of God, apt in her learning, tender hearted and

loving, an obedient child to us it was free from the rudenesse of little children, it was to us a boxe of sweet ointment, which now its broken smells more deliciously then it did before, Lord I rejoyce I had such a present for thee, it was patient in the sicknesse, thankfull to admiracion; it lived desired and dyed lamented, thy memory is and will bee sweete unto mee.

Procreation was universally regarded as the primary purpose of marriage. The statistician Gregory King reported that London marriages produced fewer children than country ones. He listed as reasons 'the more frequent fornications and adulteries', 'a greater luxury and intemperance', 'the unhealthfulness of the coal smoke' and 'the greater inequality of age between husbands and wives'. To be childless was a cause of great distress.

Children were very much wanted and valued. The precariousness of life might have led parents to be even more loving and protective towards their children than if they had lived in a more secure environment. Contrary to the notion that the English did not much like children and subjected them to harsh discipline, Henri Misson found that 'they have an extraordinary regard in England for young children, always flattering, always caressing, always applauding what they do; at least it seems so to us French folks, who correct our children as soon as they are capable of reasoning; being of the opinion that to keep them in awe is the best way of doing them a good turn in their youth'.

John Locke noted this tendency of the English to spoil their children: 'and having made them ill children, we foolishly expect they should be good men. For if the child must have grapes or sugar-plums when he has a mind to them, rather than make the poor baby cry, or be out of humour; why, when he is grown up, must he not be satisfied too, if his desires carry him to wine or women?' He advocated 'restraint and discipline', which were to be tempered by the child's age. 'Nor indeed should the same carriage, seriousness, or application be expected from young children, as from those of riper growth. They must be permitted the foolish and childish actions suitable to their years, without taking notice of them. Inadvertency, carelessness, and gaiety is the character of that age.'

London mothers of the upper and middling classes have been criticised for ignoring medical advice and sending their babies off to wet-nurses, under whose care thousands of them died or had their health put in jeopardy. This tragedy may be attributed more to ignorance than indifference. It was genuinely considered better for babies to be reared in the purer air of the countryside. Mothers were not to know that inadequate feeding might cause rickets in their children. It was a common occurrence in children who had been left to wet-nurses. Anxious mothers might turn to Hannah Woolley's recipe 'for young children who by reason of the weakness of their limbs can neither stand nor go':

> Take marjoram and sage, of each a like quantity, beat them well together, then strain out the juice, and put it into a double glass vial, filling the glass as full as it will hold; stop it then with paste very close all over, set it into an oven, and there let it stand the time of an household-loaf's making; taking it out, let it stand till it be cold; then breaking the paste round about it, see if the juice be grown thick; if so, breast the glass, and put what was therein contain'd, into a galley-pot, and keep it. When you use it, take the quantity of two spoonfuls at a time, and as much marrow of an ox-leg, melt them together, and mingle them well, and both morning and evening anoint therewith, as warm as can be endur'd, the tender parts of the childs legs, knees and thighs, chafing them with your hands; and in a short time (*Deo volente*) the child will be able to go and stand; this receipt hath been ever found successful.

It is surprising how little supervision parents gave those supposedly in charge of their offspring. Indeed, parents might leave children in the care of nurses and servants for weeks or months at a time. Elizabeth Freke left her ten-week-old son behind with his nurse while she travelled to Ireland. Eventually she received the alarming news from her father of 'my son being cripled by the carelessnes of his nurse, and about 14 of December brok his legg shortt in the hackle bone [hip], which she kept pryvatte for neer a quarter of a yeare til a jelly was grown between itt; She keeping him in his cradle, and everybody believed he was breeding of his teeth'. The nurse was dismissed, the bone reset and the child made a full, if miraculous recovery. The situation cannot have been unusual in that Dean Swift's *Directions to Servants* tells the nurse: 'If you happen to let the child fall, and lame it, be sure never to confess it; and if it dies, all is safe.'

Hannah Woolley describes the ideal nursery-maid: 'You ought to be of a gentle and good disposition, sober in your carriage, neat in your appeal; not sluggish nor heavy-headed, but watchful and careful in the night season, for fear any of the children should be ill.'

Above all, she was to be on the alert for worms in her charges: 'Take special care that they eat nothing which may over-charge their stomacks. If you observe their faces at any time paler than ordinary, or complain of pain in their stomack, conclude it is the worms that troubles them; and therefore give them remedies suitable to the distemper; do this often whether you see these symptoms or no, the neglect of which hath been the destruction of many hopeful children.'

The philosopher John Locke had been apprenticed in his youth to the leading physician Sir Thomas Sydenham, so that in his seminal work *How to Bring Up Your Children, Being Some Thoughts on Education*, he placed particular emphasis on the importance of health care. He advocated plenty of sleep, fresh air and warm clothing. He was extremely critical of the restrictive nature of children's dress. 'The child has hardly left the mother's womb, it has hardly begun to move and stretch its limbs when it is deprived of its freedom,' he complained. 'It is wrapped in swaddling bands, laid down with its head fixed, its legs stretched out, and its arms by its sides, it is wound round and round with linen and bandages of all sorts, so that it cannot move.'

After the removal of swaddling clothes at about three months, boys fared better than girls. From their earliest years, girls were literally pressed into the desirable shape for marriage by the use of whalebone corsets. When a four-year-old girl in John Evelyn's family died, the autopsy revealed that her corset had broken her ribs, which in turn had pressed into her lungs and killed her. Locke warned of the danger to health from 'straight-lacing'. 'Narrow breasts, short and stinking breath, ill lungs, and crookedness, are the natural and almost constant effects of hard bodice, and clothes that pinch. That way of making slender waists and fine shapes, serves but the more effectually to spoil them.'

Just as the adults around them loved fine clothes, children were brought up to love them too. And so clothes 'are made matters of vanity and emulation'. In vain, Locke warned of the consequences:

> A child is set longing after a new suit, for the finery of it; and when the little girl is tricked up in her new gown and commode, how can her mother do less than teach her to admire herself, by calling her, her little queen, and her princess? Thus the little ones

are taught to be proud of their clothes, before they can put them on. And why should they not continue to value themselves for this outside fashionableness of the tailor or tire-woman's making, when their parents have so early instructed them to do so?

By the same token, progressive thinkers deplored the way sexism played its part in the upbringing of children: 'Miss is scarce three years old, but she is spoke to every day to hide her leg, and rebuk'd in good earnest if she shews it; while little master at the same age is bid to take up his coats, and piss like a man.'

Hannah Woolley urged the nursery-maid to keep her children 'sweet and clean'. None of the advice manuals mentioned potty training. This is not altogether surprising in an age when adults might defecate in the fireplace or odd corners of the house if caught short, when they might use the chamber pot in company in the dining room, or when public conveniences simply did not exist. Children were left to use the pot as and when they felt inclined.

In his advice on the best way to feed children, Locke revealed the ignorance and bad habits of the adults. Children were habitually fed solids too early, and some died as a result. Locke was adamant that a child should eat no meat 'as long as he is in coats, or at least until he is two or three years old'. 'But whatever advantage this may be to his present and future health and strength, I fear it will hardly be consented to by parents, misled by the custom of eating too much flesh themselves, who will be apt to think their children, as they do themselves, in danger to be starved if they have not flesh at least twice a day.' Children would 'breed their teeth with much less danger, be freer from diseases whilst they were little, and lay the foundations of a healthy and strong constitution' if they were not 'crammed so much by fond mothers and foolish servants, and were kept wholly from flesh, the first three or four years of their lives'. Parents were urged to ensure the child chewed his food well. 'We English are often negligent herein; from whence follow indigestion, and other great inconveniences.'

Children's breakfast and supper should consist of milk, milk-pottage, water gruel, or flummery. Sugar and salt were to be used sparingly. 'I should think that a good piece of well-made and well-baked brown bread, sometimes with, sometimes without butter and cheese, would be often the best breakfast for my young master.' There were to be no snacks between meals. In a London where no one drank water, Hannah

Woolley advised that children be restrained from 'drinking too much wine, strong liquors'. Locke maintained that a child's 'drinks should be only small beer; and that too he should never be suffered to have between meals, but after he has eaten a piece of bread'. Lest he fall into the bibulous habits of the older generation, he should not be permitted to drink without eating, to 'prevent the custom of having the cup often at his nose; a dangerous beginning, and preparation to good fellowship'.

Fruit was to be treated with caution. 'But strawberries, cherries, gooseberries, or currants, when thoroughly ripe, I think may be pretty safely allowed them.' Children were not to be permitted to eat fruit 'after meals, as we usually do, when the stomach is already full of other food'. It was to be given them between meals or for breakfast. 'Apples and pears, too, which are thoroughly ripe ... I think may be safely eaten at any time, and in pretty large quantities; especially apples, which never did any body hurt, that I have heard, after October.' Sweetmeats of all kinds were to be avoided. Children were not to be asked, 'What will my dear eat?' and 'What shall I get thee?'

As a reflection of the strictly hierarchical society in which they lived, children were brought up to respect their parents, to show them reverence, love and obedience. César de Saussure observed that 'well-brought-up children, on rising and going to bed, wish their fathers and mothers "good morning" or "good evening", and kneeling before them ask for their blessing. The parents, placing their hands on their children's heads, say "God bless you", or some such phrase, and the children then kiss their parents' hands. If they are orphans the same ceremony is performed with their grandparents or nearest relations.'

Hannah Woolley in *The Gentlewoman's Companion* advised mothers to instil in their children a sense of awe of their father: 'Breed up your children in as much or more obedience to him than your self; and keep them in so much awe that they shew no rudeness before him, or make any noise to his disturbance. Make them shew him all awful regard, and keep them sweet, clean, and decent, that he may delight himself in them.'

Locke described the ideal relationship between parents and children: 'I imagine every one will judge it reasonable, that their children, when little, should look upon their parents as their lords, their absolute governors, and as such stand in awe of them; and that, when they come to riper years, they should look on them as their best, as their only sure friends, and as such love and reverence them.'

Of course, in this age of high mortality many children lost one or both parents in their early years and might be brought up by one or even two step-parents. Many London households were of this hybrid character. They were not always happy arrangements. Men feared that their second wives would not treat their children by the first with the same kindness as they did their own. Unfairly or otherwise, the notion of the wicked stepmother was current.

Parents of the upwardly mobile middling classes took a great deal of interest in their children, not least because they were their investment in the future. The upbringing of children was expensive – providing an incentive to limit the size of a family – but parents were willing to spend the money on education and accomplishments such as music and dancing, on apprenticeships and marriage portions if their children's advancement saw the realisation of their own social and economic ambitions.

Although the literacy rate among London women in 1700 was only about 48 per cent, mothers had the care of their offsprings' early education until it was time for children of all classes to attend dame school at seven. Children would be taught their letters using a horn-book. This measured about four by three inches, on which was printed the alphabet in capitals and small letters, the vowels, a few simple combinations of letters and the Lord's Prayer. The printed paper was laid on a flat piece of board with a roughly shaped handle, and covered with a thin plate of horn, fastened to the board by copper tacks driven through an edging of thin copper. It could stand a great deal of rough usage. In 1694 'J.G.' had published 'a play-book for children to allure them to read as soon as possible. Composed of small pages on purpose not to tire children and printed with a fair and pleasant letter. The matter and method plain and easier than any yet extant.' It consisted of wide margins and large type, simple language, the content being within the child's experience. In 1700 the first educational playing cards arrived from France. The pack taught carving lessons with hearts for joints of meat, diamonds for poultry, clubs for fish and spades for mince pies.

This was a brutal age in which beating was commonplace. Masters might beat servants and apprentices to within an inch of their life, public beatings were inflicted by the authorities on unmarried mothers and the 'undeserving poor' in the house of correction. Even the king's sister-in-law Princess Anne's precious only son, William, who suffered from encephalitis and found it difficult to keep his balance, was beaten by his father until he managed to walk up the stairs by himself. Despite his physical impairments this small boy loved to review his company of boy soldiers. His parents were devastated when he died at only eleven years of age in 1700; with him died their hopes of a Protestant Stuart succession. More enlightened thinkers, however, sought to discourage parents and teachers from the common practice of beating children. Locke noted that 'those children who have been most chastised, seldom make the best men', that 'if the mind be curbed, and humbled too much in children; if their spirits be abased and broken much, by too strict a hand over them, they lose all their vigour and industry'. Hannah Woolley urged her nursery-maid to 'Be loving and chearful with them, not bumping or beating them as many do, contrary to the knowledge and pleasure of their parents: That mother is very unwise that will give liberty to servants to strike her children.'

Beating was counter-productive. 'The usual, lazy, and short way by chastisement, and the rod, which is the only instrument of government that tutors generally know, or ever think of,' wrote Locke, 'is the most unfit of any to be used in education.' Children would come to hate what had first been acceptable to them if they were continually punished. Evelyn practised many such ideas on his own son, preferring a system of rewards, incentives, emulation and self-discipline to physical punishment or verbal chastisement. Beating should be reserved for only the most heinous or obstinate crimes, such as lying. They should fear the shame and disgrace of chastisement rather than feel the pain. These more enlightened theories were beginning to appeal to a growing section of the middling classes anxious for their children's welfare and future prospects.

Nevertheless, when boys exchanged the sheltered world of the home for school, they were often victims of a brutal regime. Robert Campbell, the author of a careers guide entitled *The London Tradesman*, was disgusted to find 'a base custom at Westminster school – the tyrannical subjection under which the junior scholars are kept by the senior. They are mere slaves; are obliged to fetch and carry, like spaniels; and do all the drudgery of menial servants, under the penalty of being severely beat by their seniors.'

Children were to be steered away from the wanton cruelty of the adult world. They should 'be bred up in abhorrence of killing or tormenting any living creature'. Keeping a pet would teach children how to care for inferior creatures. Locke cites an example of a mother who 'was wont always to indulge her daughters, when any of them desired dogs, squirrels, birds, or any such things'. They must be 'sure to keep them well, and look diligently after them, that they wanted nothing, or were not ill used; For if they were negligent in their care of them, it was counted a great fault, which often forfeited their possession, or at least they failed not to be rebuked for it; Whereby they were early taught diligence and good nature.'

Locke advised parents to keep their children away from the servants, who 'by their flatteries ... take off the edge and force of the parents' rebukes, and so lessen their authority'. They might learn bad habits from 'unbred or debauched servants, such language, untowardly tricks and vices, as otherwise they possibly would be ignorant of all their lives'. However, children must learn to be gentle, courteous and affable with others. Parents were to 'accustom them to civility in their language and deportment towards their inferiors, and the meaner sort of people, particularly servants'.

Toys were available from fairs and from street hawkers. Little girls played with dolls, then called 'babies' or 'poppets', commonly bought at Bartholomew Fair. A horse on a stick or a spinning top were popular. Locke suggested that children had only one 'plaything' at a time. 'This teaches them betimes to be careful of not losing or spoiling the things they have; whereas plenty and variety in their own keeping makes them wanton and careless, and teaches them from the beginning to be squanderers and wasters.' Little children had no need of bought toys. 'A smooth pebble, a piece of paper, the mother's bunch of keys, or anything they cannot hurt themselves with, serves as much to divert little children as those more chargeable and curious toys from the shops, which are presently put out of order and broken.' Older children should be encouraged to make their own toys. 'If they have a top, the scourge-stick and leather-strap should be left to their own making and fitting.'

Despite Locke's admonishments, the child of the future had arrived: 'I have known a young child so distracted with the number and variety of his play-games, that he tired his maid every day to look them over; and was so accustomed to abundance, that he never thought he had enough, but was always asking, What more? What more? What new thing shall I have?'

The new, improved world of the child outlined in the conduct books did not extend to all children. As in Defoe's *Moll Flanders*, some were

Little girls played with dolls, called babies or poppets. This one (c. 1700) is wearing
an extremely fashionable striped silk dress, and leading reins like her owner
(*Museum of London*)

victims of crime: 'Edward Tinker of Stepney, was indicted for robbing
John Wheatly an infant of two years old, on the 10th of June, of a coral
necklace, with a gold locket value 50s in a common footway.'

Others were victims of abuse and exploitation. Cases of child rape
frequently reached the courts:

Robert Ingrum of the parish of St Gregory's, was indicted for
feloniously ravishing and carnally knowing Elizabeth Raden a girl

71

of 11 years of age, against her will and consent. Elizabeth Raden declared, that as she was going home, by the prisoners masters shop-door, he lifted her up in his arm and carried her into the shop. Where he tyed her to a chair till he made fast the doors and windows, and then taking her up upon the chair kept her legs betwixt his till he had tore her private parts with his fingers; after which he laid her down on the ground, and putting himself on her body, pull'd something out of his breeches and put it into her body, which together with his former usage hurt her extreamly; and said that she cryed out several times, after which he let her go, but followed her till she was near home, when he took her by the arm, and threatening to do her mischief, made her promise not to tell her parents what had been done, or to discover him, which she did, and kept it up out of fear till her mother discovered some alteration in her body, and viewing her, discovered the matter.

The perpetrator was found guilty and condemned to death, as was:

Henry Simpkins of the parish of St Giles in the Fields ... indicted for ravishing and carnally knowing Grace Price, a girl of ten years of age, against her will. It appeared that the prisoner pickt up the girl and carry'd her to an alehouse where he made her drink, and afterwards carry'd her to an empty house in New Buildings ... and sitting down upon the stairs, took the girl upon his lap, and committed the villany, and gave her the pox. The chirugeon, who has the girl under cure, gave his judgment that she was spoiled in her privy parts, and that she could not be infected with the venereal distemper but by carnal knowledge of the man.

In the latter part of the seventeenth century the nonconformists had led the way in introducing a kinder attitude to children. The Quaker William Penn advised parents 'to love them with wisdom, correct them with affection, never strike in passion, and suit the correction to their ages as well as the fault'. Far from being the products of original sin, which must be broken in by brutal discipline, children were seen by the more progressive thinkers as a blank sheet on which good or evil could be printed. Locke wrote his treatise for parents willing 'to consult their own reason in the education of their children, rather than wholly to rely upon old customs'. He found a receptive audience among the middling classes, who had the money and the ambition to invest in their children's future.

Children were now identified as a special status group, distinct from the adults. For the entrepreneur, children represented a new market. Their concerned parents would be easily persuaded to buy them more toys and books and games and clothes as the new century progressed. Portraits of children gradually reflected the softer attitudes, moving from the formal poses of children as little adults in the seventeenth century to the informal portraits of children at play in the eighteenth century. But although parents were more open in showing their love and affection for their children, the peculiar English practice of farming children out was still prevalent. Children continued to spend many of their formative years away from home, in the households of relatives and others, as servants and apprentices, and, of course, at a variety of schools.

When Samuel Pepys was a rising young civil servant in the Navy Office, he decided to invest in arithmetic lessons. Mr Cooper, mate of the *Royal Charles*, was hired to teach him the basics and it seems the first lesson went well: 'After an hour's being with him at arithmetique, my first attempt being to learn the multiplicacion table, then we parted till tomorrow.' Pepys had been a pupil at one of London's most prestigious schools, St Paul's, and yet he lacked this fundamental skill. By the end of the century London's many endowed free schools, grammar schools, were still in a dither as to whether to concentrate on the classics or branch out into a more modern curriculum.

The new emphasis on vocational training was best epitomised at Christ's Hospital, where a mathematical school had been opened to cultivate navigational skills – as was appropriate in a city at the heart of unprecedented commercial and colonial expansion. After watching the pupils in their distinctive uniforms, Zacharias Conrad von Uffenbach paused to inspect the new school of mathematics:

> In it there stood several cupboards with glass doors, in which were various globi and a certain number of mathematical instruments, though for the most part geometrical. There stood also here a couple of fairly large wooden models of ships of most elegant and curious workmanship; they can be taken to pieces, so that the children, who make a special study of ship-building,

may be shown all the parts of a ship. In a great cupboard near the door were some four hundred mathematical books.

Although London possessed such fine free 'publick' schools as Westminster, Charterhouse, St Paul's and Merchant Taylor's, it became fashionable for boys of the upper and middling classes to be sent to private academies in and around London, where they would receive more individual tuition. When twelve-year-old Ralph Verney was attending Mrs Moreland's boarding school in Hackney, he showed great promise. His uncle Ralph Palmer sent him a parcel:

> Dear Nephew, – You give your friends such extraordinary hopes of your making a fine gentleman, as well by your early inclinations to goodness, as your industrous progress in learning, that you deserve the greatest encouragement. The books I here send you I desire you to accept as a pledge of my affections, they are the works of the author of the Hole Duty of Man. I need not desire you to read them, because I know you will make the best use of them, and when I see you next I will furnish your closet with some books of another kind that may be serviceable to you in the way of your studys, and I doubt not but in due time you will be very ornamental to your family, as well as truly serviceable to your selfe & country; which are the hearty wishes of your most affectionate uncle, R. Palmer.

Where boys had at least some chance of a good education, to go on to the Universities of Oxford and Cambridge and the Inns of Court, it was not thought necessary to waste it on girls. Hannah Woolley bitterly resented this. 'I cannot but complain of, and must condemn the great negligence of parents, in letting the fertile ground of their daughters lie fallow,' she fulminated, 'yet send the barren noddles of their sons to the university, where they stay for no other purpose than to fill their empty sconces with idle notions to make a noise in the country.'

In *The Gentlewoman's Companion*, she describes a mode of behaviour for a young schoolgirl:

> Hasten to school, having first taken your leave of your parents with all reverence. Do not loyter by the way, or play the truant

Edmund Verney took his eight-year-old daughter Molly to Bartholomew Fair as a treat before leaving her at boarding school in Chelsea (*British Museum*)

... Leave not any thing behind which you ought to carry with you, not only things you learn in or by, but also gloves, pocket-handkerchiefs ... neglect not what you are to do, by vain pratling in the school: make no noise, that you may neither disturb your mistress, or school-fellows ... If you write, be careful you do not blot your paper; take pains in the true forming or cutting your letters, and endeavour to write true and well after your copy. Preserve your pens, spill not your ink, nor spurt it on your own or others clothes, and keep your fingers from being polluted therewith.

Contemporary education was designed to snare girls a husband, not to turn them into blue stockings who would remain spinsters and a financial burden on their families. At boarding schools in villages such as Hackney and Chelsea, daughters of the gentry and middling classes learned such accomplishments as calligraphy, accounts, cookery, housewifery, drawing, painting, music, dancing, needlework. When Edmund Verney's daughter Molly was eight years old he brought her to London in order to attend 'Mrs Priest's school at Great Chelsey'. But first she was to receive some treats: 'Tomorrow I intend to carry my girle to schoole, after I have showd her Bartholomew Fayre & the tombs [at Westminster Abbey] & when I have visited her and a little wonted her to the place, I'll come home,' he wrote.

75

Before long, Molly wanted to learn the new art of japanning, painting boxes in the Japanese manner, and her father agreed to pay for this 'extra': 'a guiney entrance & some 40s more to buy the materials to work upon'. He wrote to Molly:

> I find you have a desire to learn to Japann, as you call it, and I approve of it; and so I shall of any thing that is good & virtuous, therefore learn in God's name all good things, & I will willingly be at the charge so farr as I am able – tho' they come from Japan & from never so farr & look an Indian hue & odour, for I admire all accomplishments that will render you considerable & lovely in the sight of God & man; & therefore I hope you performe yr part according to yr word & employ yr time well, & so I pray God bless you.

Privileged girls might receive extra tuition in French, which had become very fashionable, but no Latin or Greek. They would be turned into ornamental wives. So much so that the feminist Mary Astell was compelled to ask, 'How can you be content to be in the world like tulips in a garden, to make a show and be good for nothing?'

The children of the 'deserving poor' were to be flung a bone in the form of charity schools, which they might attend between the ages of seven and fourteen. There was serious alarm at the increase in poverty in London and the threat to social order posed by the great disorderly mass of the poor. Charity-school boys and girls were to be indoctrinated early to avoid the 'habits of sloth, debauchery and beggary' so typical of their class. Benefactors could rest assured that these children of artisans, small shopkeepers and labourers would be turned into pliant servants. They would be constantly reminded of their subordinate position in life.

Social and moral reform was driven by religious revival. The Anglican Church wanted to arrest the drift towards atheism and win back the souls of the poor. The Society for Promoting Christian Knowledge was founded in 1699 with the avowed intention of establishing charity schools 'in each parish in and about London'. There was no better place to start than in the sprawling out-parishes where the presence of the Anglican Church was at its weakest through lack of churches, and by 1704 there were fifty-four charity schools catering for 1,386 boys and 745 girls.

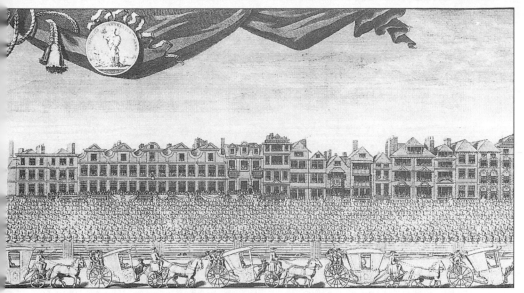

Charity school children, seen here at a parade in the Strand, were left in no doubt as
to their future destiny as servants
(*Guildhall Library, Corporation of London*)

Charity school pupils would be provided with a suit of clothes. It is
evident from *An Account of the Methods Whereby the Charity Schools Have
Been Erected and Managed, and of the Encouragement Given to Them* that the
main purpose of this uniform was so as to be able to identify pupils
misbehaving in public. 'The children shall wear their caps, bands,
cloaths, and other marks of distinction every day,' it stated, 'whereby the
trustees and benefactors may know them, and see what their behaviour is
abroad.' Parents were urged to send their children 'wash'd and comb'd to
school, least otherwise they be offensive there; and they be frequently
exhorted to give them good examples, and keep them in good order
when they are at home.'

At the charity schools teaching took place between 7 a.m. and 11 a.m.
and 1 p.m. and 5 p.m. in summer, and from 8 a.m. to 11 a.m. and 1 p.m.
to 4 p.m. in winter. Children would be taught the 'knowledge and
practice of the Christian religion, as profess'd and taught by the Church
of England'. They would learn 'the true spelling of words, and
distinction of syllables, with points and stops' and to write a fair and
legible hand. The curriculum would offer a grounding in arithmetic 'to
fit them for services and apprentices', but girls might sit out of the
arithmetic classes in order to learn sewing. Children were also given

work during school hours – 'some to spinning of wool, others to mending and making of shoes, others to sewing, knitting, etc' – so that there could be no doubts as to their future destiny. There would be three school holidays a year but 'by no means during Bartholomew Fair, for fear of any harm by the ill examples and opportunities of corruption at that season'. Perhaps not surprisingly under such a weight of patronage and frequent bouts of corporal punishment, there was a high incidence of truancy, for which the only remedy was expulsion.

Many London children fell through the educational net altogether. John Hall, born in Grays Inn Lane in Holborn, was 'descended of very mean parents, his mother at this time carrying a basket in Brook's-Market, and living upon the alms of the parish, he was depriv'd of the advantages of any education, in so much that he could neither read nor write; so that for want of going to school, and imbibing good principles in his juvenile years, he took to pilfering as soon as ever he was able to go playing about the streets'. Richard Low was born 'near the Horse-ferry, Westminster, of parents of pretty good credit and reputation'. Apparently they would have 'given him some education, as reading and writing, yet being an untoward child, he would never addict himself to learning, but always play'd truant'.

If educational excellence was to be found at all, it was at the dissenting academies. They gave not merely an education to dissenters, but a 'dissenting' education – an education much broader than that offered in the schools established by the law and controlled by the Church. The young Daniel Defoe first attended a dissenting school as a boarder at Dorking, and then at the probable age of sixteen entered Charles Morton's Academy at Newington Green, a few miles north-east of the City of London. Here Defoe mastered five languages, studied arithmetic, geometry and astronomy, natural philosophy, rhetoric and logic, geography and history and read 'politics as a science'.

As a nonconformist, Defoe was barred from the Universities of Oxford and Cambridge, where the emphasis was still firmly placed on the classics. No wonder he advocated the establishment of a University of London based on the collegiate system: 'Why should such a metropolis as London be without a university? ... Will not London become the scene of science ... Knowledge will never hurt us, and whoever lives to see an university here, will find it give quite another turn to the genius and spirit of our youth in general.' His idea had to wait until the

nineteenth century when University College London became the first university to admit Roman Catholics, Jews and nonconformists. Meanwhile, Charles Morton had become the first Vice-President of Harvard College in New England, and, like so many of his fellow citizens whose childhood had come to an end, nineteen-year-old Daniel Defoe entered the world of work in the wholesale hosiery business in the City of London.

Disease

'These gentlemen of the faculty are pensioners to death...'tis the physician has the honour of killing him and expects to be well paid for the job'

I N THE GLOOM of the apothecary's shop, John Seal felt distinctly queasy as he stared at the stuffed alligator hanging above the counter. William Rose's apprentice seemed to be in no hurry as he prepared his medicine. With the studied concentration of somebody far older than his sixteen years, he was opening jars, taking a whiff, shaking the contents and preparing another of his concoctions. No doubt it would make him horribly sick, but surely that was the point, to purge the system? Seal was anxious to get home. He had been feeling ill for the best part of a year now. At the outset of his illness, it had not occurred to him to send for a physician. He was only a poor butcher. How could he afford a physician's fees? Haughty creatures, with their full-bottomed wigs, their velvet suits and their university education. Seal had never had a coach and four at his door. But still, he had now spent the best part of £50 on the apothecary's medicine and if anything he was feeling worse than when he started. If this did not do the trick, he ruminated, he would definitely try that new dispensary the physicians had opened in St Martin's Lane.

In the event, this is exactly what Seal did. This being an open market where consumers took responsibility for their own health and voted with their purses, he shopped around for a cure elsewhere. He ended up suing the hapless apothecary into the bargain:

> This is to certify, that I, John Seal, being sick, and applying myself to this Mr Rose the apothecary for his directions and medicines, in order for my cure; had his advice, and medicines

The sight of the stuffed alligator as well as some of the potions themselves probably
made many visitors to the apothecary's shop feel worse
(*Wellcome Institute Library, London*)

from him a year together: But was so far from being the better for them, that I was in a worse condition than when he first undertook me; and after a very expensive bill of near 50l. was forc'd to apply my self to the Dispensary at the College of Physicians, where I receiv'd my cure in about six weeks time, for under forty shillings charge in medicines.

The sudden cure was surely fortuitous – nature finally doing its work – for very little medicine of the time, from whatever source, was efficacious. How could it be, when the causes of disease were not understood? Patients did not necessarily expect doctors or medicines to cure them. Whether from sickness or injury, it took an inordinately long time to get better. Hippocrates taught that nature was its own best healer. The physician's duty was merely to aid it. Nature herself would cure many diseases, and luck or accident cured many more.

As Londoners suffered chronic ill health, they were easy prey to any who promised a cure. There was a lot of money to be made from the desperate and gullible. The wit Tom Brown suggested in his *Amusements Serious and Comical* that a wise man should steer clear of a greedy medical profession who had a vested interest in over-prescribing: 'When a sick man leaves all for nature to do, he hazards much; when he leaves all for the doctor to do, he hazards more; and since there is a hazard both ways, I would much sooner choose to rely upon nature. For this, at least, we may be sure of, that she acts as honestly as she can, and that she does not find her account in prolonging the disease.'

The College of Physicians, jealous of so many encroachments on its privileges, pounced on the William Rose case. Here was an opportunity to assert its hegemony and frustrate the ambitions of its many competitors, licensed and otherwise, in a booming business:

> The practice of physick in London and seven miles round, being for near two hundred years settled by law, wholly in the College of Physicians in London, and such as they approve of upon examination, and licence; 'tis worth the while to enquire by what means they come to enjoy so small a part of it. Chymists and distillers, astrologers and mountebanks, midwives and nurses, and the whole train of broken-tradesmen doctors have everyone their share. There are not a few that are their own

doctors, and practice upon themselves; and there is hardly any one so unkind, as not to recommend to his sick friend what has done himself good. The College can only blame these last for indiscretion: And the former are the most of them hardly worth the charge of prosecution; yet the College have been ever and anon making an example of one or other of them, to strike terror into the rest.

The Rose case gave the physicians their chance to put the apothecaries in their place. 'The College of Physicians, observing that their forbearance to prosecute the apothecaries who practis'd physick, was so far abused by them, as to be interpreted as submission, that the apothecaries had a right to do so. And that every apothecary in the town pretended to undertake even the most dangerous diseases; they thought it time to stop this growing evil.'

How dare these subordinates to the physicians, these mere tradesmen who knew no Latin and Greek, presume to diagnose and prescribe medicine? Only the physicians, who had spent up to fourteen years at the Universities of Oxford or Cambridge, had the necessary classical education to enable them to study Hippocrates and Galen, upon whose theories the practice of medicine was still based. Some of them had even attended more scientifically oriented medical courses at the Universities of Padua, Montpellier and Edinburgh, and incorporated these degrees into an Oxbridge degree for a fee. Most of London's physicians were either fellows or licentiates of the College of Physicians, housed in Wren's fine new building in Warwick Lane.

Members of the Worshipful Society of the Art and Mystery of the Apothecaries of the City of London, however, merely served a seven-year apprenticeship. An apprentice accompanied his master to attend sick patients and observed the physician at work, he learned to make up physicians' prescriptions in the shop and he made the occasional 'herbarizing' excursions into the country. He could also study botany at the Apothecaries' Physick Garden by the river at Chelsea. If he were very keen and had the time to spare, an apprentice apothecary could also attend the public anatomy lectures at Surgeons' Hall.

Originally members of the Grocers' Guild, who stocked and sold spices, the apothecaries had won the sole right to dispense and sell medicines in London and within seven miles of it. At their newly built

headquarters in Black Friars Lane, they had a laboratory for the preparation of medicines. Their shops comprised a front room for sales, often
displaying a stuffed alligator or crocodile amidst a bewildering jumble of
labelled jars, and a back room for preparations. Together with the College
of Physicians, the society had the right to inspect an apothecary's stock
and to burn any defective items at the door of his shop.

Although they were trying to retain a monopoly of medicine, the
physicians were far outnumbered by the apothecaries and barber-
surgeons and had no hope of servicing over half a million sickly and
hypochondriac Londoners by themselves. By 1700 there were about
1,000 apothecaries and sixty to eighty physicians in London. As the
apothecaries were spending so much time touting for customers in the
coffee-houses, they tended to leave the running of their shops to two or
three apprentices, bringing more into the business than it could sustain.
According to the author of *The Present Ill State of the Practice of Physick in
this Nation*, a member of the College of Physicians: 'When any trade is
overstockt, those who are of it will naturally either invade the business of
other men, or strive to raise the prices of their own work or
commodities.'

The physicians doggedly argued that the apothecaries were not
qualified to practise, that there was more to medicine than merely
observing the physician at work and copying his methods. When the
William Rose case came to trial in 1701, the jury hesitated before
coming down on the side of the physicians. But clearly there were not
enough physicians, they were expensive, and they were unlikely to leave
their beds to attend sick patients in the middle of the night. This was
the opinion of the House of Lords. When the Rose case went to appeal,
the Lords ruled it 'against the public interest to prevent the giving of
advice and treatment by members of the Apothecaries Company' and
reversed the verdict.

The pretensions of the physicians were a cause for scorn and
amusement. It had not been forgotten that many of them had abandoned
Londoners to their fate during the plague of 1665, following their rich
patients to Oxford and the countryside. They were hardly more
successful than anyone else in curing disease. Tom Brown was highly
scathing of the profession:

These gentlemen of the faculty are pensioners to death, and

travel day and night to enlarge that monarch's empire; for you must know, notwithstanding distempered humours make a man sick, 'tis the physician has the honour of killing him, and expects to be well paid for the job... So that when a man is asked how such a man died, he is not to answer, according to corrupt custom, that he died of a fever or a pleurisy, but that he died of the doctor.

It was difficult for the physicians to reduce their fees without reducing their worth in the public eye. But in a bid to prove that they had the interests of the poor at heart and to undercut the apothecaries, a group of physicians set up public dispensaries, where advice and treatment were offered for a fraction of the normal costs. As the author of *The Necessity and Usefulness of the Dispensaries Lately Set Up by the College of Physicians in London for the Use of the Sick Poor* expressed it:

That the physicians might clear themselves of this false charge, they have been obliged to set their care of the poor more in the eyes of the world than heretofore; not only giving advice gratis to the poor at their own and the patients lodgings, but appointing public dispensaries also for the poor to resort to every day of the week (except Sundays) where they may both have the best advice gratis, and also proper medicines, for their respective cases at the lowest value; whereby the poor are at once delivered from the danger of the apothecaries ignorance in practice, and also from the oppressive charge of their medicines.

The dispensaries were advertised widely, and it was presumably at the one in St Martin's Lane that John Seal received his cure, after his resort to an apothecary had proved a false economy.

For those physicians who did not subscribe to the dispensaries, there was profit to be made from colluding with the apothecaries. The one could charge for attendance, the other for the medicine, imposing a huge mark-up: 'a vomit is 1s.6d. when it is not intrinsically worth above 1d. or 2d', complained the author of *The Necessity and Usefulness of the Dispensaries*. Worse than that, he continued, 'they shall either of them pour in upon the patient three times as much physick as the subscribers to the dispensaries usually prescribe in like cases, the greatest part whereof ... is nothing to the purpose of the cure, but serves only for the pomp, and to raise the apothecaries bill, or perhaps does the patient a great deal of harm'.

Tom Brown describes such an unholy alliance:

> See a consult of 'em marching in state to a patient, attended by a diminutive apothecary that's just arse-high, and fit to give a glyster [enema]. How magisterially they look and talk of the patient's recovery, when they themselves are but death in disguise, and bring the patient's hour along with 'em. While the patient breathes and money comes, they are still prescribing; but when they have sent the patient hence ... they'll say his body was as rotten as a pear, and 'twas impossible to save him.

As a consequence of their growing involvement in medical practice, the apothecaries neglected 'chymistry'. According to the author of *The Present Ill State of the Practice of Physick in this Nation*: 'And though they make no scruple to let their boys make up physick of all sorts for their patients, while they are abroad visiting; yet they dare not leave furnaces and glasses to their care, for fear they might sustain some loss. Whence it comes to pass, that not one in twenty knows anything of this part of their trade.' Just at this time when the medical regime was embracing chemical as well as traditional herbal medicine, the 'chymists' and druggists diverged from the apothecaries into a separate trade and confined themselves to their shops.

The barber-surgeons did not escape the physicians' censure, although ironically their study of anatomy was giving them a far more practical knowledge of the workings of the body than the physicians could draw from their reliance on ancient texts. Surgical practice in the London area was restricted to those who had served a seven-year apprenticeship to become members of the Worshipful Company of Barber-Surgeons, although the Bishop of London or the Dean of St Paul's sometimes granted licences to surgeons who had not been approved by the company. The barbers and surgeons formed one company, but each was to keep to his separate part of the business.

The physicians forbade the surgeons to practise internal medicine, but this was clearly impractical. An eminent London surgeon such as Joseph Binns always began his treatment of an injury with the administration of a vomit (emetic), a purge (purgative) or a clyster (enema) to clean out the stomach and bowels and set the body on the path to healing itself. According to the precepts of Galenic medicine that were still current, an individual's mental and physical condition was believed to depend on the balance of the humours. The four humours, or bodily fluids – blood, phlegm, yellow bile and black bile – corresponded to the four elements of earth, fire, air and water, whose qualities were dryness, heat, cold and wetness. An imbalance of the humours caused dis-ease. As excess humours must be evacuated to restore the body to equilibrium, surgeons were kept busy with the traditional treatments of bloodletting, cupping and blistering. The body of a woman whose periods had stopped, for instance, was considered to be awash with ill humours, which would affect the brain and cause melancholy and troubled spirits. Blood would be drawn from the sole of her foot to 'bring down the menses'.

Ned Ward, author of *The London Spy*, was persuaded to undergo 'cupping' for a shoulder injury:

> Upon this the operator fetched in his instruments, and fixed three glasses to my back, which, by drawing out the air, stuck to me as close as a Cantharidid plaster to the head of a lunatic till I thought they would have crept into me, and have come out t'other side. When, by virtue of this hocus-pocus stratagem, he had conjured all the evil blood out of my body under his glass juggling cups, he plucks out an ill-favoured instrument and begins to scarify my skin, as a cook does a loin of pork to be roasted, but with such ease and dexterity that I could have suffered him to have pinked me all over full of eyelet holes had my malady required. When he had drawn away as much blood as he thought necessary for the removal of my pain, he covered the places he had carbonaded with a new skin, provided for that purpose, and healed the scarifications he had made instantly.

Few physicians and surgeons appreciated that bloodletting was likely to make the sick weaker. Just to be on the safe side, many people elected to be bled once a year as a spring clean, whether they were ill or not. As the need for sterilisation was not understood, they risked infection from the surgeon's unclean hands and tainted instruments.

Injuries from accidents in the traffic-congested streets were common as pedestrians were pushed off the narrow pavements into the path of iron-wheeled vehicles. Burns from cooking fires and overturned candles in the home were a frequent hazard. Fussy headdresses did not help, as a friend reported to Sir John Verney: 'I have just now heard a sad story of your Aunt Verney, who being at her prayers, had her head cloths fired, & narrowly escaped being burnt herself, no help comeing to her presently, but at last she was assisted after having suffered much in her hands & face.'

The bills of mortality for 1700 record: 'Burnt and scalded ... 8' and 'Killed by several accidents ... 28.'

Severely damaged limbs required immediate amputation before the onset of gangrene. 'Gangrene, fistula, & mortification ... 36'. The English were notorious for their pugnacity, quick to draw a sword or a firearm in a tavern or street brawl, as Ned Ward observed: 'They are seldom free from thumps, cuts and bruises, and part to their surgeon with pounds as freely as fools did with their pence to the Wheel of Fortune Lottery.' Penetrating wounds to the head, chest and abdomen were usually fatal.

Surgery was limited to the most superficial of internal operations. Fortunately, since it was such a common complaint, it was possible to cut for the stone, although as many died from the operation as did from renal calculus itself: 'Cut of the stone and the stone ... 43.' John Evelyn's brother Richard died of 'the stone in the bladder' after having suffered increasing agony for well over a year. Evelyn described his pain as 'such exceeding torture ... that he now began to fall into convulsive fits'. He refused to undergo surgery, even though he received a visit from Samuel Pepys who had survived the experience and 'carried a stone as big as a tennis-ball' to prove it. The removal of an appendix or gall-bladder was beyond the surgeon's scope. Severe internal inflammation brought on by such a condition might be described as 'Stoppage of the stomach' in the bills of mortality. Death was inevitable.

Superficial tumours could be removed. A mastectomy was possible. Pepys learned from his wife that 'my poor aunt James had her breast cut off here in town – her breast having long been out of order'. The art of plastic surgery, pioneered by an Italian in the sixteenth century, was used to conceal the effects of a nose eaten away by the pox. Performing an operation on a table in the patient's home and relying on alcohol to relax the patient, the best surgeon was a speedy worker.

The barber-shops were a male resort. Bloodletting, the extraction, cleaning and scraping of teeth, nail paring, ear waxing, shaving of beards and heads and wig-making, were the original purpose of the shops. They provided music, gaming, news and conversation, and tobacco, believed to cure toothache. They also offered their male customers sexual advice and condoms, so that it was the surgeons rather than the physicians who acquired a virtual monopoly of the treatment of venereal disease.

There was no consensus that licensed healers were the sole authority in medical matters, while naturally they vigorously resisted the opposite tendency towards do-it-yourself medicine. 'People are not competent judges of what they ail, or what will help them,' pronounced the author of *The Necessity and Usefulness of the Dispensaries*. Not surprisingly given their precarious state of health, people were obsessed with it, exhaustively examining their symptoms and confiding them in diaries and correspondence. Every household had its medicinal recipe book passed down from mother to daughter. But now this knowledge was boosted by the publication of a spate of medical books in the vernacular.

Gideon Harvey produced *The Family Physician and the House Apothecary* specifically so that the layman could select and compound his own treatment and 'save nineteen shillings in twenty, comparing it with the extravagant rates of many apothecaries'. William Salmon's *English Physician: Or, The Druggist's Shop Open'd* is a dictionary of medicines informing the layman what they are, where they are from, and what they do. Cannabis, for instance, although readily available over the counter, comes with a note of caution: 'The seed, which heats and dries, and by much using abates seed in man, cures coughs, asthma, jaundice, and other like diseases.'

Opium, too, was on sale and was being advertised: 'Lately published, *The Mysteries of Opium Reveal'd* by Dr John Jones, a Member of the College of Physicians in London, and formerly fellow of Jesus College in Oxford. Shews its noxious principle, and how to separate it; thereby rendering it a sage and noble panacea.' Less lethal tonics which were great favourites were the Queen of Hungary's water, a rosemary-flavoured brandy, and Daffy's Elixir, consisting of canary wine, oranges, lemons, rhubarb and borax.

The College of Physicians reserved its greatest venom for the theories of the late 'physician-astrologer' Nicholas Culpeper of Shoreditch, labelling him a quack. Even if breakthroughs in medical science had not yet filtered down to general practice, most physicians had abandoned the use of astrology in diagnosis. They relied increasingly on close observation of the patient's symptoms and the meticulous recording of case notes.

Herbal rather than chemical remedies were still the preferred option for the majority of practitioners. However, Culpeper's *The English Physician Enlarged* included an English translation of *Pharmacopoea Londinensis* in which he describes the preparations recommended by the College of Physicians – they ranged from indigenous wild flowers to sparrow's brains and frog's liver to pearls and, most precious of all, gold – and adds his own comments and criticisms of its compilers. Culpeper was a keen advocate of the Doctrine of Signatures, believing that God had shaped plants specifically to suggest their curative purposes – for instance, cyclamen for ear disease, liverwort for liver disease, eyebright for eye diseases – and however quirky his 'alternative' theories his works have proved enduring bestsellers.

In this volatile and suggestible market quacks such as the notorious Dr John Case thrived. 'On a little shelf among phials and gally-pots, were half a dozen long bottles of Rosa Solis, with an advertisement of a rare whitewash for the face nailed to one side, and a brief account of the excellencies of Doctor John Case's pills for the speedy cure of violent pains without loss of time or hindrance of business on the other,' observed Ned Ward in *The London Spy*. Over Case's door was announced: 'Within this place/Lives Doctor Case', a jingle which Addison remarked made the 'doctor' far more money than Dryden ever did from his poetry. Unlike licensed practitioners, the quacks had no compunction in advertising. Newspapers, the walls of coffee-houses, even the Royal Exchange itself were littered with their advertisements: 'The wainscot was adorned with quack's bills, instead of pictures; never an empiric in the town but had his name in a lacquered frame, containing a fair invitation for a fool and his money to be soon parted.'

Excessive claims were made for the efficacy of their cures:

Present Remedy after Misfortune: Or, an immediate Cure for the French Disease and Clap; and all other of its numerous attendants, which oftentimes are the product of other grievous lasting distempers, to the utter ruin of many, besides frequently, unsealy death, procured by them through grand abuses, committed by the base and irregular methods and medicines of foolish and unskilful pretenders. Good medicine and advice may be had of a physician of 40 years practice, living at the Blue-ball in Whale-bone Court, the lower end of Bartholomew-lane, behind the Royal Exchange.

The least reputable quacks were the travelling mountebanks, who sold their medicines from a portable stage in the street and were usually accompanied by a clown and sometimes a monkey. The clown was nicknamed a merry-andrew after Dr Andrew Boorde, who as physician to Henry VIII had needed a good sense of humour. His purpose was to entertain the audience and put them in the mood to purchase the mountebank's wares. The poor were his particular targets. Ned Ward thought it scandalous that such rogues could make it their 'business to cheat the common people not only out of their money, but often out of their health, which is far more valuable'.

He describes a scene at the Fleet Bridge where a rowdy crowd had gathered to watch a fight between two women who were hurling insults at each other:

Just as the squabble was ended and before the rabble was dispersed, who should be stumbling along upon his hidebound prancer, but a horse-mountebank, who seeing so rare an opportunity to hold forth to a congregation already assembled, spurred up his foundered Pegasus, and halting in the middle of the crowd, plucked out a packet of universal hodge-podge, and thus began his oration to the listening herd.

The mountebank was selling a sixpenny parcel of treatments shrewdly calculated to embrace the common ailments of the average Londoner. A small pill guaranteed that 'if you have twenty distempers lurking in the mass of blood, it shall give you just twenty stools, and every time it operates it carries off a distemper'. Then there was 'an excellent outward application, called a plaster, good against all green wounds, old fistulas and ulcers, pains and aches in either head, limbs or bowels, contusions, tumours of King's evil, sprains, fractures or dislocations, or any hurt whatsoever, received either by sword, cane or gunshot, knife, saw or hatchet, hammer, nail or tenterhook, fire, blast or gunpowder, etc.'

Any quack offering a cure found a receptive audience among chronically sick
Londoners (*British Library*)

The next 'unparalleled medicine ... is an admirable powder, good to fortify the stomach against all infections, unwholesome damps, malignant effluvias that arise from putrid bodies, and the like'. It will overcome any problems associated with gluttony and an unbalanced diet: a man might pack away 'a pound of Suffolk cheese, and twice the quantity of rye bread, and still have as good an appetite to a sirloin of roast beef, as if he had not eaten a bit in a fortnight'. It was also 'the most powerful anti-verminous medicine' and 'if either yourselves, or your children are troubled with that epidemical distemper, worms, which destroy more bodies than either plague, pestilence or famine, give or take this, infused in a little warm ale, instead of wormseed and treacle, you will find these death's agents, that burrow in our bodies, come creeping out both ends'.

He offers an antidote to the poison inflicted by the new 'Paracelsian', or chemical, treatments of mercury, arsenic and opium. It will work on colds and fever by 'gentle perspiration'. For those in the crowd sporting rotten teeth and diseased gums, 'it is also a most rare dentifrice, and cleanses all foul, and fastens all loose teeth, to a miracle'.

Ward continues:

> This impudence so tickled the ears of the brainless multitude that they began with as much eagerness to untie their purses, and the corners of their handkerchiefs, and to be free of their pence, as they usually are to buy apples by the pound, or to purchase the sight of a puppet show, that it was as much as ever the doctor could do to hand out his physick fast enough. Thus they continued flinging away their money, showing there were fools of all ages, from sixty to sixteen, many of them looking as if they could scarce command as much more till next Saturday night when they received their wages; till at last, either the doctor broke the crowd of their money, or the crowd the doctor of his physick. Then away he trotted on horseback with their pence, and left his patients to trudge away on foot with his packets.

Londoners recognised that they had to pay for medical treatment. It did not occur to them to do otherwise. They confined themselves to their chambers at home – out of necessity since treatment was designed to rid the body of its ill humours by constant vomiting and purging – nursed by the women of the family or by hired nurses and receiving obligatory visits from friends and neighbours. 'If the person you visit be sick, and in bed, let not your stay be long,' Hannah Woolley advised, 'for sick persons are unquiet; and being tied up to physick, and controul'd by its operations, you may offend them by their being offensive to you: you must remember likewise to speak low.' She was also at pains to remind her readers that it 'much discourageth and dejecteth the sick person to lie in foul linnen, making them even loath themselves in that stinking condition'. The sick chamber would be fumigated with pitch and frankincense and sometimes sulphur.

Free health care was limited to the aged poor. The hospitals that survived the dissolution of the monasteries in the sixteenth century – St Bartholomew's and St Thomas's – were there to serve their needs alone, to provide them with beds as much as treatment. Nursing was indifferent. At St Bartholomew's a matron presided over a dozen nurses, called sisters in continuation of monastic custom. The hospital diet was supposed to include meat, bread, butter, milk, cheese and beer. People, beds and clothing were infested with vermin, and infection was rife.

The third survivor of the dissolution was Bethlehem Hospital, popularly known as Bedlam, for 'the distracted and lunatick'. While Bedlam was the country's only public asylum, many private asylums were springing up in response to demand – as much for men eager to put away unwanted wives as for the truly insane. Those who failed to find a cure at any of the asylums might put this newspaper advertisement to the test:

> In Clerkenwell-Close, where the figure of mad people are over the gate; liveth one, who by the blessing of God, cures all lunatick distracted and mad people, he seldom exceeds 3 months in the cure of the maddest person that comes in his house, several have been cur'd in a fortnight, and some in less time; he has cur'd several from Bedlam and other mad-houses in and about this city, and has conveniency for people of what quality soever. *No Cure No Money!*

The inmates of Bedlam could stay for one year. In a rare instance of government benevolence, the property of a lunatic was kept safe for him until his discharge. The public could visit the new building in Moorfields, passing through a gateway topped with the statues of three chained maniacs, and tipping a particularly rapacious porter on the way out. The magnificence of the building, based on the Palace of the Louvre no less, prompted Tom Brown to comment, 'the outside is a perfect mockery to the inside, and admits of two amusing queries, whether the persons that ordered the building of it, or those that inhabit it, were the maddest?'

A visit to Bedlam was a good day out for Londoners, who derived real enjoyment from observing the 'frantic humours and rambling ejaculations of the mad folks'. César de Saussure made such a visit:

> Many inoffensive madmen walk in the big gallery. On the second floor is a corridor and cells like those on the first floor, and this is the part reserved for dangerous maniacs, most of them being chained and terrible to behold. On holidays, numerous persons of both sexes, but belonging generally to the lower classes, visit this hospital and amuse themselves watching these unfortunate wretches, who often give them cause for laughter.

Travellers approaching London were warned of their imminent arrival by the overwhelming stink. Along the roads leading to the capital lay mounds of sewage and other waste, dumped there by the 'night-soil men', so that it was imperative to hold a handkerchief to the nose and mouth. In the city itself, streets and ditches were awash with human excrement and urine, which might be deposited on hapless passers-by from open windows or thrust out into the streets at night. Sheep, cattle, pigs and poultry were led through the muddy streets to slaughter and added their excrement to that of the horses. Dead animals were left to putrefy were they lay, and the vicinity of markets and butchers' premises was littered with discarded remains. Overflowing vaults flowed into cellars and cesspits leaked into wells and contaminated the water supply.

John Evelyn also warned of the threat to health from London's overcrowded graveyards: 'I am perswaded, that the frequency of church-yards, and charnel-houses contaminate the aer, in many parts of this town, as well as the pumps and waters, which are any thing near unto them, so that those pipes and conveyances which pass through them (obnoxious to many dangerous accidents) ought either to be directed some other way, or very carefully to be looked after.'

Apart from the smells, there was the all-pervasive, choking, sulphurous coal smoke which belched out of thousands of domestic fires and industrial furnaces – the 'brewers, diers, lime-burners, salt and soap-boilers' – who operated within the metropolis. It played havoc with King William's asthma, so that even before Whitehall Palace was destroyed by fire in 1698 he was compelled to move out to the village of Kensington for its purer air. All Londoners were affected by the pollution, as Evelyn noted with understandable distaste:

> For is there under heaven such coughing and snuffling to be heard, as in the London churches and assemblies, where the barking and the spitting is uncessant and most importunate the inhabitants of London, and such as frequent it, find it in all their expectorations; the spittle, and other excrements which proceed from them, being for the most part of a blackish and fuliginous colour.

In this unhealthy environment an attempt was made to identify and record the causes of death in the bills of mortality; these elementary statistics would prompt someone as far-sighted as Sir William Petty to advance their use as an index of public health so that the community could be protected. At this early stage, however, even the medical profession had trouble in defining a disease, plague and smallpox being the only two recognised for certain. Physicians were not obliged to issue death certificates. As the 'searchers' employed by the parishes to make these returns were poor, ignorant lay women who gave the deceased only the most cursory external examination and relied on hearsay and guesswork, the bills offer only a rough guide. The equation of their findings with our definitions of sickness and disease can only be tentative.

There were the diseases Londoners lived with – chronic, debilitating and disfiguring. And there were the diseases that killed. The low standard of personal hygiene meant that fleas and lice were commonplace, even on the bodies, wigs and clothing of the wealthy. They were blissfully unaware of the connection between plague, rats and

(*Opposite*) The bills of mortality gave Sir William Petty a starting point in the field of public health (*Guildhall Library, Corporation of London*)

A General BILL of all the *Christnings*
and *Burials*, from the 19. of *December*, 1699.
to the 17. of *December*, 1700.

According to the Report made to the *KING* His
Most Excellent MAJESTY:

By the Company of Parish-Clerks of London, *&c.*

Parish	Bur.	Pl.	Parish	Bur.	Pl.	Parish	Bur.	Pl.	Parish	Bur.	Pl.
St Alban in Woodstr	29		St Clement near Eastcheap	12		St Margaret in Newfishstr.			St Michael in Crookedlane	27	
Alnallows Barkin	83		St Dionis Backchurch	28		St Margaret Pattons	22		St Michael at Queenhith	36	
Alhallows in Breadstreet	17		St Dunstan in the East	82		St Martin in Ironmongerla.	3		St Michael at Quern	16	
Alhallows the Great	63		St Edmund the King	15		St Martin at Ludgate	49		St Michael Royal	27	
Alhallows in Hony-lane	4		St Ethelburga's Parish	28		St Martin Orgars	18		St Michael in Woodstreet	8	
Alhallows the Less	14		St Faith under St Paul's	37		St Martin Outwich	9		St Mildred in Breadstreet	22	
Alhallows in Lombardstr.	23		St Gabriel in Fenchurchstr.	5		St Martin Vintrey	33		St Mildred in the Poultry	18	
Alhallows Staining	27		St George in Botolph-lane	13		St Mary Abchurch	24		St Nicolas Acons	2	
Alhallows on LondonWall	60		St Gregory by St Paul	77		St Mary in Aldermanbury	26		St Nicolas Coleabby	12	
St Alphage near Sion-Coll.	37		St Helen near Bishopsgate	30		St Mary Aldermary	22		St Nicolas Olive	7	
St Andrew Hubbard	14		St James in Dukes-place	14		St Mary le-Bow in Cheapsi.	18		St Olave in Hartstreet	45	
St Andrew Undershaft	39		St James at Garlickhith	41		St Mary Botaw at Dowg.	2		St Olave in the Old Jury	13	
St Andrew Wardrobe	53		St John Baptist by Dowg	19		St Mary Col church			St Olave in Silverstreet	28	
St Ann within Aldersgate	30		St John the Evangelist	4		St Mary Hil near Billinsg.	28		St Pancras in Pancras-lane	6	
St Ann in Blackfriers	125		St John Zachary	26		St Mary Mag. in Milkstreet			St Peter in Cheapside	9	
St Anthony vulg. Antholin	12		St Katharine Coleman	52		St Mary Mag in Oldfishstr.	34		St Peter in Cornhil	25	
St Augustin vulg. Austtin	16		St Katharine Creedchurch	61		St Mary Mounthaw	7		St Peter near Paulswharf	13	
St Bartholom. Exchange	15		St Laurence Jewry	53		St Mary Somerset	29		St Peter Poor in Broadstr.	33	
St Benedict v. Bennet Fink	18		St Laurence Pountney	17		St Mary Staining	14		St Stephen in Colemanstr	47	
St Bennet Gracechurch	16		St Leonard in Eastcheap	5		St Mary Woolchurch			St Stephen in Walbrook	16	
St Bennet at Paulswharf	29		St Leonard in Foster-lane	38		St Matthew in Fridaystr.	33		St Swithin at Lond. stone	27	
St Bennet Sherehog	5		St Magnus by Lond. Bridg	49		St Michael Bassishaw	27		St Thomas the Apostle	18	
St Botolph at Billingsgate	10		St Margaret in Lothbury	21		St Michael Cornhil	21		Trinity Parish	23	
Christ's Church Parish	125		St Margaret Moses	5		St Michael in Cornhil			St Vedast alias Foster	29	
St Christophers Parish	31											

Christned in the 97 Parishes within the Walls—1790   Buried—2656   Plague—0

Parish	Bur.	Pl.	Parish	Bur.	Pl.	Parish	Bur.	Pl.	Parish	Bur.	Pl.
St Andrew in Holborn	906		St Botolph by Bishopsgate	465		St George in Southwark	342		St Sepulchres Parish	554	
St Bartholomew the Great	41		Bridewel Precinct	23		St Giles by Cripplegate	1193		St Thomas in Southwark	55	
St Bartholomew the Less	22		St Bridget vulg. St Brides	278		St Olave in Southwark	581		Trinity in the Minories	12	
St Botolph by Aldersgate	188		St Dunstan in the West	171		St Saviour in Southwark	480		The Pesthouse		
St Botolph by Aldgate	502											

Christned in the 16 Parishes without the Walls—4580   Buried—5812   Plague—0

Parish	Bur.	Parish	Bur.	Parish	Bur.	Parish	Bur.
Christ-Church in Surry	141	St John at Hackney	84	St Leonard in Shoreditch	447	St Mary in Rotherheth	211
St Dunstan at Stepney	1818	St John at Wapping	272	St Mary at Islington	99	St Mary in Whitechappel	715
St Giles in the Fields	1200	St Kathar. near the Tower	152	St Mary Mag. Bermondsey	376	St Paul at Shadwel	331
St James at Clerkenwel	294	Lambeth Parish	240	St Mary at Newington	167		

Christned in the 15 Out-Parishes in Middlesex and Surry—5053   Buried—6647   Plague—0

Parish	Bur.	Parish	Bur.	Parish	Bur.
St Ann in Westminster	496	St Margaret in Westminster	794	St Mary Savoy in the Strand	104
St Clement Danes without Templebar	403	St Martin in the Fields	1424	St Paul in Covent-Garden	180
St James in Westminster	927				

Christned in the 7 Parishes in the City and Liberties of Westminster—3216   Bur.—4328   Pl.—

The Diseases and Casualties this Year.

Abortive and Stilborn	546	Grief	5	Stoppage in the Stomach	320
Aged and Bedridden	1242	Griping in the Guts	1004	Strangury	9
Ague and Fever	3676	Headach	1	Surfeit	70
Apoplexy and Suddenly	104	Head-mould-shot	6	Swelling in the Neck	1
Bleeding, Bloody-flux, and Flux	13	Jaundies	73	Teeth	1159
Cancer, Canker, and Thrush	124	Imposthume	59	Twisting of the Guts	2
Chicken-Pox	1	Lethargy	5	Vapours and Water in the Head	7
Childbed	240	Livergrown	11	Vomiting	15
Chrisoms and Infants	78	Looseness	5	Worms	53
Colick	72	Overlaid	69		
Consumption and Tissick	2819	Palsie	31	**CASUALTIES.**	
Convulsion	4631	Plurisie	30		
Cough and Chincough	7	Quinsie	10	Bruised	1
Cut of the Stone and Stone	43	Rheumatism	16	Burnt and Scalded	8
Diabetes	1	Rickets	393	Deceased (so reported in the Coroners Warrant)	1
Distracted and Lunatick	35	Rising of the Lights	101		
Dropsie and Tympany	659	Rupture	18	Drowned	48
Evil	83	St Anthony's Fire	9	Found dead in the Streets, &c.	9
Executed	29	Scarlet-Fever	1	Hang'd and made away themselves	28
Falling-Sickness	1	Scurvy	5	Hang'd by Misfortune	1
Flox, Small Pox, and Measles	1031	Shingles	1	Kill'd by several Accidents	38
French Pox	69	Sores and Ulcers	62	Murdered	11
Gangrene, Fistula, & Mortification	36	Spleen	3	Smothered and Suffocated	3
Gout and Cramp	15	Spotted Fever and Purples	189	Stabbed	1

Christned: Males—7578, Females—7061, In all—14639
Buried: Males—9653, Females—9790, In all—19443, Plague—0.
Decreased in the Burials this Year—1352

97

fleas. After the plague of 1665, London rats seem to have become resistant. Coincidentally, the plague-carrying black rat was in the process of being overtaken by a new species of brown rat. There was no need therefore for plague-carrying fleas to abandon dying rats for human hosts. There would be no more outbreaks of plague in London, although no one realised this for some considerable time. Even as late as 1720 when plague broke out in Marseilles, Londoners feared its spread. Daniel Defoe's *A Journal of the Plague Year*, published in 1722, found a receptive audience.

Contaminated food and drinking water caused frequent outbursts of bacterial stomach infections. Flies travelled from faeces to food. It did not occur to those preparing or handling food to wash their hands after defecating. The bills of 1700 recorded only those cases that proved fatal, rising to a peak in the heat of August: 'Griping in the guts ... 1004', 'Twisting in the guts ... 2', 'Bleeding, bloody flux and flux ... 13', 'Looseness ...1'. The following recipe 'to cure a great flux or looseness of the belly' from *The Queen's Closet Open'd* can hardly have alleviated the condition: 'Take a hard egg and peel off the shell, and put the smaller end of it to the fundament or arsehole, and when that is cold take another such hot, fresh, hard, and peeled egg, and apply it as aforesaid.'

Dysentery killed within hours or days. Infants under the age of two were highly vulnerable. Diarrhoea might be accompanied by high fever leading to convulsions. The eminent physician Sir Thomas Sydenham prescribed his own highly popular remedy: two ounces of strained opium, one ounce of saffron, one drachm each of cinnamon and cloves in a pint of canary wine. Many deaths occurred because there was no understanding that severe diarrhoea, usually with blood and mucus in the stools, called for the replenishment of liquids and salt in the body.

Intestinal worms, described as 'round, flat or threadlike', was a condition especially common in children:

> Oftentimes children are extremely troubled with worms; they
> are generated of a viscous and flegmy humor; are sometimes
> round, and then children are commonly troubled with a feaver,
> and grow lean, their appetite fails them, they start in their sleep,
> they have a dry cough joyned with it, with a stinking breath,
> and an ill colour in their faces; the eyes hollow and dark with a
> kind of irregular feaver, which comes three or four times a night,

and they often rub their noses; if they be little worms, they have
always a desire to go to stool, and their excrements are very
purous.

It is unlikely that people actually died of 'worms', despite the fifty-
three cases listed in the bills of 1700. But as their eggs might be
repeatedly relayed into the mouth from unwashed hands, worms could
be a long, debilitating condition. The 'flat' worms might be tapeworms
from undercooked beef and pork. We know from Pepys' *Diary* that
meats brought in from the cook shops – the contemporary take-away –
were frequently found to be undercooked. Those from pork could pass
into the brain and be responsible for epileptic fits, described in the bills
as the 'falling sickness'. Hannah Woolley in *The Queen-like Closet*
advised:

> For the falling-sickness:
> Take a live mole, and cut the throat of it into a glass of white-
> wine, and presently give It to the party to drink at the new and
> full of the moon (viz.) the day before the new, the day of the new,
> and the day after, and so at the full. This will cure absolutely, if
> the party be not above forty years of age.

Other stomach disorders might be down to overindulgence in food
and drink – 'Surfeit ... 70' – and to an unbalanced or inadequate diet.
Those who could afford it ate large helpings of meat, scorned vegetables,
and suffered from chronic constipation. Pepys was constantly worried by
constipation and wind. Good living and a tendency to drink anything
but water also led to gout with its painful swollen big toe. Sir Thomas
Sydenham suffered from the condition himself and wrote a paper on it:
'The gout most commonly seizes such old men as have liv'd the best part
of their lives tenderly and delicately, allowing themselves freely
banquets, wine, and other spirituous liquors: and at length, by reason of
the sloth that always attends old age, have quite omitted such exercises
as young men are wont to use.' 'Dropsie and tympany' described
swellings from excessive fluid retention.

Gideon Harvey erroneously thought that scurvy with its swellings,
sores and ulcers was a new disease and called it 'the disease of London'.
John Woodall, the first surgeon-general of the East India Company,

astutely recommended the juice of lemons as a prevention, but this was not adopted until the end of the eighteenth century. St Bartholomew's Hospital used spoonwort growing on the banks of the Thames to make scurvy-grass ale for scurvy sufferers.

Children of all classes suffered from rickets through a deficiency of Vitamin D, essential for the absorption of calcium. There was little chance of Vitamin D being generated by the sun's rays in London's dark rooms and polluted atmosphere. Lack of calcium and other minerals caused aberrant bone growth and skeletal deformity. Splints were applied to try to correct bowed legs, but there was no remedy for a hunched back or a deformed or enlarged head. Girls with pelvic deformity would later suffer in childbirth.

The King's Evil, or scrofula, described tuberculosis of the lymph glands of the neck – bovine tuberculosis transmitted in milk. 'Swelling in the neck ... 1', 'Evil ... 83'. All the Stuart monarchs had adhered to the old superstition of 'touching' to cure the condition. As with so many instances of 'magical' healing, the power of suggestion was at work. Or else the illness went into abeyance. Only the rational and dispassionate William III declined to touch, telling his disappointed subjects, 'God give you better health and more sense.'

The bills list 'Ague and fever ... 3676', one of the highest causes of mortality. Malaria was borne by mosquitoes from marshy land, ditches and stagnant water, causing intermittent fevers of varying severity. It was treatable with Peruvian bark containing quinine, which was scarce and expensive. Those who could not obtain it had to rely on less exotic remedies: 'Take feverfew and sage and bruise them half a pennyworth of pepper. One little spoonful of chinny [chimney] soot and ye white of an egg mingle them together and lay it to ye wrist.'

'Fevers' and 'convulsions' are indiscriminately used to cover a multitude of infections causing high temperature. 'Convulsions ... 4631'.

In an age when the slightest sign of fever in the morning might result in death within hours or days, even the common cold was taken seriously. Diarists such as Pepys, Evelyn and Josselin never failed to mention a cold. Pepys found a concoction of honey and nutmeg very soothing. The French visitor Henri Misson noted: 'When a cold grows inveterate in England, you may reckon it the beginning of a mortal distemper, especially to strangers; you must beware therefore how you neglect a cold.' Those suffering from a sore throat might suck Dr Sydenham's lozenges.

Influenza certainly existed but it was not identified until the mid eighteenth century, when an epidemic in Italy swept through the population with such sudden ferocity as to suggest it came as the result of the influence of a particular constellation of the stars, hence 'influenza'. Earlier in seventeenth-century London, Thomas Willis had a similar impression and described the symptoms of an epidemic:

> About the end of April, suddenly a distemper arose, as if sent by some blast of the stars, which laid hold on very many together: that in some towns, in the space of a week, above a thousand people fell sick together. The particular symptoms of this disease, and which first invaded the sick, was a troublesome cough, with great spitting, also a catarrh fallin down on the palat, throat and nostrils; also it was accompanied with a feaverish distemper, joyned with heat and thirst, want of appetite, a spontaneous weariness, and a grievous pain in the back and limbs.

Meningococcal meningitis, listed as 'Spotted fever and purples ... 189', was common in crowded conditions such as prisons. Typhus, otherwise known as gaol-fever because of the prevalence of this louse-borne infection in prisons, had first been identified and recorded in the garrisons during the civil wars. Judges and juries were exposed to the disease in the courtroom, and a particularly bad outbreak would be known as a 'Black Assize'. It was a common misfortune for a prisoner in the dock to be 'seiz'd with the jayl-distemper, which is a violent feaver, attended with a delirious light-headedness, and so was not in a capacity to give any account of himself'. Typhoid, transmitted in contaminated drinking water, was sometimes confused with typhus because of the rash and fever that could occur in both diseases.

There was a virulent new strain of smallpox – called *small*pox to differentiate it from the great pox, or syphilis – and it was highly contagious among London's closely packed population. The virus was inhaled from the exhalations of people incubating the disease, or transmitted through contact with the pox pus or scabs of a sufferer. The Queen Regnant Mary died from smallpox in 1695. Thousands of migrant workers, who had never been exposed to it in the countryside and had no immunity to it, inevitably succumbed soon after arriving in London. The adolescent children of the Essex clergyman and diarist Ralph Josselin – Ann and Elizabeth who came as servants, and John and Thomas who came to serve apprenticeships – all survived the disease.

Traditionally the chamber in which a smallpox victim lay would be swathed in bright red fabric to draw out the infection. The early stages brought a raging fever and severe pains in the head, back and muscles. Some died from haemorrhages in the lungs and other organs before the appearance of the rash. Pimples turned into full-scale pustules which were sometimes so dense that the skin was eliminated. In less severe cases where the pustules were more widely spaced, there was hope of recovery once the fever broke. The scabs would fall away after a few weeks. Smallpox scars left facial disfigurement for life and led to the fashion of applying patches to the face, which English women did to ridiculous excess. Tom Brown scoffed: 'Some of them having scabbed or pimpled faces wear a thousand patches to hide them, and those that have none, scandalize their faces by a foolish imitation.'

Because of the rash, smallpox and measles were sometimes confused or lumped together in the bills: 'Flox, small pox, and measles … 1031.' Thomas Sydenham described measles as a disease of childhood, and it would have caused many deaths.

Those Londoners who survived the perils of infancy and young adulthood and built up immunity to a whole arsenal of infectious diseases remained vulnerable to respiratory droplet infections. Evelyn noted the propensity of any gathering of Londoners to cough and spit. Those in the vicinity of a consumptive's phlegm would be treated to a host of airborne bacilli. Consumption, or tuberculosis, was one of the biggest causes of death in London: 'Consumption and tiffick … 2819.' Overcrowded and unclean living conditions and airless rooms were ideal breeding grounds. The physician Thomas Sydenham was alone in recommending fresh air. *The Queen-like Closet* recommended:

> For a consumption an excellent medicine:
> Take shell-snails, and cast salt upon them, and when you think they are cleansed well from their slime, wash them, and crack their shells, and take them off, then wash them in the distilled water of hyssop, then put them into a bag made of canvas, with

some white sugar-candy beaten, and hang up the bag, and let it drop as long as it will, which if you bruise the snails before you hang them up, it is the better; this liquor taken morning and evening a spoonful at a time, is very rare.

Diaries recorded numerous eye problems, such as the 'rheum'. The dimness of candlelight must have added to the strain. It was failing eyesight that prevented Pepys from continuing his diary from 1669 to his death in 1703. Household books contain recipes for 'sore eyes', 'dim eyes', 'watery eyes' and 'pain in the eyes'.

'Teeth' is listed in the bills as a cause of death. Mortality was high among infants at teething stage. Often mothers and nurses took pity and sought to alleviate their suffering by rubbing the gums with a coin, causing infection, fever and death. Sometimes poisoning from pewter dishes and lead nipple-shields killed a child at teething stage. Adults suffered from toothache and gum disease. Septicaemia and abscess could kill.

Tobacco was thought to cure toothache. Alternatively, *The English Housewife* advised:

> Take sage, rue, smallage, fetherfew, wormwood, and mint, of each of them half a handfull, then stamp them well all together, putting thereto four drams of vinegar, and one dram of bay-salt, with a pennyworth of good aquavitae, stir them all well together, then put it between two linnen clouts, of the bigness of your cheek, temples, and jaw, and quilt it in a manner of course imbroydery. Then set it upon a chassing-dish of coals, and as hot as you may abide it, lay it over the side where the pain is, and lay you down upon that side, and as it cools warm it again, or else have another ready to lay on.

Dental hygiene was woefully inadequate. 'If you will keep your teeth from rotting, or aching, wash the mouth continually every morning with the juyce of lemons,' *The Queen's Closet Open'd* advised, 'and afterward rub your teeth with a sage leaf, and wash your teeth after meat with fair water.' The returning court at the Restoration had introduced toothbrushes from Paris, but there is little evidence that they were widely used. Toothpicks were part of the toilette. It was possible to have the teeth scraped, but it was a painful and costly business. Extraction must have been all too tempting for those suffering toothache. False teeth, of human or animal origin, were available, but were so ill-fitting that speech became pretty much incomprehensible.

Physicians and surgeons were consulted about a variety of 'female disorders'. Although the female menstrual cycle was regarded as a 'sickness', a 'monthly disease' or 'infirmity', the absence of periods was seen as alarming. Women menstruated to rid their bodies of impurities. Bloodletting was considered advisable to relieve the body of ill humours if the woman did not menstruate naturally. There were lots of recipes 'to provoke the terms'. 'Take wormwood and rue each a handful, five or six pepper-corns,' Hannah Woolley directed, 'boil them altogether in a quart of white wine or malmsey; strain it and drink thereof.' Compared to endless discussion on how to stimulate menstruation, little attention was paid to the 'cessation of the flowers' in women who lived long enough to reach the end of their childbearing years. The health of menopausal women was assumed to be precarious, deprived as they were of the regular, necessary discharge of blood.

Adolescent girls who had just started to menstruate were prone to chlorosis, or the green sickness because of the greyish-green tinge of their complexion. They suffered from palpitations, breathlessness, indigestion, constipation, irregular periods, and odd eating habits, often with difficulty in swallowing. The problem may have been attributable to diet, iron deficiency, and lack of fresh air and exercise. But their general malaise might also have been one of the consequences of excessively tight corseting from earliest childhood. There was no known cure for the green sickness. Contemporaries advocated marriage and vigorous sexual activity.

Vaginal infections, such as 'the whites' producing a copious and unpleasant discharge, were treated with pessaries of shorn sheep's wool steeped in herbal remedies or fine linen or silk bags containing the same inserted into the vagina. Women were advised to attach a string for their removal. It is just possible that some women in menstruation adopted this early approximation of an internal tampon.

Many innocent married women discovered they had contracted venereal disease from their husbands, who were under the illusion that they had been cured. Venereal disease was a social disgrace and relatives went to considerable lengths to persuade the searchers not to record the 'French disease' or 'pox' as the cause of death. The statistician John

Graunt suspected that after 'the mist of a cup of ale and the bribe of a two-groat fee', the searchers were very obliging about this. Venereal disease was far more widespread than the figures in the bills would indicate. Deaths from 'sores and ulcers' could have been syphilitic. Sufferers could also have gone down as 'lean and emaciated'. Graunt, who made a study of the bills of mortality, believed that 'only *hated* persons, and such, whose very noses were eaten off, were reported by the searchers to have died of this too frequent malady'.

Venereal disease was rampant and it was known to be sexually transmitted and even passed from mother to baby. But it was misunderstood owing to the long delay between the appearance of the first symptoms – a chancre or sore on the genitals – and the subsequent symptoms which were likely to appear many years later in skin, joints and nervous system. Thomas Sydenham was unique in making a distinction between syphilis and gonorrhoea, which might be transmitted at the same time. Gonorrhoea was treated by purgation. The bagnios, or bath-houses, were used for sweating treatments and gradually through their association with venereal disease became places of ill-repute.

Sydenham described the progress of syphilis:

> The patient is affected with an unusual pain in the genitals ... a spot, about the size and colour of a measle, appears on some part of the glans ... A discharge appears from the urethra ... the aforesaid pustule becomes an ulcer ... Great pain during erections... Ardor urinae ... Bubos in the groin ... Pain in the head, arms and ankles .... Crusts and scabs appear on the skin ... The bones of the skull, shin-bones, and the arm-bones, are raised into hard tubers ... The bone becomes carious and putrescent ... Phagadaenic ulcers destroy the cartilege of the nose. This they eat away; so that the bridge sinks in and the nose flattens ... At length, limb by limb perishing away, the lacerated body, a burden to earth, finds ease only in the grave.

Surgeons routinely treated syphilis by administering mercury by mouth and applying it in ointments to rashes, scabs and ulcers and by injection to the nose and genitals. Mercury is highly toxic and the dosage was regulated by the side-effects, which included nausea, diarrhoea and salivation. It was a long, costly and distressing business.

Mercury relieved the symptoms and might even have saved some people from developing the tertiary disease.

By 1700 medical science had not found the remedies for disease. The fact that the role of hygiene or even organisms themselves were not understood meant that the medical profession was far from being able to tackle the fundamental problems. Indeed, they could offer little more than the 'cunning men and women' of the past. Without hope or

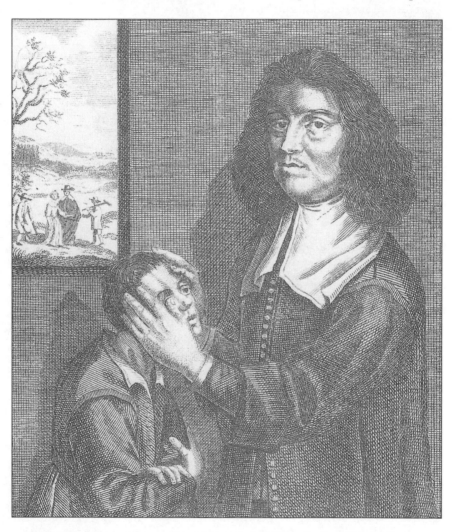

Touching, the laying on of hands, was part of the healer's art then and now
(*British Library*)

106

conviction that their doctors could cure them, people of all educational hues clung to superstitious remedies. Samuel Pepys attributed a sudden spell of good health 'to my fresh hares foot' worn as an amulet and even as late as 1697 a friend was writing to Sir John Verney:

> I am sorry to find by my Mother's letter that your familly has been in such a crazy way & particularly that my Lady's teeth have been so troublesome ... & for the pain in her breast, my mother thinks herself obliged to prescribe to her & 'tis whot a lady in this house has experienced with great success when the Doctors feared a cancer for her; & which is only a tanned hareskin worn allways upon it, with the furr next her skin.

Even after all the massive strides in medical science and technology of the last hundred years, the old 'alternative' theories remain. Touching, the laying on of hands, and stroking, drawing the energy down to the body's extremities in order to restore the balance, or equilibrium, are back in vogue. Sales of Nicholas Culpeper's books on herbal remedies are brisk. Health shops in every high street offer the sort of wide array of non-prescription remedies that were once obtained from the apothecaries. In this scientific world, magic, the power of suggestion, faith and holistic healing, are still components in the repair of the delicate mechanism of mind and body.

CHAPTER FIVE

Death

'The searchers repair to the place where the dead corps lies …
they examine by what disease or casualty the corps died'

THE BELL TOLLED nine times, there was a brief pause, then thirty-six chimes. A thirty-six-year-old man was dying. Did he hear the signal of his imminent demise? His passing-bell was less of a warning to him than to the living bustling about their daily business in the parish: 'The beating of thy pulse is just the tolling of thy passing-bell.' The bell might toll many times in a day, striking six times for a woman and three for a child, followed by one stroke for each year of their age.

The words of the Anglican burial service – 'in the midst of life we are in death' – never rang so true as in this age of high mortality. The death rate among people of all ages was higher than it had been a century earlier. London could not sustain its population without constant immigration. Death was not confined to the old. About one-third of the population died well under fifty. Husbands lost young wives, children their mothers, mothers their babies. An epidemic might wipe out several children in a family within days. Thousands of children and adolescents failed to reach adulthood. Adults in their twenties and thirties, often family breadwinners, were surprisingly vulnerable. Sickness was a constant presence in every home. Death was never far away. Medicine was powerless to prevent it. A fever in the morning could bring death by the evening. A simple cut or broken bone might be the harbinger of infection and death. The killer epidemic smallpox had become especially virulent. So contagious was it that it was very difficult to get a clergyman to bury a smallpox victim.

Life was a mere prelude to death. Regular attendance by relatives, friends and neighbours at death-beds and funerals reminded all to hold themselves in daily expectation of their own demise and to make spiritual preparation for it. Even in this more secular society innumerable diaries record frequent self-examination of the soul, a desire to keep one's relationship with God fresh and immediate. People clung to the idea of the after-life.

'Our lives are very short, they fly away like a shadow, and fade like the flowers of the field; and this were a very unsupportable thought, were there either no life after this, or not so happy a life as this,' stated one of many contemporary manuals on the art of preparing for a good death. 'We now call it death to leave this world; but were we once out of it, and instated in the happiness of the next, we should think it were dying indeed to come into it again.'

Yet in this post-Reformation world there was a lingering anxiety at the loss of Purgatory. No longer were the living able to relieve the dead of their sins by saying masses for their souls. This powerlessness translated itself into elaborate funeral rituals to assuage the grief of those left behind.

A spiritual need became inextricably linked with materialism. Funerals had become big business, attracting entrepreneurs. London's first professional undertaker, William Boyce, opened shop in 1675 'at ye White Hart & Coffin, in ye Grate Ould Bayley, near Newgeat'. William Russell, painter and coffin-maker, showed greater business acumen by linking up with the College of Arms in 1689. Hitherto, the college had arranged the funerals of the nobility under strict guidelines stipulated by the crown. The nobility was chafing at the expense of it all and would soon release itself from its grip. Now William Russell would pay members of the college to attend certain funerals he had arranged. He scooped the biggest share of the upmarket trade. Others followed in his wake.

The average undertaker was no more than a speculative cabinet-maker and joiner, who bought wholesale all the accoutrements a funeral required. Closely related, the funeral furnisher would buy the coffin ready made, and provide all the other accoutrements. Items such as the pall and wall coverings were more likely to be hired than bought by the client. Both undertaker and furnisher were in the business of 'undertaking' all the arrangements for the funeral. Trade cards elaborately designed with grinning skulls and shroud-clad corpses, bones, pickaxes and hearses were distributed to describe their functions. It was not the done thing to advertise, and anyway the funeral itself was the best advertisement. Coachmen, footmen and other servants received tips for early warning of an impending or actual death. Undertakers tended to restrict their business to their own parishes, such as 'Eleazar Malory, joiner at the Coffin in White Chapel, near Red Lion Street end',

Funerals were becoming big business and the first professional undertakers supplied
all the material needs from off-the-peg shrouds to tickets to mourning wear
(*British Museum*)

who opened in 1700 and 'maketh coffins, shrouds, letteth palls, cloaks, and furnisheth with all other things necessary for funerals at reasonable rates'.

There was comfort in the fact that death was a social occasion. Plague had been terrifying because it meant dying in isolation from others as sufferers were locked up in their houses in a misguided attempt to prevent the spread of infection. It was a social and religious duty for all to visit the sick and pray with the dying. People of all classes, even children, would attend a series of death-bed scenes before their own. Constant exposure bred resignation in the face of death. It was no less grievous for that. Grief was sometimes recorded as a cause of death in the bills of mortality. Some women lamented their husbands had been taken from them because they loved them too much.

Parents mourned their children, the more severely the longer they were with them. Children were accorded funerals only slightly less elaborate than those of adults. Infants who died before their mothers had been churched were buried in their chrysoms, pieces of white cloth held round the body with bands or pins that had been worn at their baptism. Such burials were described in the parish registers as 'chrysoms'. Even stillborn babies – who had not been integrated into Church and society through baptism – were to receive proper burial, albeit in the north side of the churchyard alongside suicides, excommunicates and executed felons. The midwife's oath stated that 'if any child be deadborn, you yourself shall see it buried in such secret place as neither hog, dog nor any other beast may come unto it ... you shall not suffer any such child to be cast into the lanes or any other inconvenient place'.

The legacy of plague was the introduction of the searchers, ignorant old crones employed by the parish to visit the dead and determine the cause of death. The London haberdasher John Graunt, founder of the science of statistics, observed:

> When anyone dies, then, either by tolling, or ringing of a bell, or by bespeaking of a grave of the sexton, the same is known to the searchers, corresponding with the said sexton. The searchers hereupon (who are ancient matrons, sworn to their office) repair to the place where the dead corps lies, and by view of the same, and by other enquiries, they examine by what disease or casualty the corps died. Hereupon they make their report to the parish clerk.

Their findings were duly recorded in the weekly bills of mortality.

The Frenchman Henri Misson was an avid observer of English funeral customs. In 1678 the government had introduced a highly controversial bill stipulating that the dead be buried in woollen shrouds to boost the native industry, and imposed a penalty of £5 on those ignoring it. As £5 was a fraction of the cost of a well-heeled funeral, many members of the upper and middling classes could afford to defy the law. Some felt so strongly that they stipulated in their will their wish to be buried in linen. The merry widow in Steele's *The Funeral* extracts the promise: 'If you shou'd, as I hope you won't, out-live me, take care I an't buried in flannel, 't would never become me I'm sure.' Unwittingly, the government had created a whole new industry in off-the-peg funeral wear. The undertakers took full advantage of it. Misson takes up the story:

> There is an act of Parliament which ordains, that the dead shall be bury'd in a woollen stuff, which is a kind of a thin bays, which they call flannel; nor is it lawful to use the least needleful of thread or silk. This shift is always white; but there are different sorts of it as to fineness, and consequently of different prices. To make these dresses is a particular trade, and there are many that sell nothing else; so that these habits for the dead are always to be had ready-made, of what size or price you please, for people of every age and sex.

Funeral wear was undergoing some adjustments. Instead of the winding-sheet with its top and bottom knots, there was the open-backed, long-sleeved shift with drawstrings at wrist and neck, either with or without an integral hood. The knot at the feet remained. Misson continues:

> After they have wash'd the body thoroughly clean, and shav'd it, if it be a man, and his beard be grown during his sickness, they put it in a flannel shirt which has commonly a sleeve pursled [tied] about the wrists, and the slit of the shirt down the breast done in the same manner. Where these ornaments are not of woollen lace, they are at least edg'd, and sometimes embroider'd with black thread. The shirt shoul'd be at least half a foot longer than the body, that the feet of the deceas'd may be wrapped in it, as in a bag. When they have thus folded the end of this shirt close to the

feet, they tye the part that is folded down with a piece of woollen thread, as we do our stockings; so that the end of the shirt is done into a kind of tuft. Upon the head they put a cap, which they fasten with a very broad chin cloth; with gloves on the hands, and a cravat round the neck, all of woollen... Instead of a cap, the women have a kind of head-dress, with a forehead cloth.

Once the corpse was dressed, it was time for another visit from the authorities. 'The body being thus equipped, and laid in the coffin, it is visited a second time, to see that it is bury'd in flannel, and that nothing about it is sowed with thread.' An affadivit had to be sworn to the effect that the corpse was attired according to government regulations, or that a fine had been paid instead, and this was entered into the parish record. Half the fine would be allocated to poor relief in the parish.

The time between death and burial varied according to the wealth of the deceased. A large elaborate funeral took some time to arrange. Funeral tickets adorned with leering skeletons, scythes and admonitions such as 'Remember to Die' were left at the houses of those invited to the funeral. These woodcuts were mass-produced with blank spaces left for the name, date and place of the funeral to be filled in by hand. Those who could not afford funeral tickets relied on word of mouth to alert relatives, friends and neighbours to the forthcoming event. A wealthy citizen might not be buried for two or three weeks. Fortunately, embalming techniques were showing some improvement and this too was boosting the undertaker's business. John Evelyn recorded in his diary:

> I went to see the corpse of that obstinate creature, Col Vrats, the King permitting that his body should be transported to his own country ... and one of the first embalmed by a particular art, invented by one William Russell, a coffin-maker, which preserved the body without disembowelling, or to appearance using any bituminous matter. The flesh was florid, soft, and full, as if the person were only sleeping. He had now been dead near fifteen days.

For the majority, who could not afford to be embalmed, swift interment was desirable, particularly during the summer months. Funerals could take place on any day of the week, even on Christmas and Easter Days. Sundays were especially popular. But first the corpse had to lie in state at home.

The bottom of the coffin was lined with several inches of bran to absorb any seepage from putrefaction. There was a purpose to the delay in burial, as Misson explained: 'They let it lye three or four days in this condition; which time they allow, as well to give the dead person an opportunity of coming to life again, if his soul has not quite left his body, as to prepare mourning, and the ceremonies of the funeral.'

It was *de rigueur* to view the body and offer condolences to the family. The widow, wearing her black mourning with peaked headdress symbolic of her retirement from the world, would receive visitors in her room, which was draped in black and lit by a single taper. Black mourning clothes would have been provided for the household servants and all members of the family. Even babies would be wrapped in black crêpe. The whole house would be swathed in yards of black cloth. Black was the colour of oblivion. All reflective surfaces such as mirrors had to be covered or turned to the wall – this was a vulnerable time for the soul. Glittering jewels had to be eschewed in favour of less shiny pearls.

In wealthy households, ceremonial mourners or hired mutes would be posted at intervals from the hall door to the top of the stairs. Steele could not resist satirising this custom in *The Funeral*: 'Come, you that are to be the mourners in the house, put on your sad looks, and walk by me that I may sort you. Ha you! A little more upon the dismal. This fellow has a good mortal look, place him near the corpse ... Did not I give you ten, then fifteen and twenty shillings a week to be sorrowful? And the more I give you, I think the gladder you are!'

Misson describes the scene in households of the middling sort:

> A little before the company is set in order for the march, they lay the body into the coffin upon two stools, in a room, where all that please may go and see it; then they take off the top of the coffin, and remove from off the face a little square piece of flannel, made on purpose to cover it, and not fastened to anything: Upon this occasion, the rich equipage of the dead does honour to the living. The relations and chief mourners are in a chamber apart, with their more intimate friends; and the rest of the guests are dispersed in several rooms about the house.

Not all mourners behaved with fitting decorum in the house of the dead, as the Old Bailey Sessions Papers record:

Elizabeth Bird and Rebeccah Dalton were both indicted for robbing one William Milledge of St Giles Cripplegate of one alamode hood, value 2s [an item of mourning wear] another old hood, value 6d. a dowlace smock, value 4s. The evidence was, that Bird came to the house, under a pretence of seeing a child of Mrs Milledge that lay dead, and whilst her back was turned, she directed Dalston to take the goods, which she afterwards pawn'd at the brokers in White-cross-street.

Funerals were an important indicator of the wealth and status of the deceased and reflected on the family left behind, so that no expense was spared to impress the mourners and the neighbourhood. Hatchments replete with the armorial bearings of the deceased were hung outside the house and, even for those not entitled to bear arms, undertakers generally kept some in stock ready for hire. On the day of the funeral the mourners were presented with black scarves and gloves and hatbands.

Appropriately, the Huguenot silk weavers at Spitalfields were producing a new kind of silk, which came to be known as mourning crêpe. The industry received an enormous boost when 'for the encouragement of our English silk called alamodes, His Royal Highness the Prince of Denmark, the nobility, and other persons of quality [appeared] in mourning hatbands made of that silk, to bring the same in fashion, in the place of crapes, which are made in the Pope's country where we send our money for them.'

Gold and black enamel mourning rings with inscriptions costing as much as £1 each would be widely distributed. When his daughter Mary died, Evelyn records that 'there were distributed among her friends about sixty rings'. At Pepys's funeral in 1703, 123 mourning rings of varying value were handed out. Rings acted as a constant reminder not just of the deceased but of what was to come for all.

Full mourning would be provided for the pall-bearers. When Samuel Pepys died, Evelyn lamented that 'Mr Pepys had been for near forty years so much my particular friend, that Mr Jackson sent me complete mourning, desiring me to be one to hold up the pall at his magnificent obsequies; but my indisposition hindered me from doing him this last office'. Obviously it was an honour to be a pall-bearer. The pall represented the cloak that had once been used to cover the body in the absence of a coffin. Now that the use of coffins was almost universal, the pall was retained to cover the coffin as the cloak had once done the body. Misson commented that:

> These cloths, which they call palls, are some of black velvet, others of cloth with an edge of white linen or silk a foot broad, or thereabouts: For a batchellor or maid, or for a woman that dies in child-bed, the pall is white. This is spread over the coffin, and is so broad, that the six or eight men (in black clothes) that carry the body are quite hid beneath it to their waste; and the corners and sides of it hang down low enough to be borne by those who, according to custom, are invited for that purpose.

Many of the items associated with the funeral – the pall, the mourning cloaks, the sconces, the silver candlesticks and the black hangings – could be hired. The pall, in particular, was expensive. Some of the City guilds had their own palls magnificently embroidered with the company's coat of arms to lend out to their deceased. Misson noted that 'the parish has always three or four mortuary cloths of different prices (the best is hir'd out at 5 or 6 crowns)'. A notorious thief known as the German Princess, who was eventually captured and hanged for her crimes, once persuaded a landlady to allow a friend of hers to lie in state in her lodging house. The landlady was dispatched to hire a velvet pall at the cost of 20s, and set up the chamber with silver candlesticks, a silver flagon, gilt bowls and several other pieces of plate. The night before the intended burial the German Princess absconded with all these items through the window, leaving the landlady with the coffin containing a bogus corpse. To add to her losses, the undertaker sued her for the pall that had cost him £40.

Drinks would be provided for the assembled mourners. 'Before they set out, and after they return,' Misson noted, 'it is usual to present the guests with something to drink, either red or white wine, boil'd with sugar and cinnamon, or some other such liquor; Everyone drinks two or three cups.' Before leaving the house, a servant would present each guest with a sprig of rosemary. Rosemary was for remembrance, but its scent also helped mask the more unpleasant odours of death. 'Everyone takes a sprig, and carries it in his hand 'till the body is put into the grave, at which time they all throw their sprigs in after it.' Flowers and garlands placed on the coffin and later on the grave represented the green symbols of rebirth.

It was fashionable to hold funerals in the evening. This meant that the

It was fashionable to hold funerals at night. Mourners were sometimes mugged for their expensive wax torches (*British Museum*)

undertakers benefited from the extra expenditure on heavy wax torches. They must have been expensive because on at least one occasion they excited a robbery at the funeral. The mourners were literally mugged for their wax candles. 'Riots and robberies,' ran a notice in the press, 'committed in and about Stepney Church Yard, at a funeral solemnity, on Wednesday the 23rd day of September; and whereas many persons, who being appointed to attend the same funeral with white wax lights of a considerable value, were assaulted in a most violent manner, and the said white wax lights taken from them.' A reward was promised if the perpetrators were brought to justice. 'Whoever shall discover any persons, guilty of the said crimes, so as they may be convicted of the same, shall receive of Mr William Prince, wax chandler in the Poultry, London, ten shillings for each person so discover'd.'

The procession through the streets to the church was supposed to take the most direct route, but it was tempting to impress the neighbourhood with the pomp and panoply by taking the long way round. The chief mourners would travel by coach and scores of people followed the hearse on foot. Misson describes the procession:

> Every thing being ready to move, one or more beadles march first, each carrying a long staff, at the end of which is a great apple or knob of silver. The ministers of the parish, generally accompany'd by some other minister, and attended by the clerk, walks next; and the body comes just after him. The relations in close mourning, and all the guests two and two, make up the rest of the procession. The common practice is to carry the corpse thus into the body of the church, where they set it down upon two trestles, while either a funeral sermon is preach'd, containing an elogium upon the deceased, or certain prayers said, adapted to the occasion.

The question now was whether the burial would take place in the vaults of the church itself, as was the prevailing fashion for the wealthy, or out in the churchyard. In the churchyard, the south and east sides were considered the most holy and so the most coveted. On top of the fees to the minister, clerk and sexton, each burial place either inside the church or out in the churchyard demanded a specific fee. An additional burial tax of 4s was payable to the government. 'By special clause in his will,' wrote Evelyn of his son, 'he ordered that his body should be buried in the churchyard and … he being much offended at the novel custom of burying everyone within the body of the church and chancel … this excess of making churches into charnel houses being of ill and irreverend example, and prejudicial to the health of the living, besides the continual disturbance of the pavement and seats, and several other indecencies.' Burial within the church meant that the parishioners would have to suffer the stench of decomposing bodies for weeks.

Out in the overcrowded churchyards of many of the London parishes, however, ghoulish ingenuity had to be employed by the gravediggers to secure space for another corpse. Decaying bodies were constantly disturbed to make way for others. The parish of St Martin-in-the-Fields, for instance, comprised only twenty-six acres. In an eleven-year period at the end of the seventeenth century, there were 15,856 burials, an annual average of 1,400. Many graves were not deep enough, sometimes inviting the attentions of grave robbers. The barber-surgeons and teaching hospitals were in desperate need of fresh corpses. The large, deep pits, such as the one near Tottenham Court in which the bodies of the poor were laid in rows in open-sided coffins or none at all were not covered with earth until they had received their full quota. 'How noisome the stench is that arises from these holes so stowed with dead bodies, especially in sultry seasons and after rain.' The air of the neighbourhoods surrounding all burial grounds was polluted and foul.

The body was interred in the presence of the mourners standing round the grave. It was customary to bury the corpse face up in a grave that was oriented east–west, so that the deceased was ready to rise up on the day of judgement. Suicides were the exception. If they made it into the churchyard at all, they would be buried face down in a north–south grave in the north side of the churchyard. At the burial site, mourners waited until the earth was 'thrown in upon it' before leaving. Only by the late seventeenth century were tombstones being used to mark graves in churchyards.

The mourners returned to the house in the same order in which they had left. Drinks and biscuits were handed around. Misson noted that men and women split into separate groups for 'the drinking', which had become an essential part of the funeral ritual. He was impressed by the amount of alcohol the women managed to consume, particularly when one Butler, the tavern keeper of the Crown and Sceptre in St Martin's Street, told him that the women attending his wife's funeral sank 'a tun of red port, besides mull'd white wine'. 'Such women in England will hold it out with the men,' Misson commented in admiration, 'when they have a bottle before them, as well as upon t'other occasion, and tattle infinitely better than they.'

The 'drinking' was also the occasion for the reading of the will to assembled relatives and friends. The first charges on the estate were the deceased's debts and the burial costs. When John Dryden died in May 1700 the Kit-Cat Club picked up the bill for his funeral, which Russell the undertaker presented to Jacob Tonson for payment:

Double coffin £5
Hanging the hall with a border of bays £5
Six dozen paper escutcheons for the hall £3 12s
Ten silk escutcheons for the pall £2 10s
Three mourning coaches and six horses £2 5s

Silver desk and rosemary 5s
Eight scarves for the musicians £2
Seventeen yards of crape to cover their instruments £1 14s
Archievement for the hearse £3 10s

The total was £45 17s.

Obviously Dryden's funeral was a grand occasion. The following account from a case in the ecclesiastical court gives some idea of the funeral outlay for a 'middling' citizen:

> Five pounds two shillings payd for the duties of St Andrews Church in Holborne and for opening the vault as also twenty shillings payd to Mr Goods for preaching the deceased's ffunerall sermon and seventeene shillings payd for fflamboys used at ye ffunerall, and five shillings for ye use of two mourning clokes and ... there was nine pounds payd and noe more for gloves and hatbands used and given away ... and three pounds ten shillings for ye deceased's shroud and coffin ... Mary Smith [got] the summe of tenn pounds for mourning.

A funeral commensurate with status was considered so important that executors had been known to authorise its expense even if there were insufficient funds in the estate to cover it. By the custom of London, a man's widow received one-third of his estate. His children received equal shares in the next third. The final third was 'the dead man's share' and could be bequeathed by will. If the man died intestate, this last share was divided half to the widow and half in equal proportions to the children. Small legacies might be left to friends. Servants rarely feature, perhaps as a reflection of their quick turnover. It is significant in this materialistic age, when the old medieval funeral dole to the poor had been abandoned, that very little was left by London's citizens to charity.

For the poor, anxious to avoid the ignominy of being buried in the 'poor hole', there was every incentive to subscribe to a burial club or society. Their development ran parallel to the growth of the undertaking trade.

> This is to give notice, that the office of society towards a burial, erected upon Wapping Wall, is now removed into Katherine Wheel Alley in White Chappel, near Justice Smiths, where sub-

scriptions are taken to compleat the number, as also at the Ram in Crucifix Lane in Barnaby Street, Southwark; to which places notice is to be given of the death of any member, and where any person may have the printed articles after Monday next. And this Thursday about 7 o'clock evening will be buried by the undertakers the corpse of J.S. Glover over against the Sun Brewhouse, in Golden Lane; as also a child from the corner of Acorn Alley in Bishopsgate Street, and another child from the Great Maze Pond, Southwark.

The funerals of paupers were paid for by the parish in which they had lived, from a rate levied on all property owners. The parish would also provide a 'drinking' for those attending.

By 1700 suicide seemed to have reached epidemic proportions. John Evelyn noted in his diary towards the end of his life that suicide seemed to have reached an all-time peak among all classes. Foreigners were amazed at the casualness by which English men and women took their own lives. As Beat Louis de Muralt reported: 'You must know, the English die by their own hands with as much indifference as by another's: 'Tis common to hear people talk of men and women, that make away with themselves, as they call it, and generally for reasons that would appear to us but trifles: The men, perhaps, for the cruelty or inconstancy of their mistresses; and the women for the indifferency of the men.'

Another foreign visitor, César de Saussure, wrote that he was perplexed by 'this mania' until he spent a few months in London and became unutterably depressed by the dreary weather and the coal smoke. 'Had I been an Englishman, I should certainly have put myself out of misery,' he wrote, 'the desire and thought of putting an end to my sorrows by a speedy death was ever in my thoughts, and it required all my strength of mind to resist its deadly attraction.' De Saussure was invited to stay in the nearby village of Islington, where the cow pastures reminded him of his native land; and the gloom lifted.

Foreign visitors and Londoners themselves might have received the impression that suicide was more prevalent because incidents were so frequently reported in an expanding press. Newspapers described every detail with evident relish.

On Thursday last a maid servant who lived in Norfolk Street

(being discontented) went into the kitchen, and having lock'd the door she cut a piece of the jack-line, and getting upon a joint-stole very dexterously endeavour'd to save the executioner labour by hanging herself on an iron hook, as if she had been used to it; but as fate would have it, the hook being rusty it broke before she made her exit, and she struggled so that she fell down, in the mean time the master sent his man to call her up (not dreaming of this accident) but he found the door shut, and heard some groaning, of which he acquainted his master, who immediately ran down, and breaking open the door found her sprawling half dead, yet not so bad, but they soon brought her to life again. They attribute the laying thus violent hands on herself to her being in love.

On Monday a Welsh taylor, who was come to town to see fashions, happening to have some words with his brother, took it so much to heart, that he went immediately and threw himself into the New River Head near Islington privately, where he was drowned; and being missing, by his landlady she dreamt the night following that he was drowned there, and that his hat was swimming over him, which accordingly was found, and soon after his corps.

Suicide notes, rare before 1700, could now be read in the press by an audience of thousands. Such reports attracted the same sort of avid readership as did the accounts of the criminals going to the gallows on execution day. Suicide was demystified. Far from being victims of some supernatural demonic force, these men and women suffered the same reverses as everyone else: they were adolescents at the mercy of cruel masters, they had no wish to live after the death of a dearly loved spouse, they were unlucky in love, they were old and could not support themselves, they were poor and desperate, they could not bear the shame of an illegitimate baby, their honour had been called into question, they had lost all on the gaming tables. More and more, people reserved the right to individual expression, to feel happy or sad, to take their own life.

Many killed themselves to escape destitution. A poor woman of Clerkenwell driven to despair because she could not feed her children killed one of them, then herself and the other child, because the parish would not afford her any further relief. Wealth and happiness were so closely associated in the contemporary mind that there was genuine bewilderment when a suicide was found to have the means of an adequate living. 'The corps of a person drowned is taken up, within these few days, at Greenwich, having money, and a bill for a sum of money in his pockets,' ran one report. And: 'Yesterday morning a woman near White-chappel, who workt to a throwster in those parts, and earned 8 shillings a week, hanged herself in her lodging; but nobody can guess at the reason of her despair.'

Understanding brought sympathy. Coroners and juries increasingly returned a *non compos mentis* verdict. The deceased had not been in his or her right mind and could not be held responsible for his or her actions. Suicide was far more likely to be the result of mental illness than the work of the devil. A suicide should be pitied not scorned. Without forensic medicine, it was not always easy to determine the cause of death: suicide, murder or accident. The rich would shoot themselves. Hanging was the preferred method of most ordinary people. Deaths by drowning could be just as plausibly returned as accidents when they could have been either suicide or murder: 'On Tuesday last a gentleman was taken up dead at Black Friars Stairs, but his money and watch being found in his pocket, 'tis not known by what accident he was drowned.' Where an element of doubt existed, the more sympathetic verdict prevailed. An application would be made to the church to bury such a person in the churchyard, so that he or she joined the community of the dead.

Coroners and jurors were less inclined to bring in a verdict of *felo de se,* calculated self-murder, which brought secular and religious penalties. By ancient custom, the crown would confiscate the property of a suicide and his family would be left destitute. In the wake of the Glorious Revolution, a subject's rights over his own property were considered unalienable. Defoe caught the popular mood when he said that 'the children should [not] be starv'd because the father has destroy'd himself'. Friends and neighbours went to inordinate lengths to hide the possessions of a suicide so that they could not be forfeited.

The Church still retained the right to refuse a Christian burial in the case of *felo de se*. Even in this more secular age, pagan ritual survived. The traditional belief was that suicide was instigated by the devil, it had supernatural associations. The corpse would be buried naked at a crossroads with a stake thrust through it to prevent the unquiet, malevolent spirit haunting the living and rising on the day of judgement. Just as crowds congregated at the gallows, so they did at this macabre ritual – an indication that superstition was not dead.

CHAPTER SIX

The Home

*'Englishmen build their houses with taste; it is not possible to
have more comfortable houses'*

WHEN SIR THOMAS GROSVENOR died in 1700, his thirty-five-year-old widow Mary was already showing signs of the mental instability that would make her easy prey to an unscrupulous fortune hunter and cast the Grosvenor estate into jeopardy before it was even built. Mary had been a vulnerable seven-month-old baby when her father Alexander Davies died of plague in 1665, leaving her in the care of an ambitious mother. Her inheritance had seemed only vaguely promising at the time. But with the relentless growth of London and its westward expansion, the marshland stretching from the Oxford Road between the Westbourne and Tybourne springs down to the river at Millbank soon became some of the most valuable real estate in the metropolis. It was a slice of land worth fighting for and became the subject of lengthy and expensive litigation between Mary's alleged second husband and her Grosvenor heirs.

In his *A Tour through the Whole Island of Great Britain*, Daniel Defoe breathlessly described the expansion of London, the monster city. 'New squares, and new streets rising up every day to such a prodigy of buildings, that nothing in the world does, or ever did, equal it. Surrounding villages that had once stood in the countryside were being 'joined to the streets by continued buildings'. And 'how much farther it may spread, who knows?'

The Great Fire of 1666 offered the opportunity for a new London with more uniform housing, wider streets and fine squares. The rebuilding programme also coincided with a shift to the west. Not everyone abandoned the City's square mile, however, where approximately 9,000 new houses replaced the 13,000 that were lost. The great financiers and merchants, the first Governor of the Bank of England, Sir John Houblon,

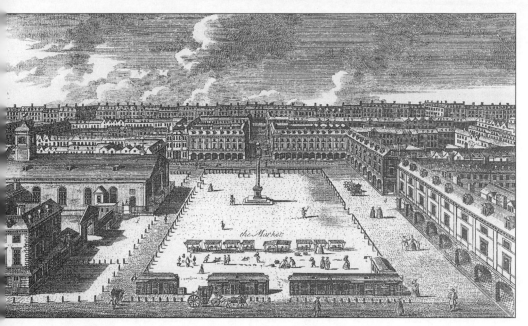

Covent Garden was graciously designed by Inigo Jones but first the market and then the brothels and gambling dens let down the tone (*Guildhall Library, Corporation of London*)

in Threadneedle Street, for instance, remained in their fine houses in the reconstructed City, where they were convenient for the whole apparatus of financial, commercial and municipal government. Although most people had to live at or near their place of work because of the difficulty of travelling any distance, those who could afford it sent their families to the more salubrious suburbs of Hampstead, Highgate and Hackney for the summer or escaped to their country houses. Daniel Defoe noted a growing trend for 'the middle sort of mankind, grown wealthy by trade, and who still taste of London; some of them live both in the city and in the country at the same time'.

As early as the 1630s the fourth Earl of Bedford had led the way in creating new developments west of the City, hiring Inigo Jones to design Covent (originally a convent) Garden with its elegant Palladian architecture. Like Lincoln's Inn Fields with its imposing houses and first garden square, Covent Garden had been a fashionable place to live. By the end of the century, however, the neighbourhood bordered by Long Acre, St Martin's Lane, Drury Lane and the Strand was dominated by the playhouse, brothels, bagnios and gambling-dens. Prostitutes, male and female, plied their trade in the streets and alleys. A fruit and vegetable market had received the royal seal of approval, prompting French visitors to rename the area common garden. The rich might find it amusing to visit Covent Garden, but they no longer wished to live there. Just south of Covent Garden, the aristocracy had abandoned their grand but impractical palaces along the Strand during the 1660s and 1670s and moved westwards. The area developed by the courtier Henry Jermyn, Earl of St Albans, around St James's was highly sought after. As the author of *A New View of London* described it:

> St James's in Westminster has a very large share of the nobility and gentry, yet a person of an indifferent rank, may find a vacant seat in the church on the Sabbath. The quality, who fly about here with their sumptuous equipages, imagine themselves to be the admiration of the vulgar sort. On the contrary, they are the objects of their ridicule, they being too well acquainted with their most private affairs.

While housing in the manufacturing and industrial districts outside the City walls and in pockets such as St Giles in the Fields (lying just east of Tottenham Court and Oxford Road) decayed into sleazy, overcrowded rookeries or grew up in a haphazard, untidy sprawl, that in the west arose from well-planned squares and wide streets. Given the motley assortment of speculators who were willing to invest their money in the rebuilding and expansion of London after the fire, and the stop-start nature of the enterprise, it is a wonder that it turned out as well as it did. Foremost among the speculative builders was Nicolas Barbon, son of the Puritan zealot Praise God Barebone, who gave his name to one of Cromwell's slimline parliaments. Nicolas Barbon was a doctor of medicine and had been involved in the early insurance business. In *An Apology for the Builder*, he put the case for London's expansion: 'The citizens, nay the whole nation is astonished at the flourishing condition of this metropolis, to see every year a new town added to the old one; and like men affrighted are troubled with misapprehensions, and easily imposed on by the false suggestions of those that envy her grandeur, and are angry with the builders for making her so great.'

Barbon argued that 'there are no more houses built every year than are occasion for; because there are tenants for the houses, when built, and a continuance every year to build more.' New buildings meant more taxes and higher rental income.

> New buildings are advantageous to the City, for they raise the rents of the old houses. For the bigger a town is, the more value are the houses in it ... Houses are of more value in Cheapside and Cornhill, than they are in Shoreditch, White-Chapel, Old Street, or any of the out-parts; and the rents in some of these out-parts have been within this few years considerably advanced by the addition of new buildings that are beyond them. As for instance, the rents of the houses in Bishopsgate-street, the Minories, etc are raised from fifteen or sixteen pounds per annum, to be now worth thirty, which was by the increase of buildings in Spittle-Fields, Shadwell and Ratcliffe Highway. And at the other end of the town those houses in the Strand and Charing-Cross are worth now fifty and threescore pounds per annum, which within this thirty years were not let for above twenty pounds per annum; which is by the great addition of buildings since made in St James's, Leicester-Fields, and other adjoining parts.

Barbon believed that 'houses are of value, as they stand in a place of trade'. Of course, new houses provided employment, not just for those engaged in the building and endless repair of them, but for the whole gamut of tradesmen and craftsmen who supplied the needs of the new occupants. Unlike in the old City, the rich would not live side by side with those who served them. The lower orders were to be there, but out of sight. Not everything turned out according to plan. In a grand new development such as Barbon's Soho Square, the rich did not stay long, because of the high population of shopkeepers and artisans – particularly Huguenot immigrants – who had fled City trading restrictions and dominated the surrounding area right down to Leicester Fields.

The Rebuilding Act of 1667, which provided strict guidelines for house building to prevent the spread of domestic fire, applied only to the City, not the West End. Nevertheless, landlords, financiers and builders wanted a quick return on their investment and so specialised in a known saleable commodity: the standard terraced house, which had been very much Barbon's concept. According to Roger North, he was 'the inventor of this new method of building by casting of ground into streets and small houses and to augment their number with as little front as possible and selling the ground to workmen by so much per foot front, and what he could not sell build himself'.

Under the Act, the principal streets were to feature four-storey houses, while those of two and three storeys were relegated to correspondingly lesser streets. On none of these streets did the houses have numbers; well into the eighteenth century Londoners relied on convoluted directions and overhanging signboards to find their way around. When young Ralph Verney came to London to study law, he had an address of imposing length that was not untypical: 'In Barbon's building, up the steps and one pair of stairs, number 8 over the door, by the Water Gate in the Middle Temple, London. To be thrust under the door if shut.'

However many storeys the terraced house contained, there tended to be only two or three rooms a floor, and Londoners had to become accustomed to vertical living and climbing up and down stairs. The terraced house gave London a uniform character which impressed foreign visitors such as César de Saussure:

> I must own that Englishmen build their houses with taste; it is not possible to make a better use of ground, or to have more comfortable houses. It is surprising to see in what a small space they will build, and in what an incredibly short time. The houses are of bricks; the walls are thin, most of them having only one foot and a half thickness. The finest houses sometimes have cornices and borders to divide the floors, and round the doors and windows you occasionally see a sort of polished marble. In all the newly-built quarters the houses have one floor made in the earth, containing the kitchens, offices, and servants' rooms. This floor is well lighted, and has as much air as the others have. In order to accomplish this a sort of moat, five or six feet in width and eight or nine deep, is dug in front of all the houses, and is called the 'area'. This moat is edged on the side next the street with iron railing. The cellars and vaults where coal is stored are very strongly built beneath the streets, and to reach them you cross the area. Almost all the houses have little gardens or courtyards at the back.

In the majority of homes, space was taken up with the essential functions of cooking, eating, working and sleeping. Londoners did very little entertaining at home. A terraced house might be divided as follows. In the basement, a kitchen, a cellar and servants' quarters. A wash-house might be attached or stand outside. The ground floor contained the parlour in the better homes, and the shop, workshop and apprentices' sleeping quarters in a tradesman's residence. The first floor consisted of the dining room, a drawing room, and possibly a house of office – the equivalent of today's lavatory. Note that the dining room was some way from the kitchen, giving the servants endless running up and downstairs at mealtimes. On the second floor, family bedrooms and a closet. In a life where privacy was almost unknown, the closet was small, cosy and private. Here an individual might indulge his or her taste in decor – be a little audacious even – and keep curiosities or collections. In the garrets, the servants' rooms. In the silk weavers' homes at Spitalfields the garrets were often turned into workrooms containing the looms. Light came through skylights.

Few Londoners owned the freehold of their houses. The normal practice was for the landlord who owned the ground to lease it to a speculator or builder who would pay for its development. Barbon specialised in the development side and divested himself of the lease even before the building began. Often the builder sold on the lease to the future occupant before the house was finished. This way none of the parties had to wait long for a return on their capital investment, which was just as well as many of them had borrowed the money at interest. The practice did not prevent some spectacular bankruptcies, however, notably that of Barbon himself. He stipulated in his will that none of his creditors was to be paid. Mortgaging made ground rents high. Leaseholding encouraged a tendency to build cheap, short-term housing with inferior bricks, which was quite likely to collapse on or before the expiry of the lease. De Saussure explains:

> I think I have already told you that houses are built for a term of years, and I must tell you the reason why; it rarely happens that the person who builds also possesses the ground. The ground is habitually let for ninety-nine years, but sometimes also for sixty-six years, or even less. The contractor builds according to the term of years. Should the ground be leased for sixty years, he will not build so thoroughly as for ninety-nine, and he knows so exactly what is required, that houses are often on the point of

tumbling down a short time before or after the term has expired,
The proprietor of the ground then regains possession of his
property and of the house, good or bad.

Aristocratic landlords such as the Russells and, in due course, the
Grosvenors were able to take a long-term view. Each generation had a duty
to protect the estate and hand it on intact to the next. The practical value
of an entailed estate was its current rental return. However, the value of
the estate could be enhanced in several ways. The owner could ensure that
the building was of a sufficiently high standard to outlast a whole series of
leases and he himself might set up house there, encouraging the 'best
elements in society' to follow suit. Stow's *Survey* describes 'Smith Street, a
new street of good buildings, so called from Sir John Smith, the ground
landlord who has here a fine house'. Residents gained prestige from living
near a titled landlord, while from the success of the development the
landlord increased both the rental income and the capital value of his land.

Landlords and speculators had to make a choice between building
more houses with narrow frontages realising lower rent per unit or fewer
houses with wide frontages whose rent could be pitched correspondingly
higher. Most developments surrounded a square, such as Lincoln's Inn,
Red-Lyon, Southampton, St James's, Leicester Fields, and King's or Soho
Squares. Initially these squares were open spaces where vagrants camped
and others dumped their rubbish. Residents campaigned for garden
squares to be contained within railings and eventually succeeded.
Thomas Neal's development at Seven Dials deviated from the norm. He
sold leases direct to building tradesmen to build seven streets radiating
in a star shape from a central Doric column. This gave each house more
street frontage than a square would allow, although the houses at the
corners of the triangles had cramped plots. The development went the
way of all failures, with subletting and overcrowding the only means of
paying the rents necessary to cover the high ground rents fixed by Neal
who, incidentally, held the right to conduct the national lottery.

The aristocracy who owned London property betrayed their true
loyalties by lending it the names of their titles and country seats.
Aristocracy and gentry were quite happy to rent a house for the season.
The removal to town involved a great deal of organisation. In May 1700,
Lady Verney wrote to her husband that 'I have taken lodgings at Mrs
Gatesheads. I have all the romes I had the last yeare & 2 garrits more,

they will be ready for the two maids to come into them Wensday night, & for the children on Friday night, Pray let all lenning [linen] come up with the carryer, as sheets, towells, servants' table cloathes & all other things as is wanting, & take care of they dear self and bring wine enough in the coach for your use.' A few months later, the whole process was about to be repeated as Sir John Verney wrote that 'I am now with all my family going to London as soon as a house is taken for me'.

London tradesmen were reluctant to tie up capital in buying houses when it could be more usefully ploughed into the business. The majority of them rented directly from the ground landlord or his lessee. Rents were high. In major thoroughfares such as Cheapside or the Strand, a good property would cost £50 or £60 a year, while the rents for middle-class houses in lesser streets were about £20 to £30 – a vast amount of money when a family of the middling class could be expected to live on £50 a year. When Elizabeth Bauer sought a separation from her husband Christian Bauer for cruelty, she told the court that the rental value of his house was £60 a year, that he received £16 a year from a tenant in Charles Court in the parish of St Martin-in-the-Fields, that besides 'the King's Tax and all parish duties as Church poor', he paid ground rent of £36 14s a year on the two properties.

Although rents were high, the majority of Londoners expected neither space nor privacy. These were unfamiliar concepts. Tall and narrow with two or three rooms a floor, a typical terraced house might be home to a husband and wife, two to four children, two to four servants including apprentices, and lodgers. Rooms were small and fully peopled. A householder, especially a shopkeeper, was often reluctant to keep an entire house to himself when he might earn money from lodgers. In *A View of London and Westminster* there is a description of such a shopkeeper in St Anne's, Soho:

The man's income, I believe, might amount to about seventy pounds per annum, and his family consisted of one wife and a daughter of about eighteen; they were extraordinary oeconomists, brew'd their own beer, wash'd at home, made a joint hold out two days, and a shift three; let three parts of their house ready furnish'd, and kept paying one quarter's rent under another. In such like circumstances had they gone on for some years, and the worst the world could say of them was, That they liv'd above what they had, that their daughter was as proud a slut as ever clapt clog on shoe leather, and that they entertained lodgers as were no better than they should be.

Widows invariably took lodgers as a source of income.

Sometimes relations within the household were less than cordial. The records of the consistory court tell us that Henry Leonard, a shoemaker, 'took a house ready furnisht situated in Vere Street near Clare Market where he set up the trade of leather cutter and let most part of the house to lodgers'. His wife Jane 'did quarrel with the people that lodged in this house and give ill language to her husband'.' Jane's extravagance led to several visits from the bailiffs, so that her husband was forced to quit the house and his trade.

A respectable lodger occupying the first floor, that is a couple of furnished rooms, in a middle-class home, might pay as much as half a guinea a week. Dean Swift was paying 8s a week for two rooms in 1710. When Sir John Verney's aunt, Betty Adams, moved into lodgings in Covent Garden in the autumn of 1697, he gently admonished her for her extravagance:

> Madam, – I may now congratulate your returne to your paradise, Covent Garden. Paradise of old was indeed a garden, and that produced delightfull fruite, but there was a devilish sting accompanied it. This hath the pleasures of the playhouse, beau church (tho' indifferent preaching), good company & plenty of it, fine cloathes, deare provisions and sleeping place, all which needs a good large income to bear the expenses, & that's the sting. But I ned say nothing of this to you, but only to fill up a letter, for I knoe your prudence & managry soe good that you can waid throw any waters you goe into ...

Aunt Adams was defensive in her reply:

> Sir John, – I rit this by the first post to give you thankes for your care to let me have sum money, that being wellcum I believe to most in the world, espesiley to one whos wonts are great and incums small. As for my paradise as you coll it, I could willingly have bin out of it much longer than I was ...& as to the plais & fin

cloths this plas affords, they have none efect on me, for I nither frequent the one nor weare the other ... my great greef is wont of money to pay my deats & feed my familey ... my rent I own is to hey for my in cum ... but when I must give dear I rather chos to doo it in a plas whear I have injoyed my health most ...

Needless to say, she could not sustain the extravagance and her kind nephew had to bail her out. As he explained to his steward: 'My Aunt Adams hath had much trouble of late, her goods being twice seized, first by the head landlady for rent, due from her landlady (for my aunt owed none), then a second time for taxes and parish duties ... You may be sure I have great moan made to me about it, others of the same relation to me are alsoe frequently asking, soe that I have a dull time on't.'

Lodgers were not always of the same social class as the householder. For instance, Betty Adams's daughter wrote to her cousin Sir John Verney quite matter-of-factly: 'My mother continues in her lodging, & I hope we have got good honest people for our landlord and lady. He is a periwig maker & did worke to my uncle & your brother & nephew, his name is Stone, he lived neare Red Lyon Street in Holborn, so the trouble & feare of removing I hope we shall be free from, & I am sure it is high time.' Different classes of lodgers could occupy different parts of the house.

Many lodgers seemed to lead a peripatetic existence. The alleged bigamist Walter Whitfield 'in company with a gentlewoman who went for his wife' lodged at 'Master Robert Halls house in Beaufort Street in the Strand' for about six months. Before that 'they lodged at one Mr Burhridges house an apothecary in ye Strand, and since they left [Mr Halls] they lodged at Mr Hanwell's house at ye Frying Pan in Russell Street'.

The poor took over the abandoned homes of the rich as they fell into decay, or crowded into rookeries in dark courtyards and alleyways off the main thoroughfares. They might pay 6d a week for lodgings, sharing a bed and a room with several others. As London became more crowded, whole families lodged in cellars without adequate light and air or in freezing garrets.

Lodgers were a trial in many ways. They could not always be relied on for their honesty. When the aforementioned Jane Leonard came to live in Mary Callow's house in Magpie Alley in Fetter Lane, she rented a room 'up three pairs of stairs'. Before long she moved in a man purporting to be her son and his 'pretended' wife (who Mary Callow came to conclude was 'a whore'). Two weeks later they stole the sheets and 'run from the lodgings without paying one farthing of their rent'.

Lodgers stole from each other and from the landlord, as the Old Bailey Sessions Papers record:

> Simon Betts was indicted for felony in stealing from Richard Finney, of the parish of St Lawrence Jewry, one gold watch, one necklace of pearl, one diamond ring, two lockets, a silver girdle, a silver buckle, and a pair of ruffles. It appeared that the prisoner took lodgings of the prosecutor, and the goods being in a box, he took advantage to carry it away.

And:

> It appeared, that the prisoner Clerk took a lodging in the prosecutor's house, whither he brought a trunk full of stones, which he seem'd very earnest to have kept safe; and taking occasion when all the family were at church but the maid, to knock at the door, it was opened; and another gagging and binding the maid, Clerk broke open nine locks, and took out the goods, while the other staid in the room with the maid, and carried them off, which were shared afterwards at a tavern in Sheer-lane.

Whether in a private home or a lodging house, lodgers enjoyed little privacy. As ever, there was the nosy landlady. When Thomas Plummer and Margaret Sheffield came to view a room in a house in Thieving Lane, the landlady 'asked the said Thomas if the woman was his wife and he replied yes'. Not long afterwards Thomas's real wife got a friend to come with her to Thieving Lane, where she found her errant husband 'keeps company with the said Margaret Sheffield in a suspicious and scandalous manner'. Landladies and other tenants knew everything that was going on in a house: 'There came a man who went by the name of Thomas Phillips in company with a woman who went for his wife to lodge at the house of Robert Showers in Chick Lane in the parish of St Sepulchre, where this deponent did likewise lodge,' the court records state, 'they did live together at the said house about a year as man and wife, and this deponent hath seen them in naked bed together.'

There were the usual fallings-out between those sharing lodgings. Elisabeth Smith and Annabella Brown found lodgings at the house of Mary Wood at the sign of the Blue Perriwig near Charing Cross. Annabella had a frequent male visitor, one Sir John Magrath. Within a month of moving in, Elisabeth 'one morning saw the said Sir John in bed with Annabella Brown, and the said Sir John the next day came and lodged in the same house and [Elisabeth] perceiving [Annabella] to be with child and thinking it not suitable for her to continue to lodge with [her], she thereupon about two months after left [Annabella] and the said lodgings leaving Sir John and Annabella Brown lodgers in the same house'. Meanwhile, Sir John's abandoned wife Ellen was living by herself in lodgings in Rupert Street 'in a very poor condition and destitute of any maintenance'.

Inside the houses generally the gloom was alleviated by the new 'double sliding-sash windows', which were Dutch in origin but took their name from the French, *fenêtre à châssis à coulisse.* The Window Tax of 1696 deprived many Londoners of air and light, as they bricked up windows, to the detriment of their health. The impression of brightness was enhanced by looking glasses. They were all the rage, significantly at a time when there was a new self-awareness, a focus on the individual. Pepys had once splurged on 'a looking glass by the Old Exchange which costs me 5l 5s – and 6s for the hooks. A very fair glass.' He does not reveal the size of this novelty, but it is unlikely to have been very large because of the difficulty of producing large panes of glass. On a more intimate scale, no lady's *toilette* was complete without a looking-glass propped on her dressing table and lit by a pair of candles.

The fashion for looking-glasses, as with so many other items that were considered to be in the best of taste for the home, came from France. The Huguenot immigrants helped to reinforce this ideal and spread the influence of all things French. In the 1690s the Parisian émigré architect Daniel Marot, who designed complete houses down to their decoration and furnishings and accompanying gardens, published a set of engravings entitled *Nouvelle cheminées à panneaux de glace à la manière de France.* William and Mary employed him to carry out large-scale renovations at Hampton Court and Kensington Palace, where panels of glass duly made their appearance above chimney pieces.

By 1700 the French claimed to be able to make a plate of glass measuring

This satire on the tea-table illustrates the interior of a prosperous London home. There is a new sash window, a single curtain, a looking-glass and a display of oriental porcelain. The tightly corseted ladies are supported by high-backed cane chairs – just as well, as it looks as if they will be engaged in 'chit chat' for some time
(*British Museum*)

a hundred by sixty inches. But thanks to the arrival of Huguenot immigrants, the London glass-making industry would not lag behind:

> Proceedings upon the petition to the King of Richard Lawrence Du Manoir and Lewis Anne de St Marie, glass makers; shewing that they lately lived at St Gobins in France, and there invented and brought to perfection several new engines and instruments, never before used, for making large rough looking glass plates, glass panels and chimney pieces for rooms, much larger, better, and cheaper than any now used or made; and being desirous the same art should be known and put in practice in this nation,

they have erected and set up several of the new engines, and made plates from 50 to above 100 inches in length, and proper breadths, and can make them much larger, etc. They pray for a grant of the sole exercise of the invention for 14 years.

Even so, it would be a while before overmantels graced the home as a matter of course. Looking-glasses were placed between the sash windows. They looked particularly effective with the candlelight reflected in them.

Misson enthuses about the 'lightsome stair-cases, fine sash-windows, and lofty ceilings' of London's newly built houses. Painted plaster ceilings, at least in the principal rooms, gave a brighter look. Pepys had the decorators in quite often and on one occasion 'set my plasterer to work about whitening and colouring my musique roome'. Although white may have been the intention, it is unlikely to have been pure white, more a pale grey. 'Plastered ceilings,' wrote Miege, 'make by their whiteness the rooms so much lightsomer, and are excellent against a raging fire. They stop passage of dust, and lessen the noise overhead.'

Rooms were at first painted in bold colours, but these softened towards the end of the seventeenth century. Walls were wainscoted, 'for so damp a country as England is, nothing could be better contrived than wainscot, to keep off the ill impression of damp walls'. It was possible to buy wallpaper in London, but it was not much used. Only as late as 1712 was it considered worth imposing a tax on it. The rich might use wall hangings of silk, crimson damask being popular at the end of the century, while lower down the scale they were of gilt leather, tapestry and wool. London's damp atmosphere meant that hangings were subject to mildew.

While the homes of many Londoners were still extremely bare, wills, inventories and divorce papers of the upper and middling classes indicate a surge in material goods for the home in the period 1690–1720. Ownership of clocks increased threefold in this period, marking an obsession with timepieces. The interiors of the grander houses were receiving more attention than ever before. Upholsterers – many of whom were French or of French extraction in the London of the 1690s – had come into their own as interior decorators. In *The London Tradesman*, a guidebook for responsible parents wishing to find the right apprenticeship for their sons, there is a rather fulsome description of his role:

This tradesman's genius must be universal in every branch of furniture; though his proper craft is to fit up beds, window-curtains, hangings, and to cover chairs that have stuffed bottoms: He was originally a species of taylor; but, by degrees, has crept over his head, and set up as a connoisseur in every article that belongs to the house. He employs journeymen in his own proper calling, cabinet-makers, glass-grinders, looking-glass frame-carvers, carvers for chairs, tests, and posts of bed, the woollen-draper, the mercer, the linen-draper, several species of smiths, and a vast many tradesmen of other mechanic branches.

Valuable upholstery spent a great deal of its time under loose covers of serge or bays to protect it, and rooms had lighter or heavier hangings according to whether it was summer or winter.

Curtains were by no means universal. They were still considered sufficiently rare and valuable for thieves to dislodge them with a grappling hook and pull them through an open window. Curtains were secured by tape to the hooks or rings. Originally it had been the practice to use a single curtain pulled to the side and secured by a cord or ribbon to a hook. Divided curtains had been introduced in the 1670s, although they were not universally adopted even by the end of the century. Pull-up curtains topped by valances were occasionally used in royal homes. Imported Indian chintzes, painted calico, might be used for window curtains, as well as for wall and bed hangings and table coverings. When Martha Cole left husband Thomas, she took 'two pairs of callico window curtains'. Linen such as 'buckram' and 'soultwich' was used in curtains to give a translucent look and act as sun-blinds. Foreign visitors noted that white table linen was a matter of pride in the better homes. Linen ranged from the coarse to the fine. Martha Cole had 'damask table cloths and twelve napkins of damask'. There was an art in folding table napkins and Pepys was willing to pay for his wife to take lessons.

All but the humblest beds had hangings – for privacy, for warmth and to keep out dust – and consisted of a feather mattress, sheets and 'ruggs' or blankets of wool, cotton or even silk, and a quilt to match the hangings. Holland sheets were the best – and the whitest – and very often the object of theft. Both Martha Cole and Elizabeth Bauer made sure they absconded with 'severall fine Holland and callico sheets' and 'fine Holland pillow doors' when they left their husbands. Childbed linen was expensive – reckoned to be worth £15 4s 7d in Elizabeth's case – and

Martha was determined not to leave behind 'a cradle silk quilt and a little Holland sheet with a suit of childbed linen'. In England two pillows were the norm, whereas in the rest of Europe multiplicity of pillows was seen as a sign of rank. Eiderdowns – bags filled with the feathers of the eider duck, a forerunner of the duvet – were in use in Germany and Scandinavia but would not be adopted in England until the eighteenth century.

The bedchamber might contain one or two easy chairs in which the occupants could sit by the fire. A chair or stool rather than a table would be placed beside the bed to hold a night candle or a chamber pot. The bedroom chest had been fitted with tiers of drawers to provide easier access to the items it contained. In a further refinement, the chest of drawers would be fitted on to legs to become a 'tall boy'.

Clothes were kept in the *garde-robe*, the closet or dressing room leading off the bedchamber. The 'wardrobe' derived from this. The close-stool was sometimes kept in the *garde-robe*. As a dressing room it would feature a dressing table, covered with a carpet and the lady's *toilette*, a lavish affair consisting of a looking glass, silver candlesticks and innumerable vessels, a patch box, a brush and comb, and a muslin cloth to protect the carpet from her cosmetics. The *toilette* was a costly but essential wedding present. The closet might also contain one of the new reclining easy chairs, a clock, a writing desk and cabinets in which to store jewellery and documents and to display the blue and white Oriental porcelain that the late Queen Mary had made so popular. As it was a small room, it could also be the recipient of some of the more experimental decorating techniques: for instance, Oriental lacquer work on the walls to match the lacquer-work cabinets.

The turn of the century coincides with the revolution of the chair. Advances in padding and covering so that it moulded the contours of the body at last offered comfortable seating. Chairs had to have high straight backs. A woman unable to bend in the middle owing to the rigidity of her stays and bearing the weight of a high-tiered headdress needed decent support. For the rich, chairs would be covered in silk damask and silk velvet, while woollen cloth, Turkeywork and leather were cheaper and more durable for the ordinary home. Toddlers also had their own little wooden chairs, in which they could stand upright and push themselves about the room. The simple single bed, the *couche*, evolved into the single-ended day bed or couch and the double-sided sofa. The term 'sofa' seems to have been introduced in the 1690s when someone explained: '*Un sofa est une espèce de lit de repos à manière des Turcs.*' Such seating was admirably suited to a growing leisure class, as were the card tables and cabinets for decorative ornaments, which became essential furniture for the parlour.

In the dining room, the table might now be round or oval in shape. A white linen cloth covered it at mealtimes. The dining room contained a buffet or cupboard, from which drinks would be carried to the table during and after the meal. Gradually cupboards had acquired extra shelves, on which a full range of cups and plates were stored, with a door in front. Pots and delicate porcelain cups for the new beverages of tea and coffee were imported from the East and graced the richer homes by the end of the century. Dining chairs were upright and cane-backed. The heavy oak furniture of the past had given way to lighter woods such as walnut and mahogany, and the surfaces of occasional tables were decorated with intricate marquetry. The heavier Dutch style of William and Mary's reign would be superseded by something more delicate in the time of Queen Anne, more in keeping with English taste. It was no longer necessary to cover such tables with carpets. Dining-room walls were the usual place to display paintings, which tilted forward, while the wall hooks were disguised with ribbon bows.

The fireplace was the dominant feature in a room. The chimney pieces in Queen Mary's apartments at Hampton Court and Kensington were adorned with panelled glass and tiers of blue and white porcelain ornaments, which acted as ballast in the tea ships coming from the East. Delft tiles were commonly used to line the fireplace surround. The sole form of heating was the fire: 'The English use no outward remedy against cold weather but a chimney-fire, which is both comfortable to the body, and cheerful to the sight,' Misson noted. Although the rich might burn wood, the majority of Londoners used sea-coal shipped down from Newcastle. 'The smell of the sulphur caused by this is somewhat offensive to those that are but just come from abroad,' Misson wrote, 'but one is soon used to it.' When Elizabeth Bauer set up home apart from her husband, she ordered from 'a woodmonger', 'one chaldron of coales and one hundred of ffaggotts' to the value of 50s.

Even with a coal fire in the parlour, the bedrooms and the kitchen, it is hard to imagine just how bitterly cold a London house would feel for a large part of the year, especially as winters in the late seventeenth century were considerably colder than they are now — so much so that

WILLIAM HALL,

Chimney-Sweeper and Nightman,

No. 1, SMALL-COAL ALLEY,

Near SPITAL SQUARE,

NORTON-FALGATE.

The poorest parish children often became apprentices to chimney sweeps
(*Museum of London*)

the Thames froze over several times. Miege alludes to the thinness of the
walls, which 'if there happens to be a long fit of excessive heat in
summer or cold in winter ... become at last so penetrated with the air,
that the tenant must needs be uneasie with it'. In the few months when
the grate was empty, a large glass of flowers or porcelain or Delftware
jars embellished the fireplace in the better homes.

Heat and light – and food – consumed most of the average household
budget. The fire itself lent most light to the room. Wax candles were
expensive, tallow candles were cheaper but had an unpleasant smell.

Pepys tried them both. 'This night I begun to burn wax candles in my closet at the office, to try the charge and to see whether the smoke offends like that of tallow candles.' Servants carried on a brisk trade in half-used candles, as Swift noted when addressing the butler in his *Directions to Servants*: 'Never let the candles burn too low, but give them as a lawful perquisite to your friend the cook, to increase her kitchen-staff; or if this be not allowed in your house, give them in charity to the poor neighbours, who often run on your errands.' People were used to the dim light, so much so that on a special occasion when many candles were lit, it was a matter of wonder and exclamation.

Households went to bed early to conserve candles. In the Old Bailey Sessions Papers, it is striking that so many burglaries took place as early as nine o'clock at night in the certainty that all the occupants would be asleep. It was just as well that a new sort of clock had been invented for early risers on dark mornings. Pepys – always keen to get to the office before everyone else – tells us he was 'up betimes by the help of a larum-wach, which by chance I borrowed from my watchmaker today'. By the time Conrad Zacharias von Uffenbach visited London in 1710, he came across an altogether more sophisticated version:

> In the afternoon we drove to another clockmaker's ... to see a new kind of alarum that can be used with all manner of clocks. He has two varieties; one for large clocks, having a dial on which the hand can be set according to the number of hours one wishes to sleep. E.g. if I go to bed at nine o'clock and want to get up at four, this would be seven hours out of twelve; so if I set the hand at seven, it will wake me at exactly four o'clock. The other variety for watches has no dial and consists of a lacquered case in which the watch hangs; the peg projecting from it is put into the key-hole behind the watch, which it fits exactly. But before one fixes the watch on it, this peg must be turned round from left to right until the hour desired appears below. E.g. if I go to bed at nine o'clock at night and wish to get up at five, there are eight hours between nine and five; so I turn it until the number eight is exactly in front of the small hole; then, if I place my watch on the peg, it will wake me punctually at five o'clock, and my watch will still go without anything amiss. Both of us purchased one of these alarms for watches for twelve shillings apiece.

London was well supplied with water. 'To supply this city with water,' wrote Miege, 'there's the Thames, and the New-River; that serving the south, and this the north parts of it. Besides the conveniency of several conduits of spring-water, and the use of pump water in all parts of the town.' Sir Hugh Myddleton's New-River water was carried in a channel from Amwell and Chadwell in Hertfordshire sixty miles away through the village of Islington and over the last remaining fields to the City. Those taking their water from the Thames fared better in the west, before it picked up the raw sewage, dead animals and industrial waste that poured into it from the Fleet and other sources. No house had running water. Water was available from public standpipes and water carriers. In the wealthier houses water was carried through leaky elm-wood pipes and stored in lead cisterns in the basement. The supply, for which householders paid a rate, was not constant. There were hours, even days, when water was not forthcoming. It was essential to collect rainwater in water-butts.

No house contained a bathroom as such. When Pepys visited Mr Povy's well-appointed house in Lincoln's Inn Fields, he exclaimed at 'his bath at the top of the house', but this is unlikely to have been a bathroom as we understand it. The Duke and Duchess of Devonshire's newly installed bathroom – marble with hot and cold taps – at Chatsworth was a tourist attraction at the end of the seventeenth century. Closer to London, Ham House also displayed a marble bathroom at this time. The fact that hot running water was not available in the home does not necessarily mean that people did not wash. But washing piecemeal in lukewarm water from a ewer or basin in cold rooms cannot have been a tempting prospect. When more privileged Londoners took a bath at home, they made do with a wooden or copper tub that was carried up to their chamber from the basement for the occasion. Servants had the unenviable task of heating gallons of water over the kitchen fire and making repeated journeys upstairs with it.

It was much more practical to go to the public bath, or hummums, as Elizabeth Pepys did on occasion. Pepys remarks: 'My wife being busy in going with her woman to a hot-house to bathe herself, after her long being within doors in the dirt, so that she now pretends to a resolution of being hereafter very clean – how long it will hold, I can guess'. He did not get off without a bit of a douse down himself. This merited a diary entry: 'At night late home and to clean myself with warm water; my wife will have me, because she doth herself, and so to bed.'

New River Water
Qui veut de l'eau
Chi vuol acqua di fiume

Maoron delin:

P Tempest ex:

Only the most fortunate had water piped to their houses, others had to carry it from conduits in the streets or bought it from water carriers (*British Museum*)

Celia Fiennes was most impressed by a very early example of the water closet at Windsor Castle, finding in the royal apartments 'a closet that leads to a little place with a seate of easement of marble with sluces of water to wash all down'. This was a rare luxury. In the average London house, chamber pots made of pewter, faience or porcelain would be kept in the scullery along with the washbasins and candlesticks and brought to the room when needed. Their use was not confined to the bedchamber. Pepys once carried on a conversation with Lady Sandwich as she used the chamber pot in the dining room. Male guests would use the pot in full view of others in the dining room during a drinking session. Close-stools were rather more elaborate and comfortable. Just as well, as the recipients of 'physick' spent many hours sitting on them. The one in William III's apartment at Hampton Court has a seat covered in red velvet. The Groom of the Stool would stand by with a linen cloth dipped in a ewer of water to wipe the royal bottom. The close-stool, containing one or two pans, would be kept in the bedchamber or in some more obscure corner or 'little house of office' nearby. The French nickname for the close-stool room or *lieu d'aisance* was *le lieu*, from which comes the English derivation 'the loo'.

Chamber pots and close-stools had to be emptied, either in the vault in the basement or in the cesspit outside. Many servants saved themselves the trouble and chucked the contents out of the window. With luck they landed among the other nastiness in the kennel, or open ditch in the middle of the street, whose noisome stink would only be alleviated when a shower of rain dispelled the contents. Otherwise they might bless some hapless passer-by, or join the ubiquitous mud to suck at the shoes of those foolhardy or desperate enough to travel by foot. Swift was wise to all the short cuts of servants. 'Never empty the chamber pots until they are quite full,' he advises the housemaid, 'if that happeneth in the night, empty them into the street; and if in the morning, into the garden; for it would be an endless work to go a dozen times from the garret and upper rooms down to the backside; but never wash them in any other liquor except their own; what cleanly girl would be dabbling in other folks' urine?'

The vault in the basement or the cesspit in the back yard was to be emptied by the night-soil men, but it seems their visits were irregular and sewage overflowed into cellars and seeped into the water supply. When Pepys stepped into his cellar one day he put his foot 'into a great heap of turds, by which I find that Mr Turner's house of office is full and

RICHARD HARPER,

NIGHT-MAN,

In *Clerkenwell-Green*, near *Turnmill-Street* End,

WITH the Care and Affiftance of his Son, who is always in the Bufinefs, carefully and decently performs what he undertakes, with proper Carriages that hold two Tuns.

He likewife cleanfes Funnels and Trunks, and empties Sefs-Pools, to the Satisfaction of all who pleafe to employ him.

N. B.   *Any Gentleman fhall be waited on by directing a Penny-Poft Letter, or fending a Meffage, as above.*

The night-soil men had a revolting job, but this trade card almost makes it sound a pleasure (*Museum of London*)

comes into my cellar'. Something had to be done, and he invited Mr Turner in 'to see where his vault for turds may be made bigger, or another made him'. Failure to dispose of one's household sewage effectively caused rows with the neighbours. Pepys records that he 'went to Sir W. Batten, where my Lady and I [had] some high words about

146

emptying our houses of office'. The occupants cannot have remained indifferent to the foul smells that drifted through the house. Perfume burners were employed to combat them.

The night-soil men had no enviable task. So bad was the stink of their load that it caused an incident which made newspaper headlines: 'Last night, several bullies of the town, meeting with a night-cart, in the Strand, were so offended at the stench thereof, that they drew their swords, and stabbed all the horses; whereby they died, immediately, after which the sparks run for it, and are not yet heard of; a valiant achievement!' Human waste was eagerly taken up by the market garden-ers, proliferating in the outskirts of London, or dumped in highway ditches, advising visitors of their imminent arrival in the capital.

In one of her many household advice books, Hannah Woolley deplored the fact that 'most in this depraved later age think a woman learned and wife enough, if she can distinguish her husband's bed from anothers'. The duties of the seventeenth-century housewife were labour-intensive, and in addition to the chores themselves she had to be able to organise her servants.

She had to be able to manage the household budget, to know how to buy 'all things at the best times and seasons'. Samuel Pepys kept a watchful eye on Elizabeth's housekeeping: 'And then rose and settled my accounts with my wife for housekeeping, and do see that my kitchen, besides wine, fire, candle, soap, and many other things, comes to about 30s a week or a little over.' A wife's expenditure must not exceed her husband's income. 'Be careful to manage what money he doth trust you with, to his and your own credit,' Woolley urged, 'abuse not the freedom you have of his purse, by being too lavish; and pinch not the guts of your family at home, that you may pamper yourself abroad; or throw away that money in buying trifles, which shall evidence your vanity as well as luxury.'

She had to make sure that her husband's meal was on the table on time:

> Be careful to keep your house in good order, and let all things with decency be in readiness when he comes to his repast; let him not wait for his meals, least by so staying, his affairs be disorder'd or impeded. And let what ever you provide be so neatly and cleanly drest, that his fare, though ordinary, may

engage his appetite, and disengage his fancy from taverns, which many are compell'd to make use of by reason of the continual and daily dissatisfactions they find at home.

Pepys complained of 'the inconvenience that doth attend the increase of a man's fortune, by being forced to keep more servants, which brings trouble'. Servants were essential for the sheer time-consuming drudgery of housework in an age lacking any mechanical tools for the job. As London's citizens became more prosperous and their wives increasingly inured to a life of leisure, servants were much in demand. While a promising young civil servant like Pepys at the start of his career had to be content with one servant, and that servant carried out all household tasks, by the beginning of the new century servants were dictating their terms.

Defoe commented that 'two servants now, will scarce undertake the work which one might perform with ease, yet notwithstanding they have rais'd their wages to a most exorbitant pitch'. They had also become very particular about job specification. He describes a girl being interviewed for a job as a housemaid: 'If you wash at home, you should have a laundry-maid,' she asserted. 'If you give entertainments, you must have a cook-maid; if you have any needlework, you should have a chamber-maid; for such a house as this is enough for a house-maid in all conscience.'

The layout of London houses increased the workload. Coal had to be brought up from the basement to light the fires and the ashes taken down again. Water had to be carried up to the bedchambers and chamber pots brought downstairs and emptied. The emptying of the vault or cesspit by the night-soil men was not a tidy process and someone had to sweep up after them. In the kitchen, the cook spent many hours every day supervising the baking, boiling and roasting of food over an open coal fire. Meals had to be carried up from the kitchen to the first floor, served, and the remains brought down again.

Water had to be heated to wash the cooking utensils, plates and crockery. Pewter plates were meant to shine: 'Wash your plate first in soap-suds and dry it, then if there be any spots, rub them out with salt and vinegar. Then when you have so done, anoint your plate all over with vinegar and chalk, and lay it in the sun or before the fire to dry, then rub it off with warm clean linnen cloths very well, and it will look like new.' In the absence of a nursemaid, children had to be minded, while in the households of ordinary tradesmen servants had to help out in the shop. With all these chores, it would seem to be superfluous for Hannah Woolley to advise, 'do not suffer any servant to be idle'.

Great efforts were made to keep houses clean in a city begrimed by coal smoke. César de Saussure was impressed:

> The amount of water English people employ is inconceivable, especially for the cleansing of their houses. Though they are not slaves to cleanliness, like the Dutch, still they are very remarkable for this virtue. Not a week passes by but well-kept houses are washed twice in the seven days, and that from top to bottom; and every morning most kitchens, staircases, and entrances are scrubbed. All furniture, and especially all kitchen utensils, are kept with the greatest cleanliness. Even the large hammers and the locks on the door are rubbed and shine brightly.

Cleaning was done on Saturday. In *A Description of the Morning*, Swift tells us: 'Now Moll had whirl'd her mop with dextrous airs, Prepar'd to scrub the entry and the stairs.' But while householders might strive to keep the interiors clean, they were less particular about the outside. John Evelyn referred to the 'dust and ordure daily cast out of their houses'. Swift advises the housemaid that 'when you wash any of the rooms towards the street over night, throw the foul water out of the street-door; but, be sure not to look before you, for fear those on whom the water lights, might think you uncivil, and that you did it on purpose'. The streets were someone else's problem. Kitchen waste was collected for pigs, but this was a haphazard arrangement. Hogs roamed the city streets and probably did rather well from household refuse.

Laundry was the most arduous chore. Even the humblest household that had no other servants tried to get some help with the washing. In 'good citizens' houses', washing of clothes and linen took place once a month. 'Observe due times for washing and smoothing up the linnen quickly, that it may not be thrown up and down, and be mildewed and spoil'd,' Woolley advised.

Monday washdays started well before dawn with the heating of the water. On a cold, dark March morning, Pepys observed, 'This day the wench ris at 2 in the morning to wash.' On another occasion, he 'slept pretty well, and my wife waked to ring the bell to call up our maids to the washing about 4 a-clock and I was, and she, angry that our bell did not wake them sooner, but I will get a bigger bell'. The washing was not finished before nightfall, because when he came home 'I found my wife and maid a-washing. I sat up til the bell-man came by with his bell, just under my window as I was writing this very line, and cried, "Past one of the clock on a cold, frosty, windy morning." I then went to bed and left my wife and the maid a-washing still.'

'All their linnen, coarse and fine, is wash'd with soap,' wrote Misson. 'When you are in a place where the linnen can be rinc'd in any large water, the stink of the black soap is clear'd away.' Expensive fabrics such as silk and lace needed special care. For just one pair of silk stockings, Hannah Woolley advised:

> Make a good strong ladder [lather] with soap, and pretty hot, then lay your stockings on a table, and take a piece of such cloth as the seamen use for their sails, double it up and rub them soundly with it; thurn them first on one side, and then on the other, till they have past through three ladders, then rinse them well, and hang them to dry with the wrong sides outward; and when they are near dry, pluck them out with your hands, and smooth them with an iron on the wrong side.

After the gargantuan task of washing everything by hand in coarse soap, there was the problem of getting it dried in the damp and polluted atmosphere. In *Fumifugium*, John Evelyn referred to the coal smoke that soils 'the clothes that are expos'd a drying upon the hedges'. Ironing must have been a lengthy process, using either a flat smoothing iron heated over the fire or a hollow iron kept hot by a lump of coal. It might all be over by Thursday. In addition to washing the linen, Hannah Woolley urged the housewife or her chambermaid to 'forget not to darn it and mend it every week, that it may not run to tatters before it be half worn'.

One of the grievances against servants was that they gossiped and were indiscreet about the family. Defoe describes them congregating in the kitchen where 'the grand affairs of the family ought to be consulted'. In his *Directions to Servants*, Swift advised the footman: 'In order to learn the secrets of other families, tell those of your master's; thus you will grow a favourite both at home and abroad, and be regarded as a person of importance.'

Servants could not be relied on when it came to security, as noted by Swift: 'When you step but a few doors off to tattle with a wench or take a running pot of ale, or to see a brother footman hanged, leave the street door open, that you may not be forced to knock, and your master discover you are gone out: for a quarter of an hour's time can do his service no injury.'

The carelessness of servants and servants themselves were responsible for many burglaries. In *Every-body's Business Is Nobody's Business*, Defoe remarked that 'our sessions papers of late are crowded with instances of servant maids robbing their places, this can only be attributed to their devilish pride; for their whole enquiry nowadays, is how little they shall do, how much they should have.' Servants were 'constantly pilfering, helping themselves to food and drink and slipping some money out of the market money for themselves'. Former servants who knew the household might return to rob it. In the Old Bailey Sessions Papers, Jane Blair was indicted for stealing three silk gowns, three silk petticoats, six silver porringers, a salt, six castors, a cup, a tankard, six guineas, and £11 17s 6d in silver:

> The prosecutor declared that the prisoner had been her servant a little before, but was gone from her; that when they were all in bed, the prisoner came into the house by a false key, and took the goods, and was going away, but being heard, they cried out, Thieves, upon which the prisoner ran downstairs, and lock'd the front door after her, and was making her escape, but was stopt by the constable, who mistrusting her, searched her, and found the false key about her and the rest of the goods; upon which he committed her to the counter.

Revenge and resentment might be incentives for crime:

> It appeared, that Hays being the prosecutors servant, but upon some faults committed by him, was threatened to be turned away; the night before the robbery was committed, having seen the prosecutor to bed, and how he placed his watch, ring, and other of the goods, took occasion before morning to steal the

goods and was gone, but being discovered was brought to confess his taking them.

There was no insurance against household burglaries. Insurance pertained only to fire, the major hazard. Contents insurance did not come in until 1708. 'There are two societies of insurers,' wrote Misson, 'that for so much in the pound upon the rent of the house, are oblig'd to rebuild or repair such as are destroy'd by fire, or demolish'd to stop the progress of it.' Guy Miege went into more detail:

> For insuring of houses in case of fire, here are two societies; the one known by the name of insurance-office, the other by that of the friendly society. In the first, for six pence the pound rent, a house is insured for one year, or else (by way of purchase) a house of ten pound a year is insured seven years for twenty-five shillings, eleven years for thirty-five, twenty one years for fifty, and so proportionably of all houses of greater or lesser rents. If a house thus insured happens to be burnt down within the time 'tis insured for, the insurers are to pay a certain sum, for the rebuilding of it; If only damaged by fire, then to repair the damages ... In the friendly society, the way is for every member thereof to pay yearly at the office, before hand, sixteen pence for every hundred pound secured on brick houses, and much more for timber houses.

Householders were responsible for the lighting outside their houses. 'To supply the light of the sun in the dark nights, London is singular in the use of convex lights, commonly called lamps,' Miege enthused. 'The reflexion whereof is so gloriously luminous, and of so long a reach, that they may be called the little suns of the night.' Householders paid lighting companies for street lighting, but it was not kept on all night. Defoe noted in *An Effectual Method to Prevent Street Robberies* that such lighting as there was failed to prevent crime. Added to which, the watch, paid for by householders to patrol the streets during the night and call out that all was well upon the hour, was quite unequal to the task: 'Our streets are so poorly watch'd; the watchmen, for the most part, being decrepid, superannuated wretches, with one foot in the grave, and the t'other ready to follow; so feeble, that a puff of breath can blow 'em down.'

CHAPTER SEVEN

Fashion

*Although Paris still dictated fashion, London was a
shopper's paradise*

WHEN THE LONDON hangman was arrested for debt on the way back from Tyburn, he was able to buy his freedom instantly with the clothes he had stripped off the corpses as one of the perks of the job. The clothes were soiled, of course, but no self-respecting criminal would go to the gallows wearing anything less than his or her best. They would fetch a good price in the thriving second-hand market and join the vast wardrobe from which all but the very richest Londoners dressed themselves. Fabrics were expensive and through a long life clothes might be cut up, altered, repaired and fashioned into different outfits for different wearers. Industry had still not managed to supply cheap manufactured clothing for all. But all could emulate their betters by buying their cast-offs as they descended the clothes chain.

Londoners had a passion for fine clothes; their outward appearance meant everything to them. 'English women are fond of luxury,' wrote César de Saussure, 'they spare no trouble to be becomingly attired.' Tom Brown described the dazzling sight of the women in the Mall, arrayed like fine birds in all their plumage. De Saussure observed in the parks that the 'women walk fast and well, but in reality I think they do it more in order to show their clothes than for the pleasure of exercise'. He suspected that 'this is the case too with plays and concerts, in which they do not really seem to take much interest'.

In *The English Lady's Catechism*, it was clear that fashionable women attended church for one purpose only. '"How often do you go to church?" "Twice a year or oftener, according as my husband gives me new cloaths." "Why do you go to church when you have new cloaths?" "To see other people's finery, and to show my own, and to laugh at those scurvy, out of fashion creatures that come there for devotion."'

The fop took all morning to perfect his appearance and was then rewarded with cries of 'French dog!' as he walked down the street (*Victoria and Albert Museum*)

And it was not just the women who loved to dress up. No one in London could fail to notice an effeminate breed of men wedded to fashion. The Frenchman Misson described them: 'These gentlemen in English are call'd fops and *beaux*. The play-house, chocolate-houses, and park in spring, perfectly swarm with them: Their whole business is to hunt after new fashions. They are creatures compounded of a perriwig and a coat laden with powder as white as a miller's, and a face besmear'd with snuff, and a few affected airs.' They were all the more remarkable, Misson noted, because generally 'the Englishmen dress in a plain uniform manner'.

Everyone poked fun at the fops. The feminist Mary Astell was merciless in her description:

> His glass is the oracle that resolves all his mighty doubts and scruples. He examines and refreshes his complexion by it, and is more dejected at a pimple, than if it were a cancer. When his eyes are set to a languishing air, his motion all prepar'd according to art, his wig and his coat abundantly powder'd, his gloves essenc'd, and his handkercher perfum'd and all the rest of his bravery rightly adjusted, the greatest part of the day, as well as the business of it at home, is over; 'tis time to launch, and down he comes, scented like a perfumers shop, and looks like a vessel with all her rigging under sail without ballast. A chair is brought within the door, for he apprehends every breath of air as much as if it were a hurricane.

Tom Brown observed the fops at the theatre which they attended mainly to survey the fashions and to attract the admiring glances of the ladies: 'There sits a beau like a fool in a frame, that dares not stir his head nor move his body for fear of incommoding his wig, ruffling his cravat, or putting his eyes or mouth out of the order his *maître de dance* set it in.'

That other sardonic commentator, Ned Ward, described a visit to a coffee-house frequented by the *beaux*: 'A very gaudy crowd of fellows ... walking backwards and forwards with their hats in their hands, not daring to convert them to their intended use, lest it should put the fore-tops of their wigs into some disorder.' He derived enormous amusement from watching their mannerisms, the 'strut and toss of the wig, the carriage of the hat, the snuff-box, the fingering of the foretop, the hanging of the sword'.

Whatever his nationality, a fop was likely to invite shouts of '*French dog!*' as he walked down the street.

Londoners defined themselves by their dress. In *The Fable of the Bees: Or, Private Vices, Publick Benefits*, Bernard de Mandeville was to sum up the situation succinctly:

> Handsome apparel is a main point, fine feathers make fine birds, and people, where they are not known, are generally honour'd according to their clothes and other accoutrements they have about them; from the richness of them we judge of their wealth, and by their ordering of them we guess at their understanding. It is this which encourages every body, who is conscious of his little merit, if he is any ways able, to wear clothes above his rank.

Londoners were so intent on aping their betters that foreign observers found it difficult to distinguish one rank from another. 'The women indeed, who value themselves most upon a fine outward appearance ... go still in rich silks, with all the set-offs that art can possibly invent,' wrote Guy Miege. 'And herein the citizens wives, and maidservants, do run into such excess as makes a confusion. So hard it is sometimes to know a tradesman's wife from a lady, or the maid from the mistress.'

Tom Brown's visitor was equally confused. 'I have not learnt to distinguish female quality from the wives and daughters of mechanics any other way than by their coaches and attendance,' he confessed, 'for the former dress with as much gaiety as the latter, speak as contemptuously of all persons beneath them, and as enviously of those above.'

Sumptuary laws were a thing of the past. When he was a rising young official in the Navy Office in the 1660s, Samuel Pepys, the son of a tailor, paid the closest attention to his wardrobe. He spent far more on his clothes than he allowed his wife for hers, and overall clothes ate up no small part of his carefully hoarded savings, as Pepys discovered when preparing his monthly account in October 1663:

> and to my great sorrow, find myself 43l worse then I was the last month; which was then 760l and now is but 717l. But it hath chiefly arisen from my layings-out in clothes for myself and wife viz., for her, about 12l; and for myself, 55l or thereabouts – having made myself a velvet cloak, two new cloth-suits, black, plain both

– a new shag-gown, trimmed with gold buttons and twist; with a new hat, and silk top[s] for my legs, and many other things, being resolved henceforward to go like myself. And also two periwigs, one whereof costs me 3l and the other 40s … So that I hope I shall not now need to lay out more money a great while, I having laid out in clothes for myself and my wife, and for her closet and other things without, these two months … besides household expenses of victuals etc, about 110l. But I hope I shall with more comfort labour to get more, and with better success then when, for want of clothes, I was forced to sneak like a beggar.

In 1665 he paid £24 – about half a year's income for a family of the middling class even in 1700 – on 'my new silk camelott sute, the best that ever I wore in my life'. Four years later he was sporting gold-lace sleeves – unmistakably the mark of a gentleman – and was given to understand that he had gone too far in dressing above his station.

By the turn of the century, conservatives such as John Evelyn might reflect nostalgically on a time when women were less extravagant in their dress, but progressive thinkers such as Bernard de Mandeville equated private vice with public prosperity. 'Pride and luxury,' he argued, 'are the great promoters of trade.' Yes, Londoners were spendthrifts, but it 'is impossible there should be a rich nation without prodigals'.

The manufacturing industry would be fuelled by the impetus from below as each section of society emulated those above them:

The poorest labourer's wife in the parish, who scorns to wear a strong wholesome frize … will half starve herself and her husband to purchase a second-hand gown and petticoat, that cannot do her half the service; because … it is more genteel. The weaver, the shoemaker, the tailor, the barber and every mean working fellow … has the impudence with the first money he gets, to dress himself like a tradesman of substance… The druggist, mercer, draper, and other creditable shopkeepers can find no difference between themselves and merchants, and therefore dress and live like them. The merchant's lady, who cannot bear the assurance of those mechanicks, flies for refuge to the other end of the town, and scorns to follow any fashion but what she takes from thence. This haughtiness alarms the court, the women of quality are frighten'd to see merchants' wives and daughters dress'd like themselves: this impudence of the City, they cry, is intolerable; mantua-makers are sent for, and the contrivance of fashions becomes all their study, that they may have always new modes ready to take up, as soon as those saucy cits shall begin to imitate those in being.

The rapacity of women when it came to dress prompted Daniel Defoe to warn aspiring tradesmen to be very careful in their choice of a wife. The elderly John Evelyn was appalled at the cost of a bride's trousseau. In *Mundus Muliebris; The Ladies Dressing-Room Unlock'd* his daughter Mary evidently derived more fun than he did from listing all the essentials. Her work is an invaluable record of the contents of a fashionable lady's wardrobe.

Most formal portraits of the period have their subjects wearing 'undress', the loose nightgown worn over the smock that the beauties of the Restoration court had made fashionable, so that one has to turn to prints to see what women actually wore in public. The French noted how fond the English were of this form of *négligée*. 'She does want a gown indeed!' exclaimed Wycherley's dancing master in the play of that name. 'She is in her *deshabille* ... a great mode in England.' Tom Brown noted near the Mall women 'of the common profession in dishabille and night-dresses, either for want of day-clothes, or to show they were ready for business'.

Generally worn only in the privacy of the home, 'undress' had gradually evolved into less formal daytime wear in the form of the mantua gown, the name deriving from the French, *manteau*, meaning a cloak or tunic. The lady's mantua, although worn over a corset, was a fairly loose garment. It was open at the front to reveal an embroidered corset or stomacher laced with ribbons, *échelles*, which like the bodice of the mantua converged in a V shape at the waist. The belt or girdle might be tied with a jewelled buckle. The skirt was looped up behind to reveal a petticoat of a contrasting pattern and colour, sometimes adorned with frills. A change in the pattern of the fabric heralded a new fashion as much as did a new cut of the outfit. There was no shortage of choice when it came to fabric. The Huguenots in Spitalfields were producing intricately woven silks of increasing richness and complexity, so that the fashion trade was hardly affected by the ban on imported French silks.

The three-quarter sleeves of the mantua ended in *engageants*, deep double ruffles hanging down to the wrists. They could be removed and washed.

In 1696 the late Queen Mary II's sister, Princess Anne, was planning what to wear for the celebration to mark William III's birthday — the high point of the social calendar. The decision would depend on whether the entertainment was to be a play or a ball. She very much wanted to indulge in the new fashion for the mantua. Inevitably, she relied on her friend Sarah, Duchess of Marlborough, to resolve her dilemma:

> Without doubt there are people that will find fault with mantoes, for one must expect every new thing will be disliked at first, the generality of the world disapproving of every fashion they do not bring up themselves. I did not think my Lady Fitzharding would have been of the number of those that did not approve of mantoes, not being at all formal herself, but she speaks of it with an air as if she did not think it respect enough. She thinks people can't be so fine as in gowns, and since mantoes are to be worn, that a play would be best, for mantoes cannot be worn at a ball. I told her since they were the dress, it was as much respect to be in them as gowns and that I might certainly be as fine in them; but she did not seem wholly to approve of what I said.

Three years later all such doubts were brushed aside and Elizabeth Adams was writing to Sir John Verney:

> I heare Sir E.D. will be in towne this night, it may be he will be at the ball at the Princess's [Anne] cort this night, I am told ther has not for many yeares bin seen so much fin clothes & rich liveris as will ther appear this night, the Princess' mantua & petycoat cost A thousand pounds & the triming of her petycoat five hundred, & the Duk of Norfock in scarlit imbrodreid with gold, & the Duk of Southamton in black imbrodreid with silver. Sum saies the King seems to dislick the extavent fin cloths that apears in his sit [suite] and saies sure ther is non of money wonting in Ingland.

The tall headdress known as the commode reached its peak in the 1690s. It was a high-tiered wire frame decorated with lace or linen frills and worn at a slight forward tilt. It set off a whole new mode in dressing the hair with appropriate Frenchified language. There were *confidants*, the smaller curls near the ears; *crèves-coeur*, or heartbreakers, the two small curled locks at the nape of the neck; *cruches*, the smaller curls placed on the forehead; *favorites*, the locks dangling on the temples; *passagères*, curled locks next to the temples; *meurtrières*, murderers, or a knot in the hair which ties and unites the curls. The headdress and hair might be adorned by a *firmament*, a mass of diamond-headed pins. Without the headdress in the home the hair was tied up in an arrangement at the top of the head and the loose curls allowed to flow casually over the shoulders.

To complete her wardrobe, Evelyn's fashionable lady also had to have two dozen Holland smocks, a dozen nightdresses with Flanders lace, a dozen laced and a dozen plain 'pocket *mouchoirs*' (only the vulgar called them handkerchiefs). The *mouchoir* would hang at her waist or reside in a pocket in her petticoat. She had to have embroidered velvet slippers, and at least three painted and perfumed fans.

Perfumed gloves were an essential accessory for both men and women of fashion – a curiously fastidious note at a time when a good overall body wash was less than frequent. The Earl of Bedford's household account books reveal that he had several pairs of 'jessemy' gloves, or gloves scented with jasmine. In one year alone he bought six pairs perfumed with frangipane. The most expensive scented gloves were made by the Parisian Martial and cost 30s a pair, while ordinary gloves cost 2s 6d. It was possible to buy from hosiers and glovers the sweet ointment called 'jessemy butter' to rub into the leather, and scented powder to rub on the hands before slipping them into the gloves. Queen Mary had a standing order for two dozen white pairs of gloves a month.

Fur muffs were worn by both men and women to keep out winter chills so severe that the Thames frequently froze over – far colder than the present climate. Wool was scorned by the upper classes, hence the outcry when the government made it compulsory for burial wear. They might at a pinch wear a mixture of silk and wool. Heavier silks would be worn in winter and a fur-lined shoulder cape over the mantua. Evelyn's lady had to have 'dozens of hoods, coiffs and velvet scarfs to keep her back warm'.

The umbrella had been invented, although no fashionable lady would venture out into London's muddy streets in a downpour. The weather seemed to present no challenge to the Earl of Bedford who made quite an investment in umbrellas:

Jonathan Hibbert's Bill

	£.	s.	d.
August 1689.			
For wood and iron work to two umbrellas to rule.	1	7	0
For 17¾ yards of ticking to make the umbrellas at 1s. 3d. per yard.	1	5	0
For 16¾ ounces of worsted fringe to the umbrellas at 5d. per ounce.		6	8
For making the umbrellas.		6	0
For a piece of tape and tacks.		2	0
For a sacking bottom and nails.		12	0
For 2 long screws and nuts.		2	6
For a plain mat to pack them in.		1	0

To compliment the brightly coloured silks of her mantua and petticoat, Evelyn's lady had to have diamond pendants or two pearl pears for her ears, and to set off the frilled open neckline of her gown, a pearl necklace 'large and oriental' and diamond and amber necklaces, and bracelets to sit beneath her lace-edged sleeves. Her silk stockings shot through with gold or silver thread would be held up with 'garters adorned with silver' and there had to be 'diamond buckles on the shoe'. The items for her dressing table, her *toilette*, had to be of silver. Of course she had to have a candlelit table mirror in which to peer to arrange her *mouches*, or black patches, and perhaps her plumpers, to plump out and fill up any cavities (teeth were lost early to decay) in the cheeks. Poignantly, in such circumstances, a gold toothpick completes the list.

Men had already sensibly settled into the three-piece suit of coat, waistcoat and knee-breeches, with a cravat made of linen or lace and ribbon as precursor to the tie, worn over a shirt with ruffles at the wrists. Suits could be of cloth, of velvet or of silk, with lots of buttons. In common with most county families, the Verneys of Claydon in Buckinghamshire bought most of their clothes from London and kept up a considerable correspondence about it. There was some uncertainty about buttons and Lady Fermanagh hastened to prevent a catastrophe:

Deare Mr. Verney, – I have spoke to Mr. Bedford and he tells me that nobody has such a thing as silk buttons to a silk wascoate, and that if you have it done with silver it will be very handsome, and my lord thinks so too. You have sent up one half of your briches and I must have the other half of them sent up, for one briches is too long and we want that which is too much for the briches to make the wascoate compleat, and can't doe without it, so pray don't fail to send it up by John Innes the carryer next week. Mr Bedford says he will pass his word they shall fitt you and it will come to ten shillings more than silk buttons, and your father bids me wright you word that silk will look very ugly, I will take care to doe everything for the best when I know your mind.

Hats, preferably made of beaver, were trimmed with feathers and featured a wide brim turned up at the front. A gentleman had to wear a sword around the waist beneath the coat and carry a walking stick – rather useful in the congested, filth-strewn London streets. His gloves of chamois leather were likely to have a bullion fringe; such military trappings were increasingly in vogue as the war with France was resumed. Stockings were held up at the knees by garters just below the breeches. Like the ladies, men wore moderately high-heeled shoes.

At home, men were also fond of 'undress', the loose gown worn casually over the shirt and breeches. The society painter Sir Godfrey Kneller depicted the poet John Dryden wearing an informal gown and slippers in 1698. Such 'Indian' gowns were made of fabrics of silk or cotton imported from India, but they were made up in London. Dryden wears a full-bottomed wig, despite the informality of his dress, but 'undress' was usually complimented by a fur turban to cover the shaven head and, of course, low-heeled slippers. Indian gowns would be weighted for summer or winter wear. The Earl of Bedford's gentleman of the chamber ordered them for his master from Mr Henry Kirk, Indian gown seller in St Clement Danes. They cost anything from 30s to £3. In due course they would be returned to Mr Kirk for relining; before the advent of deodorants all clothes would need lining and relining if they were to remain wearable.

Wigs had come into fashion during the 1660s, when Louis XIV began to lose his hair at an alarming rate. No real head of hair could be as luxurious as fashion demanded. Wigs were made of human (sometimes still greasy) and animal hair and anyone could sell their hair for a good price or incorporate it in their own wig. Hair pedlars plied their trade nationwide. The full-bottomed wig, huge and elaborate, reigned supreme by the end of the century. Parallel to the height of the female headdress, the male wig was swept up into two peaks either side of a centre parting, with the hair arranged into loose curls which fell lower on one side than the other. Wigs were expensive to make and to maintain. The Earl of Bedford paid £54 10s for four perriwigs costing £20, £18, £10 and £6. The cost of cleaning and repair would be about 10s. At first a wig had been the mark of a gentleman, but gradually wigs permeated down to the lower levels of society. Men thought nothing of combing their wigs in public. The breeze on the Thames made travelling about the metropolis hazardous for wig-wearers and, of course, wigs presented a sorry sight in the rain.

Although Paris still dictated fashion, London was a shopper's paradise, its principal streets sporting thousands of gaudy painted boards advertising the trade beneath. During the rebuilding of the City after the fire, many of the best shops moved west. The Strand and Covent Garden were temporarily established as the most stylish areas, although the nobility were closing up their mansions in the Strand and moving ever westwards. It was common practice to locate small shops in big buildings, such as Westminster Hall and the New and the Old Exchanges. The Royal or Old Exchange in Cornhill was the newer of the two, having been rebuilt after the fire. Upstairs were 200 shops 'full of choice commodities, especially for men and women's apparel'. They sold gloves, stockings, ribbons, fans, masks and materials. The New Exchange in the Strand thrived because of its proximity to the court, and after the burning of Whitehall Palace in 1698 it was still convenient for the rich living in St James.

Shops were looking more and more tempting. Many shops still displayed their wares on a counter open to the street and withdrew them behind closed shutters at night. Others had windows of cloudy glass panes, so that the customer had to step inside to inspect the wares and bargain for their purchase. Daniel Defoe, who had once been in business as a hosier, was appalled at the amount of money a tradesman was expected to spend on the aggrandisement of his premises. He had to sink anything from £200 to £500 'perhaps a third part, nay, a half part of his stock, in painting and gilding, wainscotting and glazing, before he

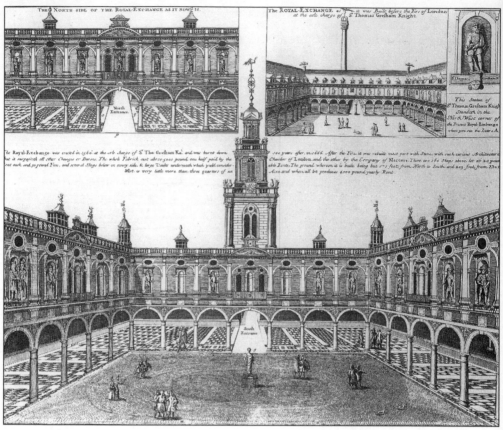

The text in the engravings reads:

THE NORTH SIDE OF THE ROYAL EXCHANGE AS IT NOW IS.

The ROYAL EXCHANGE as it was Built before the Fire of London at the sole charge of Sr Thomas Gresham Knight

This Statue of Sr Thomas Gresham Knight Standeth in the North West corner of the Present Royal Exchange where you see the Letter A

The Royal Exchange was the heart of London's cosmopolitan mercantile community and the site of some of the best shops (*Guildhall Library, Corporation of London*)

begins his trade'. There had to be looking-glasses and wall sconces and candles in silver holders to lighten the dark interior. And 'if he does not make a good show, he comes abroad like a mean ordinary fellow, and no body of fashion comes to his shop'.

Shopkeepers used their wives to charm the customers, and pretty girls were employed to encourage them to buy. Ned Ward describes them as 'begging of custom with such amorous looks, and after so affable a manner, that I could not but fancy they had as much mind to dispose of themselves as the commodities they dealt in. My ears, on both sides, were so baited with "Fine linen, sir, gloves and ribbons, sir," that I had a milliner's and a sempstress's shop in my head for a week together.' Not all customers succumbed to the charm of the vendors. Even the richest women drove a hard bargain, 'driving from shop to shop to try the market'. The expansion of newspaper advertising informed shoppers of the true value of goods, so that bargaining died out.

The late Queen Mary II's interest in fashion had been a boost for London tradesmen. She had patronised Richard Alchorn & Co., mercer, for rich fabrics; James Chase, featherman, who provided ostrich plumes for hats and headdresses, beds and coaches; the establishment of Madame Marie Cheret, sempster and milliner in Covent Garden, who provided lace bands, hat bands, cuffs, ribbons, orange and jasmine gloves, hoods, lace and scarves; George Hanbury, hatter at the New Exchange; Salomon de Medina's textile warehouse; and Samuel Tuer, milliner in Pall Mall.

She had indulged to the full in all the fripperies of a lady of fashion: dozens of yards of ribbon, painted fans and patches. From one shoemaker alone she ordered seven pairs of shoes a month, costing £68 10s in the first half of 1694. King William loved to see her dressed in rich silks and the many pearls and diamonds he had lavished on her, some of them set by her Huguenot jeweller Richard de Beauvoir, or 'Mr Bevoir' as she referred to him. Her lingerie was just as luxurious as her outward dress, her stays black embroidered and stitched with silver, her nightgowns and *négligées* of quilted scarlet and the ubiquitous red and white striped silk.

Fashionable tailors had their own establishments around the Strand, the Temple and Covent Garden. Ladies still employed tailors to make their riding habits. When he visited Epsom Races, Von Uffenbach noted the trend for English women to wear 'men's clothes and feathered hats'. The main expense for both men and women was in the purchase of the material. Lengths of fabric were bought from the mercer and sent to the tailor to be made up. Those inveterate shoppers, the Verneys of Claydon, bought their material in London. Catherine Verney writes to her husband:

> My Dearest, – I hope to hear today you got safe to your journey's end and found all well. I have sent a pattern of the cloth with an account of all you needed to buy, for here is enough of your best coloured cloth to make 'em all four wascotes and brichis, and Mr. Gurney says that the cloth briches will last a yeare very well. I think we had better use it for that purpos and not buy shag, soe you need buy but nine yards of this coloured cloth, but pray let it be as bright, and I think we used to have a finer cloth for the same price. Mr. Gurney says shalloon is much better to line

Benjamin Cole.
at the Sun in S.ᵗ Pauls-Church-Yard
LONDON.
Imports & Sells all sorts of Cambricks.
Lawn, Macklin & English Lace & Edgin,
Where all Merchants, Dealers &
Others may be Furnish'd, Wholesale or
Retail at Reasonable Rates.

The material itself, the gold and silver thread and the lace edging were the most expensive components in an outfit, while the labour of making it was comparatively cheap (*Museum of London*)

Clothes were held together by pins
and it was considered bad luck to keep
any when a bride was undressed
(*Guildhall Library, Corporation of
London*)

them than padway and he
says they cost no more a yd. I
think you had better buy it
white instead of blue because
it will look livelier, and their
briches will now be the same
as the outsides. Here is silk
and mohair enough, soe in
the note is all you need buy
besides the lace.

There was a large discrepancy
between the cost of the material
and the making-up fee. Silk
velvet would cost as much as 26s
a yard. A mixture of silk and wool such as mohair would cost 5s a yard.
Wools and worsteds such as broadcloth cost 10s 6d, serge 4s 6d, and
kersey 2s 7d. The tailor would augment his bill with the purchase of all
the other materials he supplied: the silk or fine cloth used for linings,
the wire and buckram for stiffening, and the flannel for the interlining.
He provided the ribbons for binding, the silver hooks and eyes, and the
buttons if they were ordinary. The vogue for silver, gold or jewelled
buttons meant that these items were often purchased from the goldsmith
and sent to the tailor for his use. Besides the cost of these materials, the
cost of his labour was relatively small, ranging from 10s to £1 for a suit
of clothes.

The clothes of the rich were adorned with gold and silver. The Earl of
Bedford spent £87 18s 6d on gold and silver lace and thread in one year
alone:

Bought of William Gostlin

15½ yards of rich broad gold silver wire purl lace, cost £3. 13s. 0d yard and 9s. yard to be allowed profit, which is 2s. 6d. per pound, which is £4. 2. 0 yard. £63 11s 0d

Per 75 ounces of rich gold silver purled foot, cost 5s. 10d. the ounce, which allowing 8d. the ounce profit at 2s. 6d. per pound, comes to 6s.6d. per ounce and comes to £1. 11s. 6d. per yard. £24 7s 6d.

Although the gold and silver lace men provided by far the most expensive component of a rich man or woman's wardrobe, their trade was fraught with pitfalls. Robert Campbell in *The London Tradesman* explains:

A lace-man must have a well lined pocket to furnish his shop; but his garrets may be as meanly equipped as he pleases. His chief talent ought to lie in a nice taste in patterns of lace, etc. He ought to speak fluently, though not elegantly, to entertain the ladies; and to be master of a handsome bow and cringe; should be able to hand a lady to and from her coach politely, without being seized with the palpitation of the heart at the touch of a delicate hand, a well-turned and much exposed limb, or a handsome face. But, above all, he must have confidence to refuse his goods in a handsome manner to the extravagant beau who never pays, and patience as well as stock to bear the delays of the sharping peer, who pays but seldom. With these natural qualifications, five thousand pounds in his pocket, and a set of good customers in view, a young man may commence lace-man: If he trusts moderately, and with discretion, lives with oeconomy, and minds his business more than his mistress, he may live to increase his stock; but otherwise I know no readier road to jail, and destruction, than a lace-man's business.

Apart from the expense of the gold and silver thread, every outfit had to have its lace and frills and ruffles. Fine lace was bought from a London lace man, or might be brought from Paris or Venice. The seamstress might supply muslin and ordinary lace. The Earl of Bedford employed seamstress Mary Kent to make up his cravats and paid 7s for 'a fine muslin cravat to tie and a fine large neck' and 4s 4d for '2 pair of fine muslin cuffs'. The linen drapers would provide the holland, linen and cotton for undergarments, which again would be made up by the seamstress if not bought ready-made. The earl bought his hosiery from Philip Hanbury in the New Exchange, although his housekeeper sometimes made up his socks and handkerchiefs.

The mantua was the work of the seamstress, now the mantua-maker, rather than the tailor. Again the customer would buy the material separately and this was the most expensive part of the package. Elizabeth, Duchess of Somerset, paid her seamstress, Mrs Groves, as follows:

June 19, 1686, Mrs. Grove's bill:

for making a black and gold manto trymed with loopes 1-0-0
for making a peticoat with three fringes 0-17-0
for silk to lynin the peticoat 0-11-0
for pockets 0-2-0
for making a night gown lyned with crimson 0-6-0
for making a rich peticoat with fringe upon it 0-5-0
for black sassnet to lynin the peticoat 0-8-0
for silk to lengthen it and pockets 0-4-0
for alterin a night gown llyned with whitte 0-4-0
for making a manto lyned with cherry colour and sylver 0-8-0
for making hair colour and blew manto 0-8-0
for making a peticoat of the same richly laced 0-16-0
for new platin a manto 0-8-0
for french sasenet to lynin the haire colour and blew peticoat 0-10-0
for grass taffetas 0-4-6
for two pockets 0-2-0
for making cherry colour night gown lynin whitte and gold 0-6-0
for making a lustring manto 0-8-0
for pinkin the lustring 0-6-0
for making a lustring peticoat richly laced 0-18-0
for persian to lynin it 0-12-0
for making wastcoat 0-6-0
for buttons and caligo to lynin it 0-3-0

Somme total 8-18-6

Some clothes could be bought off the peg. James Cutts, coat-seller, sold ready-made clothes at the sign of the Ape on Horseback, Henrietta Street, Covent Garden. Bourne and Harper's warehouse in Catherine Street, Covent Garden, offered riding habits, cloaks and nightgowns. Men's coats made of cloth ranged from 10s to 36s in price, waistcoats of silk from 7s to 18s, cloth breeches about 8s, breeches of stuff or serge 7s 6d, beaver hats 34s 9d, felt hats 8d to 4s, shirts from 3s to 15s, cloaks 15s to 53s. For women, silk mantuas ranged from 9s 7d to 20s, and calico mantuas about 10s 6d. A silk petticoat could cost as much as 20s or as little as 6s 3d, and a flannel petticoat 5s. Whalebone stays cost about 7s 6d.

The increasing glamour of the shop and the hunger for fine apparel presented the shoplifter with increased temptation. The Old Bailey Sessions Papers record hundreds of such incidents:

> It appeared that the prisoner came frequently to the prosecutor's shop on pretence to court her maidservant, he being her next neighbour's apprentice, and took occasion to carry off the goods which he and his accomplice pawn'd and sold, which he confesst when taken.

> It appeared that the prisoner took the head-dress out of a seamstresses shop-window, where it was sent to be made up; and being seen take out the goods by some of the neighbourhood, he was immediately pursued, and dropt the goods.

> ... It appeared there was nobody in the shop at that time but a little boy, and the prisoner and another woman came in, and askt for his master, pretending to buy some goods, but they took the opportunity, as they were talking with the boy, to take the goods and went their ways, telling the boy, they would go into Cheapside, and call again as they came back; but the boy missing the goods, pursued after them, and took the prisoner in Castle-Tavern Yard.

Tens of thousands of Londoners depended on the second-hand clothes trade. When Ned Ward was walking in Long Lane, he was suddenly accosted by a 'parcel of nimble-tongued sinners' who 'leaped out of their shops, and swarmed about me like so many bees about a honeysuckle.

In a sense all London shared the same wardrobe, some of which is seen here at a pawnbroker's operating under the sign of the three golden balls of Lombardy

(*Museum of London*)

Some got me by the hands, some by the elbows, others by the shoulders, and made such a noise in my ears, that I thought I had committed some egregious trespass unawares, and they had seized me as a prisoner.' These were the second-hand clothes salesmen – the original bearers of that name – who urged him to buy their clothes. '"A pox take you," said I, "you are ready to tear a man's clothes off his back, and then ask him whether he'll buy any. Prithee let mine alone, and they will serve me yet for this six months." But they still hustled me backwards and forwards like a pick-pocket in a crowd, till at last I made loose and scampered like a restless prisoner from a gang of bailiffs.'

Tom Brown had a similar experience:

> Now I, that am always more scared at the sight of a sergeant or bailiff than at the devil and all his works, was mortally frighted in my passage through Barbican and Long Lane by the impudent rag-sellers in those scandalous climates, who laid hold of my arm to ask me what I lacked? At first it made me tremble worse than a Quaker in a fit of enthusiasm, imagining it had been an arrest, and was just asking the customary question, "At whose suit?" But their rudeness continuing at every door, relieved me from these panic fears; and the next that attacked my arm, with "What d'ye buy, Sir, what d'ye lack?" I threw from my sleeve into the kennel, saying, "Though I want nothing out of your shops, methinks you all want good manners and civility; you are ready to tear a new suit from my back, under pretence of selling me another one. Avaunt, vermin, your clothes smell as rankly of Newgate and Tyburn, as the bedding to be sold at the ditchside near Fleet Street smells of a bawdy-house and brandy.

There were second-hand clothes shops such as George Hartley's and Daniel Jones's in Monmouth Street and Godfrey Gimbart's in Long Lane. Markets trading in second-hand clothes were to be found in Monmouth Street, Rosemary Lane, East Smithfield, Houndsditch, the Minories, Petticoat Lane, Chick Lane, Long Lane and the Barbican. The second-hand trade enabled Londoners to wear clothes above their rank and beyond their means had they been new. No one threw away used clothes. A good wardrobe was the equivalent of a savings account – it could be used to realise cash if the need arose.

The rich, for whom a new suit of clothes might cost as much as a labourer earned in a lifetime, might part-exchange old for new with their tailors. Others sold used clothes to second-hand merchants, exchanged them for goods in kind, or took them to the pawnbrokers. There were regular advertisements in the press for second-hand clothes, auctions of unclaimed pawned clothes, and sales of the effects of the dead. Hawkers paraded the streets, crying, 'Any old clothes to sell or exchange?' London remained the hub of the second-hand market, with pedlars carrying clothes back and forth between the capital and the provinces.

The love of luxury encouraged crime. Those who wanted to emulate their betters either stole or bought from the second-hand market. Thieves had a ready market on which to offload stolen goods. The market easily absorbed them. To some extent, it depended on them. Victims of crime advertised in the press, consulted the *Universal British Directory of Pawnbrokers*, and trawled the pawnbrokers and markets in search of stolen goods. Sometimes clothes were altered to disguise their origins. Thieves could not always resist the temptation to wear the clothes themselves, the attraction of the clothing overcoming the need for caution.

It seems that one section of the population was permanently preying on the other and relieving them of articles of clothing:

> Isabella Dickens ... indicted for feloniously stealing from Elizabeth Roe widow ... one gown value 30s a crape petticoat value 10s and some other goods.

> Judith Jones ... indicted for feloniously stealing from Katharine Butler ... a gown value 10s a petticoat value 5s a sable tippet value 5s a muff and several other goods.

> William Martin ... indicted for robbing Mary Jelly on the highway ... and taking from her one laced head-dress value 6l.

Thieves were forever breaking into houses, robbing fellow lodgers, snatching goods in the streets and stripping them off washing lines: 'It appeared that the goods being hung out on the hedges to dry, the prisoner and the rest of the gang were observed to take them off.' The Old Bailey Sessions Papers are peppered with the vast array of clothing that attracted the opportunistic thief:

173

Old Cloaks Suits or Coats

Second-hand clothes sellers were the original 'salesmen' (*British Museum*) 'ten hats and ten hatbands, one coat' … '24 yards of Norwich stuff, value 42s… an apron, three lace coifes, one smock' … 'one gown, four silk hoods value 20s, four yards of Flanders lace value 20s'… 'one silk petticoat, one cloth coat with silver buttons'… 'two stuff petticoats, a callico gown, a pair of stays' … 'a silk petticoat with a gold fringe, and gold spangl'd lace' … 'three pair of cimson worsted stockings' … 'an Indian sattin gown'… 'a silk gown, two stuff gowns, two stuff petticoats, a pair of buckles, set with stones, a sable tippet' …. 'a stuff manteau gown, ten laced caps, a callico apron' … 'a cloth coat, a cloth waistcoat, cloth breeches, a muslin cravat'.

A man wearing a wig was presumed to be worth robbing. Tom Brown encountered 'a pick-pocket, who measuring my estate by the length and bulkiness of my new wig (which God knows is not paid for) he made a dive into my pocket'. Thieves targeted the wigs themselves. Small boys in baskets would ride on the heads of adults and snatch the wigs of passers-by. Edward Short of St Martin-in-the-Fields was indicted for robbing Peter Newell on the highway 'of a hat value 2s and a periwig value 5s'. He had approached the victim in St Martin's Lane, 'snatch't the hat and wig off his head, and then escaped; but being pursued, he dropt the wig, but the hat was found under his arm'. Thomas Giblet was 'going under Ludgate with a perriwig in a band-box' when he was 'thrust up to the wall by the prisoner and some persons, who took the wig from him'. When John Matthews was condemned 'for privately stealing 24 ounces of hair out of Mr Trotts' shop, and 2 perruques out of Mr Newth's', he admitted that 'being without employment, and in great straights, he had of late years given himself to this way of stealing hair and perruques out of a barber's shop'.

Servants in close proximity to their employers had ample opportunity to study their mode of dress and hanker after the same. Sometimes the longing to possess became overwhelming:

Anne Hughes of the parish of St Dunstans in the West, was tried for stealing a quarter of an ell of Holland value 18d one yard of cambrick 3s one scarf 6d one pair of shoes 12d the goods of Gabriel Collins. It appeared that the prisoner had been a servant of Mr Collins, and took away the goods, which were found in her box; which matter being fully prov'd against her, and that when she was apprehended she made an attempt to cut her own throat, but was prevented.

The wages of crime were quite likely to be poured back into the trade, since fine clothes were everyone's ambition. As Bernard de Mandeville expressed it:

> A highwayman having met with a considerable booty, gives some common harlot he fancies ten pounds to new-rig her from top to toe; is there a spruce mercer so conscientious that he will refuse to sell her a thread sattin, tho' he knew who she was? She must have shoes and stockings, gloves, the stay and mantua-maker, the sempstress, the linen-draper, all must get something by her, and a hundred different tradesmen dependent on those she laid her money out with, may touch part of it before a month is at an end.

Before long, she might be pawning her new finery, setting it on its hand-me-down journey through the ranks until it reached the poorest of London's citizens. There was a sense in which all London wore the same clothes, the rich when they were new and gleaming and the poor when they were filthy, worn and tattered. As for the highwayman, he too would contribute to the trade when he reached the gallows, because, as the London hangman knew only too well, a dead man's clothes were good for recycling.

CHAPTER EIGHT

Food and Drink

*'The English eat a great deal at dinner; they rest a while, and
to it again, till they have quite stuff'd their paunch'*

A T SIX O'CLOCK IN THE morning in summer or sunrise in winter, the
London housewife or her servant was summoned by the market
bell six days a week to shop for food. There were a couple of hours
of brisk trading in which City regulations ensured she had priority before
tradesmen, hawkers and the suburban shopkeepers moved in to buy their
stocks. There were no fixed prices and she had to bargain hard, judging the
quality and weight of the goods herself. She paid in cash. Her purchases
would be handed over unwrapped and she carried them home without
help. She was lucky in at least one respect. London was a city of plenty.
Not only was there a rich variety of foodstuffs from the provinces, but
London was a great port which imported more exotic goods than could be
produced at home. 'For pleasure, or luxury, London is a magazine, where
all is at hand, and scarce any thing wanting that money can purchase. Here
is to be had, not only what Europe affords, but what is fetched by
navigation from the remotest parts of the habitable world.'

Since the Great Fire the old haphazard arrangement of congested street
markets had been superseded by four new sets of buildings, where pattern
and order replaced the free-for-all mixtures of goods. Leadenhall in the
street of that name was the grandest of these new markets, consisting of
myriad stalls in four spacious open courtyards. This was a major market
for meat. Sheep and cattle were brought into London on the hoof, sold to
the butchers at Smithfield and slaughtered behind their premises and in
back yards in the City itself and just outside the walls. In lieu of
refrigeration, slaughtering was necessarily a regular occurrence. The blood
and offal posed a constant problem in waste disposal. The stink was
particularly odious for those in the vicinity, not least the churchgoers
passing Butcher Hall Lane on the way to St Paul's on Sunday morning.

At Leadenhall beef was sold on 100 stalls, leaving 140 stalls for mutton, veal and poultry. Turkey had become popular and they were walked from Norfolk in droves of up to 1,000. Poultry was fattened up in London storehouses before being taken to market. Country wives brought in chickens and rabbits to sell. There were rows for fish, rows for butter, rows for cheese. Wholesalers could go to Queenhythe market for corn and to Billingsgate for fish – both conveniently situated along the north bank of the Thames where the cargoes were unloaded – and to the Stocks (named after the gillyflowers on sale there) in Poultry for fruit and vegetables. The Swiss visitor César de Saussure was impressed:

Nowhere can you see finer markets than in London, especially those of Leadenhall, of Stocks Market, and several others; they are vast, covered, and shut in, and in them you can find every kind of butcher's meat, the finest in all the world, and kept with the greatest cleanliness. England is celebrated, and justly so, for her excellent meats, especially beef and veal, mutton being rather coarse, often tasting of tallow, but full of juice. In these markets an abundance of every kind of salt and fresh water fish is to be found; also vegetables and poultry of every description.

For the housekeeper who did not feel up to the market, help was at hand. César de Saussure explains: 'Besides these public markets, quantities of small vendors go through the streets, especially in the morning, calling out their wares for sale; thus, if you prefer it, you need not leave your house to buy your provisions.' Against the constant thunder of iron-wheeled coaches and carts on cobbled paving, the streets rang to the hawkers' cries: 'Four for sixpence, mackerel!', 'Twelve pence a peck, oysters!', 'Cherries ripe-ripe-ripe!' and 'Pippins fine? Pippins fine?' Hawkers and itinerant pedlars were greatly resented by the shopkeepers who paid rates and rent for their premises.

The milkmaid carrying a pair of churns on a shoulder yolk was a daily visitor. 'Milk maids below!' Asses, whose milk was much sought after for young children and those with digestive problems, were led from door to door and milked straight into the customers' jugs. Cows for milking were kept in London and César de Saussure felt particularly at home when he visited the nearby village of Islington which was famous for its cow pastures and dairies. He described the milkmaids' own special day in the city:

The shopkeepers resented the street hawkers who paid no rates or taxes. This one is wearing the poor woman's version of the mantua gown (*British Museum*)

The 1st of May is a great festival for the milk-vendors, who live in great numbers in London and its neighbourhood. The milkmaids dress as neatly and daintily as possible, and in companies of from five to six visit all the houses where they are wont to carry milk. One of these maidens carries a trophy of different pieces of crockery decked with flowers, ribbons, and tinsel on her head. One or two violin players go before, playing on their instruments. The milkmaids stop before the houses and dance, and generally a few coins are thrown to them, or some food is offered. Their dance is called a jig, and is peculiar. Two maidens dance at a time, without changing places, with one foot uplifted, whilst they frisk and stamp extraordinarily quickly with the other. Some of these girls dance with great agility, grace, and measure.

Although there was a rich variety of foods available in London, its inhabitants were no gourmets. Guy Miege, whose _The New State of England Under Our Present Monarch King William III_ was a useful guide for those engaging in trade, was of the opinion that 'the less time is lost in eating, and the more saved for business. In short, if other nations live to eat, the English may be said to eat only to live'.

There was only one main meal a day. 'The generality of them (especially at London),' noted Miege, 'have used themselves to eat but one meal, the breakfast and supper being commonly made up with slight things, as chocolate, tea, coffee, and at night especially some sort of strong liquor.' Londoners saved themselves for dinner, which had originally been held at one o'clock but was gradually moving later in fashionable circles. The French visitor Henri Misson was a wry commentator on English eating habits. 'The English eat a great deal at dinner; they rest a while, and to it again, till they have quite stuff'd their paunch. Their supper is moderate: Gluttons at noon, and abstinent at night.'

Misson conceded that the 'English beef is reported to excel that of all other countries in the world' and that it was the dish of choice among all those who could afford it:

I always heard they were great flesh eaters, and I found it true. I have known several people in England that never eat any bread, and universally they eat very little: They nibble a few crumbs, while they chew the meat by whole mouthfuls. Generally speaking, the English tables are not delicately serv'd. There are some noblemen that have both French and English cooks, and these eat much after the French manner; But among the middling sort of people, they have ten or twelve sorts of common meats, which infallibly take their turns at their tables, and two dishes are their dinners; a pudding, for instance, and a piece of roast beef: another time they will have a piece of boil'd beef, and then they salt it some days beforehand, and besiege it with five or six heaps of cabbage, carrots, turnips, or some other herbs or roots, well pepper'd and salted, and swimming in butter.

Sunday was a day on which 'to feast as nobly as possible' and 'it is common practice ... to have a huge piece of roast-beef, of which they stuff till they can swallow no more, and eat the rest cold, without any other victuals, the other six days of the week'. César de Saussure noted that beef came to the table weighing 'according to the number of those who are to partake of it, ten, twelve, or fifteen pounds, though I have even seen it weigh twenty'. One wonders about the state of the beef at Sunday dinner. Much would depend on the housekeeper's astuteness in the purchase. It needed to have been recently slaughtered and properly bled by the butcher. Once home, it would be dropped in a tub of brine until it was time to cook it. Defoe complained that 'in extreme hot weather, when meat will not keep from Saturday to Sunday, we throw, or cause to be thrown away, vast quantities of tainted meat, and have generally stinking dinners, because the butchers dare not sell a joint of meat on a Sunday morning'. Perhaps it was appropriate that Hannah Woolley included recipes for beef well coated in sauces:

Beef à-la-Mode
Cut some buttock-beef a quarter of an inch thick, and lard it with bacon, having hackt it before a little with the back of your knife, then stew it in a pipkin with some gravy, claret-wine, and strong broth, cloves, mace, pepper, cinnamon and salt; being tender stewed, serve it on French bread snippets.

Alternatively:

Beef Carbonadoed
Steep your beef in claret wine, salt, pepper, and nutmeg, then

broil it on the embers, over a temperate and unsmoaky fire, in the mean while boil up the liquour wherein it was steeped, and serve it for sauce, with beaten butter.

Venison pasties were a particular favourite of Samuel Pepys. If the venison had become tainted, Hannah Woolley's recommendation was to 'take a clean cloth and wrap your venison therein, then bury it in the earth one whole night, and it will take away the ill scent or savour'.

In *Acetaria, a Discourse of Sallets*, John Evelyn expressed some concern about excessive meat-eating. Bernard de Mandeville took vegetarianism a step further: 'If it were not for this tyranny which custom usurps over us, that men of any tolerable good-nature could never be reconcil'd to the killing of so many animals for their daily food, as long as the bountiful earth so plentifully provides them with varieties of vegetable dainties.'

As may be inferred from Misson's description, Londoners were not over-fond of 'edible roots and herbs', the term vegetable not being known. Plenty were available from the market gardens edging the city – artichokes, beans of all sorts, beets, onions, cabbage, cauliflower, carrots, clary, cucumber, endives, lettuce, spinach, parsnips, turnips, peas, radish, celery, potatoes – but they were generally used as 'a supplement, or accessory to the principal'. They were expensive. Some vegetables were clearly more appreciated than others. A dish of fresh peas seems to have been something of a favourite. Princess Anne is said to have burst into tears when her brother-in-law King William failed to pass them to her and ate them all himself. Hannah Woolley offered tips for making vegetables more appealing:

> To make boiled sallads
> Boil some carrots very tender, and scrape them to pieces like the pulp of an apple; season them with cinnamon, ginger and sugar, put in currans, a little vinegar, and a piece of sweet butter, stew these in a dish, and when they begin to dry, put in more butter and a little salt, so serve them to the table; thus you may do lettuce or spinage or beets.

In *Acetaria*, Evelyn recommended the proper ingredients for a salad and tips for its preparation. He distinguished between vegetables intended for the pot and those that should only be eaten raw. The 'sauce' must be a careful mixture of mustard, oil and vinegar, with or without the hard-boiled yoke of a new-laid egg, and the only salad bowl to be contemplated was of 'porcelaine or of the Holland Delft ware', silver and pewter being quite unsuitable receptacles for the sauce. At each of the barber-surgeons three feasts held in April 1700, '2 sallets' costing 1s were served.

Occasionally beef gave way to other meats: 'A leg of roast or boil'd mutton, dish'd up with the same dainties, fowls, pigs, ox-tripes, and tongues, rabbits, pidgeons, all well moisten'd with butter, without larding: Two of these dishes, always serv'd up one after the other, make the usual dinner of a substantial gentleman, or wealthy citizen.'

The first and second courses, with the emphasis on savouries, would be served up simultaneously, so that the table might look like this:

June

First Course:
A neats-tongue [cow's tongue], or leg of mutton and colliflowers
A steak-pye
A shoulder of mutton
A fire-quarter of lamb
A dish of pease

Second Course:
Sweet-bread pye
Capon
Gooseberry-tart
Strawberries and cream. Or strawberries, white wine, rose-water
    and sugar

Food accounted for a substantial part of the household budget. In the early days of his marriage, Samuel Pepys was dismayed to discover that 'my ordinary housekeeping comes to 7l a month – which is a great deal'. Still, he did not stint when he was giving a dinner party:

So my poor wife rose by 5 a-clock in the morning, before day, and went to market and bought fowle and many other things for dinner – with which I was highly pleased. And the chine of beef was done also before 6 a-clock ... Things being put in order and the cooke come, I went to the office, where we sat till noon; and then broke up and I home – whither come ... my guests. I had for them, after oysters – at first course, a hash of rabbits and lamb, and a rare chine of beef – next, a great dish of roasted fowl, cost me about 30s, and a tart; and then fruit and cheese. My dinner was noble and enough ... I believe this day's feast will cost me near 5l.

The barber-surgeons kept meticulous accounts of the company dinners following the public anatomy lectures and these give us some idea of the costs involved in 1700:

2 large legs of mutton boyl'd 7s; 2 loyns of beef 17s.6d; 3 pigeon pyes, 12 in each pye 1s.4d; 3 large neck of veale 12s; 2 sallets 1s; 1 pint and a quarter of oyle 1s.7d; 1 pound of dish butter for ye table 1s; sampier and capers and spinage 1s.6d; 4 pound of fresh butter 2s.4d; vinegar pepper laurell flowers and severall other things to garnish 1s.6d; flower, salt and salt butter 2s; wood and coles 9s.6d; dressing ye dinner 8s. Total cost £3.12s.11d.

The statistician-economist Gregory King estimated that middling families spent between £5 and £20 per head a year on food and drink.

When her family and guests were all seated at table in the new Dutch fashion of man-woman-man-woman introduced by William III, the lady of the house would begin to carve the meat. She would probably have received carving lessons before marriage. Hannah Woolley's *The Gentlewoman's Companion* outlined the etiquette to be used and implied from its instructions on what not to do, just what its readers *were* doing: 'In carving at your own table, distribute the best pieces first, and it will appear very comely and decent to use a fork; if so touch no piece of meat without it ... avoid clapping your fingers in your mouth, and licking them, although you have burnt them in the carving.'

The best cuts were to be served to the guests in order of precedence: 'If chicken-broth be the first dish, and you would help your principal guest with a part of the chicken, the best piece is the breast; the wings and legs are the next.' If roasted pig was to be served, then 'the dainty most approve the ears and divided jaws, the neck and the middle-piece, by reason of the crackling'.

Guests might be left to help themselves. 'If you are left to your own liberty, with the rest, to carve to your self, let not your hand be in the dish first, but give way to others; and be sure to carve on that side of the dish only which is next to you, not over-charging your plate, by laying thereon a little at a time.'

In polite society, it was not done to 'baul out aloud for any thing you want; as, I would have some of that; I like not this; I hate onions; give me no pepper: But whisper softly to one, that he or she may without noise supply your wants.'

There would often be one central dish for all: 'It is not civil to be twice in one dish, and much worse to eat out of it piece by piece; and do not (for it favours of rudeness) reach your arms over other dishes to come at that you like better. Wipe your spoon every time you put it into the dish, otherwise you may offend some squeamish stomacks.'

Above all, *The Gentlewoman's Companion* urged its readers not to 'fill your mouth so full, that your cheeks shall swell like a pair of Scotch bag-pipes' and to 'close your lips when you eat; talk not when you have meat in your mouth; and do not smack like a pig, nor make any other noise which shall prove ungrateful to the company'. Also, 'gnaw no bones with your teeth nor suck them to come at the marrow: Be cautious, and not over-forward in dipping or sopping in the dish; and have a care of letting fall any thing you are about to eat between the plate and your mouth'.

Misson was rather taken aback by English manners: 'Belching at table, and in all companies whatsoever, is a thing which the English no more scruple than they do coughing and sneezing.' Hannah Woolley reminded her readers that 'it is uncivil to rub your teeth in company, or to pick them at or after meals, with your knife, or otherwise; for it is a thing both indecent and distasteful'.

Misson noted that 'when they have boil'd meat, there is sometimes one of the company that will have the broth; this is a kind of soup with a little oat-meal in it, and some leaves of thyme or sage, or other such small herbs. They bring up this in as many porringers as there are people that desire it; those that please crumble a little bread into it, and this makes a kind of potage.' Hannah Woolley warned: 'If your potage be so hot your mouth cannot endure it, have patience till it be of a fit coolness; for it is very unseemly to blow it in your spoon, or otherwise.'

While the poor would also like to have eaten beef every day, their staple fare consisted of beer, bread and cheese and the cheaper cuts of meat: tripe, offal, trotters and hogg's puddings. The English were not great bread eaters, and the quality of the bread was poor. The poor ate coarse brown bread, stamped with an H to signify 'housewife's' bread. Others preferred the dearer white, wheaten bread, stamped with a W. In the City the Assize of Bread fixed the weights of the halfpenny, penny and twopenny loaf, but its authority did not extend to the outlying parishes. Bread was baked in large brick ovens, the dough being thrust into the oven once the embers from the wood fire had been raked out. The baker might also produce baked meats, its content chopped into small enough pieces to cook while the brick oven cooled.

In London, fresh- and salt-water fish were plentiful, but according to Misson 'dearer than any other belly-timber'. Most of the sea-fish sold to Londoners was already dried and salted before it left ports far up the east coast. Dried cod or haddock and herrings dried, pickled or smoked in innumerable ways were basic fare. It was more economic to buy them in bulk when they might work out at about 6d each. Anchovies imported from Italy were a popular accompaniment to a drink of wine or beer. Fresh fish of any kind was more expensive, because of the effort of keeping it alive in fish tanks and water carts until it could be sold. There were permanent fish stalls in all the new markets. The fishwives hawked their wares around town, shrieking: 'Two a groat, and four for sixpence, mackerel! New fresh herrings! New-new cockells!' They were notorious enough to provoke Defoe's comment: 'Not only strumpets, but labouring women, who keep our markets, and vend things about the street, swear and curse at a most hideous rate.'

Oysters were cheap and plentiful, sold by the fishmongers direct and by street hawkers. One advertisement ran: 'Thomas West Fishmonger in Honey Lane Market near Blossom's Inn, gives notice, That all persons who have occasion for the choicest oysters called Colchester oysters, may be supplied for this season with the largest pick't fat and green for 3s a barrel.' Home deliveries were available for a small charge. There were lots of recipes for oysters:

Oyster pyes
Parboil your oysters in their own liquor, then take them out and wash them in warm water, dry them, and season them with

pepper, nutmeg, yolks of hard eggs and salt; the pye being made, put a few currans in the bottom, and lay on the oysters with some sliced dates in halfs, some large mace, sliced lemmon, barberries and butter, close it up, and bake it, then liquor it with white-wine, sugar and butter.

Herbs and spices were liberally used in cooking and no one could be left ignorant as to their culinary and medicinal benefits from the many household recipe books available. Black pepper should not be crushed too small 'for fear of inflaming the blood'. It 'cutteth gross flegm, dispelleth crudities, and helpeth digestion'. Ginger was 'very expedient for the expulsion of wind'. Saffron was supposed to 'unstuff the pipes of the lungs'. And cloves were good for 'the head, heart, stomach, and the eyes'.

The English were very fond of puddings. These could be savoury as well as sweet. At Christmas, for instance, Misson describes uniquely English dishes: 'Every family against Christmas makes a famous pye, which they call Christmas pye: It is a great nostrum the composition of this pasty; it is a most learned mixture of neats-tongues, chicken, eggs, sugar, raisins, lemon and orange peel, various kinds of spicery, etc. They also make a sort of soup with plums, which is not at all inferior to the pye, which is in their language call'd plum porridge.' César de Saussure did not find the Christmas porridge to his taste, but he noted its ingredients: 'You must stew dried raisins, plums, and spice in broth, rich people add wine and others beer, and it is a great treat for English people.'

Misson waxed lyrical about the English pudding:

The pudding is a dish very difficult to be describ'd, because of the several sorts there are of it; flower, milk, eggs, butter, sugar, suet, marrow, raisins, etc etc are the most common ingredients of a pudding. They bake them in an oven, they make them fifty several ways: Blessed be he that invented pudding, for it is a manna that hits the palates of all sorts of people; a manna, better than that of the wilderness, because the people are never weary of it. Ah, what an excellent thing is an English pudding! To come in pudding-time, is as much as to say, to come in the most lucky moment in the world.

Londoners consumed huge amounts of dairy produce. Butter was heavily salted and bought by the barrel or gallon pot. It was mainly used for cooking, and foreigners noted with a degree of repugnance the amount of butter that was lathered on meat and vegetables. Butter, eggs and cream were popular ingredients in puddings:

An Almond Pudding
Take a pound of almond-paste, some grated bisket-bread, cream, rose-water, yolk of eggs, beaten cinnamon, ginger, nutmeg, some boiled currans, pistages and musk, boil it in a napkin, and serve it in a dish, with beaten butter and sugar serap'd thereon.

To Make the Orange Pudding
Take the rind of a small one, pared very thin, and boiled in several waters, and beaten very fine in a mortar, then put to it four ounces of fine sugar, and four ounces of fresh butter, and the yolks of six eggs, and a little salt, beat it together in a mortar till the oven heats, and so butter a dish and bake it, but not too much; strew sugar on it, and serve it to the table. Bake it in puff-paste.

Lashings of sugar were used in the Londoners' diet. Boosted by an expanding slave trade, it cost only 5d to 6d a pound. Hannah Woolley sounded a note of caution. Not only did it 'rot the teeth and taint the breath', but 'the most part of our finest sugar, and which is the most coveted, is refined and whitened by the means of the lees of lime; how prejudicial that may be to the body, I will leave it to the rational to consider'. Sugar was cheap and easily available from the grocers' shops, alongside other non-perishable goods, such as salt, pepper, ginger, cinnamon and other spices. Sugar gave an impetus to the consumption of fruit. It was used in fruit tarts – which were very popular – and in 'candying, conserving and preserving fruits'. Tarts and sweetmeats were 'to be taken up at the point of your knives, laid dextrously on a plate, and so presented; and whatever you carve and present, let it be on a *clean* plate'.

Misson made a distinction between the pudding and the dessert. 'The desert they never dream of, unless it be a piece of cheese.' Cheese was eaten in vast quantities by all classes. It was only possible to buy a whole cheese, though the sizes varied. Ned Ward recalls: 'The conclusion of our dinner was a stately Cheshire cheese, of a groaning size, of which we devoured more in three minutes than a million of maggots could have done in three weeks.' Cheese was easy to keep and to store, so that specialist shops opened to sell it. Chandlers and other tradesmen sold it as a sideline.

Misson claimed that fruit – which was expensive – was not brought to the table, but according to *The Gentlewoman's Companion* fruit was certainly offered 'when the meat is all taken away'. In summer there would be raspberries and strawberries washed in wine, three or four dishes of sweetmeats decorated with vine leaves and flowers, and jellies of several colours; in winter dried fruits, candied oranges and lemons, blanched almonds, figs, raisins, pistachios and walnuts. Apart from a wide range of home-grown fruit – apples, pears, plums, cherries, peaches, apricots, nectarines, grapes, figs, gooseberries, strawberries, mulberries, berberries, quinces – there were exotic imports. 'A parcel of choice mangoes lately come from the Indies, are to be sold by retale,' ran a newspaper advertisement, 'at 4s a dozen at Walsalls Coffee-house in Naggs-head Court, in Bartholomew-lane, behind the Royal-Exchange.'

Those who had attended dinner and lingered for the rest of the afternoon playing cards and visitors arriving in the course of the afternoon, might be offered 'one or two dishes of cream only, a whipt sillibub, or other, about four dishes of sweetmeats and fruit and wine'.

To Make a Whipt Sillibub
Take half a pint of Rhenish wine, or white wine, put it into a pint of cream, with the whites of three eggs, season it with sugar, and beat it as you do snow-cream, with birchen rods, and take off froth as it ariseth, and put it into your pot; so do till it be beaten to a froth, let it stand two or three hours till it do settle, and then it will eat finely.

To Make Thick Cream
Take sweet cream, a little flower finely searced, large mace, a stick of cinnamon, sugar and rosewater, let all these boil together till it be thick, then put into it thick cream, the yolks of eggs beaten, then let it seethe but a little while for fear of turning, then pour it out, and when it is cold serve it.

189

In more prosperous households the table would be covered with a white linen cloth and diners might wipe lips and fingers on fringed linen napkins supplied by Thomas D'Oyly of Henrietta Street, Covent Garden. Apart from pewter plates, knives, forks and spoons, and of course candles, there was no other table ornamentation. Wine or beer was kept on the cupboard, from where it could be fetched by the glass or tankard.

'When everyone has done eating, the table is cleared, the cloth even being removed, and a bottle of wine with a glass for each guest is placed on the table.' The clearing of the table after dinner was the signal for the drinking to begin. 'All our empty plates and dishes were, in an instant, changed into full quarts of purple nectar and unsullied glasses,' Ward marvelled. This was the moment to toast the king's health and as many others' as could be devised, a good excuse for a prolonged drinking bout. Misson regarded this English custom as rather quaint, as it had long gone out of fashion in France:

> To drink at table, without drinking to somebody's health, especially among the middling people, would be like drinking in a corner, and be reckon'd a very rude action. There are two principal grimaces which are universally observ'd, upon this occasion, among persons of all degrees and conditions: The first is, that the person whose health is drunk, if an inferior or even an equal, must remain as still as a statue while the drinker is drinking. If, for instance, you are about to help yourself to something out of the dish, you must stop suddenly, lay aside your fork or spoon, and wait without stirring any more than a stone till the other has drank: After which, the second grimace is to make him a low bow, to the great hazard of dipping your peruke in your sauce.

The whole ceremony struck Misson as absurd:

> I own, that to a stranger, these customs seem ridiculous; he thinks nothing can be more pleasant than to see a man that is just going to chew a mouthful of victuals, cut a piece of bread, wipe his fingers, or anything of that nature, in a moment put on a grave serious face, keep his eyes fix'd upon the person that

drinks his health, and grow as motionless as if he were taken with an universal palsy, or struck with a thunderbolt.

Again, etiquette was involved:

As civility absolutely requires this respectful immobility in the patient, so there is some caution to be used on the part of the agent: When you would drink a man's health, you should first keep your eye upon him for a moment, and give him time, if possible, to swallow his mouthful, that you may not reduce him to the perplexing and uneasy necessity of putting a sudden stop to his mill, and so sitting a good while with his mouth cramm'd with a huge load of victuals, which commonly getting all to one side, raises his cheek as high as an egg, so forming a large kind of a wen, often shining with grease, equally distorted and unseemly.

The women, too, were included in the toasts: 'The usual kick is, for the men to drink the women's health, and the women the men's; and if any one in the company should break this law, 'twould be reckon'd intolerable rudeness.' Probably because they drank with such gusto, Hannah Woolley was at pains to remind her readers to use some decorum: 'This throwing down your liquor as into a funnel would be an action fitter for a jugler than a gentlewoman.'

'After these toasts the women rise and leave the room, the men paying them no attention nor asking them to stay,' noted César de Saussure, who never ceased to marvel at the chauvinism – in both senses – of English men. There was a good practical reason for the women to withdraw, for now the men might ease the call of nature in the pot kept in the dining room for this very purpose.

Foreign observers felt that the English drank for the sake of it. César de Saussure wrote home in amazement: 'Would you believe it, though water is to be had in abundance in London, and of a fairly good quality, absolutely none is drunk? The lower classes, even the paupers, do not know what it is to quench their thirst with water. In this country nothing but beer is drunk, and it is made in several qualities. Small beer is what everyone drinks when thirsty; it is used even in the best houses, and costs only a penny the pot.'

191

Beer came in varying strengths. Strong beer was twice the price of small beer. Obviously Guy Miege had a very strong brew: 'It goes down gently and palatably; but, as if it were too noble a liquor for those lower parts, it presently flies up into the head and puts all there in confusion. So quick is the operation of those strong sorts of liquors, upon too large a dose, that they run a man out of his senses, before he can have an interval of mirth.'

The housewife would brew beer in her own home, but in London it was easier to buy it from the local 'brewhouse'. Although there was a tax on it, it was reasonably priced because no middleman was involved. Householders kept in a good supply, an eight-gallon firkin at least. Alternatively, the alehouse could supply a quart pot. No deposit was required on the pewter tankards, which were often stolen when left outside on the house railings for collection. César de Saussure spoke of ale so pale that foreigners mistook it for wine. London brewers had competition from such ales as 'right Darby', 'Sleeford of Lincolnshire' and 'North Country Pale Ale ready bottled at 4s per dozen' – all now reaching London thanks to improved inland transport. Brunswick Mum, a forerunner of stout, was popular. Cock-ale could be prepared in the home:

> To make cock-ale, take ten gallons of ale and a large cock, the older the better, parboil the cock, flea him and stamp him in a stone mortar till his bones are broken (you must craw and gut him when you flea him), then put the cock into two quarts of sack, and put to it three pounds of raisins of the sun stoned, some blades of mace, and a few cloves: put all these into a canvas bag, and a little before you find the ale has done working, put the ale and bag together into a vessel. In a week or nine days' time bottle it up, fill the bottles to just above the neck, and give it the same time to ripen as other ale.

The upper and middle classes drank French and Rhenish wines, which were heavily taxed. The French wars and an embargo on French goods promoted Spanish and Portuguese wines as an alternative.

> In the vaults under St James' Market House, going down on the west side, is a large quantity of extraordinary wines to be sold by wholesale at reasonable rates, or retail at the prices following,

viz. Red and White at 5s per gallon, Canary at 6s 6d per gallon, Sherry at 6s per gallon, Burgundia at 2s per gallon. Attendance will be given from 8 in the morning till 8 at night daily, till the whole be sold off.

Wine buffs might purchase the following volumes:

There is now published a book, entitled, *England's Happiness Improved: Or, an Infallible Way to Get Riches, Encrease Plenty and Promote Pleasure*. Containing the art of making wine of English grapes, and other fruit, equal to that of France and Spain with their physical virtues. To make artificial wine, and order all sorts of wine to keep well, and recover what is faded, etc. And the whole art and mistery of distilling brandy, strong-waters, cordial waters, etc. To make all the sorts of plain and purging ales, cyder, mead, rum, rack and many other useful liquors ... with many other things very profitable and never before made publick.

Punch had made an appearance. To make it: 'Take one quart of claret wine half a pint of brandy, and a little nutmeg grated, a little sugar, and the juice of a lemon, so drink it.' The sinister Dutch import, gin, made from the juniper berry, had just been introduced. It was cheaper than beer, so quickly gained a hold over the poor, to devastating effect.

When coffee and tea made their first appearance in England, it was hoped they would have a sobering effect on the nation. 'But I must not omit coffee and tea, two sober liquors now so prevalent in England, which take off people considerably from drinking of strong liquors,' wrote Guy Miege. 'They are both hot and dry,' he enthused, 'and therefore very proper for phlegmatick people. And, whereas strong liquors are apt to disorder the brain, these on the contrary, do settle and compose it.'

Chocolate, usually drunk first thing in the morning as part of a light breakfast, gave way to tea as the preferred drink in the home. By the end of the seventeenth century, tea kettles outnumbered coffee pots by three to one. But tea was precious. Its sale was controlled by the East India Company, which limited supplies and kept costs high. Prices varied wildly and depended on whether the tea was new or old. The average price stood at an exorbitant £1 a pound in 1700, when the annual income of poor to middling families ranged between £15 and £50. Partly because it was so expensive, tea was served in the Chinese fashion – very weak and without milk – sparingly in shallow porcelain dishes especially imported from the East. Tea drinking was a fragrant and delicate operation, largely confined to ladies in the drawing room. Servants might help themselves to the used tea leaves, but otherwise this precious commodity resided in a little chest under lock and key. It would be many years before tea became the national panacea, the universal pick-me-up doled out in emergencies and disasters. Its sister, coffee, played a far more significant part in the more boisterous male world outside the home.

CHAPTER NINE

Coffee-houses, Clubs, Alehouses and Taverns

'Debauch runs riot with an unblushing countenance'

W HEN A LONDON merchant who had been trading in the
Ottoman Empire during the Commonwealth introduced
coffee, doctors welcomed it as an antidote to drunkenness
and women suspected it made their husbands impotent. Jealous of the
amount of time their husbands were spending in the coffee-houses, the
women got up a petition against that 'black, thick, nasty bitter stinking,
nauseous puddle water'. 'Never did men wear greater breeches,' they
complained, 'or carry less in them of any mettle whatsoever.' It was the
'excessive use of that newfangled, abominable, heathenish liquor called
coffee, which riffling nature of her choicest treasures, and drying up the
radical moisture, has so eunucht our husbands, and crippled our more
kind gallants, that they are become as impotent, as age, and as unfruitful
as those deserts whence that unhappy berry is said to be brought'.

Far from waking them up, their men came home from the coffee-house
with 'nothing moist but their snotty noses, nothing stiff but their joints,
nor standing but their ears: They pretend 'twill keep them waking, but
we find by scurvy experience, they sleep quietly enough after it.'

Men were accused of spending more time in the coffee-houses than in
their own homes. As Mary Astell put it in *An Essay in Defence of the
Female Sex*, a typical coffee-house habitué 'lodges at home, but he lives at
the coffee-house. He converses more with newspapers, gazettes and votes,
than with his shop books, and his constant application to the publick
takes him off all care for his private concern. He is always settling the
nation, yet could never manage his own family.'

The men fought back. Coffee, they asserted, 'rather assists us for your nocturnal benevolencies, by drying up those crude flatulent humours, which otherwise would make us only flash in the pan, without doing that thundering execution which your expectations exact'. If they sought out other male company in the coffee-houses, it was hardly surprising. 'You may well permit us to talk abroad,' they defended themselves, 'for at home we have scarce time to utter a word for the insufferable din of your ever active tongues.'

By 1700 there were over 2,000 coffee-houses in London. They had begun under the Commonwealth as democratic establishments where for a penny entrance fee payable to *la dame de comptoir* any man who was reasonably dressed and who was prepared to obey the rules as regards swearing and fighting could sit at the common table and drink a dish of coffee – at about one and a half pence a dish – and smoke his long, clay pipe. For very little financial outlay he could spend hours sitting by the fire, read the newsletters of the day, meet friends and conduct business, and engage in discussion on everything from politics to shipping to the latest scientific inventions. Tom Brown described the coffee-house as:

> the place where several knights-errant come to seat themselves at the same table without knowing one another, and yet talk as familiarly together as if they had been of many years acquaintance. They have scarce looked about them, before a certain liquor as black as soot is handed to them, which being foppishly fumed into this noses eyes and ears, has the virtue to make them talk and prattle together of everything but what they should do.

Each coffee-house developed its own clientele and became identified as the meeting place for men of a particular occupation. 'Some coffee-houses are a resort for learned scholars and for wits; others are the resort of dandies or of politicians, or again of professional newsmongers; and many others are temples of Venus,' wrote César de Saussure. 'You can easily recognise the latter, because they frequently have as sign a woman's arm or hand holding a coffee-pot.' He noted a great number of these in Covent Garden, where 'you are waited on by beautiful, neat, well-dressed, and amiable, but very dangerous nymphs'.

Men of letters and the wits met at Will's on the corner of Bow Street

This original Delftware tile depicts all the essentials of the coffee-house: the Turkish coffee pot, the dish of coffee, the long clay pipe and the *London Gazette* (*Museum of London*)

197

and Russell Street in Covent Garden, one of the most fashionable if raunchy areas of town. Ned Ward and his companion 'adjourned to the wits' coffee-house, in hopes that the powerful eloquence which drops from the silver tongues of the ingenious company that frequents this noted mansion, might inspire us with such a genius as would better fit the perfection of our renovated clay'. Will's was made famous by the poet John Dryden, who could be seen sitting on its balcony in the summer and in his favourite chair by the fire in the winter months. Like all the coffee-houses Will's was essentially democratic, but it would be easy for someone lacking the requisite literary accomplishments to feel out of place in such illustrious company. Ned Ward was amused to find 'much company, and but little talk; as if every one remembered the old proverb, That a close mouth makes a wise head, and so endeavoured, by his silence, to be counted a man of judgement, rather than by speaking to stand the censure of so many critics, and run the hazard of losing that character which by holding of his tongue he might be in hopes of gaining'. After Dryden's death in 1700 Will's began to decline in popularity and was eventually overtaken by Button's.

Learned fellows of the Royal Society such as Sir Isaac Newton, Edmund Halley the astronomer, and Sir Hans Sloane the collector, would meet at the Grecian in Devereux Court opposite what is now the Law Courts. Thomas Twining, founder of the tea dynasty, opened Tom's Coffee-House adjoining his shop just off the Strand. Whig politicians patronised the St James's, the Tories the Cocoa-Tree, both near Pall Mall. Lawyers frequented Nandos in Fleet Street, the clergy Child's in St Paul's Churchyard. More hedonistic establishments included White's in St James, a haven for gamblers, and King's in Covent Garden, 'well known to all gentlemen to whom beds were unknown'. Young men of fashion, the *beaux*, met at Man's near Scotland Yard on the river. Man's was unique in that smoking was frowned upon. Its clientele were wholly engaged in the new art of taking perfumed snuff. Ned Ward gives a lively description:

> We squeezed through the fluttering assembly of snufflers till we got to the end of the room, where, at a small table, we sat down, and observed that though there was an abundance of guests, there was very little to do, for it was as great a rarity to hear anybody call for a dish of Politician's porridge [coffee], or any

other liquor, as it is to hear a sponger in a company ask what's to pay. Their whole exercise was to charge and discharge their nostrils, and keep the curls of their perriwigs in their proper order. The clashing of their snuff-box lids, in opening and shutting, made more noise than their tongues, and sounded as terrible in my ears as the melancholy ticks of so many death-watches. Bows and cringes of the newest mode were here exchanged twixt friend and friend, with wonderful exactness ... Amongst them were an abundance of officers ... though they looked as tender as if they carried their down beds with them into camp. At the end of the principal room were other apartments, where, I suppose, the beau-politicians retired upon extraordinary occasions to talk nonsense by themselves about state affairs.

In this rarefied company, Ned Ward and his friend dared to light their pipes:

Having sat all this while looking about us, like a couple of Minerva's birds among so many of Juno's peacocks, admiring their gaiety, we began to be wishful of a pipe of tobacco which we were not assured we could have the liberty of smoking lest we offend those sweet-breathed gentlemen, who were always running their noses into a civet box. But we ventured to call for some instruments of evaporation, which were accordingly brought us, but with such kind of unwillingness, as if they would rather to have been rid of our company ... Notwith-standing we wanted an example to encourage us in our rudeness, we ordered 'em to light the wax candle, by which we lit our pipes, and blew about our whiffs with as little concern as if we had been in the company of so many carmen. At this, several Sir Poplins that were near us, drew their faces into many peevish wrinkles. But regardless of their grimaces, by which they expressed their displeasure, we puffed on our unsavoury weed, till we had cleared one corner of the room.

Businessmen kept regular hours at a particular City coffee-house, so that their clients and associates could seek them out. The coffee-houses served as makeshift offices and provided the nucleus upon which the great financial institutions were built. The speculative boom of the 1690s, in which an unprecedented number of stocks and shares were traded, meant that an elementary stock exchange with its index listed in the press was established. A London apothecary and statistician, John Houghton, described this new financial game in a guide to share dealing:

> The manner of managing the trade is this; the monied man goes among the brokers (which are chiefly upon the Exchange, and at Jonathan's coffee house), sometimes at Garroways and at some other coffee houses, and asks how stocks go? And upon information bids the broker buy or sell so many shares of such and such stocks if he can at such and such prices: Then he tries what he can do among those that have stock, or power to sell them; and if he can, makes a bargain.

In 1697 the merchants had the stockbrokers removed from the Royal Exchange. They were in disgrace because some of the brokers had been accused of 'jobbing' – dealing on their own account – and other shady practices. Daniel Defoe had disliked the whole business from the start, likening it to 'a branch of highway robbing':

> 'tis a compleat system of knavery; that 'tis a trade founded in fraud, born of deceit, and nourished by trick, cheat, wheedle, forgeries, falsehoods, and all sorts of delusions; coining false news, this way good, that way bad; whispering imaginary terrors, frights, hopes, expectations, and then preying upon the weakness of those, whose imaginations they have either elevated or depress'd.

The stockbrokers moved their business to the neighbouring coffee-houses, Jonathan's and Garraway's in Exchange Alley in Cornhill, which had been the customary haunts of the shippers, traders, underwriters and merchants engaged in maritime trade. With the arrival of the stockbrokers, Defoe scoffed that 'Exchange Alley is as dangerous to the publick safety, as a magazine of gun-powder is to a populous city'. Before long the inhabitants and shopkeepers were complaining 'that by daily resort and standing of brokers and stock-jobbers in the same alley, not only the common passage to and from the Royal-Exchange is greatly obstructed, but encouragement is given by the tumultuary concourse of people attending the said brokers, to pick-pockets, shop-lifters, and other idle and disorderly people to mix among them'.

The various segments of London's financial community were being forced to define their influence, to concentrate their expertise, and to develop their own specialised institutions for conducting their affairs. Usurped by the stockbrokers, those engaged in maritime trade tended more and more to frequent the coffee-house of Edward Lloyd at the corner of Abchurch Lane, Lombard Street. Although the actual underwriting was done on the floor of the Exchange, it became increasingly common for the preliminary business to be done at Lloyd's. Not only did Edward Lloyd issue handwritten 'ships' lists' for the benefit of his customers, which developed into *Lloyd's News* and eventually *Lloyd's List*, but starting in 1700 ships and their cargoes were actually auctioned at Lloyd's and other coffee-houses:

> On Tuesday the 17th instant, at 3 in the afternoon, will be exposed to sale at the Marine Coffee-house in Birchin-lane, the ship *Charles the Second*, English built, square stern'd, burthen about 750 tuns, 50 guns, lying at Mr Well's wet dock near Deptford. Inventories to be seen on board the said ship, or at Lloyd's Coffee-house in Lombard-street.

Auctions of all kinds of goods were held by candle, that is, while an inch of candle burned:

> Tomorrow, the 10th of this instant April, will be exposed to sale, by candle, at Lloyd's Coffee-house in Lombard-street, at 3 a clock in the afternoon, several pieces of new cabinet-work, embellished with silver, in imitation of inlaid plate engraved.

> On Thursday the 4th January next, at 3 in the afternoon, the proprietor of the *Mary and Frances* will expose to sale at the Marine Coffee-house in Birchin-lane, the cargo of the said ship, being Guinea redwood and elephants teeth.

Coffee-house auctions were popular and convenient. The Swiss visitor Zacharias Conrad von Uffenbach was particularly interested in buying books, since English-language books were not easily found abroad: 'In the evening we drove to the so-called Latin coffee-house near St Paul's Cathedral to see an auction of books. This is most convenient. One goes there in the evening, drinks a dish of tea or coffee, smokes a pipe of tobacco, and can, when a good book appears, join in the bidding. I bought several excellent books much cheaper than they could be purchased in the shops.'

Trade was boosted by a new postal system. The penny post, which had been established by a Mr Dockwra in 1680, facilitated communication in the growing metropolis. Guy Miege praised the new service:

> All gentlemen, country chapmen, and others, can presently give notice of their arrival to town. Shop-keepers and tradesmen send for what they want to their work-men. Much time is saved in solicitation for money. Bills dispersed for publication of any concern. Summons, or tickets, convey'd to all parts and societies. Brewers entries safely sent to the Excise-office. Lawyers and clients mutually correspond, patients send to doctors and apothecaries, etc, for what they want; and the poor prisoners can now send for one penny, where they could not formerly under six, or twelve pence, or more.

Where better to direct the mail than to the 'four or five hundred shops and coffee-houses' commonly called 'penny-post houses'? For the price of a penny a pound or £10 in value payable by the sender within the metropolis and a penny payable by both sender and receiver to districts within fifteen miles of it, letters and parcels would be deposited and collected by 'messengers having their respective walks'. Collections took place every hour of the day in London and Westminster, every two hours further afield in Southwark, twice a day in 'towns near London, as Hackney, Mile-End, Islington, Newington'. Mail was conveyed to sorting-offices in Tower Hill, Charing Cross, Chancery Lane, Paternoster Row and St Mary-over-Ree in Southwark before onward distribution.

The coffee-houses were the principal male resort for discussion and the dissemination of news. Charles II had tried to suppress them as places of seditious conversation, but the Glorious Revolution brought a degree of toleration and free speech. The suspension of the Licensing Act in 1695 provided the impetus for the expansion of Grub Street. By 1700 London had several newspapers, including the *London Gazette*, *Post Man*, *Post Boy*

Apart from the *dame de comptoir*, the coffee-houses were a male preserve, where customers sat at a common table and joined in the roar of conversation (*British Museum*)

and *Flying Post*, published three times a week and distributed chiefly in the coffee-houses. Circulation of the biggest, the *Gazette*, increased from about 7,000 in 1693 to 11,000 in 1705. The first daily paper, the *Daily Courant*, arrived in 1702. Runners would be sent round the coffee-houses with news flashes. As newspapers flourished, so did literacy, which was already high in the metropolis. Foreigners such as César de Saussure were amazed at the liberty of speech among Londoners and how hotly debated were political issues by men of all classes:

> What attracts enormously in these coffee-houses are the gazettes and other public papers. All Englishmen are great newsmongers. Workmen habitually begin the day by going to coffee-rooms in order to read the latest news. I have often seen shoeblacks and other persons of that class club together to purchase a farthing paper. Nothing is more entertaining than hearing men of this class discussing politics and topics of interest concerning royalty. You often see an Englishman taking a treaty of peace more to heart than he does his own affairs.

The newspapers were an entertainment in themselves:

A lady will offer five guineas reward for a little lost dog worth five pence. A husband will warn the public not to lend or sell his wife anything on credit. Another husband, on the contrary, will be crazy enough to advertise for his beloved better half, who has abandoned him in order to follow her sweetheart, promising a reward to whoever will bring her home ... A quack will advertise that he will cure all ailments. A person who has been robbed promises a reward to whoever will help him to recover his stolen property. Entertainment and spectacles are advertised; also offers of houses, furniture, carriages, horses for sale or on hire, books, pamphlets, etc, and by reading these papers you know of all the gossip and of everything that has been said and done in this big town.

Newspapers received an unexpected boost from another quarter. John Houghton was the first to understand the commercial advantages of advertising. A city as large and complex as London needed information on goods for sale and services. Where better to advertise than in the newspapers and on the walls of the coffee-houses? Nothing lent itself so well to the exaggerated promise of advertising than quacks' medicine. Ned Ward describes his impression:

'Come,' continued my friend, 'let us step into this coffee-house. As you are a stranger to the town it will afford you diversion.' Accordingly, in we went, where a parcel of muddling muck-worms were as busy as so many rats in an old cheese-loft; some going, some drinking, others jangling, and the whole room stinking of tobacco like a Dutch barge or a boatswain's cabin. The walls were hung with gilt frames, containing an abundance of rarities, viz; Nectar and Ambrosia, May Dew, Golden Elixirs, Popular Pills, Liquid Snuff, Beautifying Waters, Dentifrices, Drops, Lozenges, all as infallible as the Pope. Where everyone above the rest, Deservedly has gained the name of best; good in all cases, curing all distempers; every medicine pretends to be nothing less than universality. Indeed, had not my friend told me 'twas a coffee-house I should have took it for Quack's Hall, or the parlour of some eminent mountebank.

The coffee-houses began as open venues, but gradually some of them employed men to bar undesirables so that they became exclusive preserves of their members. The practice of sitting at the communal table and entering into conversation with the people who happened to be sitting there was carried over into the clubs. The idea of 'clubbing', pooling together the money to pay for drinks and food, was not a new one. Pepys mentions it several times and Ned Ward records that 'I thought it high time to take our leave; which, after the payment of our clubs we did accordingly'.

The most notable of these early clubs was the Kit-Cat, a gathering of distinguished Whigs captured on canvas by their fellow member, the painter Kneller. The club is said to have first met at a tavern kept by Christopher Cat near Temple Bar and took its name from the mutton pies, known as 'Kit-cats'. The secretary was Jacob Tonson, the publisher of one of the most prestigious lists ever, topped by Shakespeare, Milton, Dryden and Pepys. The club shrewdly chose as its toast the young Mary Pierrepont, better known to posterity by her married name of Lady Mary Wortley Montagu, who in 1700 was only eleven years old.

Some of the clubs were merely gambling dens, gambling being part of the speculative fever that had the nation in its grip. Everything became the object of a bet, from horseflesh to the arrival of a ship to the outcome of a battle. Gambling was utterly reckless with everything pitched on the throw of the dice, the turn of a card. 'Money,' Ned Ward observed, 'was tossed about as if a useless commodity.' He watched the gamesters in fascination:

> They are men whose conditions are subject to more revolutions than a weathercock. They are very richly dressed one day, and perhaps out at elbows the next; they often have a great deal of money, and are as often without a penny in their pockets. They are Fortune's bubbles, for whatever benefits she bestows upon 'em with one hand she snatches away with t'other. Their whole lives are a lottery; they read no books but cards; all their mathematics is to truly understand the odds of a bet ... They are seldom in debt, because they know not where to borrow it. A pair of false dice, and a pack of marked cards sets 'em up. They generally die intestate, and go as poor out of the world as they came into it.

Whole fortunes were made and lost at the gaming tables. Tom Brown

Gambling fever gripped the nation, fortunes were made and lost overnight
(*British Library*)

observed: 'I knew two Middlesex sharpers not long ago, that inherited the estate of a west-country gentleman, who I believe would have never made them his heirs in his last will and testament.' Women had a passion for cards, for ombre and basset, and lost their husbands' money with equal abandon. Daniel Defoe thought cards the bane of all conversation and had no patience with the craze: ''Tis mere madness, and a most stupid thing to hazard ones fortune, and perplex ones mind; nay, to sit up whole nights, poring over toys of pipt ivory and painted pasteboard, making our selves worse than little children, whose innocent sports we so much ridicule.'

The proponents of the coffee-houses argued that they would bring sobriety to the nation. But many coffee-houses also served alcohol. 'To the charms of the coffee,' Tom Brown drawled, 'the wiser sort joined spirit of clary [brandy, sugar, clary-flowers, cinnamon and ambergris], usquebaugh [Irish whiskey], and brandy.' Failing that, customers like Ned Ward oscillated back and forth between alehouse and coffee-house. 'Considering coffee to be a liquor that sits most easy upon wine,' he confided, 'we went into a great coffee-house by the Temple Gate [Nando's], where a parcel of grave men were thickening the air with the fumes of their weed.' No wonder the women scoffed in their petition: 'The coffee-house being in truth, only a pimp to the tavern, thus like tennis balls between two rackets, the fopps our husbands are bandied to and fro all day between the coffee-house and the tavern.' The petition continued:

> For when people have swill'd their morning draught of more ale than a brewers horse can carry, hither they come for a pennyworth of settle-brain, where they are sure to meet enow lazy pragmatical companions, that resort here to prattle of news, that they neither understand, nor are concerned in; and after an hours impertinent chat, begin to consider a bottle of claret would do excellent well before dinner; whereupon to the Bush they all march again together, till every one of them is drunk as a drum, and then back again to the coffee-house to drink themselves sober.

Drunkenness was the national vice, even ahead of gambling. 'Debauch runs riot with an unblushing countenance,' observed César de Saussure.

'It is not the lower populace alone that is addicted to drunkenness; numbers of persons of high rank and even of distinction are over fond of liquor.' He thought that the English drank so much because of 'the thickness and dampness of the atmosphere'. Perhaps drink, like gambling and violence, was a palliative at a time when life was so precarious. Shortly after their accession, William and Mary had issued proclamations calling on local officials to enforce the laws against drunkenness, blasphemy, profanity and immorality. Their attempts at moral reform were greeted with hoots of derision by their new subjects and largely fell on stony ground.

Royal efforts to stamp out drunkenness ran counter to the fact that a significant and increasing proportion of government revenue was derived from excise duties on the sale of alcohol. In the case of strong beer the duty increased from 2s 6d a barrel in 1688 to 5s in 1710. The economist Gregory King estimated that in 1695, 28 per cent of annual per capita expenditure was devoted to beer and ale, which were the most highly taxed beverages. The excise officials noted that provincial ales with extra strength such as those from Derby and Nottingham were much in favour and even in demand for export. Customers liked to add fruits and herbs to promote different flavours, and their benefits were advertised in the press:

> At the 3 Golden Horse-shoes in Fenchurch Street, near Grace-church, is sold that excellent ale called juniper, so famous for curing the rheumatism, wind-cholick, palsy, gripes; it carries away all gravel, and is a great cleanser of the blood; it creates an appetite and helps digestion; it fortifies the stomach against all sick fumes, and foggy and unwholesome air, and infectious scents.

Consumers had both the financial ability and the discernment to demand a wide range of high-quality drink. Visitors to London were overwhelmed by the choice. After all, London was a great port through which passed the bulk of the nation's imports. Spirits such as brandy from France, rum from the West Indies, Scotch and Irish whiskies and London-distilled gin were comparatively cheap and not subject to such heavy excise duty. This may account for their growing popularity. When the government did hit French brandy with a heavy tax, it merely served to fuel the gin craze. The consumption of spirits quadrupled between 1680 and 1710. Brandy was mixed with wine and herbs to make punch. It was also used as a chaser to beer. Cheaper than beer, gin was the new drink of the poor, sold in tawdry gin-shops and from street barrows. Wine imported from France, Spain and Portugal was expensive, which may account for the fact that so much of it was doctored. César de Saussure was quick to notice this:

> Though no wine is made in England, yet I am persuaded that three times more is drunk than is imported into the country, and I will solve this problem by telling you that most wine merchants, and especially tavern proprietors, possess the art and address of doubling their wine and even of making it threefold the original quantity, for with one cask they have purchased they will fill two or three others, by addition of water and spirits ... and this so skilfully that good judges of wines and even epicures do not immediately perceive it; but if they have a drinking bout they will soon find out, and to their cost, that the wine has been tampered with.

Perhaps this explains why Pepys was able to order wine by the pint in taverns and alehouses to no ill effect.

Tax on drink meant that the English had already embarked on their enduring quest to beat the excise man, and large quantities of wine and spirits were smuggled into the country. In March 1700 the *Post Man* reported 'a great quantity of French brandy was seized on board a vessel at Falmouth' and, in a particularly good month for the authorities, 'the *Pool* frigate has brought into Plymouth a ship of 120 tons, laden with prohibited goods from France'.

The term 'public house', a contracted form of 'public alehouse', came into use around 1700. At first it applied only to the alehouses, but gradually encompassed the smaller inns and taverns (which differed from alehouses only in that they served an 'ordinary' meal), signalling a convergence of their fortunes. Alehouses were moving towards respectability. Justices and excise officials leaned on the brewers not to supply unlicensed or disorderly alehouse-keepers and those who did not pay their duty on time. The illicit tippling house was being forced out of business. Its proprietors and the poorest of its customers would find a new venue in the gin-shops. However, a proclamation of 1700 still depicts a boisterous, riotous scene in the public houses:

> Whereas many murders, manslaughters and other great disorders are frequently committed and done in divers taverns and other publick houses within this city and the liberties thereof by disorderly persons resorting thereto, and abiding therein at late and unseasonable hours of the night, to the ruin of many families: And in such publick houses are often harboured house-breakers, robbers, lewd and debauch'd men and women, by reason whereof the many thefts, robberies and other misdemeanours are frequently done and committed, to the great disturbance of the peace ... For the preventing of which great evils and mischiefs for the future. It is ordered by this court, That all vintners, coffee-sellers, alehouse-keepers, victuallers and all others keeping publick houses within this city and the liberties thereof, do not from henceforth permit or suffer any person or persons to be or continue in their respective house or houses gaming, tippling or drinking after the hour of ten of the clock in the night-time between Michaelmas and Lady-day; Nor after the hour of eleven of the clock in the night-time between Lady-day and Michaelmas; Nor on any part of the Lord's Day.

Tom Brown was of the opinion that

> a tavern is a little Sodom, where as many vices are daily practised as ever were known in the great one. Thither libertines repair to drink away their brains, and piss away their estates; aldermen to talk treason, and bewail the loss of trade ... gamesters to shake their elbows, and pick the pockets of cullies who have no more wit than to play with them; rakes with their whores, that by the help of wine they may ... do those things in their cups that would be a scandal to sobriety.

And in recognition of the common practice of concluding deals, even a simple purchase, over a drink: 'Thither sober knaves walk with drunken fools, to make cunning bargains and over-reach them in their dealings.'

Highwaymen frequented alehouses and taverns to suss out

information about goods on the move, and were often in cahoots with the landlord. Ned Ward described one such character:

He's acquainted with the ostlers about Bishopsgate Street and Smithfield, and gains from them intelligence of what booties go out that are worth attempting. He pretends to be a disbanded officer, and reflects very feelingly upon the hard usage 'we poor gentlemen meet with, who have hazarded our lives and fortunes for the honour of our prince, the defence of the country, and safety of religion; after all to be broke for the dangers and difficulties we have run through. At this rate, Zounds, who the devil would be a soldier?' At such sort of cant he is excellent.

Stolen goods found their way to alehouses and taverns. 'The clothes were left at an alehouse,' was a common admission in court, 'and one of the evidence deposed, that she had orders from the prisoner and some of the gang, to carry them thence, which she did, and left them at two other places, where they were discovered.' Landlords were still caught receiving or fencing stolen property, but they ran the risk of losing their licence and increasingly turned away from crime and sought to discourage it on the premises.

In their drive towards respectability alehouses were better furnished and equipped. They even went so far as to provide silver tankards and other items, but they were a temptation to the light-fingered. One thief boasted that he cut the bottom out of tankards while he was sitting there. Notices of stolen items would appear in the press: 'Lost on Thursday, September 12 from the Ship Tavern over against Beaufort Buildings in the Strand, a silver spoon marked NFS: If offered to be pawned or sold, you are desired to stop the party that brings it, and give notice to the master of the house aforesaid, and shall be well rewarded. It is supposed to be taken by a fresh coloured woman, fair hair, in a white stuff gown and petticoat.'

Fuelled by alcohol, fights were frequent and sometimes ended tragically:

On Friday night, being the 15th of this instant March 1700, Philip Parry, Esq, who lived in Lincolns-Inn-Fields ... drinking at the Rose Tavern in Bridges Street, near the King's Play-house,

Englishmen were quick to draw the sword and many tavern brawls were fatal
(*British Museum*)

in company of his own son, two of his sons-in-law, and one Mr
Thomas Bond; they having had some difference about Mr Bond's
keeping company with the wife of one Mr ... and reflected on
the chastity of Bond's sister, which he so highly resented, that
very provoking words happened between them: Notwithstanding which, after having stay'd till near ten of the clock,
they went out of the said tavern, in a seeming friendly manner;
but malice having no bounds when aggravated by a violent
passion, it so unfortunately fell out, that a small distance from
the Rose Tavern, Mr Thomas Bond drew his sword, and renew'd
the quarrel with Squire Parry ... and stabb'd Squire Parry in the
upper part of the left pap, the wound extending several inches,
even so far as 'tis supposed it reach'd his heart, for he thereupon
fell immediately down dead in the place, without speaking a
word.

It was the duty of constables and watchmen – who were considered a
bit of a joke for their amateurishness – to make sure landlords adhered to
licensing hours. Ned Ward describes closing time:

Each jack-a-lanthorn [watchman] was now croaking about the
streets the hour of eleven. The brawny topers of the City now
began to forsake the tavern, and stagger to their own houses.
Augusta [London] appeared in her mourning-weeds, and the
glittering lamps which a few hours before sparkled like
diamonds ... were now dwindling to a glimmering snuff, and
burnt as dim torches at a prince's funeral. Harlots in the streets
were grown a scarce commodity, for the danger of the Compter
had drove them home to their own poor sinful habitations.

Ward fell foul of the watchmen on at least one occasion:

Time taking advantage of our carelessness had pruned his wings,
and fled with such celerity that the noon of night was brought
upon our backs before we had measured out a sufficiency of the
noble creature to our craving appetites; and as we were
contending with the drowsy master for the other quart, who
should come in and put an end to our controversy but a tall,

meagre carrionly constable, and with him his crazy crew of halbardiers … When he had given us a fair sight of his painted staff of authority, which he stamped down upon the boards before him with as much threatening violence as a buffoon in a music-house … he opened his mouth: 'Look you, d'ye see, gentlemen? 'tis an unreasonable time of night for people to be tippling. Every honest man ought to have been in bed an hour or two ago.'

For answering back, Ward and his drinking companions spent an uncomfortable night in the Poultry Compter. Fortunately there were no restrictions on day-time drinking, so that in the morning they went straight to the nearest tavern to recover. 'As we had been fellow-sufferers together, there was no parting without a glass, so we went to the Rose Tavern in the Poultry, where the wine had justly gained a reputation according to its merit; and there in a snug room, warmed with brush and faggot, over a quart of good claret, we laughed at our night's adventure, and cursed the constable.'

In keeping with their improved status, the alehouse premises extended beyond a mere kitchen, where customers might congregate around the fire, to a series of rooms which could be used for private functions, business meetings and amorous intrigue. Imitating their betters in the clubs, men of middling and lower status formed clubs and societies — the florists' societies, for instance, whose 'feasts' provided the occasion for the reading of papers on all aspects of gardening. Landlords with an eye to business advertised such events in the newspapers and encouraged them to hold their meetings at the public house. Alehouses also served as short-term lodging houses for those newly arrived in town.

The personalities of the landlord and his wife were crucial in ensuring the success of a public house. Tom Brown poked fun at the landlady's pretensions:

But who pray was that opulent lady that we met in the entry coming out of the kitchen with her head so finely dressed and with glittering pendants in her ears, that so dazzled my eyes I could scarce behold her countenance?' 'That shining lamp of cloven mortality is that necessary evil in such a house, called the vintner's helpmate, whose business it is to have a super-intendancy in the bar, to overlook and direct all culinary proceedings, to scold the maids, be civil to the head-drawer for her own ends, grace the bar.

Just as shopkeepers used their wives and pretty employees to entice the customers, so it was with the landlord in the public house. Tom Brown's barmaid had 'little else to do but to dress, paint and patch, ogle her uncle's beau-customers, and tattle at the bar' with one of her admirers. She 'treats him with kind glances and a few amorous witticisms, as long as his money runs flush; as soon as that begins to fail, her shooting-horn looks and freedoms are turned into moody pouts and a scornful reservedness'.

Londoners did not entertain much at home, many of them living in lodgings. Misson explained that it was possible to have a meal brought to your lodgings, but really there was little point. Eating out was cheap and easy. There were hundreds of taverns in which Londoners could meet to talk and eat. There was a fixed price for an 'ordinary' meal. And there were the cook shops, 'where it is very common to go and chuse upon the spit the part you like, and to eat it there'. A really good meal was to be had for a shilling. 'Generally four spits, one over another, carry round each five or six pieces of butcher's meat, beef, mutton, veal, pork, and lamb; you have what quantity you please cut off, fat, lean, much or little done; with this, a little salt and mustard upon the side of a plate, a bottle of beer, and a roll; and there is your whole feast.' Although people of all ranks ate at the taverns and cook shops, a really special dinner could be had at Lockets or at Evelyn's favourite, Pontack's, for the extravagant sum of one or two guineas a head.

It was impossible to enter any public establishment without being wreathed in 'the stinking mist' of tobacco smoke. The smoking habit was so prevalent that Misson noted that 'the very women do it in abundance'. The indigenous industry was destroyed during the Commonwealth to boost trade with Virginia and Maryland. Imports doubled between the Restoration and the end of the century and were subject to duty. Tobacco was valuable enough for warehouses to be frequently broken into, as the Old Bailey Sessions Papers record:

They were a second time indicted for breaking the warehouse of a Joseph Lacy, and taking 250 pound weight of tobacco. As to the stealing of the tobacco, one of the evidence deposed, that

Macdonald told him he knew a warehouse where they might make a purchase of tobacco; and accordingly they went, and took the lock off the door and each a bag of tobacco, which they carried to Macdonald's lodgings ... they sold the tobacco for 25s in Whitechappel.

Tobacco was on sale in the alehouse, where common clay pipes were passed unwashed from customer to customer. Ned Ward braved the traffic of Fleet Street – venturing 'to shoot ourselves through a vacancy between two coaches' – to visit the famous tobacconist Benjamin Howes on the corner of Shoe Lane, who sold 'old, mild, sweet-scented Virginia tobacco for 20d, either large cut, small cut or long cut ... Spanish in the roll, for 8s. a pound, and Spanish and Virginia mixed for 3s a pound'. There he found a crowd of dedicated 'fumigators':

They behaved themselves like such true lovers of the prevailing weed, that I dare engage custom had made their bodies incapable of supporting life by any other breath than smoke. There was no talking amongst 'em, but puff was the period of every sentence, and what they said was as short as possible, for fear of losing the pleasure of a whiff, as 'How d'ye-do?' *Puff.* 'Thank ye.' *Puff.* 'Is the weed good?' *Puff.* 'Excellent.' *Puff.* 'It's fine weather.' *Puff.* 'G—d be thanked.' *Puff.* 'What's a clock?' Puff, Etc.

CHAPTER TEN

Amusements

'Anything that looks like fighting is delicious to an
Englishman'

IN FEBRUARY 1700 Londoners read in the newspaper that a
'monstrous cannibal giant' brought from overseas to entertain them
had drowned in the Thames before he could disembark. This was
disappointing. His arrival had been eagerly anticipated, so much so that
the article confidently reported that people would have paid over the
odds to satisfy their curiosity. Enormous fun was to be derived from
watching the torments of creatures less fortunate than themselves, be
they human or animal. Cruel spectacles where others were the victims
gave Londoners a sense of power, because their own lives were so
precarious. Next to watching a fellow citizen going to the gallows, the
antics of the insane at Bedlam, or pelting filth at the occupant of the
stocks, there was nothing Londoners enjoyed more than viewing freaks
and curiosities. Where better to do so than at Bartholomew Fair?

> At the corner of Hosier Lane, and near Mr Parker's booth; There
> is to be seen A Prodigious Monster, lately brought over by Sir
> Thomas Grantham, from the great Mogul's Countrey, being a
> Man with one Head and two distinct Bodies, both Masculine;
> there is also with him his Brother, who is a Priest of the
> Mahometan Religion.

> To be seen the next door to the Black Raven in West Smithfield,
> during the time of the Fair, being a living skeleton, taken by a
> Venetian Galley, from a Turkish Vessel in the Archipelago. This
> is a Fairy Child, supposed to be born of Hungarian Parents, but
> chang'd in the Nursing, Aged Nine Years and more; not
> exceeding a Foot and a-half high. The Legs, Thighs, and Arms

The rope-dancers were some of the biggest attractions of the fair, putting the
theatres out of business for the duration (*British Library*)

so very small, that they scarce exceed the bigness of a Man's Thumb, and the face no bigger than the Palm of one's hand; and seems so grave and solid, as if it were Threescore Years old. You may see the whole Anatomy of its Body by setting it against the Sun. It never speaks. It has no Teeth, but is the most voracious and hungry Creature in the World, devouring more victuals than the stoutest Man in England.

The City authorities dreaded Bartholomew Fair, a magnet for all sorts of 'idle, loose, vicious and debauched people'. Its original purpose as a trade fair was almost forgotten as Londoners from all walks of life converged on West Smithfield on 24 August for two weeks. The Lord Mayor's Proclamation forbidding booths to be used 'for interludes, stage-plays, comedies, gaming-places, lotteries, disorderly musick-meetings' seems to have been largely ignored. Actors deserted the playhouse for the fair, where they competed with the merry-andrews, the rope-dancers and tumblers for their audience:

At Mr Barnes's and Mr Appleby's Booth, between the Crown Tavern and the Hospital Gate, over against the Cross Daggers, next to Miller's Droll Booth, in West Smithfield, where the English and Dutch Flaggs, with Barnes' and the Two German Maidens' pictures will hang out, during the time of Bartholomew Fair, will be seen the most excellent and incomparable performances in Dancing on the Slack Rope, walking on the Slack Rope, Vaulting and Tumbling on the Stage, by these five, the most famous Companies in the Universe, viz., the English, Irish, High German, French and Morocco, now united. The Two German Maidens, who exceeded all mankind in their performances, are within this twelve-month improved to a miracle.

Whores and thieves did a roaring trade. Children were made giddy in 'flying coaches', swings climbing high into the pungent air. The smell of roasting pig and crackling wafted out of fly-ridden cook shops to mingle with the odour of the closely packed crowd. César de Saussure found the event too vulgar for his taste: 'for the noise and uproar is so continuous and overwhelming, besides you run a perpetual risk of being crushed to death, and also of being robbed, for I think that no cleverer pickpockets exist than in this country, and in every crowd you must beware, else your pockets will soon be picked and emptied.'

The City authorities were no doubt relieved when, after a fortnight at West Smithfield, Bartholomew Fair moved on to Southwark across the river. The Londoners' taste for strange and exotic animals imported from overseas continued to be indulged:

> The living alligator or crocodile, lately arrived from the coast of Guinea, will be seen during the time of the Southwark Fair at the Hand and Dial over against the Queen's Arms Tavern; and the Crown Bird, lately arrived, to be seen at the Lamb near St Georges Church.

Coffee-houses, alehouses and taverns competed with the fairs to exhibit freaks and curiosities, and advertised in the newspapers. It was a sure way to pull in the punters:

> At Painters Coffee-house, over against the Fountain Tavern near Stocks Market, is to be seen an Eel, the largest ever seen in London, being 68 inches long, 22 thick, and weighing 34 pound 3 quarters; it is to be seen at so low a rate (viz. one penny) that 'tis not doubted, but every one who is curious, will be willing to see such a prodigy in nature; and, for greater encouragement, if any one can say upon his word that he has seen a greater, he shall have his money return'd; not that it will be exposed to view after tomorrow night.

With so many novelties on offer, Londoners could be forgiven for leaving a trip to the Tower to see the lions to the tourists.

Perhaps the most riotous and disorderly scene of all was reserved for the May Fair, held in the fields now roughly bordered by Piccadilly, Oxford Street and Park Lane. It was so disreputable that it was about to be shut down. When Ned Ward visited the fair, he noticed the whores doing good business. Various booths were staging comedies:

> Beyond these were a parcel of scandalous boozing dens, where soldiers and their trulls were skipping and dancing to most

lamentable music, performed upon a cracked fiddle by a blind fiddler. In another hut a parcel of Scotch pedlars were dancing a Highlander's jig to a horn-pipe. Over against 'em was the Cheshire booth, where a gentleman's man was playing ticks with his heels in a Cheshire round. These intermixed here and there with a puppet-show, where a senseless dialogue between Punchinello and the Devil was conveyed to the ears of a listening rabble through a tin squeaker, which was thought by some of 'em as great a piece of conjuration as ever was performed by Dr Faustus.

The rough and tumble of London life was not confined to fairs. The slightest altercation could end in a street brawl. 'Anything that looks like fighting,' wrote Misson, 'is delicious to an Englishman':

If two little boys quarrel in the street, the passengers stop, make a ring round them in a moment, and set them against one another, that they may come to fisticuffs... During the fight, the ring of by-standers encourage the combatants with great delight of heart ... And these by-standers are not only other boys, porters, and rabble, but all sorts of men of fashion, some thrusting by the mob that they may see plain, others getting upon stalls; and all would hire places, if scaffolds could be built in a moment.

No wonder César de Saussure considered 'the lower populace is of a brutal and insolent nature, and is very quarrelsome'. Any sort of combat was an opportunity to indulge in the passion for gambling which affected all classes: 'The spectators sometimes get so interested that they lay bets on the combatants and form a big circle around them.' Street brawls and bare-knuckle fighting were not confined to men. 'Would you believe it,' De Saussure continued, 'I have actually seen women – belonging, it is true, to the scum of the people – fighting in this same manner.'

When Zacharias Conrad von Uffenbach visited London, he ventured up to Hockley in the Hole in Clerkenwell, 'to watch the fights that take place there, a truly English amusement'. The combatants were 'an Englishman and a Moor'. The entertainment he witnessed on the stage was as nothing compared with watching the spectators:

The place where the fight took place was fairly large. In the middle was a platform as tall as a man of middling height; it had no rail and was open all round, so that neither of the fighters could retreat. All round the upper part of the open space were wretched galleries with raised seats, like those on which the spectators sit at the play. But the common people, who do not pay much, are below on the ground. They tried with violence to clamber up on to the galleries and scaffolding, and when some would have hindered them, they cast up such monstrous showers of stones, sticks and filth, and this with no respect of persons, that we were not a little anxious; as we, however, were sitting on the best side, they did not come near us. They behaved like madmen and things looked very ugly.

While the two combatants fought with sword and dagger and the stage was awash with blood, Von Uffenbach fell into conversation with the couple sitting behind him. The man 'had probably drunk a considerable amount, and was making a vast uproar and throwing down whole handfuls of shillings'. His wife regaled him with how 'two years ago she had fought another female in this place without stays and in nothing but a shift. They had both fought stoutly and drawn blood, which was apparently no new sight in England.'

He was next drawn by the printed notices and news-sheets to Gray's Inn to watch a cockfight. This took place in a round tower, in which spectators of all ranks sat together in tiers. The fight was staged on a table in the centre:

When it is time to start, the persons appointed to do so bring in the cocks hidden in two sacks, and then everyone begins to shout and wager before the birds are on view. The people, gentle and simple (they sit with no distinction of place) act like madmen, and go on raising the odds to twenty guineas and more. As soon as one of the bidders calls 'done' ... the other is pledged to keep his bargain. Then the cocks are taken out of the sacks and fitted with silver spurs ... As soon as the cocks appear, the shouting grows even louder and the betting is continued. When they are released, some attack, while others run away ... and are impelled by terror to jump down from the table among the people; they are then, however, driven back on to the table with great yells and thrust at each other until they get angry. It is amazing to see how they peck at each other, and especially how they hack with their spurs. Their combs bleed terribly and they often slit each other's crop and abdomen with the spurs.

As soon as the fight is over, 'those who put their money on the losing cock have to pay up immediately, so that an hostler in his apron often wins several guineas from a lord.' Anyone foolish enough to have placed a bet he was unable to pay was put in a basket and drawn up to the ceiling accompanied by the thigh-slapping laughter of the audience.

There was no doubt that Londoners had a taste for cruel and ferocious sport, which reflected their own lives: nasty, brutish and short. Apart from cockfighting, they loved to indulge in bull- and bear-baiting, held every Monday and Thursday at Hockley in the Hole, Clerkenwell, at Marylebone Fields, Soho, and at Tothill Fields, Westminster:

First a young ox or bull was led in and fastened by a long rope to an iron ring in the middle of the yard; then about thirty dogs, two or three at a time, were let loose on him, but he made short work of them, goring them and tossing them high in the air above the height of the first storey. Then amid shouts and yells the butchers to whom the dogs belonged sprang forward and caught their beasts right side up to break their fall. They had to keep fast hold of the dogs to hinder them from returning to the attack without barking. Several had such a grip of the bull's throat or ear that their mouths had to be forced open with poles. When the bull had stood it tolerably long, they brought a small bear and tied him in the same fashion. As soon as the dogs had at him, he stood up on his hind legs and gave some terrific buffets; but if one of them got at his skin, he rolled about in such a fashion that the dogs thought themselves lucky if they came out safe from beneath him.

Londoners might more usefully have put their energies into sport, but in this they were less than enthusiastic. A leisurely game of bowls at the alehouse was acceptable, with spectators gambling on the outcome. Football was a street game with everyone joining in to kick the ball – although there was no goal – sending it high to smash against sash windows. Foreign visitors such as Beat Louis de Muralt found the game 'very troublesome and insolent'. César de Saussure was equally irritated: 'In cold weather you sometimes see a score of rascals in the streets kicking at a ball, and they will break panes of glass and smash the windows of coaches without the slightest compunction; on the contrary, they will roar with laughter.'

He was just as bemused by cricket: 'The English are very fond of a game they call cricket. For this purpose they go into a large open field, and knock a small ball about with a piece of wood. I will not attempt to describe this game to you, it is too complicated; but it requires agility and skill and everyone plays it, the common people and also men of rank.'

To someone like Ned Ward, London was a stage whose people afforded endless fascination and amusement. As for the real theatre, the actor-manager-impresario Thomas Betterton, actresses Mrs Barry and Mrs Bracegirdle, and William Congreve the playwright had defected from the Theatre Royal, Drury Lane, to the New Theatre at Lincoln's Inn Fields. Plays were generally performed in the afternoon, beginning at three o'clock with the stage lit by candles. There was music and dancing on the stage prior to the play and during the interval. Of the audience, Misson noted that 'men of quality, particularly the younger sort, some ladies of reputation and vertue, and abundance of damsels that hunt for prey, sit all together in this place, higgledy-piggledy, chatter, toy, play, hear, hear not.'

To the sardonic commentator Tom Brown, the playhouse was 'an enchanted island, where nothing appears in reality what it is nor what it should be'. The audience provided a study in itself:

> That beau there is known by the decent management of his sword-knot and snuff-box; a poet, by his empty pockets; a citizen, by his horns and gold hatband; a whore, by a vizor-mask and a multitude of ribbons about her breast; and a fool by talking to her. A playhouse wit is distinguished by wanting understanding; and a judge of wit, by nodding and sleeping till the fall of the curtain and the crowding to get out again, awake him.

He was equally scathing about the entertainment on stage. 'What are all their new plays but damned insipid, dull farces, confounded toothless satire, or plaguy rhymy plays, with scurvy heroes?' In the year when

Congreve's comedy *The Way of the World* was an enormous hit, Brown criticised popular taste:

> When the humour takes in London, they ride it to death ere they leave it. The primitive Christians were not persecuted with half the variety that the poor unthinking beaux are tormented with upon the theatre; character is supplied with a smutty song, humour with a dance, and argument with lightning and thunder, and this has often reprieved many a scurvy play from damning. A huge great muff and a gaudy ribbon hanging at a bully's backside is an excellent jest.

Before his death in 1695, the English composer Henry Purcell had enjoyed a fruitful professional relationship with Thomas Betteron. They collaborated on *The Fairy Queen*, which Roger North later described as 'a sort of plays which we called operas but had bin more properly styled semioperas for they consisted of half music and half drama'. The opera proper would not be introduced to London until the next reign.

Concerts offered more refined entertainment than the contemporary theatre and London's burgeoning music scene was attracting foreign composers to visit and settle. Where Pepys had enjoyed musical evenings at home, it was now possible to attend public concerts at Thomas Hickford's Great Room off the Haymarket and at the concert room at York Buildings which seated 200 at 5s a head. Summer evenings provided the ideal setting. 'There was on Monday night last a fine consort of musick in the gardens at Kensington, there being present abundance of nobility and gentry,' ran one newspaper report. And, 'This present Monday, being the 8th September at 3 of the clock exactly, at Richmond Wells, will be perform'd a New Consort of Instrumental Musick, by the greatest masters in Europe, for the last time this summer. Mr Abell will sing in English, Latin, Italian, Spanish and French. Tickets to be had only at the Wells at 5s a ticket.'

London provided a vast panorama of parks and pleasure gardens. Ned Ward describes a visit to St James's Park just at the time 'when the Court ladies raise their extended limbs from their downy couches, and walk into the Mall to refresh their charming bodies with the salubrious breezes of the cooling evening'. As ever, he was more moved by the people than the place:

> We could not possibly have chosen a luckier minute, to have

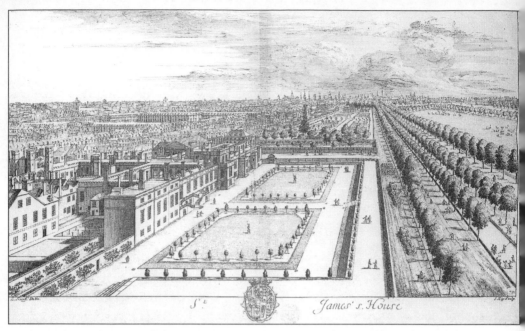

As London expanded to the west, huge vistas and parks provided the setting for society to parade itself (*Guildhall Library, Corporation of London*)

seen the delightful park in its greatest glory and perfection, for the brightest stars of the Creation were moving here, with such an awful state and majesty, that their graceful deportment bespoke 'em goddesses. Such merciful looks were thrown from their engaging eyes upon every admiring mortal; they were so free from pride, envy or contempt, that they seemed, contrary to experience, to be sent into the world to complete its happiness.

Henri Misson admired the park with its 'very fine walks of elms and lindens, a fine mall, a large canal, and several other ponds and basons of water'. There was no real woodland, but the avenues were an inviting place to walk. Respectable people stayed away on Sundays, however, when 'whole shoals' of 'the common people', who could not get there during the week, converged on the park. Red deer and cows grazed in St James's and wandered across Piccadilly to Hyde Park.

In Hyde Park, Tom Brown noted 'the quality' making its daily appearance:

Here we saw much to do about nothing; a world of brave men,

gilt coaches, and rich liveries; within some of them were upstart courtiers, blown up as big as pride and vanity could swell them, sitting as upright in their chariots as if a stake had been driven through them. It would hurt their eyes to exchange a glance up on any thing that's vulgar; and that's the reason they are so sparing of their looks that they will neither bow, nor move their hats to anything under a duke or a duchess.

Those visiting the court at Kensington – or, further afield, at Hampton Court – could admire William and Mary's gardens laid out in the formal Dutch style with box hedging, flower beds, statuary and fountains. Von Uffenbach was intrigued by the maze at Hampton Court and noted the 'wooden rollers made of thick trunks of oak, which are used to roll the lawns when they have been mown'.

The hub of London life was the Thames itself, the great thoroughfare dotted with thousands of red and green boats. Like many visitors before and since, César de Saussure loved this sight:

> You cannot see anything more charming and delightful than this river. Above the bridge it is covered with craft of every sort; round about London there are at least 15,000 boats for the transport of persons, and numbers of others for that of merchandise. Besides these boats there are others called barges and galleys, painted, carved, and gilt. Nothing is more charming and attractive than the Thames on a fine summer evening; the conversations you hear are most entertaining, for I must tell you that it is the custom for anyone on the water to call out whatever he pleases to other occupants of boats, even were it to the King himself, and no one has a right to be shocked.

The language of the watermen as they indulged in the tradition of shouting insults across the water was 'coarse and dirty'. It was all very confusing to a newcomer. Ned Ward joked that when he was first approached by watermen shouting, 'Scholars, scholars, will you have any hoars?' he was shocked, until his companion explained that the watermen distinguished themselves by the titles of Oars and Scullers.

River transport was essential, partly because the streets were so congested and also because the bone-shaking jolting of hackneys was

Many travellers opted to disembark rather than brave the rapids at London Bridge
(*Guildhall Library, Corporation of London*)

unendurable. Walking was another option, but only the principal streets
had a pavement of sorts, where it was courteous to 'give the wall' to one's
betters. Sedans were carried along the pavement with the bearers
shouting, 'By your leave, sir,' and 'Have care,' before knocking pedestrians
out of the way. Forced off the pavement, pedestrians had to walk in streets
that turned into dust in the heat and mud in the rain. The building work
that was taking place all over town added to the muck of the streets.

London Bridge was still the only bridge across the Thames. Von
Uffenbach remarked that 'one does not take it for a bridge because it has
on both sides large and handsome houses, the lower storeys of which are
shops. Well over half way across the bridge towards Southwark is a
single place about eight feet long where there is not a house and the
Thames can be seen through the iron palings.' Compressed among the
pillars of the bridge, the water was a deep, roaring torrent. It was so
treacherous that many boat passengers preferred to disembark and re-
embark on the other side of the bridge.

On a fine summer day Londoners could cross the river from London
Bridge to Foxhall paying 4d for oars and 2d for scullers. Pepys made
such a visit with his 'family':

With my wife and the two maids and the boy took boat and to
Foxhall – where I have not been a great while – to the Old
Spring garden. And there walked long and the wenches gathered

pinks ... Thence to the New one, where I never was before, which much exceeds the other. And here we also walked, and the boy creeps through the hedge and gather[s] abundance of roses. And after that long walk ... so to another house that was an ordinary house, and here we have cakes and powdered beef and ale; and so home again by water, with much pleasure.

Spas had become extremely popular by the end of the century. Von Uffenbach took the trip to Lambeth 'to see Lambethwells or the medicinal spring there':

Near it is a house where they dance on certain days, though it is frequented for the most part only by the riff-raff. Judging by its taste, the spring contains alum and iron. From here we drove further along this side of the Thames to Foxhall, where there is a large garden of matchless elegance called the Spring Garden, because it is most agreeable in spring when vast quantities of birds nest and sing there. It consists entirely of avenues and covered walks where people stroll up and down, and green huts, in which one can get a glass of wine, snuff and other things, although everything is very dear and bad. Generally vast crowds are to be seen here, especially females of doubtful morals, who are dressed as finely as ladies of quality.

Perhaps because they were so obsessed with finding a cure for their chronic ills and their own drinking water was so contaminated, Londoners flocked to sample the waters at Hampstead. Von Uffenbach wrote:

This is the nearest medicinal spring to London, and it is such an agreeable spot that not only do many people take the waters there but several have built handsome houses for themselves, where they remain for the whole summer, while many drive out from London on Mondays, Thursdays and Saturdays and divert themselves there. The spring is some way out of the town and near it are a coffee-house and assembly room where they dance ... Nothing is danced, but new English country dances, and they were, for the most part, very charming. The district is very pleasing and, if one looks from one hill over to the other, the prospect over the Thames and London is vastly agreeable.

In common with visitors to all similar pleasure spots near London – the village of Marylebone, for instance – Von Uffenbach aimed to be home before nightfall: 'As soon as it began to grow dusk we set out for London, since footpads are often abroad on this short road.'

Londoners liked to walk out to Islington Spa. It never really caught on as 'the new Tunbridge Wells', perhaps because the upper classes elected to give it a miss. However, in April 1700 notice was given of the impending entertainment:

> These are to give notice, that new Tunbridge Wells at Islington will be opened the 5th day of May, where will be musick for dancing all day long every Monday and Thursday during this summer season. No masque [meaning a vizard mask, a fashion item increasingly associated with prostitutes] to be admitted.

Misson suggested that the Islington waters 'do you neither good nor harm, provided you don't take too much of them'. The area was known for its cow pastures and dairies, so that it would be silly for visitors to leave without sampling the syllabub and cream cakes. They could pause at Sadler's Wells for the music and dancing before following the course of the New River back to London.

Londoners needed little excuse for a bout of dissipation, and eagerly anticipated the 'publick days for feasting'. Guy Miege wished that the 'holy days [holidays] of Christmas, Easter, and Whitsuntide' were 'kept with more devotion, and less intemperance'. Misson thought the English Christmas festival charming: 'From Christmas-Day 'till after twelfth-day, is a time of Christian rejoycing; a mixture of devotion and pleasure: They wish one another happiness; they give treats, and make it their whole business to drive away melancholy ... little presents begin here at Christmas; and they are not so much presents from friend to friend, or from equal to equal ... as from superior to inferior.' Old pagan customs prevailed as homes were decorated with laurels, rosemary, holly, mistletoe and other greenery.

In the City, Lord Mayor's Day on 29 October (old calendar) was 'a solemn day of public rejoicing and feasting', when the newly elected

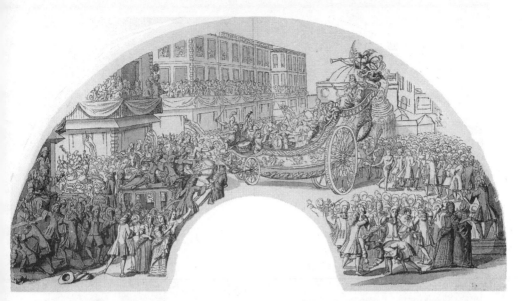

The Lord Mayor's Pageant provides the occasion for the usual disorderly behaviour: the shopkeepers in Cheapside have taken the precaution of boarding up their premises, but already fighting has broken out and pickpockets are at work in the crowd (*Museum of London*)

Lord Mayor accompanied by the twenty-six aldermen and members of the livery companies went by barge to Westminster to take the oath of office. When Ned Ward attended the show with its elaborate floats, he rose early to secure a place in Cheapside, 'where I thought the triumphs would be most visible, and the rabble most rude, looking upon the mad frolics and whimsies of the latter to be altogether as diverting ... as the solemn grandeur and the gravity' of the procession. Other days of 'public rejoicing' – although not holidays – included the king's birthday on 4 November, Coronation Day on 11 April, Restoration Day on 29 May, 'Gun-powder-treason-day' on 5 November, and Royal Oak day on 3 September, when people wore oak leaves in their hats in memory of Charles II's escape after Worcester. To mark the anniversary of William III's accession, the press in February 1700 noted that 'the morning was usher'd in with ringing of bells, at noon the great guns were fired round the Tower, and at night we had bonfires'.

During the week Londoners worked long hours. Sunday was a holiday, but a day in which amusements were severely curtailed. Theatres, concerts, shows and sports were all forbidden. Even the serious-minded Swiss visitor Von Uffenbach was hard put to find entertainment:

Women had a passion for cards, which were forbidden on Sunday (*British Library*)

Moreover no one can amuse himself here on Sundays, which are observed as strictly as in any place in the world, so that, not only is all play and frequenting of inns forbidden, but also only a few boats and hackney-coaches are allowed to ply. Thus one is forced to stay at home, and our hostess would not even permit her foreign guests to play to themselves on the viol de gamba or flute, so that she should run no risk of punishment. All this indeed is the only sign that the English are a Christian people, for it is not very apparent from the rest of their dealings.

While there was hardly a sound in the streets, behind closed doors the leisured classes were indulging in illicit card-playing and gambling – strictly forbidden on Sundays – and others spent the day 'in debauch' in illegally operating taverns.

CHAPTER ELEVEN

The Working City

The Thames was the passageway to burgeoning colonies

AT THE FIRST OUTBURST of the Bow Bell in Cheapside marking the hour of nine o'clock, fourteen-year-old John Coggs sprang from his place behind the counter to unhitch the folded shutters and close up shop. The dazzling glare of the streetlamp illuminated the sign of the Bible above his head gently swaying back and forth as if moved by the echoes of the bells which now rang out all over the City. His master John Stevens had already sloped off to enjoy a pint of wine in the tavern with some fellow stationers, printers and booksellers. His duty done, young Coggs retreated into the dark interior of the shop amidst the paper, memorandum and account books 'drawn and undrawn', pens, ink, sand, ink-pots and sealing wax that made up his master's trade. Perhaps he would spend the evening studying his notes on arithmetic, including 'What is meant by the commission of 2 per cent, how must that be done?'.

Unusually for an apprentice, John Coggs is still on his best behaviour. It is not very long since he was 'bound upon liking' to Mr Stevens for one month, that upon passing that hurdle he accompanied his master and his father to Stationers' Hall in Ludgate to have his indentures stamped. His father had paid a £250 premium for his apprenticeship and signed 'a bond for my honisty'. For the next seven years, Mr Stevens would act *in loco parentis*, guiding John's moral welfare as well as his training, and as a member of his 'family' or household the young apprentice would owe his master loyalty, discretion and diligence. Just in case things did not work out as smoothly as planned, the Chamberlain of the City of London, the guardian of all apprentices, would arbitrate in any dispute. John had been presented to the Chamberlain at Guildhall on the day his indentures were stamped.

On serving his full term he would be admitted to the Stationers'

Many stationers and booksellers operated under the sign of the Bible, a bestseller then and now

Company, perhaps as a master able to take on apprentices himself if the money could be found, but otherwise in somebody else's employ as a journeyman, literally paid by the day. At the age of twenty-four he would become a freeman of the City of London, able to vote for office-holders, perhaps even become Lord Mayor himself one day.

For many parents it was a struggle to raise the premium, although friends might contribute to this essential passport to a boy's future career. The cost of premiums had risen alarmingly. After all, the apprentice system was a means of controlling the labour supply and there was no point in overstocking a business. For those younger sons of noblemen and gentlemen not attending the universities or the Inns of Court, an apprenticeship was their only option. There was no snobbery attached to the sons of gentlemen entering trade, although they would have to embrace a different set of values from the ones they had been used to in a leisured class living off the labour of others. Their willingness to participate in the apprentice system drove up the cost for the rest. The tenets of this hierarchical society held true even for apprentices, as Daniel Defoe observed: ''Tis very ordinary to give a thousand pound with an apprentice to a Turkey merchant, £400 to £600 to other merchants; from £200 to £300 to shop-keepers, and wholesale dealers, linnen-drapers especially; and so in proportion to other trades.'

At least once a boy was apprenticed his master was responsible for his upkeep. He would be housed with his master's family, clothed and fed at his expense. Indeed, City regulations stipulated that an apprentice could wear no clothes other than those provided by his master. John Coggs's fond mother blithely ignored this rule. Not only was she slipping him extra pocket money, but also buying him clothes. All the errands her son was running in muddy streets meant that he needed no fewer than six new pairs of shoes in the first few months of his apprenticeship, costing 4s and 4s 6d a pair, while repairs set her back 1s 2d and 1s 4d a time. There was no hope of John being able to foot these bills himself, for as Henri Misson pointed out: 'An apprentice is a sort of slave, he wears neither hat nor cap in his master's presence, he can't marry, or have any dealings on his own account. All he earns is his masters.'

The flip-side of masters demanding such great sums with their apprentices, Defoe noted, was that apprentices were getting as uppity as servants. Not long ago they had cleaned their master's shoes, carried water vessels on their shoulders into the houses from the conduits in the street, waited at table, and accompanied their master to church with his Bible or prayer book in hand. Now, he says, they can barely rouse themselves to 'open or shut the shop-windows, much less to sweep the shop, or warehouses'. They 'shall not fail to tell their masters, they did not give such sums of money to be confin'd like prisoners, or to be used like foot-boys'. What's more, 'so far are they from being subjected to their masters, or to their family discipline, that they think it hard to have any enquiry made after them when they go out, and keep oftentimes later hours than their masters; and as often are pleas'd to come home in drink. Which also their masters have scarce the authority to resent, or question them about.'

One would like to assume that John Coggs's father took every care to seek out an honest master for his son and that the arrangement came to a happy conclusion. However, innumerable cases reaching the Lord Mayor's Court and the Middlesex County Sessions record the breakdown of relations between master and apprentice. James Smith was apprenticed to John Hart, a linen draper, for a premium of £250. Hart complained that 'he was a very idle and negligent servant' and 'kept company with loose and idle women and was often guilty of excessive drinking ... and did gamble for considerable sums of money and was very extravagant in his clothes and other expenses which amounted to much more than what his father allows him'. Hart suspected that Smith had been fiddling the books and pilfering from him to maintain his lifestyle. He had complained to Smith's father, who hoped it was a passing phase. Hart's advice was to send the boy to sea. Clearly he was to be discharged from his apprenticeship and it only remained for the court to decide how much of the premium would be returned.

The case of Samuel Pearse shows a promising apprentice going to ruin. He came to London from Gloucestershire and was 'bound to a pastry-cook in Shear-Lane, after he had been with him about 3 months upon liking'. His master was 'a good and religious man, kept him to his duty, and from ill company, making him go to church and employ his time well at home'. After five and a half years Pearse was given permission to visit friends in the country. On his return to town he 'became unruly, taking more liberty than he had done before ... he kept bad company, abandon'd himself to drinking, and to the sin of uncleanness, and other vices'. When his master died there was still a year of his apprenticeship to serve, and he did so with his master's widow, whom 'he wrong'd of several goods at diverse times; but she was so kind as to forgive him'. No sooner was Pearse out of his apprenticeship, than he 'fell upon the robbing of houses and shops'.

Apprentices were forbidden to fornicate or to marry. *The London Tradesman* spells out a terrible warning to an apprentice tempted by the fair sex: 'He must consider, he risks his health, and plunges himself into a sea of diseases when he embraces a common woman; not only endangers his health but his morals; their arts, their blandishments, and snares are such, that sooner or later, they tempt their votaries from one degree of vice to another, till ruin, diseases, and a shameful end finishes their catastrophe.'

Masters worried about the spread of venereal disease, but more pertinently, that an apprentice would pilfer from them to keep a mistress or pay the bawd. Nevertheless, the budding Sally Salisbury found plenty of customers as 'the beautiful little wench that sells pamphlets to the schoolboys and apprentices ... in Pope's Head Alley in Cornhill in the City of London'. Here she supplemented her income by a little juvenile prostitution, charging 'half a crown an hour'.

Apprentices who fell pregnant or contracted marriage would be discharged. Sarah Fifield was discharged from her apprenticeship to Samuel Hurst, bookbinder in Shoreditch, on the grounds that 'she is a notorious, lewd, idle and disorderly servant, now great with child, and likely to become a great charge and burthen to her master'. The author of *The Father's Counsel to His Son, An Apprentice in London* warns the young man against 'any familiarity with the maidservants of the family' because 'they catch at any appearance of a match'. *The London Tradesman* warned that an illicit marriage would be a disaster: 'An apprentice is never completely miserable till he has got a wife: He ought to consider marriage as a matter of the last consequence to his peace, not to be undertaken rashly at any age, but on no account to be entered upon till he is settled in a way of providing for a family.'

But it was not only the apprentices who fell short of the ideal. Masters could be remiss in honouring their obligations to teach their trade. Edward Green was discharged from his 'indentures of apprenticeship to Roger Gately, late of the parish of St James Clerkenwell, surgeon, upon proof that the said Gately did not practise the art of surgeon, and that he compelled the said Green to be a rope-dancer, tumbler, and jack-pudding'. John Knight, apprentice to James Cuffe of the parish of St Andrews Holborn, clockmaker, petitioned to be discharged from his indentures, 'alleging that the said Cuffe resides in Salisbury Court, near Whitefriars, for fear of being arrested for debt; that he had no work in the said trade to employ an apprentice and did not supply him with necessary food and drink'. Elizabeth Barnes was apprenticed to Mary Cope, mantua-maker in the parish of St Sepulchre, and complained that she 'had not been taught her art, but put to do the household work'.

There was a drop-out rate of 50 per cent among apprentices, either through discharge by mutual agreement or by their running away. If they were caught, they were severely punished for breaking their contract:

> Whereas Simon Smith the servant and apprentice of one Sam Manning carpenter a freeman of this City who hath deserted his master's service and now refuseth to return to his master again to serve him according to the indentures of his apprenticeship, It is ordered that the said Simon Smith be sent to Bridewell being the house of correction of this City of London there to be kept at hard labour until the next Sessions of the Peace.

Apprentices who failed to serve their full term joined the casual labour force and often drifted into crime. William Barrow, born in the parish of St Andrews Holborn, was 'bound to an upholsterer in London, he ran away from his master, and listed himself a trooper. Then he left the service, and by the enticement of bad company, turn'd thief.' John Hart, born in St John's Street in Clerkenwell, was bound 'to a card-maker in St James' Street Westminster' and 'when he had but one year and a half of his time to serve, he ran away, and became a vagabond; and so, was easily entic'd to those ill things ... which prov'd at last his ruin.'

At the gallows he 'desired all apprentices and other young men to take warning by him; and so to avoid his loose and wicked life, as to prevent their coming to an untimely end in the world'.

Thomas Browning was particularly unlucky, as recalled by the Ordinary of Newgate at his execution:

> When he was yet very young, his parents brought him up to London, and he lived a good while with them in Spittlefields: That his father (a butcher) bound him apprentice to a tripe-man, with whom having served about four years and a half of his time, he then ran away: That not long after this, he accidentally passing one day by a house in Wapping, which had been broke open and robbed the night before, and being lookt upon as an idle person, and known by some people to have run away from his master, was thereupon apprehended and committed to Newgate; where he unhappily contracted such acquaintance, and such an habit of sin and wickedness, as afterwards proved his total corruption and ruin.

The worst fate of all was reserved for those poor children who as orphans or paupers were disposed of by the parish for a trifling £5 to masters who could not in all honesty afford them. They were supposed to be provided with board and lodging in return for their labour. The deal was equivalent to an indefinite term of slave labour. Children as young as seven were apprenticed to chimney sweeps and watermen. Often the watermen sold the children for transportation to the colonies, or they were press-ganged into the navy, or sent to serve on merchant ships with the watermen taking all their wages.

As ever, there were those who treated a defenceless child at their mercy with the utmost cruelty. None was more vulnerable than those parish children with no one in the world to look out for their interests or care what happened to them. Elizabeth Wigenton, a coat-maker, was tried for the murder of her thirteen-year-old apprentice, who had been 'set a piece of work and not done it so well as she required'. She whipped the girl with a bundle of rods 'so unmercifully, that the blood ran down like rain'. She 'fainted away with crying; and of her unmerciful usage in a short time dyed'.

Richard Tate was a 'poor parish boy' apprenticed to Edward Bayly, who took a coach whip and gave him 'several stripes upon the shoulders, loyns and buttocks'. Next 'he took an iron spindle heated in the fire and ... did burn Tate in several places, in and about his body'. Bayly excused his cruelty on the grounds that the boy 'did not follow his work, so close as he expected'. He would tie a stone weighing over seven stones about the boy's neck and make him 'carry it about, lashing him forwards, with the coach whip'. Far from tempering her husband's cruelty, Judith Bayly incited it. The poor boy suffered this cruel usage for some considerable time 'by reason of which, he was brought so low and weak, that he was not able to subsist any longer; but being burnt by his mistress on the Saturday in the afternoon, he went to bed, and there continued till Sunday night, speechless, and then died'.

The River Thames was the passageway to burgeoning colonies. Ships built and repaired in London's thirty-three yards plied the far-flung corners of the world. Incoming ships queued for days, even weeks, from Blackwall to London Bridge to unload their cargoes. Tobacco, molasses, sugar and dyes from America and the West Indies, silk and spices from the Levant, printed calico and pepper from India, wine and foods from France and the Mediterranean, tea and porcelain from China, coal from Newcastle. And the port of London turned these goods over – three-quarters of the nation's trade at a value just short of £10 million – re-exporting some to Europe along with home-produced goods and importing the rest to feed London's manufacturing and industrial processes and its consumers hungry for luxury goods.

The Royal Exchange, where merchants had their separate walks according to their regions of trade, was the hub of London's highly cosmopolitan mercantile world. '"What news from Scandaroon and Aleppo?" says the Turkey merchant. "What price bears currants at Zant? Apes at Tunis? Religion at Rome? Cutting a throat at Naples? Whores at Venice? And the cure of a clap at Padua?"' quipped Tom Brown in his *Amusements Serious and Comical for the Meridian of London*. Here bargains were sealed, wholesalers contacted, ships chartered, maritime insurance arranged, news, gossip and advice exchanged. '"What news of such a ship?" says the insurer. "Is there any hope of her being cast away?" says the adventurer, "for I have insured more by a thousand pounds than I have in her?"'

Shipping was a perilous business at a time when the English colony of New York was the pirate capital of the world and when pirates roamed

The Customs House. Ships from the expanding colonies and the furthest corners of the world brought three-quarters of the nation's trade into London
(*Guildhall Library, Corporation of London*)

the high seas, preying on shipping even in the English Channel itself. Just one of many incidents was reported in July 1700 when news came in of a 'ship bound from Barbadoes to Virginia, which had two women passengers on board, which the pirates most barbarously ravished; and tyed two of her men by the neck and heels, and flung them overboard, because they espoused the womens quarrel; and endeavoured to dissuade the rogues from such villainy.'

Pirates sold English captives into slavery. In August 1700 there was a national collection for their release, as reported in the press: 'The collection that was ordered to be made throughout this kingdom, for the redemption of our poor countrymen slaves in Barbary, is now over, and is found to amount to a sum sufficient for effectually discharging them all: and the same is paid to a great Jew of this city, in order to be remitted to his correspondent in Germany, for that purpose.'

As the centre of a shipping nation on the brink of imperial greatness, London dominated the national economy. Not surprisingly, the great merchants who played so crucial a role in providing the means towards this prosperity – particularly those in the East India, the Royal African and the Levant Companies – were at the pinnacle of the income scale. The likes of Sir Peter Vansittart and Sir Theodore Janssen left fortunes in excess of £100,000. These were the merchant princes. The majority of merchants earned anything from £200 to £400 a year and left fortunes in the region of £5,000 to £15,000. But this was wealth indeed when a personal fortune of £1,000 or £2,000 was generous and a family of the lower-middling class could live comfortably on an income of £50 a year.

The rise in prosperity, fuelled partly by overseas trade and colonial expansion, needed more sophisticated financial services and extended lines of credit. Traditionally the goldsmith-bankers who congregated in Lombard Street in the City of London – named after the Lombardy bankers who operated under the sign of the three golden balls of Lombardy, which at the lowest end of the scale signified the pawnbroker – carried out the essential banking functions. They had strongrooms where merchants and others could deposit surplus cash and valuables for safe-keeping. They would lend out the sums deposited with them at interest, while the depositor obtained a receipt or note which represented a promise to pay him back the amount of his deposit. Before long these notes began to pass from hand to hand as a substitute for ready cash, although the Bank of England note which promised to 'pay the bearer' was the first bank note proper. Even so, people

were slow to make use of banking facilities. The likes of Samuel Pepys in the 1660s deposited only part of his savings with Alderman Backwell, endured sleepless nights worrying about the amount of money he had lying in the house, and even resorted to burying some in the garden.

The sign of the Grasshopper in Lombard Street, the traditional haunt of the goldsmith-bankers

Three years after the founding of the Bank of England, Daniel Defoe in *An Essay Upon Projects* was unhappy about the new banking facilities:

> Our banks are indeed nothing but so many goldsmiths shops, where the credit being high (and the directors as high) people lodge their money; and they, the directors I mean, make their advantage of it; if you lay it at demand, they allow you nothing; if at time, 3 per cent and so wou'd any goldsmith in Lombard Street have done before; but the very banks themselves are so awkward in lending; so strict, so tedious, so inquisitive, and withal so publick in their taking securities, that men who are anything tender, won't go to them; and so the easiness of borrowing money, so much design'd, is defeated; for here is a private interest to be made, tho' it be a publick one; and, in short, 'tis only a great trade carried on for the private gain of a few concern'd in the original stock.

In common with many others, Defoe was even more sceptical about the new dealers in stocks and shares as new companies – and many 'projectors', or inventors – sought to raise money for speculative enterprises. There was a general feeling that there was something fundamentally immoral about the way the 'stock-jobbers' manipulated the market. Defoe took a case in point, pointing the finger at Sir Josiah Child, 'that original of stock-jobbing':

> There are those who tell us, letters have been order'd, by private management, to be written from the East Indies, with an account of the loss of ships which have been arriv'd there, and the arrival of ships lost; of war with the Great Mogul, when they have been in perfect tranquillity, and of peace with the Great Mogul, when he has come down against the factory of Bengal with one hundred thousand men, just as it was thought proper to calculate those rumours for raising and falling of the stock, and when it was for this purpose to buy cheap, or sell dear.

When the speculative fever culminated in the disaster of the South Sea Bubble in 1720, the critics of the new money men and financial institutions felt vindicated.

*

London depended on thousands of migrant workers – for whom the streets were not paved with gold. They made easy targets for recruiting officers for the armed services and the plantations. Others led a chequered existence, caught between casual work and drifting into crime. The potted biographies of those condemned to death, written by the Ordinary of Newgate, recall the careers of those migrants who paid the ultimate penalty, ending their days at Tyburn.

Benjamin Jones, thirty-four, was 'born at Abberley in Worcestershire, a baker by trade, and afterwards kept a victualling house for above three years in London: And leaving that occupation, he apply'd himself to starch-making'. Francis Turnley, twenty-eight, was 'born near Bewdley in Worcestershire ... he was a labouring man, and had served with brick layers and brewers, both in the country and London'. Elizabeth Tetherington was 'about 29 years of age, born at Orms-Church in Lancashire, from whence coming up to London, upon the death of her mother, about six years ago, she fell upon the business of selling oysters at Billingsgate'. Alice Gray, thirty-two, born in Andover in Hampshire, had 'liv'd several years in the parish of St Clement Danes, and had since her husband's death maintain'd herself by her honest and constant labour; she making-up cloaths for souldiers, and sometimes going to washing and scowring, and at other times watching with sick folks and being a nurse to them'. Thomas Jones, twenty-three, born at Owston in Yorkshire, had 'learned the trade of barber-surgeon and perriwig-maker; but did not follow it long' and became a burglar instead.

One-fifth of London's labour force was employed in the textile and clothing industries. Enormous importance was attached to dress, so much so that it consumed one-quarter of national expenditure. Pride of place went to the silk industry concentrated at Spitalfields, which had received a shot in the arm by the influx of thousands of Huguenot immigrants bringing more sophisticated techniques. Imported raw silk passed from merchant to silk man to manufacturer, who employed women and children on low wages as throwers, twisting and winding it on to reels. Weavers were engaged in narrow silk-weaving for the ribbons that were so fashionable, and broad silk-weaving for the fabrics that would grace the persons and homes of the rich. Silk thread provided the raw material for the lace-makers and for the stocking knitters operating the knitting frames. Others were engaged in spinning and weaving silk and wool, pure woollens and worsteds, and in the finishing trades such as dyeing.

Not everyone involved in the textile and clothing industry was on low wages. A good pattern-drawer was in high demand, as described in *The London Tradesman*:

> Pattern-drawers are employed in drawing patterns for the calico-printers, for embroiderers, lace-workers, quilters, and several little branches belonging to women's apparel. They draw patterns upon paper, which they sell to workmen that want them; especially to calico-printers, embroiderers, and lace-women: They draw shapes and figures upon men's waistcoats to be embroidered, upon women's petticoats, and other wearing apparel; for all which they have large prices. This requires a fruitful fancy, to invent new whims to please the changeable foible of the ladies, for whose use their work is chiefly intended.

A pattern-drawer might earn over a £1 a week, and in common with other fashion-oriented occupations, he was employed most 'when the company are in town'.

The calico-printers were about to receive a boost by a ban on the import of printed calico from India. The Indian designs were not always to English taste, but their techniques were far superior:

> The calico-printer is employed in printing or staining cotton and linen cloath. We had the first hint of this branch of business from the Indies, where those beautiful cloths called chints are made to the greatest perfection. We have gathered of late some of the principles of this art; but fall short of the Indians in striking colours: Ours come short of theirs both in their beauty, life and durableness; They exceed in all dies, but especially reds, greens, and blues. But their patterns are wild, and all their figures, except flowers and plants, are monstrous. The Honourable East India Company have been at a vast expense to find out the secret of their dye, especially of red, but to no purpose; all trials that have been made have fallen short of the true Indian chint.

Thousands were employed in converting textiles into clothes and furnishings. There was a growing ready-made trade, with poorly paid women plying their needles in dim and overcrowded rooms to produce

A multitude of overhanging signs in Cheapside indicate that it was one of London's most fabulous shopping streets; house numbers were not used until the mid-eighteenth century (*Guildhall Library, Corporation of London*)

smocks and nightgowns, shirts and cravats, petticoats and caps. And for rich town-dwellers and county families who came to London for the season there was a whole array of specialist tradespeople to wait on them in expensively furnished shops. All along Cheapside, Fleet Street and the Strand to Charing Cross and over in St James's a multitude of painted boards hung over the streets displaying the Hand & Shears of the tailors, the Beaver of the hatters, the Civet Cat of the perfumers, the Buck of the breeches-makers, the Hand of the glovers, the Leg of the hosiers, the Peacock of the gold lace men, the Maiden's Head of the mercers, the Hood & Scarf of the milliners, the Woolpack of the haberdashers, the Indian Queen of the linen-drapers, the Lock of Hair of the perruquiers, the Golden Boot of the shoemakers, the Bodice of the stay-makers, the Golden Fan of the fan-makers.

Inside the shops customers would find the tailors to make their suits and coats and riding habits; the woollen drapers to provide the men with good cloth and the mercers to provide the ladies with silks, velvets, brocades and 'an innumerable train of expensive trifles'; there were the perruque-makers who depended on the hair merchants who depended on the pickers to sort the raw material; the hatters to make becoming shapes

246

out of hare, coney and beaver and shoemakers to mould fine leather about the foot; the cutlers to provide a gentleman with a sword; the tire-women to dress the ladies' hair; the milliners who made up linen smocks and headdresses, silk and velvet cloaks and all the trimmings and accessories from muffs to gloves. For parents contemplating apprenticing their daughter to a milliner, *The London Tradesman* carried a word of warning:

> Nine out of ten young creatures that are obliged to serve in these shops, are ruined and undone: Take a survey of all the common women of the town, who take their walks between Charing-Cross and Fleet-Ditch, and, I am persuaded, more than one half of them have been bred milliners, have been debauched in their houses, and are obliged to throw themselves upon the town for want of bread, after they have left them.

There were the male stay-makers cutting out whalebone according to a lady's measurements. The author of *The London Tradesman* was surprised that 'the ladies have not found out a way to employ women stay-makers rather than trust our sex with what should be kept as inviolably as free-masonry: But the work is too hard for women, it requires more strength than they are capable of, to raise walls of defence about a lady's shape.' Instead, female workers had to be content to stitch the cloth holding the whalebone strips together.

As for the mantua-maker who had taken over the dressing of the ladies from the tailor:

> She is sister to the taylor, and like him, must be a connoisseur in dress and fashions; and like the stay-maker, she must keep the secrets she is entrusted with, as much as a woman can ... She must learn to flatter all complexions, praise all shapes and ... ought to be a compleat mistress of the art of dissimulation. It requires a vast stock of patience to bear the tempers of most of their customers, and no small share of ingenuity to execute their innumerable whims.

Just at this precise moment in time London was pre-eminent in every branch of manufacture and industry and other towns lagged far behind. It was not only home to the textile and clothing industries. A nobleman wants a new coach? He should go to Long Acre where the coach-maker will employ a team of specialist workmen from wheelwrights to carpenters to painters to saddlers to complete the body he has fashioned. Metalworkers at Clerkenwell put together the clocks and watches, including the fine precision pieces of Thomas Tompion and Daniel Quare, for which London was becoming world-famous. London gun-makers were similarly esteemed. Pewter eating utensils, kettles and fire tongs were produced for the home, and ornate lead cisterns for the plumber to install. Glass manufacturers supplied the material for the sash windows, coach and shop windows, looking-glasses and drinking glasses, and bottles for the gin distilled in London, as well as for the new optical instruments and spectacles.

Over in Southwark were the leather workers, tanning hides to sell to the curriers and dressers who prepared the material for the saddlers and shoemakers, the manufacturers of trunks, the bookbinders, the makers of buff coats and oilskin breeches and the glovers. Just north of the Strand, London cabinet-makers fashioned increasingly refined pieces for the home and export markets. And over all these activities hung the noxious fumes emitted by the soap- and candle-makers, the sugar refiners, dyers, distillers and brewers.

London was the centre of printing and publishing. *The London Tradesman* attributed the printing boom to 'the spirit of writing that prevails now in England, and the liberty of the press', which 'has given employment to a great number of hands in this branch of business, which has arrived of late years to a great perfection'. The printer depended on the stationer to provide the paper made from 'linen-rags' that he had bought from the manufacturer. The term 'stationer' had originally applied to booksellers, who sold their wares from stations or stalls. Now some stationers combined their trade with another, such as bookseller and stationer, bookbinder and stationer, printer and stationer.

The booksellers clustered around St Paul's were in business to purchase original copies from the authors, to get them printed, and publish and sell them in their shops. Or else to buy and sell books second-hand. *The London Tradesman* was scathing about their treatment of authors:

> But their chief riches and profit is in the property of valued copies. The author, generally speaking, has but a very trifling sum for his trouble in compiling the copy; and finds himself treated with abundance of slights by many of the ignorant part

Stationers were originally booksellers who sold their wares from stations or stalls, but had now diversified (*Guildhall Library, Corporation of London*)

of the trade, who are sure to depreciate his performance, though never so well executed; with no other intention but to beat down his price ... Authors are generally poor, and perhaps know not where to get a dinner without disposing of their work, and therefore are necessitated to comply with hard terms.

In the booksellers' defence, *The London Tradesman* admitted that 'the press is loaded with so much trash of late years, that unless the work bears the name of some very eminent hand, they have very little chance to save themselves; and I believe most of them will agree with me, that of all the books now printed, taking them in the gross, where one sells to advantage there are three that do not clear the paper and print'. The market was ever fickle: 'There is a fate attending books, a whim possess the public sometimes to favour the sale of a mere trifle, when a performance of public utility and real worth is neglected.'

Wholesalers oiled the wheels of commerce between merchants and retailers and between London's food markets and their provincial suppliers. Food and other basic household items were supplied by shopkeepers who made up a large section of the comfortable middling class. An array of signs advertised their wares: the Oyster Girl of the fishmongers, the Lemon Tree of the fruiterers, the Pineapple of the confectioners, the Two Black Boys of the tobacconists and snuffmen, the Crown & Tea Canister of the tea men, Three Sugar Loaves & Crown of the grocers, the Tea Kettle of the braziers, the Three Keys of the ironmonger, and the Golden Beehive of the wax and tallow chandlers. Despite these signatures, very few neighbourhood shops specialised in any one item; most of them contained a jumble of goods. Expensive imports such as tea and coffee were still sold by a specialist dealer, but a grocer might sell tobacco alongside more usual items like sugar, dried fruits, rice and spices.

One-quarter of all London's working women were employed as domestic servants. This was not a career for life, but a career before marriage. About two-thirds of servants were under the age of twenty-five and there were virtually none over the age of forty-five. There were about 32,000 females employed as cook maids, scullery maids, chambermaids, housemaids, laundry maids and the like and 8,000 males employed as butlers, footmen, coachmen and grooms. To a certain extent, they could call the shots. Londoners accustomed to a life of luxury and ease employed more

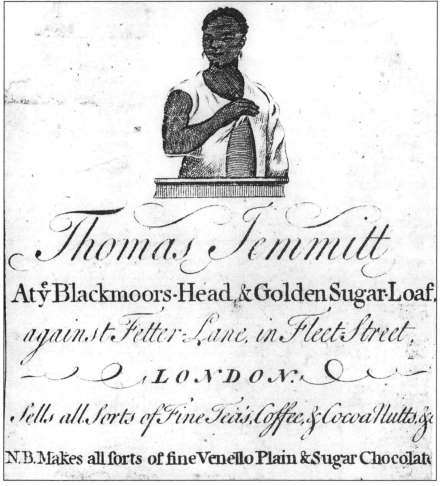

Tea and coffee were so precious that they were sold by specialist retailers (*Guildhall Library, Corporation of London*)

servants than ever before and this demand was driving up their wages. Daniel Defoe thought servants had become insufferably arrogant:

> Women servants are now so scarce, that from 30 and 40 shillings a year, their wages are increased of late to 6, 7, and 8 pounds per annum, and upwards; insomuch, that an ordinary tradesman cannot well keep one; but his wife, who might be useful in his shop, or business, must do the drudgery of household affairs: and

251

all this, because our servant wenches are so puff'd up with pride, now a days, that they never think they go fine enough: it is a hard matter to know the mistress from the maid by their dress, nay very often the maid shall be much the finer of the two. Our woollen manufacturer suffers from this, for now, nothing but silks and sattins will go down with our kitchen wenches, and it is to support this intolerable pride, that they have insensibly raised their wages to such a height, as was never known in any age or nation but this.

Defoe was an early advocate – perhaps the first – of servants wearing uniform: 'Were her dress but suitable to her condition, it would teach her humility and put her in mind of her duty.'

No sooner had a country girl arrived in a London household at £3 a year with board and lodging than the other servants were urging her to ask for an increase. The neighbourhood grapevine in the form of 'the herb woman or chandler woman, or some other old intelligencer' was quick to tip her off about a place offering £4 or £5 a year: 'This sets Madam cock-a-hoop, and she thinks of nothing now but vails and high wages, and so gives warning from place to place, 'till she has got her wages up to tip-top.'

Servants expected to eat the same food as their masters. But for many this was not enough. In his *Directions to Servants*, Swift alluded to all the trickery going on below stairs: 'If your lady forgets at supper, that there is any cold meat in the house, do not you be so officious as to put her in mind of it; it is plain she did not want it; if she recollects it the next day, say she gave you no orders, and it is eat; therefore, for fear of telling a lie, dispose of it with the butler, or any other crony, before you go to bed.' He advised the cook to keep in with the butler who held the keys to the master's cellar.

Swift was under no illusions that servants connived with tradesmen: 'If you are employed to market, do not accept a treat of a beefsteak and a pot of ale from the butcher, which, I think, in conscience, is no better than wrongdoing your master; but do you always take that perquisite in money, if you do not go on trust, or in poundage when you pay the bills.'

Guests hesitated to accept invitations to dinner because they knew they had to run the gauntlet of the servants lined up as they left and pay tips, or 'vails'. According to Defoe, the system had got completely out of hand:

Another great abuse crept in among us, is the giving of vails, to servants: this was intended originally as an incouragement to willing and handy servants, but by custom and corruption it is now grown to be a thorn in our sides ... now they make it a perquisite, a material part of their wages; nor must their master give a supper, but the maid expects the guests should pay for it, nay, sometimes through the nose.

Swift suspected that the servants made a note of a mean tipper and 'according as he behaves himself, remember to treat him the next time he comes'.

Employers had to tread warily around their servants. Swift knew just how they might be manipulated: 'If your master or lady happen once in their lives to accuse you wrongfully, you are a happy servant; for you have nothing more to do, than, for every fault you commit while you are in their service, to put them in mind of the false accusation, protesting yourself equally innocent in the present case.' No wonder servants were so insouciant as to leave the front door open while they gossiped with a fellow servant down the road, stop off for a pint of ale while on an errand, kick the mistress's dirty linen about the floor when sweeping her room, and chuck the contents of her chamber pot out of the window.

Servants often had the upper hand because they knew the most intimate secrets of their employers. They spent a great deal of time listening at keyholes, especially for any conversation that might affect them. 'When your master and lady are talking in their bedchamber, and you have some suspicion that you and your fellow servants are concerned in what they say,' Swift advised, 'listen at the door, for the public good of all the servants; and join all to take proper measures for preventing any innovations that may hurt the community.'

There was a quick turnover among servants, many keeping a place for only a year or so, and some thought nothing of leaving their employers in the lurch. Their fickleness enraged Defoe:

Nothing calls for more redress than their quitting service for every idle disgust, leaving a master or mistress at a nonplus; and all under plea of a foolish old custom, call'd warning, nowhere more practis'd than in London ... If you turn them away without warning, they will make you pay a month's wages, be the provocation or offence never so great; but if they leave you, tho' never so abruptly, or unprovided, help yourselves how you can, there is no redress.

Servants, too, were vulnerable. Employers thought nothing of administering a beating. Samuel Pepys had endless irritations with the boy he employed and was not slow to punish him: 'This morning, sending the boy down into the cellar for some beer, I followed him with a cane, and did there beat him for his staying of arrands and other faults.' It appears that he did not mend his ways because a few months later he received another beating: 'Having from my wife and the maids complaints made of the boy, I called him up and with my whip did whip him till I was not able to stir, and yet I could not make him confess any of the lies that they tax him with.' No concessions were made for age or sex. Pepys ordered his wife 'to the disturbance of the house and neighbours, to beat our little girle; and then we shut her down into the cellar and there she lay all night'.

Sir John Verney was totally exasperated by the antics of his footboy Perry:

> Yesterday Perry staying all the morning out on a small arrant onely to fetch 3 or 4 quarts of milk, as soon as he came in seeing me angry (tho' I have not strength to beate him) out of doores he went, & ran away, being then half drunck, for of late he keeps some very ill company & setts with shabby fellows at the alehouse, but never would to anybody confess who his comrades be. He hath served me this many times of late & I have often threatened to have him beate but never yet hath it been done. I heare he was yesterday in the afternoon with two fellowes at the Blew Lattice near Holborn bridge & drinking brandy, & that he lay last night at the Mitre Alehouse in Hatton Garden but left it early in the morning: I think it's a house of no good repute. Where he is rogueing today I know not, I feare he will be trapand on shipboard, & soe sent away to the West Indies, where the rogue will fetch above twenty pound … Pray see if you knowe of any pretty sightly boy about us that would be a footboy: in case Perry doth not return.

A beating could get completely out of hand and some employers were vicious in the extreme. Elizabeth Deacon, ironically the wife of a whipmaker, beat her seventeen-year-old servant maid Mary Cox to death when she would not admit the source of a shilling found on her person:

> The maid confest at first, that she had one 6d of one Mrs Baker, and the other of one Susannah Middleton; which her mistress being doubtful of, she ty'd her to the bedpost, and whipt her very sorely ... in a most violent manner, until she cry'd out murther, To prevent which, her mistress stopt her mouth with her hand ... burning her with the fire-poker upon the neck, shoulders, and back, after a most inhuman manner, and then gave her a blow on the head with a hammer, until she made her confess to have been confederate with some thieves who intended to rob her master's house ... She could no ways be prevail'd upon to take any pity upon her servant nor give her any sustenance ... The surgeon said that the stripes and wounds did contribute to her death.

Of course, servants did steal from their employers. Ann Harris was found guilty of breaking open a chest of drawers and removing sixteen guineas, a silver watch, some silver spoons, and some change in silver. Her defence is illustrative of a servant's peripatetic career:

> She said she never was guilty of any ill thing before and that she had behaved herself well in several services she had been in about London, for 12 years together, viz, first with a gingerbread baker in Aldgate; then at a victualling house in Horsey-down in Southwark; and afterwards at another victualling house in Bedford-bury in St Martins in the Fields, at each of which places she stay'd about 4 years, and never wrong'd any of her masters; till she came to live with Mr Newell in the Haymarket near St James's, where she had not been two full months before she stole the things out of her mistress's chest of drawers.

Alone in the house with the master, female servants were victims of seduction and rape. Elizabeth Chivers, condemned for the murder of her bastard, told the Ordinary of Newgate her story:

> That she being very young when her father died, and her mother

left in very poor circumstances, she was forc'd to go to service at fourteen years of age: That she had liv'd in several worthy families, where she behav'd herself faithfully and honestly in all respects: But, that about two years since the removing from the service she was then in, to another, her master perswaded her to lie with him, and got her with child: That when she began to grow big, she went from his home to another service, where she stay'd about six weeks, and then took lodgings for herself; where some time after being brought to bed of a female child, which they nam'd Elizabeth Ward, the father promis'd he would provide for bothe the mother and the child; which he did, till about three months after the devil putting it into her cruel heart to destroy the poor infant; which she suckled, carried it to Hackney, and drown'd it in a pond there.

Women too old for service still had to earn a living. Some of them must have descended to the realm of casual labour, like Elizabeth Price of the parish of St Andrew Holborn, who admitted that 'for these several years past, she had follow'd sometimes the business of picking up rags and cinders, and at other times that of selling fruit and oysters, crying hot-puddings gray-pease in the streets'. Beyond that, she could join the army of beggars on the streets or be swept up into one of the new workhouses that London's wealthiest citizens had dreamed up to keep the poor out of mischief.

CHAPTER TWELVE

The Poor

*'Seeing they have not work enough, they will not work at all and
that brings them to wander, starve, beg, steal and be hanged'*

I N JANUARY 1700 THE London Corporation of the Poor scooped a
bunch of ragamuffins off the streets, de-loused them, and placed
them in its new workhouse in Half-Moon Alley off Bishopsgate
Street. Something had to be done to tackle the problem of homeless and
abandoned children. In *The London Spy* Ned Ward describes his
encounter with 'a young crew of diminutive vagabonds' who proudly
introduced themselves as the Black-guard – a term once innocently
applied to a shoeshine boy. Ward thought it scandalous that 'an infamous
brood of vagabonds should be trained up in villainy, ignorance, laziness,
profaneness, and infidelity, from their cradles, in such a well-governed
Christian city as this, where are so many grave magistrates and parish
officers, whose care it ought to be to prevent such growing evils'.

In this thrusting commercial society there was less sympathy and
patience to spare for the poor. Busy and successful tradesmen found the
sight of the poor cluttering the streets and begging for alms at every
corner offensive. Apart from anything else, this disorderly swell of
unemployed vagrants and casual labourers posed a threat to law and
order. A new term had been coined to describe them – the mob, from
mobile vulgaris – used for the first time in the 1690s. The problem of the
poor had far outstripped the ability of the parish relief system to cope.
There had been heated debate for some time in parliament, in the newly
established Board of Trade and in the parishes themselves as to how to
deal with it.

There was a feeling that the failure of the parish authorities to provide
employment for the poor encouraged idleness which led inevitably to
vice and crime. 'Give me not poverty,' pleaded Defoe, 'lest I steal!' This
was certainly the case with Eleanor Gravenoz, who was condemned to

death for stealing six yards of silver lace out of a shop in Covent Garden. As she confided to the Ordinary of Newgate, 'her great poverty and inability to get bread for herself and four small children, had made her give way to temptation by which she fell again into this her old wicked course of seeking to supply her wants by unjust means'.

Many believed that poverty was not just a social condition. The poor must be responsible for their own situation through some moral defect. They must be *compelled* to work, to have discipline imposed upon them. Perhaps poverty was curable? The Quakers certainly thought so and were among the first to experiment with workhouses. If the poor were brought back to God, surely they would be reformed? No one could be both devout and lazy. The charitable benefactor Thomas Firmin produced a novel solution in the 1670s when he set up a workhouse in Little Britain Street for the 'imployment of the poor in the linnen manufacture' where 'children not above five or six years old ... earn two pence a day, and others but a little older, three pence or four pence, by spinning flax which will go very far towards the maintenance of any poor child'.

The children of the poor, he argued, were a menace to themselves and everyone else. No longer would they be allowed to roam the streets in gangs, frightening the horses and dismounting their riders, chucking dirt and stones at coaches, and hurling rude insults at passers-by. They must be usefully employed 'to prevent an idle, lazy kind of life, which if once they get the habit of, they will hardly leave'. Two hours a day would be allowed for reading, time they would otherwise waste in play. Children destined to earn a living as masons, bricklayers, shoemakers had no need of a fancy education. 'Is it not enough that such children are taught to read the Bible,' Firmin argued, 'and so much of arithmetic and writing, as may fit them for such trades and employments, as they are intended to be put unto?'

Firmin's workhouse failed to pay its way, but he had introduced the germ of an idea that found fertile ground in the London of the 1690s – a time of economic hardship and dislocation during the wars with France. Workhouses allowed the local ratepayers who financed them the chance to reconcile their duty to the poor with their desire to distinguish between those who deserved help and those who did not. When the Bishopsgate workhouse opened in December 1699, one hundred parish children were allocated to the Steward's Side, where they would be saved

Poor vagrant women were pushed from parish to parish and some resorted to
stealing to feed their children (*British Museum*)

from 'perishing for want'. The children would be 'taught to work as soon as they are able, whereby they at present help to support themselves, and whereby they are fitted for honest trades and services ... and made useful members of the community'.

The estimated cost of a child in the workhouse was £8 a year. The churchwardens of various parishes would contribute 12d per week towards the upkeep of every child of theirs maintained in the workhouse. Awakened by the bell at 6 a.m. for morning prayers and breakfast, the children would be engaged between 7 a.m. and noon and 1 p.m. and 6 p.m. in spinning wool flax, sewing and knitting. Two hours daily would be spent on religious instruction and learning to read, write and 'cast-accompt'. There would be three meals a day. For breakfast they could look forward to bread and beer once a week, beef broth twice a week, and bread and butter or cheese on the other days. Dinner consisted of one of the following dishes: beef broth, pease-porridge, rice-milk, plumb-dumplings, barley-broth or milk porridge. Bread and butter or cheese was served up every evening for supper. Peas, beans, greens and roots were added to the diet 'as the season affords them'.

Life on the Keeper's Side was rather less pampered. In keeping with the idea that 'if the poor are not taken in to one side of the house, when they are young, it's great odds but they will deserve to be sent to the other, when they are grown up', the inmates on this other side were of a more dangerous disposition. Here, 'vagabonds, sturdy beggars, pilfering and other vagrants, lewd, idle and disorderly persons ... have such relief as is proper for them, and are employ'd in beating hemp, picking oakum, or washing linen'. Some managed to escape, like one poor woman sent to the Clerkenwell workhouse 'and there being sick and weak, and wanting food, she follow'd other prisoners who had made a hole in the wall of the room she lay in, and so went out at that hole and made her escape with them'.

The idea of the workhouse as a deterrent, to persuade the poor to desist from seeking parish relief or begging for alms lest they be sent there, was slowly taking hold. Be self-reliant or be institutionalised was the new slogan. If the poor could not be controlled out on the streets, they must be brought into the workhouse where they would be given productive employment to keep them out of trouble. On an even more sinister note, Sir Josiah Child advocated that his 'fathers of the poor' should 'have the power to send such poor beyond the seas as they shall think fit in to His Majesties plantations'. Certainly some were desperate and gullible enough to volunteer for transportation to Virginia, signing on to work for a number of years' hard labour on the plantations in exchange for their passage money.

Not all the poor could be packed off to the workhouse – not yet, anyway – and apart from the old and infirm there remained the problem of a huge casual labour force who looked to the parishes for support. The appeal of higher wages and employment opportunities meant that London attracted thousands of migrant workers, but how were they to be maintained when unemployed? In *A New Discourse of Trade*, Sir Josiah Child recognised that the old Elizabethan system of 'leaving it to the care of every parish to maintain their own poor only' was inadequate for present needs. Instead of tackling the fundamental problem, the system encouraged each parish to 'shift the evil from their own doors ... thrusting a poor body out of the verge of their own parish'. Anyone not of that parish seeking relief would be harried into the next one, or unlucky claimants would be passed back and forth between parishes while the authorities argued which one was responsible.

In one such case in the Lord Mayor's Court, Mary Raworth and her two children were 'sent and delivered by the churchwardens and overseers of the poor of the parish of St Stephen's Wallbrooke' who disowned them and sent them back to 'St Bottolph Without Bishopsgate to be by them provided for and maintained until they can free themselves of the charge by due course of law'. Vagrant women in the throes of labour were hounded beyond the parish boundaries, so that their infant would become the responsibility of another parish. People from the countryside brought small children into London and abandoned them – children too young to remember their place of birth – expecting the parishes to maintain them. And parish authorities not only pushed claimants from parish to parish within the metropolis, but also ran them out of town altogether – an expensive and useless exercise as they simply turned round and came back.

The argument was as much about *who* was going to tackle the problem of London's poor, as *how* it was going to be tackled. Churchwardens, overseers of the poor and vestry men, who held virtual autonomy in the collection and distribution of poor relief funds, were never going to buy Sir Josiah Child's proposal to oust them from power. He wanted to replace them with a uniform system administered by a select group of 'fathers of the poor' encompassing the entire area within the bills of mortality. The administration of poor relief was a significant portion of what local government actually did in some parishes. Parish officers – local tradesmen as often as not – served on an annual basis, but some elected to pay a fee rather than serve. Officers ran the risk of being left out of pocket whenever there was a shortfall between assessment and demand. Householders were assessed for their ability to contribute to the poor rates. A heavy burden fell on the City ratepayers, for while the population of the City accounted for only a fifth of the whole metropolis they paid over one-third of the total poor relief bill.

Poor relief consisted of doles of money, supplemented by payments of rent, nursing, funeral expenses, premiums for apprenticeships, gifts of bread and fuel, and miscellaneous payments, such as the recovery of clothes or tools from the pawnbroker. The parochial basis of poor relief meant that not everyone got the same. Parishes varied in size. Some were richer than others, some carried a disproportionate number of people in need of relief. For instance, St Katherine Coleman, a poor parish, spent 60 to 80 per cent of its revenue on the poor. It could only afford Ellinor Elliston 2s 6d a week 'for maintenance of hirselfe, and hir two children, house rent and clotheing', although she did receive these payments for a seven-year period. Those pensioners living in a wealthy parish such as St Michael Cornhill could expect over £11 a year, while those unlucky enough to be living in the parish of St Andrew by the Wardrobe received only 1s to 4s a month.

Pensions did not start automatically at a certain age. They were set according to the churchwarden's perception of the person's needs. Funds were not going to be handed over without a struggle no matter how needy the supplicant, and their ability to manage some work was taken into account. If necessary, the parish would provide the work – the searchers of the dead were old women of the parish. Bernard de Mandeville summed up current thinking in *The Fable of the Bees* when he said: 'All should be set to work that are any ways able, and scrutinies should be made even among the infirm: Employments might be found out for most of our lame, and many that are unfit for hard labour, as well as the blind, as long as their health and strength will allow it.' Those who did obtain a pension surrendered their rights over their own property: parish officers took possession after their deaths.

Parish officers were understandably reluctant to give up the power they wielded over so many of their neighbours, who would have to apply personally for relief. Poor relief was often conditional on the wearing of a badge, like 'Joanna Garwood, a poor migrant woman' who 'wore a badge as one of the poor of the parish of St Andrew Holborn'. Badge-wearers lost the opportunity to boost their income by begging outside the parish. Relief was also conditional on good behaviour. Those who lost their temper with the overseer or, worse, were drunk and abusive, might find their dole reduced. Those who failed to collect in person had to do without. Relief was often supplemented by other charitable donations. In the City, the court of aldermen, livery companies and ward motes also dispensed alms to the poor. Alms and hospitals were administered by the livery companies for aged freemen and their wives or widows. St Bartholomew's and St Thomas's Hospitals were open to the aged poor for free medical care.

The immensity of London's problem and a greedier society forced contemporaries to draw a distinction between the deserving and the undeserving poor. The workshy and the downright idle were not to be tolerated in this more ruthless world. In *Giving Alms No Charity, And Employing the Poor*, Daniel Defoe identified true poverty as being not 'among the craving beggars but among poor families, where the children are numerous, and where death or sickness had depriv'd them of the labour of the father'. These should be the objects of charity, not the street beggars. London householders hated to have beggars at the door, but more often than not paid up to get rid of them. Indiscriminate charity was not the answer. 'Alms to the idle,' wrote one commentator, 'is like grease to a cart-wheel, which makes it go round the easier, but still upon the same axle.' Defoe agreed that 'alms ill directed may be charity to the particular person, but becomes an injury to the publick, and no charity to the nation'. Beggars 'can live so well with the pretence of wanting work, they would be mad to leave it and work in earnest'.

Defoe attributed poverty to sloth and was impatient with the feckless nature of the labouring poor:

> Under a stop of trade, and a general want of work, then they are clamorous and mutinous, run from their families, load the parishes with their wives and children, who they leave perishing and starving ... seeing they have not work enough, they will not work at all, and that brings them to wander, starve, beg, steal

and be hanged. In a glut of trade they grow saucy, lazy, idle, and debauch'd; they may get money enough to live well, and lay up for a time of less business; then instead of diligence and good-husbandry which might be expected from honest men, on the contrary, they will work but two days in the week, or till they get money enough to keep them the rest of the week, and all the other part of their time they lie in the alehouse to spend it.

Their reluctance to put anything away for a rainy day exasperated Defoe. Maidservants spent all their money on dressing above their station. Men spent every last penny in the alehouse or on betting. Perhaps their heedlessness was in response to the shortness and precariousness of their lives, but Defoe would have none of this:

> Want of consideration is the great reason why people do not provide in their youth and strength for old age and sickness … all persons in the time of their health and youth, while they are able to work and spare it, should lay up some small inconsiderable part of their gettings as a deposit in safe hands, to lie in store at the bank to relieve them, if by age or accident they come to be disabled, or uncapable to provide for themselves.

In *An Essay Upon Projects*, Defoe was an early advocate of people contributing to their own pension. He envisaged a Pensions Office to which subscribers would pay a 6d entrance fee and 1s a quarter as an insurance against injury, sickness, accident and infirmity in old age. By the early eighteenth century many people were subscribing to the new friendly societies and life insurance schemes to mitigate against disaster and death. Individuals could take some charge of their own destiny. As for Defoe's feckless poor, those who failed to spare 'so small a part of their earnings to prevent future misery' could well find the parish relief tap turned off just when they needed it most.

CHAPTER THIRTEEN

Huguenots and Other Strangers

*In many of the streets of Spitalfields and Soho, the immigrant
population was so dense it was rare to hear English spoken*

ON A FEBRUARY DAY of gentle frost, Louis Goujon, silk weaver, and his wife Marie left their house in Black Eagle Street, Spitalfields, to take their infant son Paul down to the French Protestant Church in Threadneedle Street in the City for his baptism. Left behind in the dimness of the small rooms, their canary's cheerful song pierced the unaccustomed silence. The loom, which clattered from dawn to dusk six days of the week, was still. The house held its breath, waiting expectantly for the return of the family.

By this year of 1700, there were twenty-eight French Protestant churches in London, their location reflecting the two main areas of immigrant settlement. That to the east encompassing the districts of Spitalfields, Aldgate, Whitechapel, Bethnal Green and Mile End, and the western district of Soho stretching from the New Oxford Road down to Leicester Fields. There were seven French churches in Spitalfields itself, so that Threadneedle Street was by no means the church nearest the Goujons' home. But it represented the very heart of the Huguenot community; here the term '*réfugiés*', which came to describe persons seeking refuge from any kind of persecution, was first coined in its minutes in 1681. Perhaps it was the one that the Goujons first attended if they came to England as children during the peak of Huguenot immigration in the late 1680s. Then the church was so crowded that some could not get inside at all, and those who did found they were 'so afflicted by the heat and the crush of people that their devotions are weakened and sometimes their health is affected'.

In those early days thousands had stood before the congregation to make their *reconnaissance* – a public confession that they had betrayed their Calvinist faith and had been forced to attend mass or sign a paper abjuring the teachings of John Calvin while still in France. Terrorised by the *dragonnades* – whose actions brought the phrase 'to dragoon' into the English language – but prevented from escaping Louis XIV's persecuting regime, the confessions of these people reveal human suffering on an immense scale.

Pierre Laurent of Picardy had 'signed to get out after two or three months in prison, had not been to mass and made efforts to leave'. Anne Popinar had been 'compelled by dragoons to attend mass'. Judith, widow of Jean Maintru of Fécamp, and their daughter had 'signed a second time after being delivered from the Barbary pirates, to escape Frenchmen who wished to transport them to America'. Madeleine Barbot and her husband 'had not been to mass and had suffered imprisonment for over two years'. Marguerite Cauvin of Caen 'signed and spent six months in prison'. Judith Daufin signed and was 'arrested twice trying to leave'. Many had not been able to leave because they lacked the means to do so. Or, like Marie Quesnal of Fécamp, 'had not left because of a sick child' or other dependant.

Altogether 40,000 to 50,000 Huguenots from all parts of France fled to England. Of course they did not all come to London. Some settled in other towns such as Canterbury, Southampton and Plymouth, or moved on to America and to Ireland with whatever financial aid the hard-pressed relief committee could spare.

Unlike so many other immigrants before or since, the Huguenots were generally welcomed as fellow Protestants. Earlier Walloon and Huguenot immigrants fleeing religious persecution in the Low Countries and France in the sixteenth century had paved the way. As urban artisans mainly in the textile trade, they had been economically self-sufficient, indeed they had introduced valuable new skills and prosperity into their adopted country. And the evident sufferings of this new wave of immigrants made an enormous impact and won the sympathy of their English hosts.

How could anyone not be moved by the story of Martha Guisard, living in Frith Street, Soho, who 'came out of France, because Jean Guisard, her father, was burnt at Nerac; being accused of having irreverently received the host'? Or of the Sieur Peyferie and his family, who had been forced to 'abandon a great estate …condemned to be hanged: and his house demolished, and his woods destroyed' ... now 'reduced to great straits' in Soho? Or of the Sieurs Dupre and Moise Du Boust, 'now living in the parish of Saint Giles in the Fields ... persecuted in their persons and their estates ... their houses demolished; before they fled into this country'?

Anti-popery was the strongest emotional force in England at the end of the seventeenth century. The plight of the Huguenots served only to reinforce it. Reports of women imprisoned and men condemned to serve in the galleys for one hundred years, of people hounded from their homes and families dispersed, and the sorry state of the refugees who managed to secure a passage and land on these shores, persuaded the English that a Catholic monarch was never to be trusted. If Louis XIV could revoke the Edict of Nantes so easily, what might his Catholic cousin James II do to endanger the lives and liberties of his Protestant English subjects? It was this conviction that helped make the revolution of 1688 possible.

The Huguenots had a vested interest in the regime of William III, who had long been acquainted with their abilities in his native Dutch Republic, and in his avowed intention to curb the power of Louis XIV. As Sir William Petty argued in *Political Arithmetic*, England's population was low – only 5 million to France's 20 million – and people were riches. Not only would these immigrants boost trade, they would lend their manpower and military expertise to William's armies in the confrontation with France. The military training that William III's Huguenot regiments had received in France transformed the fighting power of England's army.

Already the Huguenots had given their support to the newly established Bank of England, which owed its very existence to the need to finance the war. Seven out of the twenty-four original directors of the Bank of England were of Walloon or Huguenot extraction, including the first Governor, Sir John Houblon, whose family had arrived in the sixteenth century. The new banking venture depended on confidence. Of the £1.2 million raised to launch the bank, £104,000 was provided by 123 recently arrived Huguenots, who as refugees appreciated the significance of having liquid capital assets available for investment. Those refugees fortunate enough to have some ready cash were able to buy their way into the mercantile world and secure their position in society very quickly.

The Huguenot network was international. Many had dispersed to the

Dutch Republic, to the German states, and to the American colonies. Far from these aliens presenting a threat to England in time of war, as some believed, Huguenot contacts overseas would facilitate trade. Despite the manifest advantages of their presence, parliament was reluctant to grant the Huguenots full naturalisation, which would allow them to bequeath land to their heirs. Naturalisation would not be granted until 1708, and even then it was shortly rescinded. The ongoing wars with France through the eighteenth century meant that it gradually became apparent to the Huguenots that they would never return home.

The Huguenots might have fled their native land for their religious principles and to win the right to worship God as they pleased, but not all of them were models of moral probity. This was a community beset by human foibles like any other. The elders of the church who sat on the consistory spent much of their time settling marital disputes, censoring crimes of debauchery, wife-beating, unmarried pregnancy, blasphemy, obtaining money from the committee under false pretences and irreverent behaviour in church. Members of the congregation were urged to 'honour their religion in their attire and deportment, since some entered church last fast day with a proud air contrary to due humility, and a number of women came heavily adorned, some with uncovered breasts'.

Naturally the elders were concerned to make a good impression on their English hosts. They were only too aware that their welcome was not universal. There were those who resented their presence, who inevitably believed that the refugees were taking jobs away from the natives, that they were receiving charity that might otherwise be dispensed to the English poor. The elders warned that 'public feasting and dancing and games are contrary to the orderly, moderate conduct enjoined by the church, and scandalise the English nation, undermining its compassion for our poor refugee brethren. We should weep with those who weep, not undermine their cause by flaunting wealth and so discouraging charity.'

Trouble with local law officers would not be countenanced. When M. de Primrose 'reported that a Spitalfields constable complained about the unruly behaviour of some French people in that area', the elders resolved that 'debauchery will be preached against strongly, and a notice will be read in a week's time.' When there were rumours of the French frequenting taverns on Sundays, the elders decided to 'inform themselves about the facts of the matter in their *quartiers* and warn individuals to take more note of the remonstrances previously made so often on this subject'. Perhaps one of the offenders was Jean Boulay, who was 'accused of ill conduct and of being prone to becoming inebriated and shocking his neighbours'. He was to be suspended from communion 'until he leads a more edifying life'. Four quarrelsome young men, Isaac Barre, Pierre Fournier, Pierre Gatineau and Daniel Chabot, were told in no uncertain terms that 'if they did not live together and desist from their debauchery, they would be suspended from communion'.

One of the inevitable consequences of the diaspora was that many married couples had been separated. Was the lost spouse dead or alive? When Jean Faviere requested that his suspension from communion be lifted, since 'the wife he had in France is dead and so he believes his marriage here is legitimate', permission was refused. He was reprimanded for 'remarrying without assurance of the death of his first wife' and 'without informing the Consistory'. When Jean Hebert enquired why his banns had not been read a third time, it was to receive the disappointing news that 'Amaury Terin, husband of his fiancee Augustine Houson, was still alive'. And the widow of Jacques Benoit was 'blamed for remarrying to Daniel Alavoine without making certain that her first husband was dead'.

The peculiarity of the English marriage laws, which differed from those of the rest of Protestant Europe in the matter of divorce and remarriage, confounded some:

> Nicolas Hesse and Isabelle Popart sought reception into the peace and communion of the church, although they married while both their previous spouses were alive. The consistory was insufficiently knowledgeable about the causes of the dissolution of their first marriages, and knew that even in the case of adultery and desertion they could not proceed to a second marriage according to the laws of England. It therefore did not wish to get involved in this matter, and sent the parties to the parish where they were married.

Whereas when François Testu and his wife Marie Sarrazin 'complained about the insults of Charles Le Cavelier and his wife, who claim their marriage is adulterous because Testu's first wife is still alive in Geneva', the consistory was able to resolve the situation. On having the records of the consistory and the Senate of Geneva examined, it was satisfied that 'the first marriage was absolutely annulled, that Testu was at liberty to contract a new one and that consequently his marriage with Marie Sarrazin is valid and legitimate'.

The consistory had the power to make or break a contract, as Tobie Le Maistre found to his cost when 'he came to request fulfilment of the promise of marriage between himself and Anne Hauteville'. The young lady was accompanied by some of her relatives, 'who represented that her mother, who is in France, refused her consent'. The consistory judged that since 'Anne was only fifteen when she signed these promises, and was not therefore of an age to betroth herself, Le Maistre did not have the right to make her fulfil them'.

The consistory came down heavily on the side of André de Joux when his fiancée Jeanne Tibaudin sought to break their engagement: 'André de Joux, n. of Niort, and Jeanne Tibaudin were engaged before us last month on 23 November, but she now says she would never marry him. Her reasons have not been found valid, and he does not wish to consent to the dissolution of the engagement in the hope that time will bring her back to him; the consistory has left the state of affairs unchanged.' Jeanne was not prepared to accept the situation, however. André was soon back before the court to demand 'justification from Tibaudin's daughter his fiancee, and from Isaac Caillau's widow, for offensive words spoken against him'. 'After hearing both parties, the consistory urged Jeanne Tibaudin to hold to her engagement with André de Joux, or to seek means of disengaging herself by compensating her fiancee. This being refused with great stubbornness, she will be refused her *mereau* [communion token or invitation to receive communion] until she recognises her obligation.' One wonders what sort of a marriage they could possibly have had after all this.

There were cases of adultery and of incest. In the most poignant of all, Judith Godefroy confessed that 'her uncle Pierre Godefroy was the father of the child she had had before her marriage'. Her uncle had prevailed on her not to reveal their secret and anyway she had been too ashamed to do so until driven by a bad conscience to a confession. Godefroy denied the child was his, 'even taking God as his witness', but acknowledged he had had an affair with her. 'Challenged to say he had never had an affair with his niece, he replied that he could not say that, and admitted he had slept with her but in the same bed as his wife.'

In many of the streets of Spitalfields and Soho the immigrant population was so dense that it was rare to hear English spoken. Nor did many of the immigrants speak English. At his son's baptism, Louis Goujon described his occupation as *'ouvrier en soie'* and it would be some time before others like him would use the English term silk weaver. Others listed their occupations as *tailleur d'habits, imprimeur en toile, chirugien, apoticaire, chapelier, drapier, tapissier, boulanger, perruquier, tourneur en ivoire, horlogeur, marchand, cordonier, bonnetier, dresseur d'alamode, jardinier, bijoutier, distilleur, chandelier, boutonnier, charpentier, cuisinier.* Addresses were given in French or a combination of the two languages. Jean and Anne Gaudin lived at the *Rue du Moulin à Vent,* Soho. Michel Du Breuil and Marie du Puis from Dieppe said they were living *'à Pettit coste Laine'.* Others lived *'dans la rue du Lyon Rouge, paroisse* Stepney, Spitlefeilds *hameau'* and *'à l'enseigne du fromage au marché de* Spitlefeilds, Stepenay'.

Traditionally the extramural districts of Spitalfields, Bethnal Green, Whitechapel, Bishospgate, Stepney, Mile End and the liberties of Norton Folgate and the Artillery Ground attracted immigrants who could work free of City guild regulations and restrictions. The London silk industry had been established at Spitalfields by immigrants from the Low Countries and France during the reign of Elizabeth I. Weaving was a mobile skill and many of the new immigrants simply joined the existing workforce. Others brought trade secrets, new skills and techniques that would provide an enormous boost to the native silk industry. It was not just the quality of the silk that mattered, a new pattern was as important as a new cut in determining a new fashion. Leading designers such as Christopher Baudouin from Tours produced patterns of expensive flowered silks of a brilliance that had never been achieved in London before. The Mongeorges father and son from Lyon used their skills to bring a lustrous sheen to taffeta. Huguenot immigrants pioneered the making of alamodes and lustrings to such a standard that the Weavers Company eagerly admitted them:

> John Larguier and John Quet, who lately came from Nimes in Languedoc, now appeared and declared that they were ... fully enabled to weave and perfect lutestrings, alamodes, and other fine silks, as well for service and beauty in all respects as they are perfected in France, and praying to be admitted ... [Time was

The Huguenot refugees at Spitalfields produced silk of unparalleled beauty. The design of the fabric was as important as the cut in determining a new fashion (*Museum of London*)

allowed for a supervised demonstration of their skills] ... John Larguier now produced a piece of alamode silk made in England the which piece was shot with a piece of coloured silk given him by **Mr Willaw**. *This Court considered thereof, and conceiving the like* *hath never been made in England and that it will be of great benefit to this nation*, do agree that the said John Larguier be admitted a foreign master gratis, upon this condition: that he employ himself and others of the English nation in making the said alamode and lutestring silks, for one year from this day.

The River Wandle was already a centre of the dyeing industry, but now Huguenot immigrants launched the hat industry in its neighbouring suburbs of Putney, Battersea, Wandsworth and Lambeth. So successful were they in depressing the French industry, that in future Catholic cardinals in Rome had their hats supplied by Protestant refugees in England.

French taste was universally considered supreme, something for everyone else to emulate. Parisian fashion was the last word in chic, so that the Huguenot immigrants settled in Soho had no trouble in establishing themselves as purveyors of luxury goods, everything from jewellery to wigs to tailored coats to shoes to perfumes to fine wines to patisserie and cut flowers. Huguenot gun-makers such as Monlong brought the indigenous industry to a new perfection. Huguenots contributed their skills to clock-making and to paper-making. Paul Lamerie and others produced the finest gold and silver work ever seen in England. Jean Pelletier was a cabinet-maker of superb skill. He worked with Daniel Marot, the Parisian émigré who had followed William and Mary to England and refined the art of interior decoration. Louis XIV had his spies among the immigrants. The foremost among his agents, Bonrepaus, warned that the influx of so much French talent into England would depress French exports and alter the balance of trade between the two countries.

Many of the Huguenot immigrants had lost everything. Financial relief administered by the French Committee and distributed through the French churches at Threadneedle Street and the Savoy came from three sources. As head of the Church of England, the monarch was able to authorise collections in the parish churches. The sympathy of William and Mary for the refugees prompted them to set up the Royal Bounty, offering gifts of money out of the royal revenues. And parliament voted grants of £15,000 a year over so many years raised from new duties on French goods and other wines and spirits.

In this way, the Huguenot elders were able to give able immigrants a start in their new country and take care of their poor and needy in the long term. For a six-month period from the beginning of 1701 people like 'Marguerite Morisset, *veuve de* Paris *agée de 80 ans et* Marthe de Chartres *sa fille agée de 40 ans et malade*' received £2. 'Marie *femme de* François Bouchereau *d'*Angers *agée de 32 ans et trois petits enfants*' received £1. 'Jean Colomb *de* Montauban *agé de 65 ans et quatre enfants*', £2 16s 8d. 'Pierre Chastellier *de* La Rochelle *agé de 48 ans infirme sa femme et un enfant*', £1 6s 8d. And Marie Morin, for taking care of Paul Bertrand, '*fils de ministre agé de 9 ans*', 10s.

It took three to four generations for the Huguenot immigrants of the 1680s to become assimilated. Even then they remained justifiably proud of their separate identity and heritage. Some of them anglicised their names, for instance making Charpentier Carpenter and Rideau Ridout and Reynard Fox. But many others such as Olivier, Garrick, Courtauld, de Gruchy and Bosanquet remain unchanged to this day. The Huguenot contribution to their adopted country was enormous. No wonder the expression soon became current in the eighteenth century that one drop of inherited Huguenot blood was worth £1,000 a year.

In contrast to the Huguenots, the Jews were treated with a measure of prejudice and suspicion. After their long exile from England, they were invited to return in the 1650s by Cromwell, who admired their expertise in finance and commerce. These first Jewish immigrants were Sephardim, from the Peninsula, Holland, Italy and North Africa-Levant. Samuel Pepys was curious and paid a visit to their synagogue:

> After dinner my wife and I … to the Jewish synagogue – where the men and boys in their veils, and the women behind a lettice out of sight; and some things stand up, which I believe is their Law, in a press, to which all coming in do bow; and at the putting on their veils do say something, to which others that hear them do cry Amen, and the party doth kiss his veil. Their service all in a singing way, and in Hebrew. And anon their Laws, that they take out of the press, is carried by several men, four or five, several burthens in all, and they do relieve one another, or whether it is that everyone desires the carrying of it, I cannot tell. Thus they carried [it] round, round about the room while such a service is singing. And in the end they had a prayer for the King, which they pronounced his name in Portugall; but the prayer,

like the rest, in Hebrew. But Lord, to see the disorder, laughing, sporting, and no attention, but confusion in all their service, more like brutes than people knowing the true God, would make a man forswear ever seeing them more; and endeed, I never did see so much, or could have imagined there had been any religion in the whole world so absurdly performed as this.

The few, prosperous Sephardim families who settled in London and were involved in City trade and finance were swiftly followed by increasing numbers of their poorer brethren, the Ashkenazi from Eastern Europe. They settled in the outlying parishes as small manufacturers, shopkeepers and street traders. During his visit of 1698, Henri Misson noted: 'The Jews of London have by little and little quite left off the yellow hat which they were formerly oblig'd to wear; and now they have no mark of distinction at all. I don't think they are at present above sixty or seventy families. They have but one synagogue.' Two years later, the press reported that 'the Jews here are building a new synagogue in Dukes-place, which is to be very spacious'.

Daniel Defoe ridiculed national prejudices against foreigners in his best-selling satire of 1700, *The True-Born Englishman*. 'A True-Born Englishman's a contradiction, In speech an irony, in fact a fiction.' We are all the descendants of immigrants, he argued:

> From this amphibious ill-born mob began
> That vain ill-natured thing, an Englishman
> The customs, surnames, languages, and manners,
> Of all these nations are their own explainers:
> Whose relics are so lasting and so strong,
> They ha' left a shibboleth upon our tongue;
> By which with easy search you may distinguish
> Your Roman-Saxon-Danish-Norman English.

Few Englishmen were as open-minded as Sir Josiah Child, who in *A New Discourse on Trade* argued for toleration of the Jewish immigrants. He recognised that 'Fear is the cause of hatred'. Child outlined the sort of prejudices held against the Jews. They were believed to be 'a subtil people, prying into all kind of trades, and thereby depriving the English merchant of that profit he would otherwise gain'. They were 'a penurious people, living miserably, and therefore can, and do afford to trade for less profit than the English, to the prejudice of the English merchant'.

It was suspected that 'they bring no estates with them, but set up with their pens and ink only; and if after some years they thrive and grow rich, they carry away their riches with them to some other country (being a people that cannot mix with us) which riches being carried away is a publick loss to this kingdom'. This was hardly surprising, Child argued, since they were made to feel so unwelcome. He urged that the Jews be allowed the same freedom and security in England as they currently enjoyed in Holland and Germany – who were so patently benefiting from the commercial advantages of their presence.

Among the ladies of Covent Garden, the Jews were considered to be good lovers. When a friend of Tom Brown became the mistress of a Jew, he expressed surprise that 'Mrs Lucy had thrown off her old Christian acquaintance and revolted to the Jews'. The letter continues in the same anti-Semitic vein:

So then, I find, 'tis neither circumcision nor uncircumcision that avails anything with you, but money, which belongs to all religions; and you only put in practice what your keeper's ancestors did formerly in the wilderness, that is, you fall down before the Golden Calf which, the Rabbis say, was some excuse for their idolatry ... For your comfort, all the casuists agree that it is no more sin to cheat a Jew than to over-reach a Scot, or to put false dice upon a stock-jobber. And now, old friend of mine, to tell the truth, I have a great inclination upon me to be wonderfully loving to thee, and I'll tell you the reason. If thou hadst kept still within the pale of the Church, I believe you and I knew one another so intimately well before that I should have lain under no great temptation to trespass with thee. But since thou hast admitted an interloper into thy bosom, I have a wonderful longing to beat up his quarters, and am resolved to cuckold this Eleazar, this Eben-Ebra, this son of circumcision, only to shew my zeal to Christianity. Therefore meet me, dear Lucy, this very evening in the pit; for I long to know, first, how thou madest a shift to pass the Levitical muster with him; and, secondly and lastly, to be informed whether Aaron's bells make better music than ours. Adieu.

*

Standing alone on the deck of the ship that had carried him to England, African-born James Albert Ukawsaw Gronniosaw could not believe the sounds that were floating up from the quay below. Surely he could not be hearing properly? The cursing and swearing and blasphemy that were undoubtedly reaching his ears shocked him to the core of his being. All the Englishmen he had met through his master in the American colonies had been gentle, God-fearing people. The figures emitting all the ugly sounds on the quayside – and not hesitating to administer a blow to any that got in their way – did not seem like the same people at all. He stared out in perplexity at the land of Bunyan, the first doubts about his decision to come here beginning to assail him.

James was unusual among Africans coming to England in that he was a free man. It had not always been so. As a small child, grandson of the King of Zaara somewhere in the African interior, he had been lured to the coast 1,000 miles away by a promise to see the ships. No sooner was he on the Gold Coast than he was sold by its African ruler to a Dutch captain, who divested him of his gold ornaments as soon as he boarded his ship bound for Barbados. Here he was sold for fifty dollars to a young gentleman of New York, who expected him to wait at table dressed in livery.

His next master was a good, religious man, who on his death-bed gave him his freedom and £10. As James had never made his own way in the world, and had no understanding of the value of money, he stayed on with his master's widow and her sons. After their deaths, he was 'quite destitute, without a friend in the world'. Incurring a £3 debt, he was persuaded to go privateering, only for his creditor – a New York merchant – to appropriate all his £125 winnings, a sum far in excess of the original loan.

And now he had arrived in England, only to be cheated again, for his landlady kept all the money he had deposited with her for safe-keeping: 'As she had given me no receipt, and I had nothing to shew for it, I could not demand it.'

In London, he sought out a Mr Whitfield, 'who was the only living soul I knew in England'. He wanted him 'to direct me how to procure a living without being troublesome to any person'. The good Mr Whitfield duly 'directed me to a proper place to board and lodge in Petticoat Lane, till he could think of some way to settle me in, and paid for my lodging, and all my expenses'. It was here that James met the love of his life: 'The morning after I came to my new lodging, as I was at breakfast with the gentlewoman of the house, I heard the noise of some looms over our heads; I enquired what it was, she told me a person was weaving silk … As soon as we entered the room, the person that was weaving looked about, and smiled upon us, and I loved her from that moment.'

Betty was a widow with a child. James went to Holland as butler to a contact of Mr Whitfield, returned and married Betty after he had discharged her debts. 'I was resolved all my wife's little debt should be paid before we were married,' he recounts, 'so that I sold almost everything I had, with all the money I could raise, cleared all that she owed.' Besides, Betty 'got a very good living at weaving, and could do extremely well'. James did not encounter prejudice as such. Life was just very difficult. Eventually the couple moved on to Norwich, where employment in the textile industry was erratic until orders from London arrived, and they nearly starved.

Then their little girl died. It appears she had not been baptised and no one would bury her: 'This was one of the greatest trials I had ever met with, as we did not know what to do with our poor baby.' Grudgingly, the 'parson of the parish sent to tell me he would bury the child, but did not choose to read the burial service over her'. James's story ends with his wife still working hard at the loom to support their family, he being by this time 'through age and infirmity able to contribute but little to their support'.

Most Africans came to England as slaves, the property of West Indian plantation owners and sea captains who usually sold them off before departure. At first court ladies had regarded their 'blackamoors' as fashion accessories, and treated them much as they did their pets, at least until they grew up. The idea of having a free servant for life began to seem very appealing. But there was some question as to whether slavery was recognised in England. In the 1700 edition of *Angliae Notitia*, Edward Chamberlayne confidently stated that, 'Foreign slaves in England there are none since Christianity prevailed. A foreign slave brought into England, is upon landing, *ipso facto* free from slavery, but not from ordinary service.' This assumption was backed up by a spate of test cases under the supervision of Chief Justice Sir John Holt of the Court of King's Bench. They suggested that slavery was not a status recognised by the law of England. There was no precedent for it in recent history.

The law was one thing, prevailing practice another. West Indian planters who brought their black 'chattels' to England to wait on them were particularly incensed by any quibbles about their rights of ownership. The law did not quite dare gainsay them. When Katherine Auker appealed to the Middlesex Sessions for justice, therefore, she was to be disappointed:

> Upon the petition of Katherine Auker, a black. Shows she was a servant to one Robert Rich, a planter in Barbadoes, and that about six years since she came to England with her master and mistress; she was baptised in the parish church of St. Katherine's near the Tower, after which her said master and mistress tortured and turned her out: her said master refusing to give her a discharge, she could not be entertained in service else where. The said Rich caused her to be arrested and imprisoned in the Pulletry Cempter [Poultry Compter, where blacks were imprisoned usually before their return to their masters or transportation to the American colonies or West Indies], London. Prays to be discharged from her said master, he being in Barbadoes.

A reasonable request, but denied. The law allowed Katherine to work in service only until the return of her master from Barbados, when she must return to him as her rightful owner.

The very fact that financial transactions were taking place making one man the property of another meant that it was a condition in practice. In 1698 the Royal African Company lost its monopoly of the slave trade. Now it was a free market with an infinite profit incentive. Where the Royal African Company had been transporting about 5,000 Africans a year to the West Indies, the figures now shot up drastically. In the first nine years of free trade, Bristol alone transported 160,950 blacks to the sugar plantations.

Greed knew no bounds. The original intention of the English in Africa – to civilise the 'savages' and introduce them to Christianity – was shown up for the hypocrisy it was once those people became a saleable commodity. The idea that African slaves might gain their freedom once baptised was quickly refuted. Ministers were actively discouraged from converting the Africans, servants were instructed not to discuss religion with them. From now on, they would be property at the disposal of their masters, to be bought and sold like any other goods. Notices of runaways littered the press:

> A Negro girl of six years of age, speaks good English is very comely and witty, and has abundance of very taking little actions, is to be sold. Enquire at the Surgeons Sign in Flaggon Row in Deptford near London, where she is to be seen, and her proprietor to be spoken with.

The only way the Africans could rebel was to run away. But hue and cry notices were quickly posted and their chances of escape were slim:

> A Negro named Quoshy, aged about 16 years, belonging to Capt, Edw. Archer, run way from Bell-Wharf the 25th instant, having on a plush cap with black fur, a dark waistcoat, a speckled shirt, old breeches, branded on his left breast with E.A. but not plain, and shaved round his head. Whoever brings him to Mr Roland Tryon in Lime-Street shall have a guinea reward, and charges.

> Whereas a Negro boy by name Guy, about 14 years old, very black, with a cinnamon colour'd serge coat, waistcoat, and breeches, with a silver lace'd black hat, speaks English very well, hath absented himself from his master (Major Robert Walker) ever since the 4th instant, Whoever shall bring the above said Negro boy into Mr Lloyd's Coffee-house in Lombard-street London, shall receive a guinea reward, with reasonable charges.

The symbol of slavery was the silver collar:

> A black boy, an Indian, about thirteen years old, run away the 8th instant from Putney, with a collar about his neck with this inscription: "The Lady Bromfield's black, in Lincoln's Inn Fields." Whoever brings him to Sir Edward Bromfield's at Putney, shall have a guinea reward.

Of course some fell foul of the law in more conventional ways. The Old Bailey Sessions Papers records:

Mary Harris, a black-woman of the parish of St Giles in the Fields, was indicted for feloniously stealing a pair of Holland sheets, three smocks, and other goods of Nicholas Laws, gent, on the 30th November last. It appeared that she was a servant in the house, and took the goods, which were afterwards pawned by the prisoner; she had little to say for herself and it being her first offence, the jury considering the matter, found her guilty to the value of 10d. To be whipt.

These were only the beginnings. The forthcoming war between England and France over the Spanish succession would give England the Asiento, the exclusive right to import slaves from Africa into the King of Spain's dominions in South America and the Indies. At that point, Daniel Defoe reckoned that 40,000 to 50,000 slaves a year were being transported in British ships and sold at an average price of £25 a head. Aphra Behn had been one of the first to attack slavery in her novel, *Oroonoko*. As the eighteenth century got into its stride, her voice of protest dwindled to a distant echo as the full horror and shame of the British slave trade began to unfold.

CHAPTER FOURTEEN

Religion and Superstition

*'No city in the spacious universe boasts of religion more, or
minds it less'*

THE MAN IN THE PILLORY at the Royal Exchange is standing on
tiptoe. It is not a position he will be able to maintain for long,
but for the moment it eases the discomfort as his neck is wedged
into the 'wooden ruff' and his arms are twisted at an unnatural angle
into the holes on either side of his head. He is aware of the excitement of
the heaving crowd around him, of those jostling for a position at the
front, but he keeps his eyes shut tight. Any second now and the mob
will release their arsenal of filth and brickbats as thick and fast as hail at
his defenceless body. He is already finding it difficult to breathe. How
much worse will it be under the coming torrent when mud and
excrement cover his nose and mouth. Involuntarily he cringes against the
imagined stones injuring his face and head, damaging his eyesight,
pounding his legs and the small of his back. There is a dreadful moment
of pause. Something soft brushes his cheek. It is as if warm snow is
descending on him. He dares to open his eyes a fraction, then opens
them fully in amazement. The Londoners are pelting him with flowers.

The City oligarchs whom he has insulted by alluding to their
corruption in *The Reformation of Manners* have finally had the satisfaction
of condemning Daniel Defoe to stand in the pillory three times. One
way and another Defoe has played right into their hands. He has
managed to antagonise everyone. He can claim the unique distinction of
prompting such irreconcilable parties as High Church Tories and Whig
nonconformists to unite against him. His latest biting pamphlet, *The
Shortest Way with the Dissenters*, has incensed the High Church Tories, the
'high fliers' who in this first year of Queen Anne's reign, 1702–3, feel
they are finally in a position to put the late King William's Whig
supporters and their nonconformist allies back in their place.

Once again the pendulum swings and now it is time for an Anglican comeback, especially in London where they are so weak: the nonconformists are too numerous and too rich and powerful in the City. They must be cut down to size. There are not enough Anglican churches in the outlying parishes. Fifty new churches will be built. The nonconformists are winning the allegiance of the poor. Their children must be brought back into the fold of the Church of England. Charity schools are being set up throughout the metropolis to indoctrinate them in the tenets of Anglicanism.

Defoe wrote *The Shortest Way with the Dissenters* in the guise of an extreme churchman. So convincing was he that at first everyone thought it was genuine, which made churchmen and politicians all the more enraged when they realised they had been fooled. All the bitter quarrels and resentments of the seventeenth century – in which politics and religion are so inextricably linked – are aired in the pamphlet. James I should have rooted out the Puritans while he had the chance. Look at the damage they have done! 'You have butchered one king!' it thunders, 'deposed another king, and made a mock king of a third! And yet, you could have the face to expect to be employed and trusted by the fourth!' Referring to the Toleration Act of 1689 allowing freedom of worship to Protestant dissenters, it claims the Church of England has been 'huffed and bullied with your Act of Toleration!' 'If ever you will leave your posterity free from faction and rebellion,' it urges, 'this is the time! This is the time to pull up this heretical weed of sedition, that has so long disturbed the peace of the Church!'

The pamphlet's recommendation to hang a few nonconformists in order to bring the rest into line was too close to the truth of reactionary Anglican sentiments. The idea was not altogether fanciful when those other dissenters, the Huguenots, had been similarly persecuted in neighbouring France. 'If one severe law were made, and punctually executed, that whoever was found at a Conventicle should be banished the nation, and the preacher be hanged; we should soon see an end to this tale! They would all come to church again, and one age would make us all one again!' It ends resoundingly: 'Alas, the Church of England! What with popery on one hand, and schismatics on the other, how has she been crucified between two thieves. Now, let us crucify the thieves! Let her foundations be established upon the destruction of her enemies! The doors of mercy being always open to the returning part of the deluded people, let the obstinate be ruled with the rod of iron!'

Defoe's swingeing attack on the Anglican extremists also brought his powerful nonconformist brethren into disrepute, because it addressed the question of 'occasional conformity' – just at the moment the House of Commons was considering a bill to prevent it. In 1698 Defoe had nailed the first edition of his pamphlet *An Enquiry into the Occasional Conformity of Dissenters* on to the door of St Paul's. This way that old hypocrite the Lord Mayor, Sir Humphrey Edwin, would be bound to see it when he attended divine service in the morning wearing his mayoral robes before nipping off to the Pinner Hall Conventicle in the afternoon. A second edition of an *Enquiry* in 1700 similarly embarrassed the Lord Mayor Sir Thomas Abney, another 'occasional conformist'. In his *Reformation of Manners* Defoe had been scathing about the double standard surrounding religion: 'No city in the spacious universe boasts of religion more,' he wrote, 'or minds it less.'

Defoe blamed the Test Act of 1673 – by which no one could hold public office of even the meanest kind unless participating in the Anglican Communion – for leading ambitious men into such hypocritical behaviour. The Act debased communion, he argued, 'the most sacred thing in the world into a political tool and engine of state'. By the same token, to expect people to pay fines rather than to attend the Church of England was the greatest obscenity. 'To talk of five shillings a month for not coming to the Sacrament, and one shilling per week, for not coming to Church; This is such a way of converting people as was never known! This is selling them a liberty to transgress for so much money!'

As a practising nonconformist, Defoe was disgusted by the hypocrisy of the 'occasional conformists'. Men like Sir Thomas Abney, he felt, betrayed their principles for worldly gain, they sullied the purity of nonconformist faith. In his youth Defoe had seen his father and other good men such as his teacher Charles Morton of Newington Academy treated as second-class citizens – barred from the universities and public office of any kind – because they refused to conform to the Church of England or to compromise their beliefs. By compromising, Abney and others let down the side. Needless to say, the Anglicans were triumphant at nonconformist disarray. Although it had landed him in Newgate and the pillory, Defoe felt he could do nothing less than employ his pamphlet warfare to win the right for himself and everyone else to worship according to their conscience without being penalised.

The religious wrangling at the beginning of Anne's reign was a depressing backward step. The Glorious Revolution of 1688 had brought a refreshing measure of toleration – at least for Protestant dissenters, who had suffered since the Restoration when the Anglican-inspired Clarendon Code had expelled them from the Established Church: payback time for the civil wars, regicide and republicanism. King William III, a Calvinist himself, needed to unite the nation, and one of the best ways to do this was by promoting religious harmony. He understood the advantages of bringing the dissenters, people of enterprise, initiative and drive with proven business acumen, inside the national fold.

The new mood was best personified in John Locke's *A Letter Concerning Toleration,* published in 1690. Religion, it stated, was the business of the individual: 'No man can so far abandon the care of his own salvation, as blindly to leave it to the choice of any other, whether prince or subject, to prescribe to him what faith or worship he shall embrace. For no man can, if he would, conform his faith to the dictates of another. All the life and power of true religion consists in the inward and full persuasion of the mind: And faith is not faith without believing.'

In a radical new departure, Locke stated that a man's religious belief was no business of the state, nor should it jeopardise his civil rights: 'No private person has any right, in any manner, to prejudice another person in his civil enjoyments, because he is of another church or religion. All the rights and franchises that belong to him as a man, or as a denison, are inviolably to be preserved to him. These are not the business of religion.'

Church and state were to be quite separate, and an individual's religious belief need not impinge on the body politic:

> If a Roman Catholick believe that to be really the body of Christ, which another man calls bread, he does no injury thereby to his neighbour. If a Jew do not believe the New Testament to be the word of God, he does not thereby alter any thing in mens civil rights. If a Heathen doubt of both Testaments, he is not therefore to be punished as a pernicious citizen. The power of the magistrate, and the estates of the people, may be equally secure, whether any man believe these things or no. I readily grant, that these opinions are false and absurd. But the business of laws is not to provide for the truth of opinions, but for the safety and security of the Commonwealth, and of every particular mans goods and persons.

In contrast to the passions of the extreme Anglicans and committed nonconformists, Samuel Pepys personified the phlegmatic mindset of the conventional Anglican, observing the outward ceremonies without too much heart-searching. He usually attended church twice on a Sunday, but his main concerns seem to have been his placement in the hierarchical pew system and whether his wife was attracting unwarranted attention from some imagined rival. 'My wife and I to church in the afternoon and seated ourselfs, she below me; and by that means the precedence of the pew which my Lady Batten and her daughter takes, is confounded.' Frequently the sermon was not up to scratch – 'an ordinary lazy sermon of Mr Mills' – and more often than not, Pepys found it difficult to stay awake: 'a young simple fellow did preach [and] I slept soundly all the sermon.'

Whatever their religious affiliation, religion permeated everyone's lives. All the key stages of life – baptism, marriage, burial – took place within the embrace of religion. The Established Church was a major landowner, with its representatives sitting in the House of Lords. Its tentacles reached into everyday life. If a teacher or midwife or sometimes a surgeon wanted a licence to practise, they applied to the ecclesiastical court. If a couple wanted to separate, they went to the ecclesiastical court. If someone defamed his neighbour, they answered the charges in the ecclesiastical court. If a woman bore a bastard or a man refused to maintain his child, they would be punished by the ecclesiastical court. In the absence of national media, the pulpit played its part in disseminating views on politics, morality and current affairs.

Nonconformists were part of the parish even if they did not attend church. The parish was the basic administrative unit in town and country, doling out poor relief as one of its secular functions. Parishioners paid their tithes, church rates and miscellaneous fees to maintain the Church and the poor. Nonconformists, who ministered to the needs of their own congregations, paid double dues – to the parish churches and to their own organisations. And, of course, they maintained their own schools and academies and used their own burial ground at Bunhill Fields, just outside the City boundary.

While some measure of compromise might be reached among Protestants, anti-Catholicism was the strongest emotional force in England at the end of the seventeenth century. The presence of thousands of Huguenot refugees in London was a constant reminder of

Popular sentiments equating 'popery' with 'slavery' even appeared on this new triumphal arch in Cheapside (*Guildhall Library, Corporation of London*)

the supposed Catholic threat to liberty. English Catholics were not numerous and kept a low profile. Nevertheless, they were objects of suspicion and likely to incur the severest penalties:

February 8, 1700. Kensington. By the king a proclamation. Whereas his Majesty hath been informed, that great numbers of papists and other disaffected persons, who disown his Majesty's government have lately resorted to and assembled in London and Westminster contrary to the known laws, he has thought fit to issue this proclamation, and does hereby command all popish recusants, natives or denizens, above 16 years, to repair to their places of abode, and, if they have none, then to the places where their father or mother is dwelling, and do not remove above five miles from thence.

The laws were to be stepped up:

22 April, 1700. Hampton Court. By the king, a proclamation. Whereas by an Act made the last session of this present parliament, intituled, *An Act for the further preventing the growth of Popery*, it is enacted that after March 25, 1700, every person who shall apprehend one or more popish bishop, priest or jesuit, and prosecute him until he or they be convicted of saying Mass or of exercising any function of a popish bishop or priest within these realms, shall receive, for every such offender £100. And it is thereby enacted that if any popish bishop, priest or jesuit, shall say Mass or exercise any function of a popish bishop or priest within these realms, or the dominions thereunto belonging, or if any papist or other persons making profession of the popish religion, shall keep school, or take upon themselves the education or government, or boarding of youth in any place within this realm, or the dominions thereto belonging, [that every such person] shall on conviction be adjudged to perpetual imprisonment.

On this eve of renewed warfare with Catholic France, Roman Catholics could well be considered to hold primary allegiance to the papacy and sympathy with a foreign power. They were to take the oaths of allegiance and supremacy, otherwise be declared incapable of inheriting or buying land. Children of Catholic parents were not to be sent overseas to be educated 'in the Romish religion'.

The London Post reported: 'We hear several hundred strings of popish beads are lately seized, by one of the officers of the Customs, coming for London from France, for the use of the papists in this kingdom.'

The author of *The Danger of the Protestant Religion Consider'd, From the Present Prospect of a Religious War in Europe* summed up general opinion in 1701: 'The growth of popery is certainly dangerous to the Protestant religion; They are the two buckets in the well, the two scales on the beam of power; if one comes up, the other must go down; if you add to the weight of one, it will lift the other out of its place.' The old English belief that Protestantism was equated with liberty was still prevalent: 'Popery and slavery are like sin and death; direct consequences of one another; and whenever we think fit to admit the first, any body may promise us the last.' It has to be remembered that the siege mentality was not inappropriate. Louis XIV's France was seen as all-powerful, he housed the Stuart Catholic Pretender who might yet claim the English throne as James III, and Marlborough's victories still lay in the future.

After the turbulence of the mid seventeenth century it became inherent in the national psyche to avoid fanaticism of any kind. Too much enthusiasm was seen as un-English. Of all the sects that came to prominence during the Interregnum, only the Quakers – so called because their congregations were said to shake and tremble at the word of God – found a permanent place in national life. Quakers maintained that as the spirit moved them they had no call for the intercession of priests. Their refusal to remove their hats to a superior, to acknowledge titles, and their insistence on the use of the common forms of address 'thou' and 'thee' in speech to their betters were considered dangerous and anarchic. Their dress and furniture reflected such simplicity. They eschewed pagan and Catholic rituals of all kinds, including the days of the week, preferring to use 'First Day' for Sunday, and so on. Their charismatic leader George Fox carried out many cures of the sick, even encroaching on the royal prerogative to cure scrofula. Because they had the courage to be different, the Quakers were ridiculed and ostracised, the most persecuted minority of the 1660s and 1670s.

Persecution shaped the future of this Society of Friends. While George Fox and his brethren spent many years in prison for their beliefs, they became wedded to non-violence. They became highly organised, converging on London for the Yearly Meeting to discuss their strategy and other matters. This habit of organisation, their isolation, and the practice of mutual support gradually transformed them into highly successful business people. Deprived of a university education and unable to become freemen because of their inability to swear on oath (a handicap that would be rectified in the Act of 1708), the Quakers turned to alternative, practical ways of earning a living. They might take exception to participating in certain luxury trades, but they could produce soap and chocolate. And to finance these new enterprises, they needed banks: Barclays and Lloyds had Quaker origins. Material success could be offset by philanthropy.

For people of all religious persuasions God was a real presence in everyday life. Disasters such as the Great Plague and the Fire of London were attributed to God's displeasure at the sinful lives of its citizens. After the plague in 1665 the diarist John Evelyn had recorded 'a solemn fast throughout England to deprecate God's displeasure against the land by pestilence and war', while a year later the fire prompted the following entry: 'This day was ordered a general Fast through the nation, to humble us on the late dreadful conflagration, added to the plague and war, the most dismal judgments that could be inflicted; but which indeed we highly deserved for our prodigious ingratitude, burning lusts, dissolute court, profane and abominable lives, under such dispensations of God's continued favor in restoring church, prince, and people from our late intestine calamities, of which we were altogether unmindful, even to astonishment.' Well into the eighteenth century public fast days were designated to allay God's wrath.

At the end of the seventeenth century the newly formed Society for the Reformation of Manners and the Society for the Promoting of Christian Knowledge were animated by the conviction that if man did not reform, God's vengeance would fall upon the land. There was an unwillingness to accept the randomness of misfortune, or indeed, to put wrongdoing in a social and economic context. The prime function of the official Accounts of the Ordinary of Newgate was to prove that while virtue was rewarded, vice did not go unpunished. Over and over again, the 'malefactors' are seen to have transgressed the moral laws: they have been 'sabbath-breakers', they have indulged in swearing and profanity, in drunkenness, lechery and vice. And so they must die.

At the Protestant Reformation men had renounced the miraculous solutions to the problems of life offered by the medieval Church without having any technical or medical remedies to put in their place. The gradual rejection of 'magic' made such advances imperative. Before 1700 the world was agreed to be a purposive one, responsive to the wishes of the Creator. Once the universe began to be conceived as a great clock, however, governed mechanically by the wheels a distant God had set in motion, it was logical to assume that the belief in miracles, the power of prayer and faith in divine intervention in human affairs would be diminished. It is significant that even Sir Isaac Newton was slow to comprehend this; and his secret alchemical investigations are a reminder that change did not happen overnight. There was a reluctance to relinquish the role of providence in daily life. On the other hand, the members of the Royal Society insisted that all truths be demonstrated, laid emphasis on the need for direct experience and showed a disinclination to accept inherited dogmas without first putting them to the test.

Although the educated class had relinquished a belief in witchcraft so that it was no longer prosecuted effectively in the courts, it still persisted at a popular level. Even as late as 1704, it was reported in London:

Sarah Griffith who lived in a garret in Rosemary-lane was a long time suspected for a bad woman ... some of the neighbour children would be strangely effected with unknown distempers, a vomiting of pins, their bodies turn'd into strange postures and such like, many were frighted with strange apparitions of cats, which of a sudden would vanish away, these and such like made those who lived in the neighbourhood both suspicious and fearful of her; Till at last the Devil (who always betrays those that deal with him) thus brought the truth to light.

When Sarah went to the local shop, the apprentice made some quip about the scales being affected by her presence, and she vowed she would wreak vengeance. Sure enough, during the night, the shopkeeper came downstairs to find the contents of the shop in disarray. The local lads decided to take matters into their own hands:

The young man and some companions saw Griffiths near the New River Head. They consulted together to try her, and one of them said let us toss her into the river, for I have heard that if she swims 'tis a certain sign she is a witch; in short they put their design in execution, for coming up to her they tossed her in; but like a bladder when forc'd under water pops up again so this witch was no sooner in but swam like a cork; they kept her in some time, and at last let her come out again; she was no sooner out, but she smote that young man on the arm, and told him he should pay dear for what he had done; Immediately he found a strange pain on his arm, and looking on it found the exact mark of her hand and fingers as black as cole; he went home where he lay much lamented and wonderfully affrighted with the old woman coming to afflict him, and at last died with the pain, and was buried in St Sepulchres churchyard.

As in any sort of healing process, the power of suggestion in witchcraft was still enormously strong.

By the end of the seventeenth century magic was thought to be in decline because of the growth of urban living, the rise of science, and the spread of the ideology of self-help. The environment was more amenable to control. Progresses in agriculture – largely bolstered by the need to feed a great city such as London efficiently – meant that man relied more on practical planning and less on superstition. Strenuous efforts were made to predict the weather. Divination declined as other means were devised to find lost goods; at the most mundane level, Londoners could advertise in the press and in the coffee-houses. Where rational solutions were found, magic declined. Yet medical science was slow to advance; women still clung to an eaglestone in childbirth and a hare's foot was still worn to protect the wearer from ill-health. And people continued to rely on horoscopes to show them a better future.

But fortune need not depend on superstition or be random. The work of John Gaunt, Sir William Petty and Edmund Halley on the science of statistics meant that tables of life expectancy could be devised. People could mitigate against ill-fortune by taking out insurance. It is paradoxical that the word 'coincidence' – meaning the juxtaposition of causally unrelated events – should have been coined just at a time when probability odds were becoming the objects of scientific understanding. In this brave new world, God would sometimes be forgotten.

CHAPTER FIFTEEN

Prostitution and Vice

*'Some thousands of lewd persons have been imprisoned, fined
and whipt ... many of our streets have been purged of that
pestilent generation of night walkers that used to infest them'*

A MAZE OF DARK ALLEYWAYS lay between the Strand and his destination in Drury Lane. Striding up through Katherine Street, the gentleman impatiently shook off importunate fingers tugging at his sleeve and tossing a corner of his wig over his shoulder. A fan tapped his cheek. The unspoken code of the streetwalkers. He ignored obscene whispered suggestions from disembodied voices in dark doorways. A figure sprang into his path and the smoky glare of an oil lamp revealed a gross parody of a woman, pockmarks barely concealed by a frenzy of black patches and sunken cheeks made determinedly cheerful by a splatter of rouge. The mouth opened to reveal black teeth and gums eaten up by the mercury cure; it issued an invitation to follow her into an alley out of sight of prying eyes. Warding her off, he strode on towards a fine house near the Drury Lane theatre, where he knocked with his cane to gain admittance. The turning of a key in the lock, the sliding of bolts, and a quick scrutiny of the visitor to ensure he was neither the constable on a raid nor some snoop from the new vigilante Society for the Reformation of Manners, and he was inside.

Our gentleman has just entered one of the most notorious brothels in London, the premises of that pox-ridden bawd Elizabeth Wisebourn, respectfully known to the girls she has inveigled into her service as Mother Whybourn. The production of a letter of recommendation from a previous customer takes him past the Bible lying open on a table in the hall – after all, Mother Whybourn is the church-going daughter of a clergyman – into the dining room. The portraits of beauties *en déshabillé* – dressed ready for business – adorn the walls. Which one shall he chose? Perhaps one of those rich City wives 'who loath their husbands and who

London's prostitutes used their fans in soliciting
(*Guildhall Library, Corporation of London*)

love the sport'? Or that fresh-cheeked country girl who Mother Whybourn lately picked up at the Holborn coaching inn? Either will cost a guinea to the bawd and whatever sum he feels inclined to pay the girl herself. Does he want a virgin? The girl must have ten guineas for 'parting with her maidenhead'. No matter that she parted with it many years before. Lost maidenheads are ten a penny when they can be surgically restored by Mrs Lydia Bennet at her Knightsbridge clinic-cum-convalescent home and 'sold to new customers several times over'. Upstairs each room contains a looking-glass 'so conveniently plac'd, that those who have a mind to it, may see what they do: for some take as much delight in seeing as in doing'.

Bible in hand, Mother Whybourn made a daily round of inns and taverns 'to see what youth and beauty the country had sent to London'. Such innocent girls should not be left on their own at the mercy of the town. She would take them under her wing – house them, clothe them, feed them – in return for their bodies and souls. She would spring promising young recruits from the bridewells with cash payments to the gaolers. Street urchins would be cleaned up and taught to please a gentleman. Sundays were not for idleness. Mother Whybourn's girls would be sent to church. Where better to tout for customers? As one of her girls recalled:

> We'd take all opportunities, as we came down stairs from the galleries, or as we past over the kennels in the streets, to lift up our coats [skirts] so high, that we might show our handsome legs and feet, with a good fine worsted or silk pair of stockings on; by which means the gallants would be sure either to dog us themselves, or else to send their footmen to see where we liv'd; and then they would afterwards come to us themselves; and by that means we have got many a good customer.

Nor should her girls worry about a dose of the pox. A bit of an expert herself, Mother Whybourn relied on the friendly advice of one of her clients, Dr Richard Meade, to keep her informed of all the latest treatments. All good brothels have 'surgeons and apothecaries, with whom we are in fee, who, if we but suspect the least miscarriage straight gives us something that may carry it off'. Some were luckier than others: 'She used to change her strumpets once a year, and sometimes would exchange them with others of the trade, but such as were poor, sick, poxt, or old she would turn out of doors, yet if now and then some of her young and handsome strumpets were clapt, she would take care of their cure.'

The pox was an old enemy, but now there was an insidious new one: the Society for the Reformation of Manners. It was recruiting thousands of secret informers – small tradesmen such as James Jenkins and Bodenham Rewse down in the Strand were two of the most active – to help them wage their anti-vice campaign. The principles of the society appealed to thousands of small shopkeepers and skilled craftsmen, indignant at the loose morals of the upper classes and uneasy at the disorderly lewdness of the lower orders. Informers were to be ever vigilant 'by taking notice of all those, that for the time to come, shall impudently dare, in rebellion against the laws of God and man, to swear and curse, to profane the Lord's day, or be guilty of the loathsome sin of drunkenness, also by searching out the lurking holes of bawds, whores, and other filthy miscreants, in order to their conviction and punishment according to law'. Such sinfulness would surely bring down divine retribution on the whole nation.

In his 1698 Proclamation for Preventing and Punishing Immorality and Profaneness, King William himself had voiced an apprehension that 'the open and avowed practice of vice' might 'provoke God to withdraw his mercy and blessings from us, and instead thereof to inflict heavy and severe judgements'. At least with the demise of the fornicating Stuarts and the accession of the morally upright William and Mary, the anti-vice movement could depend on royal support for its actions. But this was no good if the upper classes failed to offer a good example. The author of *The Night Walker, Or, Evening Rambles in Search after Lewd Women*, John Dunton, felt that the society faced an uphill struggle:

> Blessed be God, tho' the debauchery of the nation in the last two reigns was justly chargeable upon the throne, its so far from being so in this, that the present government have always declared their abhorrence of that vice, and of that foul crime in particular, which like good subjects and Christians you have so heiniously endeavour'd to reform; but to the disgrace of the nation, it must be said, that we are nothing so ready to obey the commands and follow the example of a good prince, as to be infected with the lascivious practices of a bad one.

As the author of *The Poor Man's Plea* pointed out, there seemed to be one law for the rich and another for the poor:

> These are all cobweb laws, in which the small flies are catch'd, and the great ones break through. My Lord Mayor has whipt about the poor beggars, and a few scandalous whores have been sent to the house of correction; some alehouse-keepers and vintners have been fin'd for drawing drink on the Sabbath day; but all this falls upon us of the mob, the poor plebeii, as if all vice lay among us; for we don't find the rich drunkard carried before my Lord Mayor, nor a swearing lewd merchant punish'd. The man with a gold ring and gay cloaths, may swear before the Justice, or at the Justice; may reel home through the open streets, and no man take any notice of it; but if a poor man gets drunk, or swears an oath, he must to the stocks without remedy.

The informers had gone to work with a will, hunting down their prey and applying for warrants to be signed by magistrates and served on the offenders by the constables, who might be zealous in their duty or open to bribes. No longer would the town ring with obscenities, with shameless hussies brawling in public places and insulting each other with defamatory remarks like: 'You are a whore and a hott salt arse bitch and such private whores as you spoyle the common whores trade.' The streets would be cleared of such idle, lewd and disorderly creatures. Mary Dickenson was one of those committed to Bridewell, 'charged on oath for being a lewd woman and for being picked up by a gentleman in the street late last night and [being] one that can give no good account of herself or her lawful way of living and hath no legal settlement but is a common vagrant'.

By 1699 the society was able to boast:

> Some thousands of lewd persons have been imprisoned, fined and whipt; so that the Tower-End of the town, and many of our streets, have been much purged of that pestilent generation of night walkers that used to infest them ... forty or fifty of them having been sent in a week to Bridewell, where they have of late received such discipline, that a considerable number of them have chose rather to be transported to our plantations, to work there for an honest subsistence.

A Black Roll,

Containing the real (or reputed) Names and Crimes of several *Hundred* Persons that have been Prosecuted by the *Society* , this last Year, for *Whoring*, *Drunkenness*, *Thefts*, *Sabbath-breaking*, &c. as Delivered unto Them by their *Clerk* : And been published for the satisfaction of many who have been desirous to know what progress we have made in this *Reformation of Manners*.

Some of these Persons have kept Bawdy-Houses ; some of whom have been Indicted and some Fined.

Mary Adams	Mary Smith	Sarah Moor	William Harper
Mary Arrundell	Rebecca Trimmer	Samuell Parker	John & Elizabeth Hedges
Sasah Allin	Mary Thorogood	John & Mary Parker	May Hill
Mary Abbitt	Jane Winchcomb	Mary Quarles	Ann Holbrook
Mary Anderson	Sarah Whitaker	Elizabeth Raice	Dorothy Howes
Jane Armstrong	Mary Wilden	John & Sarah Rigway	Catherine Flower
Elizabeth Avean	Elizabeth Ealy	Alice Sprinkfield	Elizabeth Johnson
James and Sarah Ayres	Thomas Bowater	Susanna Stanley	Sarah Keath
Elizabeth Ealy	Tho. and Sarah Burton	Sarah Scoot	Elizabeth Leel
Elizabeth Earle	Elizabeth Brown	Margaret Seale	Elizabeth Michel
Margaret Eaten	Jane Brickstock	Sarah Thompson	Tho. and Jane Pettit
Mary Evnall	Henry Body	Richard and Mary Thomas	Elizabeth Purtree
Amey Eliot	Mirtha Blefford	Alice Wilson	Ann Raye
Sarah Edwards	Elizabeth Bushell	Elizabeth Wheler	Temperance Reed
Alice Jones	Ann Bradbery	Hannah Ware	Mary Reves
Christian King	Ann Brewrick	John and Eliz. Hedger	William and Eliz. Smith
Mary Kirk	Mary Bone	Margaret Tillard	Susanna Stuobs
Wm. & Eliz. Moolularum	Mary Banfield	George Codd	Millicent Still
Elizabeth Oliver	Joan Horsnaile	Bridget Cotton	Mary Swan
Hannah Pannel	Mary Hughes	Elizabeth Chettham	Elizabeth Watts
Mary Main	Mary Harrisson	Mary Cole	Mary Vincent
Joan Reffe	Dorothy Howell	Mary Copinger	Ann Watte
William Remnant	Elizabeth Faugh	Mary Chetham	Elizabeth White
Ann Semer	Elizabeth Jones	Ann Chandler	Mary White
Charity Squish	Elizabeth King	John and Ann Coleman	John and Mary Pannell
Elizabeth Shift	Susanna Lewis	Mary Dawson	

And some Cured, Viz.

Dorithy Furlon	John Hix Alias Hurst	Mary Moor	Elizabeth Topta
John and Judith Frost	Many Harris	Mary Palmer	Elizabeth Taylor
Mary Fairfax	Mary Hall	Ann Mack	Dorothy Williams
Thomas & Alice Gibbons	John and Mary Hind	Alice Randoll	Elizabeth Williams
William Groves	Geo. and Mary Harrel	Sarah Rose	Elizabeth Whores
Sarah Gorry	Mary Jones	Mary Randford	Ann Winchcomb
Mary Gayrish	Peter & Elizabeth King	Elizabeth Star	James Delasoy
Mary Garret	Mary Knight	Susan Spritgfield	
John Durnbit	John & Elizabeth Long	Arrundel Turner	

Night

In seeking to clean up the streets, the Society for the Reformation of Manners persecuted many women driven to prostitution by poverty while ignoring the reprobates in high society (*Guildhall Library, Corporation of London*)

Night Walkers and Plyers in Bawdy-Houses, all or most of whom have been Whipt in *Bridewell* this Year.

Elizabeth Bates
Elizabeth Biſſel
Elizabeth Brown
Lidia Buckler
Martha Bolt
Mary Carr
Mary Carroll
Jane Deſow
Suſanna Edwards
Elizabeth Elliot
Dorothy Flander
Ann Goulding
Elizabeth Harris
Sarah Hilliard
Margaret Heiger
Elizabeth Hedger
Elizabeth Heath
Ann Kettle
Mary Kempe
Katherine Lewis
Elizabeth Mills
Jane Peters
Ann Preſton
Ann Palmer
Elizabeth Sammon
Mary Turner
Martha Tucker
Ann Vickar
Catherine Chilver
Hannah Ribbey
Mary White
Elizabeth Thome
Hannah Powell
Elizabeth Lee
Mary Madſon
Jane Glover
Mary Jenkins
Suſanna Tates
Jane Bayley
Ann Bonuſs

Mary Bennet
Mary Baker
Katherine Dodd
Mary Dupper
Martha Davis
Mercy Dickenſon
Jane Gloves
Elizabeth Green
Elizabeth Ginney
Ann Harreſs
Dorothy Hall
Martha Hariſon
Hannah Jackson
Alice Jones
Martha Morgan
Elizabeth Meſſenger
Ann Pearce
Elizabeth Partre
Elizabeth Poor
Ann Sheldrick
Elizabath Smith
Sarah Slaughter
Mary Tanner
Judith Trumbold
Mary Truelove
Sarah Varrey
Suſadna Wilſon
Mary Weſt
Mary Osborne
Frances Haughting
Frances Palmes
Patience Webbes
Mary Jeffreys
Elizabeth Prince
Alice Springfield
—— Phendal
Mary Gibbs Alice Gibbs
—— Stanly
Mary Peach
Cib l Godwin

Elizabeth Bird
Mary Haughton
Alias Haughtry
Thomes Newton
John Stow
Ann Green
Sarah Moon
Alias Thompſon
Mary Downing
Katherine Lewis
Wid. Wing
Tho. Gibbon
Ann Morris
Alias Haber
John Lockyer
Edward Newby
—— Wynn
Margaret Tylard
Mary Kinde
Mrs Oram
Mary Clark
—— Gatton
Mary Raughby
Alias Haughton
Alice Gobbons
William Monday
George Peter
Katherine Moor
Ann Worball
Mary Long
Mary Summers
Ann Worrel
Iſabel Perry
Alice Springfield
Hugh Wilkinſou
Lucy Michel
Mrs. Arran
Mary Tanner
Mary D.
George Peacock

Samuel Jones
Ann Jones
Ann Newman
Elizabeth Pierce
Sarah Jefferis
Hugh Wilkinſon
Ann Londay
Jobe Laud
Margaret Smith
Hanna Lewis.
Ann Reed

January 161⅘
Sarah Ellis
Wm. Griffeth
Thomas Bowater
Ann Worrel
Martha Flitcher
Mary White
Johanna Playſhad
Mary Osbourne
    Rainſborow
Mary Kempe
Mary Stevens
Mary Baker
Mary Alderman
Alice Fendal
Mary Clark
Ann Slaughter
Elizabeth Gouge
Mary Reed
Rebecca Bowman
Lucy Baſly
Martha Griffen
Rebecca Foſter
Jane Bluit
Elizabeth Prince
Sarah Cook
Sarah Lacy

F I N I S.

But Bridewell, it was argued, was not the answer. The more successful whores were immediately released on posting of bail with very little interruption to business. Those too poor to raise bail were only made poorer, so that they were 'under a greater necessity than ever of continuing whores'. Ned Ward visited the bridewell by the Fleet behind Bride Lane – there were others in Westminster and Clerkenwell – and describes one of the scenes Londoners loved best: 'A grave gentleman whose awful looks bespoke him some honourable citizen, was mounted in the judgement seat, armed with a hammer, like a 'Change broker at Lloyd's Coffee House, and a woman under the lash was in the next room, where folding doors were opened so that the whole court might see the punishment inflicted. At last went down the hammer and the scourging ceased.'

But the thirst for punishment was not yet assuaged: 'Another accusation being then delivered by a flat-cap against a poor wretch, who had no friend to speak in her behalf, proclamation was made, viz.: "All you who are willing E—-th T—ll should have present punishment, pray hold up your hands."' The self-righteous audience gleefully assented. The woman was stripped to the waist – her nakedness exposed to the leers of the men and boys 'as if it were designed rather to feast the eyes of the spectators than to correct vice, or reform manners' – before turning her white back to the court to be shredded and torn by the lash.

As for the women committed to Bridewell to beat hemp and pick oakum until their fingers bled, Ned Ward describes a visit to their apartment:

> We followed our noses and walked up to take a view of these ladies, who we found were shut up as close as nuns. But like so many slaves they were under the care and direction of an overseer, who walked about with a very flexible weapon of offence, to correct such hempen journey-women as were unhappily troubled with the spirit of idleness. They smelt as frowzily as so many goats in a Welsh gentleman's stable ... They were all cheerful over their shameful drudgery, notwithstanding their miserable circumstances. Some seemed so very young that I thought it exceeding strange they should know sin well enough to bring them so early into a state of misery. Others were so old that one would think the dread of the grave, and thoughts of futurity were sufficient to reclaim 'em from all vice, had they been trained up

never so wickedly. Some between them both were in the meridian of their years, and were very pretty, but seemed so very lewd that, Messalina-like, they might be tired, but never satisfied.

Some streetwalkers used the decoy of carrying something as if on an innocent errand. Those who plied their trade among the lawyers at the Temple had the best cover, as Ned Ward explains:

These are ladies that come to receive fees, instead of giving any. They have now extraordinary business upon their hands, with many of the young lawyers, though nothing to do with the Law; for you must know, these are nymphs of delight, who only carry papers in their hands for a blind. They are such considerable dealers, that they can afford to give credit for a whole vacation, and now in term-time, they are industrious in picking up their debts. You are now, I assure you, in one of the greatest places in town for dealing in that sort of commodity; for most ladies who, for want of fortunes, despair of husbands, and are willing to give themselves up to love, without waiting for matrimony, come hither to be truly qualified for their mercenary undertaking. By the time any condescending nymph has a month's conversation with the airy blades of this honourable society, she will doubtless find herself as well fitted for the employment, as if she had had a twelvemonth's education, under the most experienced bawd in Christendom; and if you ever chance to meet with any of the trading madams, and ask her who was her first lover it's ten to one but her answer will be *A Gentleman of the Temple.*

The vigilantes were determined to stamp out sex in public places and the playhouses were an obvious target. These dens of iniquity encouraged 'delight in idleness, excessive vanity, revelling, luxury, wantonness, lasciviousness, whoredoms'. The long association between prostitution and the stage made the playhouse a favourite haunt of whores such as Deborah Churchill, who 'appear'd in a very great splendid manner' as she touted for custom. Bawds would send their pimps along, knowing that those who 'did most frequent those places were the surest pillars of the bawdy-house'. Dryden summed up the scene in his *Prologue* to Thomas Southerne's comedy *The Disappointment* in 1700:

> The playhouse is their place of traffick, where
> Nightly they sit to sell their rotten ware
> Tho' done in silence and without a cryer
> Yett he that bids the most is still the buyer!
> For while he nibbles at her am'rous trap
> Shee gets the mony: he gets the clap!

The plays themselves came under fire for their lasciviousness. Jeremy Collier's *A Short View of the Immorality and Profaneness of the English Stage* won many adherents when it castigated Wycherley's *Country Wife* and *The Plain Dealer* and Vanbrugh's *Provoked Wife* for their 'smuttiness of expression ... swearing, profaneness and lewd application of scripture ... abuse of clergy ... making of their top characters libertines and giving them success in their debauchery'.

The Society for the Reformation of Manners was concerned as much with religious revival as with social reform. Large-scale immigration from the provinces, casual and insecure employment and economic hardship created unprecedented social instability with poverty and crime spiralling out of control. Without a police force, such a society lived on a knife-edge between law and disorder. Street prostitution was seen as both a symptom and a cause of London's problems. Far from understanding that many women turned to prostitution as a desperate means of earning a living, the 'moral police' and reformers believed that if they were not indulging in 'lewd and disorderly practices', these idle creatures would be doing a decent day's work.

In *Augusta Triumphans* Daniel Defoe fulminated against insubordinate servants who quit their place on a whim and turned to casual prostitution with all the attendant consequences:

> A girl quits a place, and turns whore; if there is not a bastard to be murder'd, or left to the parish, there is one or more unwary youths drawn in to support her in lewdness and idleness; in order to which, they rob their parents and masters, nay, sometimes any body else, to support their strumpets; so that many thieves owe their ruin and shameful deaths to harlots. Not to mention the communication of loathsome distempers, and innumerable other evils, to which they give birth.

Before long, he warned, 'our streets will swarm with impudent shameless strumpets; the good will be molested; those, prone to evil, will be made yet more wicked, by having temptations thrown in their way.' It is high time 'to clear the streets of nightwalkers, who are grown to such a pitch of impudence, that peace and common decency are manifestly broken in our publick streets'.

In mitigation, the author of *The Night Walker* argued that employment was not always that easy to come by — not only servants but actresses might be laid off after the season when the rich left town — and that it was difficult for a vulnerable woman without means to avoid the determined onslaught of 'bawds and procurers'. One prostitute told him that although she felt uneasy about her occupation, 'poverty, and not knowing otherwise how to subsist, forc'd her to continue in it; that many times, when she endeavoured to get into a good service, she found those who pretended to help her to them, to be nothing but bawds and procurers'. Many women were tricked into prostitution — particularly virgins who were kidnapped and raped — by these predatory creatures who 'made a perfect prey and a sale of them to lascivious fellows, that hired them to do such things'.

Some young women were corrupted by their employers and continued on a downward spiral of prostitution and vice. Deborah Churchill, going to the gallows for killing someone who had insulted her, confessed that 'when she grew up she went to wait on a lady here in town; where in the family she was debauch'd, and taken from thence and kept in great state for two or three years; being in her younger days a very beautiful woman; but being deserted by this gentleman, and her splendour decaying, she took to the town, in which wicked trade of life she continued a long time'.

Whores were corrupting youth, Defoe feared, and leading silly old men astray:

> While we want servants to do our work, those Hundreds [of Drury], as they call 'em, are crowded with numbers of idle impudent sluts, who love sporting more than spinning, and inveigle our youth to their ruin: Nay, many old lechers (beasts as they are) steal from their families, and seek these harlots' lurking holes, to practice their unaccountable schemes of new invented lewdness: Some half hang themselves, others are whipt, some lie under a table and gnaw the bones that are thrown 'em, while others stand slaving among a parcel of drabs at a washing-tub. Strange that the inclination should not die with the power, but

that old fools should make themselves the prey and ridicule of a pack of strumpets!

No one knew better than Mother Whybourn the horrors of venereal disease. After all, it cost her her beauty and a fortune to cure. Perhaps that was why in her will she left 'To His Grace the D— of — a gross of right Dutch c—ms, newly imported from Holland, by M—ez the Jew'. But condoms were not easily available or widely used in London generally. Syphilis was so prevalent that the author of *The Night Walker* suggested that 'instead of saying the French pox ... there is as good reason to call it the English pox, and the London disease ... indeed we come very near appropriating it to ourselves, by calling it in our common proverb the Covent Garden Gout ... it is become an epidemical distemper amongst us'.

There was general concern that men caught venereal disease from consorting with prostitutes and passed it on to their wives and unborn children. A case from the consistory court illustrates the human tragedy. Mary Hill, a servant in a house in Mile End Green, Stepney, attested that she was alerted by her mistress crying, 'What will you murder me?' She ran into the parlour to find her master Isaac Pewsey 'twisting and squeezing his wifes hands over a cane chair'. Sara Pewsey was 'then very bigg with child and near the time of her delivery', but Isaac kicked her 'all the way from the said parlour into the kitchen'. Apparently Isaac had been undergoing a salivation treatment 'by the order of Dr Salmon for the ffoul disease'. Sara had tried to look after him 'yett notwithstanding he would often curse and swear at [her] and call her a bitch, whore ... without any provocation or cause, and [he] did during his salivation, throw a bason of nasty spittle on her ... which stunk so intolerably that [the maid] could hardly come near her to help her off with her cloaths'. Sara had contracted the disease from her husband.

Another woman living in Clerkenwell was similarly afflicted: 'Thomas Ashworth had often had the carnall knowledge of the said Joanna's body and ... he had given her the pox by which she was reduced to so very great weakness that she could not go without crutches.'

Of course, all the costly mercury and salivation treatments in the world could not guarantee a cure for syphilis. Resorting to the bagnios in and about Long Acre for a good sweat was useless. Once places of assignation, many of them were now brothels. Although it was all too common, syphilis was held in opprobrium, a social disgrace. Merciless playwrights could not resist a joke at the expense of the members of the 'no-nose club'.

Many harboured doubts about the effectiveness of the Society for the Reformation of Manners. Some thought it ridiculous, others distasteful. There was something un-English about all this informing. The author of *A Modest Defence of Public Stews* told the 'gentlemen of the Societies for the Reformation of Manners' that 'your endeavours to suppress lewdness, have only served to promote it'. None of these problems occurred in the past, he argued, before Henry VIII closed down the 'public stews' in Southwark. King William would be familiar with the system, since licensed brothels existed in the Dutch Republic. Public stews would be endowed with 'such privileges and immunities' as to discourage 'private whoring' and 'turn the general stream of lewdness into this common channel'. There would be several price tiers ranging from 2s 6d to a guinea and funds would be put aside for 'the maintenance of bastard orphans and superannuated courtezans'. Health checks would be rigorous: 'No woman that has been twice poxed shall ever be readmitted [after a spell in the infirmary]. Note, That three claps shall be reckoned equivalent to one pox.'

When London closed down for the summer, homosexuals were lured into a false sense of security, plying on the Exchange and soliciting in the Covent Garden Piazza in daylight. The 'Mollies houses' or gay clubs used taverns in the Covent Garden area, particularly in Clare Market near Drury Lane. For once, Ned Ward was mildy shocked: 'There are a particular gang of Sodomiticall wretches in town who call themselves Mollies and are so far degenerated from all masculine deportment ... that they rather fancy themselves as women, imitating all the little vanities ... of the female sex ... not omitting the indecencies of lewd women ... to commit these odious bestialities that ought for ever to be without a name!'

Sodomy was considered the vilest of crimes and the punishment was death. Of course, some were not slow to resort to blackmail. George Skelthorp, up before the bench for assault and robbery, knew there was 'a certain publick house about Covent Garden, where ... those Sodomites us'd frequently to meet':

> That he knowing the time when, and the places where some Sodomites were resorting about Covent Garden, he went to stand in their way, and when any of them would (as they often did) carry him to a by-place thereabouts to commit their foul acts with him, he went with them; and then he taking hold of them,

threaten'd them, that he would presently bring them before a Justice, unless they gave him satisfaction. By which means he got a great deal of money at several times, of such persons; who rather than suffer themselves to be exposed gave him either money, rings, or watches, or what else they had about them.

London in the early eighteenth century was if anything more licentious than in the 1690s when the Society for the Reformation of Manners got into its stride. Prostitution and crime were well and truly in bed together. Social degradation seemed complete. Far from reforming morals, the society's legacy might have been to accentuate a strain of prudery in English society, to encourage a disgust with bodily functions and to drive sex underground.

CHAPTER SIXTEEN

Crime and Punishment

*Eight times a year London's church bells were rung muffled to
alert the city it was time for a hanging match ... an eagerly
awaited and unofficial public holiday*

IT IS 20 JANUARY 1700 AND the court has convened at the Sessions
House in the Old Bailey, a narrow street running north from Ludgate
Hill. A stench fills the covered outdoor court, as the prisoners are
brought up from the hold. The youngest of the crew has had to stump up
12d to buy his fellows' Dutch courage, but neither the liquor on their
breath nor the pungent nosegays lining the bench can disguise the smell or
ward off the prisoners' gaol-fever. It is a motley crew. Thieves,
highwaymen, counterfeiters and killers, although the distinctions are moot
in a society where taking property is as grave as taking a life, and both
warrant the death penalty. Today they will answer to the law for their
crimes, but justice in the London of 1700 makes for bizarre reading. The
correspondent of the *Post Man* is here to capture it for an avid readership.

The King's Justice pronounces sentence, in ascending order of severity.
In accordance with King William's new laws, some will be burned on the
hand; thirteen are to be branded immediately on the left cheek, the large
'T' proclaiming a thief. Those lucky enough to have 13d on them can
ensure that the branding iron is at least dipped in cold water, to reduce
the scorching of the flesh. Metal skullcaps are used to keep the head
steady during the branding. As the prisoners' skin blackens and smokes
and their shrieks fade into agonised groans, the brander turns to the judge
and declares with professional pride, 'A fair mark, my lord!'

Those condemned later in the list are less indulged. Seven men and four
women are sentenced to death. A woman up for the common practice of
clipping and counterfeiting the currency, a capital offence, 'pleads her
belly', claiming pregnancy as a ruse to buy time. She knows that the
matrons employed by the court to check out her claim will be open to

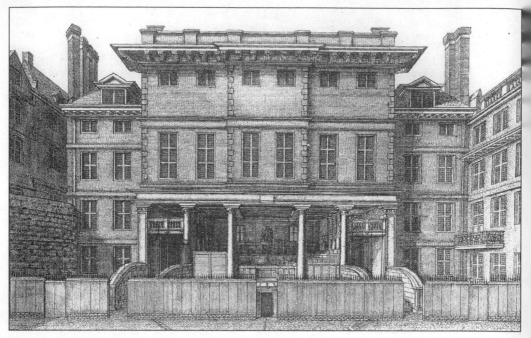

Prisoners were tried in an outdoor courtroom in a vain attempt to ward off the typhus fever they brought in their wake (*Guildhall Library, Corporation of London*)

bribes, she knows too that the birth of the baby guarantees the death of the mother: and eventually she will be burned alive at St Bartholomew's in Smithfield. A highwayman opts for transportation, then changes his mind and pleads benefit of clergy, that strange legacy of the ecclesiastical courts whereby any man who can read the words of the 51st Psalm, the so-called 'Neck Verse', can escape the full weight of the law. The prison chaplain moves behind him, perhaps whispering into the prisoner's ear the words that will save his neck – for a small fee. Money talks in this courtroom. 'Does he read?' asks the judge in Latin. 'He reads like a cleric,' pronounces the chaplain. And like a cleric, he is merely burned in the cheek.

The lucky ones who escape the noose will probably see the courtroom again. Many of the criminal fraternity prepare for this eventuality by taking another name, so as to make their return to court seem like a first appearance. As the eighteenth century dawns, the steady growth of crime brings a new plethora of laws on to the statute books each year. John Locke's philosophy that 'Government has no other end but the preservation of property' is taken literally by the governing class. Between the 1680s and the 1720s the number of offences punishable by death rises from about eighty to over 350; indeed, there are so many that no one can be absolutely sure what you can or cannot be hanged for.

It is worth stating, however, that executions do not keep pace with convictions; a few hangings inculcate fear, too many will harden or repel a populace that has to assent, in some measure at least, to the rule of property. 'Thou instrument of fate and law,' Defoe writes of Tyburn, 'Contriv'd to punish some, and keep the rest in awe.' The use of benevolent pardons and the threat of transportation are other weapons of law enforcement in a society without a police force or large standing army. Even for the most minor offences, the law brands those it condemns, and the telltale wounds make honest employment impossible. Branded as criminals, these men and women become criminals. It is a near-certainty that they will reoffend.

For those condemned, their last days will be spent preparing for death amidst the noise, overcrowding, filth and stink of the condemned hold of Newgate Gaol next door. To the anonymous author of *The History of the Press Yard*, the hold was 'a noisome vault underground' with boarded places 'whereupon you may repose your self if your nose will suffer you to rest, from the stench that diffuses its noisome particles of bad air from every corner'. Chains and iron staples were attached to the cockroach-strewn floor to 'bring those to a due submission that are stubborn and unruly'. Darkness could be escaped 'only by the help of a candle, which you must pay through the nose for'. Those with money might secure themselves a cell away from the others, but real privacy could not be bought. Even as the condemned unburdened themselves to the prison chaplain, prisoners and visitors pressed their ears to the grille to catch their words.

Prisoners entering Newgate for the first time might have been forgiven for thinking they had entered hell itself. There were about 150 prisons in London, but Newgate was the most notorious. Newgate was described by a contemporary as 'a dismal prison ... a place of calamity ... a habitation of misery, a confused chaos ... a bottomless pit of violence'. New prisoners were first struck by the uproar, the raucous noise of hundreds of inmates crowded together with the sounds of fetters scraping across stone floors. Then there was the noxious stink of unwashed bodies mixed with the ubiquitous fug of tobacco smoke in the ill-ventilated surroundings.

While their senses reeled, they were grabbed by the gaolers and frisked, undergoing what prison jargon described as 'Making the Black Dog Walk'. 'Rhino', cash, was the lifeblood of the place. In common with all office-holders of the time, the keeper had to buy his position – it had cost the princely sum of £5,000 and he was bound to recoup it from the prisoners – so that no prisoner could enter without first paying 'garnish'. Those who resisted would be stripped of all their possessions and thrown into a stinking cesspit. Water being in short supply, the new prisoners' degradation was instant and their discomfort likely to linger for some time.

An official investigation into conditions elicited:

> We do find that the prisoners in the common side of the prison of Newgate pretend to demand money of every new prisoner that comes in, under the notion of garnish money, which was formerly but 9s and is now advanced to 17s ... that if any prisoner comes in and has not wherewith to pay the garnish money he or she is presently conveyed into a place they call Tangier, and there stript, beaten, and abused in a very violent manner.

Prisoners were housed according to their ability to pay. Superior accommodation was available in the Keeper's House overlooking the Press Yard and it was among the most expensive in London. The author of *The History of the Press Yard* paid a deposit of 20 guineas, 11s a week rent and a further 10s a week for furniture. A bed with clean sheets was available for another 5s. He might also hire a cleaning woman for 1s a week, a whore for 1s a night and pay the gaoler 6d to allow a friend to visit. Newspapers could be ordered. However, the majority of prisoners were not so fortunate. They resided on either the master side or the common side, where in the lower ward the highwayman John Hall described them as lying 'upon ragged blankets, amidst unutterable filth ... the lice crackling under their feet'. Since everyone was lice-ridden Newgate cant included the expression 'Squeeze the chats', that is, kill the lice. Typhus was so prevalent that only one in four prisoners actually survived long enough to make the journey to Tyburn.

And the expense of Newgate did not end with garnish. Prisoners who could not afford to have food brought in from the outside depended on the meagre supplies granted by the authorities and charitable donations, but even then the cook demanded 3d to cook it, so that it had to be eaten raw or cold. The prison meal was served mid afternoon. One of the solaces of the prisoners was drink and Newgate had its own bar, which charged rip-off prices. It was far cheaper to have drink and tobacco brought in by friends or, as certain women prisoners did, beg for the money so as to pay the victualler 'who fetch their drink in tubs every brewing day'.

Even when they had served their sentence, prisoners could not leave without paying a departure fee. Some debtors languished for years, unable to scrape together the necessary cash and subsisting 'on the rats and mice they have catched', and if they died in gaol, the body would lie rotting in its cell until relatives scraped enough money together to pay keeper and turnkeys for its release. A prisoner of state such as Major Bernardi spent more than forty years in Newgate, where he married a second time and brought up ten children. It was not unusual to find children and pets in this prison.

Prostitution was rife. In 1700 the Lord Mayor and Aldermen were appalled to discover that William Robinson, the deputy keeper, was busy transforming the gaol into a brothel, permitting 'lewd and common strumpets ... to constantly lay there all night'. It was said that 'he locked up a whore with one Peter Flower, alias Bennett, alias French Peter, and she often lay with him, even when he was under sentence'. Not to miss a trick when it came to making money out of his office, he charged 6d to allow the male prisoners to enter women's cells. Many of the female prisoners competed with prostitutes brought in from outside to have sex with male prisoners. Pregnancy would buy a stay of execution.

If a Newgate baby survived, it would be passed on to the workhouse or parish for its upbringing. Defoe's heroine Moll Flanders was such a child, though her mother was transported rather than executed. The irony of her situation, born in Newgate and ending her days there, was reflected in the real lives of many criminals. The highwayman Tom Merryman's mother was a 'common prostitute' imprisoned in Newgate for theft and robbery, who pleaded her belly and was later executed, leaving her son to the care of the parish.

In *An Enquiry into the Causes of the Frequent Executions at Tyburn*, Bernard de Mandeville deplored the depravity of Newgate:

> It is an encouragement to vice, that the most dissolute of both sexes, and generally young people too, should live promiscuously in the same place, and have access to one another. For the rest, the licentiousness of the place is abominable, and there are no

Newgate provided some of the most expensive board and lodgings in London and debtors were reduced to eating rats and mice (*Guildhall Library, Corporation of London*)

low jests so filthy, no maxims so destructive to good manners, no expressions so vile and prophane, but what are utter'd there with applause, and repeated with impunity.

It was easy to get swept up and arrested in the London of 1700. Once in the prison system awaiting trial, prisoners inevitably became part of the criminal underworld. The author of *Hanging Not Punishment Enough* deplored the fact that prisons 'are now known to be the sanctuaries of villains, from whence their emissaries are dispatch'd, and a regular and settled correspondence is said to be fix'd and carried, through the whole fraternity of rogues in England'.

Many of the prisoners, especially the old hands, spent 'their most serious hours ... in mock tryals, and instructing one another in cross questions, to confound witnesses'. *The Memoirs of the Right Villanous John Hall, The Late Famous and Notorious Robber* depicts a vivid picture of Newgate life:

> In the boozing ken ... the students, instead of holding disputes in philosophy and mathematicks, run altogether upon law; for such as are committed for house-breaking, swear stoutly they cannot be cast for burglary, because the fact was done in the day-time; such as are committed for stealing a horse-cloth, or coachman's cloak, swear they cannot be cast for felony and robbery, because the coach was standing still, not stopp'd; and such as steal before a man's face, swear they value not their adversary, because they are out of the reach of the new act against private stealing. Thus with an unparallell'd impudence every brazen'd face malefactor is harden'd in his sin, because the law cannot touch his life.

In these grim surroundings torture as such did not exist, which led foreign visitors to think the English were very advanced and lenient. But prisoners who refused to plead in court (the 'Not Guilty' plea came in later, and meanwhile a prisoner who stood mute could not be tried without his consent) underwent another sort of trial known as *peine forte et dure*. Guy Miege in *The New State of England* explains that the prisoner was sent back to the prison:

> there to be laid in some low dark room, all naked but his privy members; his back upon the bare ground, his arms and legs

stretched with cords, fastened to the several quarters of the room, and as much irons and stone laid upon his body as he can well bear. The next day he is allowed but three morsels of barley-bread, without drink; and the day after as much ... water, and that without any bread. And this is to be his diet, till he die.

As a last resort, his friends might add their own weight to the load to ensure a speedy death. By keeping silence, such prisoners could not be found guilty and so could 'save their estates for their children'.

Transportation to the colonies in North America or the West Indies was considered a fate worse than death. In the late 1690s the prisons were full of women arrested on coining and clipping charges, but pardoned from the death sentence on condition of transportation. Although the West Indian islands might be persuaded to take male convicts – who would be useful in defence or out in the plantation fields – women were not wanted. Immigration and settlement policy had largely been left to the colonies themselves, and 'persons of bad character were not wanted in Jamaica'. While the wrangling continued, some of those concerned decided to take matters into their own hands. In July 1700 the *London Post* recorded: 'That night about 12 of the clock, several women who lye under sentence of transportation in Newgate, attempted to make their escape from the top of the prison, by a rope down into a neighbour's leads, but were discover'd; and two of them who had got down were again seized and recommitted.' Eventually the Leeward Islands agreed to take fifty of the women, and William III's exasperated government promised to pay £8 a head to get rid of them.

It was almost certainly a myth that a gallows wedding might save the life of a criminal. However, this lingering notion could have prompted the action of a group of women – symbolically wearing white – as reported by the press in July1700: 'On Tuesday last 12 women all in white went in a body to the Lords of the Admiralty, to beg the life of Griffin, one of the pirates that are to be executed tomorrow, but their lordships could give them no great comfort; and this day 19 went to the Lords Justices upon the same errands, but could obtain nothing.'

Visitors travelling to and from the capital had to run the gauntlet of the highwaymen. Newspapers, diaries and correspondence regaled their readers with the latest incidents. Sir John Verney wrote to a friend:

Six forraigners goeing for France were robb'd in the Dover stage coach at Shooters Hill, & lost about 300 pound, & one of them kill'd by the rogues who gott off with the prize. The gentln returned to London with their dead comrade. Severall other robberies have been lately committed on the roads about this towne, soe that it is very dangerous travelling at present. On Sat. on Hounslow Heath 3 highwaymen robbed 3 chariots and servants as they returned from the Wells at Richmond. The D. of Northumberland rob'd. Lord Osultstone was on his coachbox, his man in the coach snapt a blunderbuss but it went not off, soe the rogues kill'd one of my lord's horses and rob'd him too ... & about 20 persons as they dropt into their hands.

Nor was it much safer in the capital itself, as Nancy Nicholas confided to Sir John Verney:

I could not be well enough all last week to wright to my dear cosen ... we have at London most dismall robeing almost every night and abought Hid Park cornor, & last weeke a gentilman & two ladys coming from Chelsy turning the cornor of St Jeamses Park had six naked swords thrust into the coch in severall places att a time.

No one could have failed to notice that the severity of the law for offences against property was having little effect in stemming the rising tide of crime. As César de Saussure observed: 'Executions are frequent in London ... notwithstanding this, there are in this country a surprising number of robbers. They may be classed in three divisions – highwaymen, foot pads and pickpockets, all very audacious and bold.'

In a nation intent on the expansion of commerce through an improved road system and the use of inland bills of exchange, there was growing impatience with the 'frequent interruption given to trade and business, by robbing of packets, and intercepting letters of correspondence and advice; to say nothing of the insecurity of sending Exchequer and bank-bills by the publick conveyances'. The author of *Hanging Not Punishment Enough* suggested that 'if some remedy be not found to stop this growing evil, we shall shortly not dare to travel in England.'

He admitted that the economic dislocations following the war with France were partly responsible, the increase of highwaymen being attributed to 'the great numbers of soldiers, without employment and plunder, and in poor pitiful pay':

> that after so many thousands of soldiers disbanded, and mariners discharged, many of them are driven upon necessity, and having been used to an idle way of living, care not to work, and many (I fear) cannot, if they would. Besides, the poor are exceedingly numerous ... lewd women abound, to the great scandal of good people, and ... they are very often the chief causes, that these men murther, plunder, rob and steal.

Nevertheless, he said, 'they have ruined several, and have brought fear on almost all. They have wounded and maimed divers, and have left many bound and naked in cold weather, to the hazard, and often the loss of their lives.' They were now robbing with 'that impudence, assurance, and leisure, as if they did it legally and with commission; and as if they came not to steal and rifle, but rather by authority to seize and distrain'.

The myth of the dashing highwayman had already been born. According to César de Saussure: 'With one hand he will present a pistol, with the other his hat, asking the unfortunate passengers most politely for their purses or their lives. I have been told that some highwaymen are quite polite and generous, begging to be excused for being forced to rob, and leaving passengers the wherewithal to continue their journey. All highwaymen that are caught are hanged without mercy.'

When he was caught and hanged, the legendary highwayman Claude Du Vall's torch-led funeral had been attended by hundreds of weeping women. His epitaph at St Paul's Covent Garden read:

> Here lies Du Vall: Reader, if Male thou art,
> Look to thy Purse; if female, to thy Heart.
> Much Havock he has made of both; for all
> Men he made stand, and women he made fall.
> The second Conqueror of the Norman race
> Knights to his Arms did yield, and Ladies to his face.
> Old Tyburn's Glory, England's illustrious thief,
> Du Vall, the ladies' Joy, Du Vall the ladies' grief.

De Saussure noted a curious practice that explains the term 'daylight robbery': 'If a person is robbed of a considerable sum in the daytime and on the high road, and if he declares the theft to the sheriff of the county before the sun sets, and can prove that the sum has been taken from him in such and such a place, the county in which he has been robbed is obliged to refund him the sum.'

In London itself footpads roamed the ill-lit streets. It was said that no man might dine out unless armed to the teeth with swords, pistols, muskets and blunderbusses. Link-boys employed to light the way could not always be trusted: a 'moon curser' led the unwary right into the path of those who would rob them. De Saussure warned that should footpads 'meet any well-dressed person at night in some unfrequented spot, they will collar him, put the muzzle of a pistol to his throat, and threaten to kill him if he makes the slightest movement or calls for help'. It was up to the victims themselves to pursue them and bring them to justice, often through a notice offering a reward in the press:

> Whereas, on yesterday morning between eight and nine a clock in the morning, three footpads between Islington and Holloway, committed a robbery on the body of one Thomas Waller, and took from him the sum of three and twenty shillings in silver, one of the said footpads, being a tall black man with straight hair, long visaged, and a large red nose, and full of pimples about the mouth, and a small blew spot on the bottom of his chin; whoever secures him, and gives notice to the said Mr Waller (so as he may be had before a Justice of Peace) shall have 2 guineas reward, and reasonable charges.

Sometimes the press reported footpads taking on an extraordinary disguise: 'On Sunday and Monday night 4 footpads disguised in women's apparel, robbed several persons between Pancras and Highgate, but I hear that 2 of them are since seized and committed.'

Women themselves were the perpetrators of muggings. The Sessions Papers record that 'Elizabeth Brown, alias Latham, was tried for robbing one Alice Haman in the Strand, making an assault upon her, taking away a silver medal value 10s and 5s in money. It was declared against her, that she met the prosecutor in the street, and set upon her in company with some other women ... she was lookt upon as an idle housewife, so she was found guilty.'

The forces of law and order in London were weak since there was no central authority. There was no police force as such. Policing was seen as un-English; in neighbouring France it was an instrument of royal tyranny. Policing in London then was sporadic and piecemeal. There were the King's Messengers, responsible directly to the Privy Council. Their brief was treason and other political matters. As coining and counterfeiting were treasonable offences, they were kept busy. The Court of Aldermen of the City employed the City Marshals to deal with vagrants. They had power to execute warrants of arrest over the counties surrounding London. Their work was duplicated to some extent at parish level by the constables, beadles and watch, although they were greatly restricted in their powers of arrest. Constables were unpaid and elected annually from rotas of citizens; in practice, citizens paid deputies to do the job on their behalf and some became regulars. Watchmen earned only 6d a night for a very dangerous job.

Much of the onus for police work fell on private citizens, who formed neighbourhood watch groups in their localities, did their own sleuthing and set out to catch the criminals. The *London Post* reported:

> I am told the gentlemen of Hackney being desirous to clear the roads leading to that place of highwaymen, and foot-pads, have, since the promised gratuity for apprehending of any of those rogues, hired a lusty porter to carry some goods in the duskish, between London and that place, on purpose to see if he should be set upon; and at the same time ordered 3 or 4 lusty fellows to follow him at some distance, in order to assist him if attacked; which had so good effect, that the porter, being stopt by 3 foot-pads, he, after throwing his burden upon the ground, made his party good with them, till the others came to his assistance, and took them all 3 prisoners, who are since committed to prison.

As society grew richer and crime increased, the criminal underworld produced a thriving counter-culture with its own codes and language. Moll Raby specialised in the 'buttock and twang'. She would pick up 'a cull, cully or spark' in an alehouse and take him to some dark alley. While 'the decoyed fool is groping her with his breeches down, she picks his fob or pocket of his watch or money. And giving a sort of Hem! as a signal she has succeeded in her design, then the fellow with whom she keeps company, blundering up in the dark, he knocks down the gallant and carries off the prize.' Moll Raby was up to all sorts of tricks, such as being a 'night sneak' and burgling a house in Downing Street, lying under the bed all the time the family was at supper. Once she removed a pearl necklace from a sleeping woman and swallowed it, then innocently offered to be searched.

Moll Hawkins practised the 'question lay', dressing up as a milliner's or sempstress's apprentice and arriving at the homes of 'persons of quality' on the pretext that 'she had brought something for her ladyship'. While the maid went to fetch the mistress, Moll robbed the house and made her getaway. Visiting the house of Lady Arabella Howard in Soho Square with gloves and fans, she made off with £50 worth of plate from the parlour.

Nan Holland went in for 'service lay', hiring herself out as a servant and then robbing the household. Although she was young, Nan could 'wheedle most cunningly, lie confoundedly, swear desperately, pick a pocket dextorously, dissemble undiscernibly, drink and smoke ever-lastingly, whore insatiably and brazen out all her actions impudently'.

César de Saussure noted that 'pickpockets are legion, with extra-ordinary dexterity they will steal handkerchiefs, snuff-boxes, watches — in short, anything they can find in your pockets'. Thieves might 'bite the bill from the cull': take the sword from a gentleman's side as he turned the corner. They might take 'lobs' from behind 'rattlers': remove a trunk or box from a moving coach. They might 'nim the nab': steal a man's hat off his head and run away with it. They might be 'clouters': removing handkerchiefs out of people's pockets; or 'files': diving into pockets for money or watches. They were not above 'kid lay': robbing a child.

Burglary had reached epidemic proportions. To 'mill a ken' was to rob a house. Burglars might 'mill the gig with a betty': break open the door with an iron crow; or 'mill the glaze': break open the window. They might opt for 'faggot and stall': gag all the occupants while they made away with the goods. Shops were a magnet for thieves, despite the fact that a new Shoplifting Act made stealing goods worth 5s or more from a shop a capital felony. Thieves might employ a 'drag' — a hook fastened to the end of a stick — to drag goods out of the shop window on a dark evening.

Stolen goods might find their way to a 'fencing cully', a broker or

319

receiver. William and Mary's policy was to set a thief to catch a thief. By offering rewards for the capture of thieves, they encouraged thieves to inform on each other and broke up gangs. Receivers of stolen goods became accessories after the fact, liable to branding, whipping or transportation for seven years. Paradoxically, this created the 'thief-takers', men such as Jonathan Wild who were 'double-crossers', pretending to enforce the law while in fact profiting from criminal activities. Their army of professional informers had power of life and death over the thieves who came into their orbit.

For those Newgate inmates under sentence of death, the squalor of the condemned hold finally gave way to the glory of execution day. For many, it was a point of proud principle to affect an air of gallant indifference to their fate. They played a central role in the state's execution drama, in those rituals of sacrifice and renewal that formed part of the contract between governors and governed. Far from feeling the shame and degradation that was intended, many drew courage from their moment of fame, even gloried in their public notoriety. They faced death with bravado and intended to aquit themselves well in the role allotted to them.

Bravado did not come cheap. Cash had to be found for this grand exit, and Newgate was notoriously efficient at stripping its inmates of their possessions. But the crowds must not be disappointed. Among a people used to lavishing a large proportion of their wealth on appearance, and for whom the symbolism of dress and colour had meaning, it was customary to dress gaily for the gallows. There were coffins to be bartered for and new clothes to be ordered.

Most of the condemned were young and single, textbook examples of the flotsam lured to London with dreams of gold-paved streets and then cast into the capital's underworld. This was their first and only big day. Since their lives were to be cut off so abruptly, they chose to go to their death dressed as if to their wedding. Or, as the notorious robber John Hall puts it in his memoir, 'so that one would take them for bridegrooms going to espouse old Mrs Tyburn'. Even more affluent offenders followed the tradition. Lord Ferrers wore his white satin wedding suit when he was executed for shooting his steward. At least one gentleman highwayman had his tailor hard at work right up to the eve of execution. Some of a more practical bent, however, went to the gallows wearing their shrouds.

The Frenchman Henri Misson was such a keen observer of English customs he could hardly be expected to ignore a public hanging:

> He that is to be hanged or otherwise executed first takes care to get himself shaved and handsomely dressed, wither in mourning, or in the dress of a bridegroom. This done, he sets his friends at work to get him leave to be buried, and to carry his coffin with him, which is easily obtained. When his suit of clothes, or night-gown, his gloves, hat, perriwig, nosegay, coffin, flannel dress for his corpse, and all those things are bought and prepared, the main point is taken care of, his mind is at peace and then he thinks of his conscience.

The magistrate and novelist Henry Fielding, one of the first to question the efficacy of public hanging, felt that this attention to dress served only to glamorise the criminal. He proposed that the condemned should be assigned 'a particular habit (black the most proper colour) ... at least at their executions; and that they might not be suffered to make their exits in gay clothes ... but rather as becomes those, who are just going to undergo the curse of the law.'

The public wanted their villains glamorous, and – with that peculiarly English tendency to regard criminals as heroic rebels against authority, free men in an exploitative, oppressive society – there was a huge audience that extended beyond the crowds at Tyburn. The adventures of highwaymen, pirates and other outlaws fired the popular imagination, and by 1700 a publishing industry had realised that there was an avid and lucrative readership for their memoirs. Competition to print them was fierce, and started right at the Old Bailey Sessions. Beat Louis de Muralt commented ironically: 'Tho' these criminal proceedings are very moving, yet we see them often attended with such gay and airy circumstances ... that the printed accounts of them are in the opinion of many people one of the most diverting things a man can read in London.'

And so every Old Bailey trial was a media event, with its own newsletter hard on its heels. The more sensational the cases, the more sensational the titles: 'A full and true account of the discovery and apprehending of a notorious gang of sodomites in St Jamses's, 'A full and true account of the discovering, apprehending and taking of a notorious witch' and 'A true and wonderful relation of a murther committed in the parish of Newington by a maid who poysoned herself and cut the throat of a child'. Inaccurate and exaggerated they may have been, but these pamphlets were reliably racy, reasonably priced, and guaranteed to hit the streets on execution day, when demand was at its highest.

Some of the more astute condemned sold their own memoirs to pay for a coffin, settle prison debts and leave a little over for their families. In their moment of fleeting glory, some liked to read their published memoir before they died, even in the cart on the way to Tyburn. Others bequeathed their writings to friends and family to publish, or ostentatiously handed the manuscript to the chaplain as they stood on the gallows.

But the real profiteers were not the prisoners, but the prison officials. Newgate's prison chaplain, the so-called Ordinary of Newgate, took home a salary of £35 from the Lord Mayor and Aldermen of the City of London, but his greatest perk was his monopoly on the 'official' accounts of the condemned, the 'accounts, behaviour, confessions, and dying-words' of the named criminals, each of which sold for between 3d and 6d in their thousands. The Ordinary had of course the advantage of the 'exclusive interview': conversing with the prisoners over many hours, hearing last confessions, and accompanying them right to the gallows. Unfortunately, by the time he had performed all his clerical duties to the condemned, the market for his account had died along with its subject, The chaplain published earlier and earlier on the following morning in a desperate drive to mop up sales. And he was no slouch when it came to advertising his forthcoming publications in the newsletters at the end of the Old Bailey proceedings.

In the first months of 1700 John Allen occupied this prestigious position, supplementing his income with a lucrative funeral business on the side, and taking it upon himself to offer reprieves to condemned men in exchange for the most lurid accounts. His replacement Paul Lorrain, one-time clerk to Samuel Pepys, was no more scrupulous, though tireless in urging the condemned to 'speedily and sincerely forsake their evil ways and repent; and in order to this, patiently and submissively, take that temporal shame and punishment which is due to them; ingeniously acknowledging their faults, and as far as they are able, making all satisfaction and reparation to the world.' Many found the pressure intolerable. A few proved obdurate, like the pirate Dalziel who threatened to kick him downstairs.

But it was in the legendary pirate Captain Kidd that Lorrain met his match. By execution day, things were not going to schedule. Imagine the scene: low-water mark, Execution Dock, Wapping. Here pirates were hanged until three tides had washed over them. The River Thames was packed with spectator-filled barges, while others stood on the opposite bank with their spy-glasses trained on the scene. Lorrain had left Kidd at Newgate and reached Execution Dock first. By the time the captain arrived, however, it was clear that something was very wrong. Lorrain discovered 'to my unspeakable grief' that Kidd was 'inflamed with drink; which had so discomposed his mind, that it was now in a very ill frame, and very [resistant] to the great work, now or never to be perform'd on him'.

Kidd was counting on a reprieve from his former business associates in the government, who had been in for a share of the profits from his piracy operating out of New York. None was forthcoming. 'I suspected his sincerity,' Lorrain continues, 'because he was more reflective upon others, than upon himself, and still would endeavour to lay his faults upon his crew and others, going about to excuse and justify himself, much about the same manner as he did upon his trial.'

But thanks to 'a remarkable accident', Lorrain got a second crack at this nut. As he told it:

> the rope with which Captain Kidd was ty'd, broke, and so falling to the ground, he was taken up alive; and by this means had the opportunity to consider more of the Eternity he was now launching into. When he was brought up, and ty'd again to the tree I desired leave to go to him again, which was granted. Then I shew'd him the great mercy of God to him in giving him (unexpectedly) this further respite, that so he might improve the free moments now so mercifully allotted to him, in perfecting his faith and repentance. Now I found him in much better temper than before.'

Only when he was back on the top of the ladder, finally and horribly sober, with Lorrain clinging precariously to its lower rungs urging repentance, did Kidd declare 'openly that he repented with all his heart, and dy'd in Christian love and charity with all the world'.

As Lorrain's story of Kidd shows, these official accounts are laced with sanctimonious moralising; unsurprisingly, because Lorrain, unlike many of his predecessors, wrote most of them himself. Previous incumbents had given a greater share of the writing to the subjects. The Ordinary Samuel Smith collaborated with the highwayman Jackson, for example, to produce one of the most entertaining accounts. The input of each is obvious and roughly sewn together. Smith condemns highwaymen as 'those devouring and destroying caterpillars of a corrupt and polluted nation', but Jackson's tongue is visibly in his cheek as he describes Smith as 'a minister, or rather a charitable physician for my sin sick soul'. Women seem to have been Jackson's downfall. He lets slip that his late partner in crime had 'bequeathed to me his wench'. 'I accepted of the legacy, and took possession immediately, without forcible entry; for she made presently a willing surrender.' But it is clear who is really in control of this pamphlet. Smith, of course, has the last word: 'God I hope hath forgiven him his sins, and may we all amend his errors, for which he now hangs in chains at Hampstead, a sad and dreadful spectacle to all beholders.'

In this way the criminal was ultimately depicted as a sinner, whose sins had led inevitably and inexorably to his downfall. John Allen's account of the burglar John Titt is typical: 'His life of late was very irregular, addicted to swearing, lewdness, and debauchery, for which he said he was exceeding sorrowful, and his vices were now as detestable in his sight as before they seem'd pleasant.'

Lorrain made it his business to deliver a series of hellfire and brimstone sermons to the prisoners in the run-up to their execution. He used such salutary texts as Matthew 25:46: 'And they shall go away into everlasting punishment; but the righteous into life eternal.' On the day before execution he preached to the condemned for the last time as they sat in the prison chapel in front of the black-shrouded caskets that would carry them to their graves. A solemn occasion, yet morbid curiosity-seekers bought tickets from the turnkeys at the chapel door, and the prisoners' attitude was anything but solemn: 'The very morning before they were executed, when they were in the chapel, they did not at all seem affected with their condition; but while the Ordinary was at prayers, Stone took a louse out of his bosom, and putting it on an open book, which lay before Chickley, says to him, see how he is galloping over the prayers.'

Eight times a year London's church bells were rung muffled to alert the City and suburbs that it was time for a 'hanging match', an eagerly awaited and unofficial public holiday when business came to a total halt. As Beat Louis de Muralt observed: 'You would, perhaps, think that they look upon these executions as so many publick shews due to the people, and that a stock of thieves must be kept up and improved for that end.'

Outside the prison the air was thick with street hawkers' cries advertising their criminal broadsheets, ballads and refreshments. On the ground, thieves made their way through the throng, gleefully undeterred by the manifestation of the awful power of the law unfolding before them. Execution days were guaranteed income for the pick-pockets. César de Saussure wrote in some awe that 'these rascals are so impudent; they steal even under the gibbet. There never is any execution without handerkerchiefs and other articles being stolen.'

The festive atmosphere made its way even into the gaol, where many of the condemned became increasingly rowdy and defiant, fuelled by liberal amounts of alcohol designed to dull their fear. One observer, Bernard de Mandeville, found this to be the 'most shocking' aspect of the affair; the condemned, he wrote, were 'either drinking madly, or uttering the vilest ribaldry, and jeering others that are less impenitent ... the Ordinary bustles among them, and ... distributes scraps of good counsel to unattentive hearers; and near him, the hangman, impatient to be gone, swears at their delays.'

The progress to the gallows was highly ritualised. First, the prisoners were brought into the Press Yard, where their chains were struck off, before a crowd of onlookers. Then the gaol gates were thrown open and the procession of carts swung out into the roaring, excited crowd. The parade was led by the City marshal on horseback and the under-sheriff, flanked on all sides by a cavalcade of peace officers and constables armed with staves, with a company of javelin men bringing up the rear. The prisoners, many perched on their own coffins, were accompanied by the Ordinary and the hangman. Among the carts there was a strict order of precedence according to the severity of the crime, with first place in the hierarchy granted to those who had robbed the Royal Mail. The rich could arrange to travel to the gallows by coach, although they had to climb up on to the cart beneath the gallows once they got there. Those who had committed treason were dragged backwards in a hurdle. For anyone who had earned the people's hatred, it was a journey fraught with danger from the jeers, abuse, rotten vegetables and more lethal missiles hurled at them.

The prisoners stopped at the church of St Sepulchre's, where by ancient custom the bellman rang a handbell twelve times, before making his address: 'All good people, pray heartily unto God for these poor sinners, who are now going to their death, for whom this great bell doth toll. You that are condemned to die, repent with lamentable tears; ask mercy of the lord for the salvation of your souls through the merits, death, and passion of Jesus Christ, who now sits on the right hand of God, to make intercession for as many of you as penitently return unto Him. Lord have mercy upon you! Christ have mercy upon you!'

The bellman then handed each of the prisoners flowers and a cup of wine. The procession moved down Snow Hill, took a sharp left at the bottom and crossed the Fleet Ditch, and proceeded up the hill to High Holborn. It made slow progress through the narrow streets bordered by the rookeries of St Giles. All along the route spectators leaned out of windows and thronged rooftops for a better view. As excitement mounted, rakes fresh from a night on the town joined the rest of the mob in throwing dead cats and dogs in the air. The only people still at work were the pick-pockets, making the most of their opportunity while their quarry's attention was riveted on the parade.

Despite their precautionary imbibing, the effects of alcohol wore off for the condemned. As Bernard de Mandeville explained: 'The courage that strong liquors can give, wears off, and the way they have to go being considerable, they are in danger of recovering, and, without repeating the dose, sobriety would often overtake them: For this reason they must drink as they go; and the cart stops for that purpose three or four, and sometimes half a dozen times, or more, before they come to their journey's end.' Hawkers of the new Dutch import, gin, ran alongside, but the procession itself halted several times along the route so that its occupants could take another fortifying drink either at the houses of friends or at the many inns which, while dispensing free drinks to the condemned, benefited from the publicity. Even the drinking became part of Tyburn legend. On the way to his execution some years previously, the highwayman Captain Philip Stafford had made the crack that he would pay for his drink on the way back, and by now it had become a gallows tradition. One unfortunate man did not take the time to stop for a drink, and missed his reprieve, which arrived five minutes after he was 'turned off'.

Some of the condemned occupied themselves with prayer. Others, mere boys and girls in their teens, wept. One fifteen-year-old boy had his father accompany him in the cart and lay, his head in his lap, weeping the whole way. More often that not the occupants of the carts elicited admiration and pity from the crowd, defeating the whole purpose of public execution as a crime deterrent. The frequency of executions had inured the public to the sight of death, so that it had lost its power to instil terror. Instead, it had become 'more a holiday for, and to entertain the mob', a massive public bunfight. The criminal and the crowd seemed to collude in their defiance of authority, the more so perhaps because of the absurdity of so many new crimes against property, drawing punishments out of all proportion to the size of the offences. As this became apparent to the authorities, it was suggested by the mid eighteenth century that executions should take place within the prison precinct because, as Fielding put it, 'that would be more dreadful to the criminals themselves, who would thus die in the presence only of their enemies; where the boldest of them would find no cordial to keep up his spirits, nor any breath to flatter his ambition.'

The end of the procession regularly deteriorated into chaos. The last portion of the route, along the busy Oxford Road to Tyburn at its most westerly end, saw the crowds at their thickest and most disorderly. The authorities had to resist attempted rescues, and contend with riots, brawls and violent arguments from those whom de Mandeville described as the 'most sturdy and resolute of the mob'. Sometimes the carts were abandoned in the press of bodies and the condemned had to finish the journey on foot. Injury and even death were real possibilities. In the *London Post*'s account of the execution of a Dutch vintner and his 'pretended wife, and drawer' for the murder of one Norris, there was 'so great a crowd of spectators ... that there was a great deal of mischief done ... One scaffold fell, which killed one boy, and wounded several people more; one of the sheriff's officers, though on horseback, was so crowded, that his horse fell down under him, and he was carried off dead; and there was nothing to be heard but shrieks and out-cryes of murder.'

If they could get through, the carts carrying the condemned drew up at the triple tree, the deadly nevergreen, the three-legged mare, the fatal treegallows – London's many nicknames for the triangular wooden gallows that allowed eight people to swing side by side from each beam at once, twenty-four at a time. Then, as de Saussure noted, 'The chaplain who accompanies the condemned men is also on the cart; he makes them pray and sing a few verses of the psalms. The relatives are permitted to mount the cart and take farewell.' This pause gave the hangman the opportunity to size up the value of the prisoners who were about to become his property; in John Hall's words, 'putting them into lots for the easier accommodation of the sale'.

The hangman earned about £90 a year, accrued from a small fixed salary, from 'piecework', and from the perks of the job. As de Saussure put it: 'The bodies and clothes of the dead belong to the executioner; relatives must, if they wish for them, buy them from him.' Another source of the hangman's income came from 'unclaimed bodies' which could be 'sold to the surgeons to be dissected': more often, the income came in the form of tips from the Worshipful Company of Barber-Surgeons for helping their beadles to secure the corpses allotted to them and convey them to Surgeons Hall.

The liberal alcohol intake made for some farcical moments. By the time he reached Tyburn, the hangman was quite likely to be as drunk as those he was about to hang. On one notorious occasion he was so inebriated that he threw the rope round the neck of a clergyman who was praying with the condemned. The name of the 1680s public executioner, Jack Catch, or Ketch, who had made such a botch-up of the Duke of Monmouth's beheading, became a byword for savagery and incompetence. Children were terrorised into good behaviour by the threat that 'Jack Ketch will get you.' He was even drafted into the Punch and Judy puppet play. There was a thin line between the hangman and the hanged. At least two hangmen were arrested as they went about their duties, one on the way to Tyburn, so that the condemned had to be returned to Newgate.

The hanging process could last several minutes – an inefficient and agonising death. As Misson noted: 'The hangman does not give himself the trouble to put them out of their pain; but some of their friends or relations do it for them. They pull the dying person by the legs, and beat his breast to despatch him as soon as possible.' The crowd watched awestruck as the hanged men and women writhed in their death throes. They cheered or groaned, depending on whether he or she was popular or not, to the alarm of foreigners like Misson: 'The English are a people who laugh at the delicacy of other nations who make it such a mighty matter to be hanged.' The phenomenon provoked a black humour; in criminal cant, hanging was 'only a kick' or 'a wry neck with wet breeches'.

Foreign observers did not consider the English cruel, at least not by their own standards. De Saussure was impressed that 'it is thought that the taking of life is sufficient punishment for any crime without worse torture.' However, a more terrible death than hanging was meted out for high treason. The prisoner was hanged for only a few minutes, then cut down alive and disembowelled, his body carved into four parts, both head and quarters being 'at the disposal of the Crown'. By 1700, there was a reasonable possibility that the executioner would show some mercy in making sure the prisoner was dead before being cut up, naturally for a prearranged fee.

There is a stomach-churning description in John Hall's memoir of the several body parts being treated for their better preservation and longevity in Jack Ketch's kitchen in Newgate. Here the carcass and other parts were thrown into a cauldron of boiling pitch, then withdrawn and 'cold riveted' in what was known as 'his last suit' of tar, before being put on display in prominent sites – to become 'city surveyors', as Hall so wittily puts it – as a warning to others.

No sooner had the hanged men and women stopped kicking, about fifteen to twenty minutes after they were 'turned off', than a desperate struggle broke out for possession of the bodies between 'the people who do not like the bodies to be cut up, and the messengers the surgeons have sent for the bodies'. De Saussure described these 'most amusing scenes': 'blows are given and returned before they can be got away, and sometimes in the turmoil the bodies are quickly removed and buried. The populace often come to blows as to who will carry the bought corpses to the parents who are waiting in coaches and cabs to receive them.'

The Royal College of Physicians and the Worshipful Company of Barber-Surgeons were entitled to a maximum of ten criminal corpses a year free of charge for purposes of dissection. There are occasional hints that representatives of these learned institutions visited Newgate to pick out the best specimens before death and tipped the clerk of the court to ensure that their executions coincided with a scheduled anatomy lecture. It was crucial that the corpse be fresh. While the official allotment of corpses was hardly adequate for these two institutions, no provision at all was made for the growing needs of the private teaching hospitals, St Thomas's and St Bartholomew's, and the hangman had a profitable sideline in selling them unclaimed corpses.

In this highly competitive environment, the cost of acquiring a corpse rose steeply. Although their work was to prove so valuable in the advancement of medical science, the surgeons found themselves violently opposed by a people who believed that the dissection was an impediment to resurrection on the day of judgement.

The accounts of the Worshipful Company of Barber-Surgeons bear witness to the trouble and expense they took in securing bodies:

> The hangman's Christmas-box 2s 6d.
> Paid Charles Window for fetching four dead bodies from Tyburn this year and expenses £2 8s 0d.
> Paid to bring a skeleton from St Giles' to the hall in a coach 2s.
> Paid the beadles expenses for going to Tyburn for a body for the muscular lecture when they could not get one by reason of a great mobb of soldiers and others 13s.
> Paid the high constable of St Giles' parish for assisting the beadles in recovering a body which had been taken from the beadles by the mobb 7s 6d.
> Paid the hangman for the dead man's clothes which were lost in the scuffle and for his Christmas-box 15s.
> Paid Mr Babbage for making a skeleton of Malden's bones £3 3s.
> Paid the beadles for their being beat and wounded at the late execution £4 4s 0d.
> Paid for mending the windows broke upon bringing the last body from Tyburn 6s.

The hanged sometimes regained consciousness after being taken down, revived as they were being put into the coffin, or, most alarming of all, on the dissection table itself. A criminal known as 'half-hanged Smith' was reprieved after hanging for fifteen minutes and found to be still alive when taken down. He was bled and treated until he recovered and later gave an account of his remarkable experience. He recalled that he was

> Sensible of very great pain occasioned by the weight of his body, and felt his spirits in a strange commotion, violently pressing upwards: that having forced their way to his head, he saw a great blaze or glaring light, which seemed to go out at his eyes with a flash, and then he lost all sense of pain. After he was cut down, and began to come to himself, the blood and spirits forcing

The last chance for the condemned to make their peace with God and society, nudged by the Ordinary of Newgate (*Pepys Library, Magdalene College, Cambridge*)

themselves into their former channels, put him, by a sort of pricking or shooting, to such intolerable pain, that he could have wished those hanged who had cut him down.

The greatest shame of all attached, not to the gallows, but to the gibbet. To be hanged in chains until the flesh should rot or be picked clean from the bones by the 'fowls of the air' was the ultimate disgrace, and families and friends took enormous risks to give their dead a decent burial. Once darkness fell, they competed with the body snatchers in the illegal (not to say gruesome) task of trying to free the remains from the chains. The authorities, well aware of this possibility, took to studding the gibbet with sharp nails. The *London Post* reported how when two men were hanged in chains on a gibbet at Mile End, many of the numerous spectators were 'so terrified at the dismal sight, that they were forced to call in at the Golden Cabbage ... to take a cup of the precious mortals' reviving liquors' on the way home.

From time immemorial the bodies of the executed were popularly believed to contain mystical properties, beneficial to health. Extraordinary scenes took place at the gallows. A foreign visitor once saw 'a young woman, with an appearance of beauty, all pale and trembling, in the arms of the executioner, who submitted to have her bosom uncovered, in the presence of thousands of spectators, and the dead man's hand placed upon it'. Women held children up to the gallows, to have them stroked by the hands of the executed criminals as a general guarantee of good health. Even now, in the reign of the rational and pragmatic William III, the 'death sweat' of executed criminals was believed to possess the power to cure scrofula, otherwise curable by the monarch's touch.

Bibliography

Adams, John, *An Essay Concerning Self-Murther* (London, 1700)

Addison, *Selections from Addison's Papers Contributed to the Spectator.* Edited with introduction and notes by Thomas Arnold (Oxford, 1886)

Akber, Edward, ed., *The Torment of Protestant Slaves* (London, 1908)

Allen, John, *A full and true account, of the behaviour, confessions, and last dying-speeches of the condemn'd criminals, that were executed at Tyburn, on Friday the 24th May, 1700* (London, 1700)

Allen, Robert J., *The Clubs of Augustan London* (London, 1933)

Allestree, Richard, *The Whole Duty of Man* (London, 1658)

Anon, *The Women's Petition Against Coffee. Representing to Publick Consideration the Grand Inconveniencies Accruing to their Sex from the Excessive Use of That Drying, Enfeebling Liquor. By a Well-willer* (London, 1674)

Anon, *The Men's Answer to the Women's Petition Against Coffee* (London, 1674)

Anon, *The Compleat Servant Maid, or, The Young Maiden's Tutor* (London, 1677)

Anon, *The New Whole Duty of Man* (London, 1680)

Anon, *Account of the Barbarous Murther of Philip Parry, Esq, committed by Mr Thomas Bond, Near Covent Garden, on Friday night last, being the 15th March, 1700* (London, 1700)

Anon, *The Present Ill State of the Practice of Physick in this Nation Truly Represented, and Some Remedies Thereof Humbly Proposed to the Two Houses of Parliament by a Member of the College of Physicians* (London, 1702)

Anon, *The Necessity and Usefulness of the Dispensaries Lately Set Up by the College of Physicians in London for the Use of the Sick Poor* (London, 1702)

Anon, *A Full and True Account of the Discovering, Apprehending and Taking of a Notorious Witch* (London, 1704)

Anon, *The London Bawd: With Her Character and Life, Discovering the Various Intrigues of Lewd Women* (London, 1711)

Anon (possibly Daniel Defoe), *The History of the Press-Yard Or, a Brief Account of the Customs and Occurrences that Are Put in Practice in that Ancient Repository of Living Bodies Called Newgate etc* (London, 1717)

Anon, *Account of Several Workhouses for Imploying and Maintaining the Poor* (London, 1725)

Anon (probably Paul Lorrain, Ordinary of Newgate), *A Select and Impartial Account of the lives, behaviour, and dying-words of the most remarkable Convicts, from the year 1700* (2nd edition, London, 1745)

Anon, *The Malefactor's Register, or, The Newgate and Tyburn Calendar Containing the Lives, Trials, Accounts of Execution, and Dying Speeches, of the Most Notorious Violators of the Laws of Their Country; Who Have Suffered Death and Other Punishments from 1700, to Lady Day 1779*, 5 vols (London, 1780)

Anon, *Hanging Not Punishment Enough For Murtherers, Highwaymen, and House-Breakers*. Edited by Basil Montagu (London, 1812)

Appleby, A., 'The Disappearance of Plague: A Continuing Puzzle', *Economic History Review*, 2nd series, 33 (1980)

Aristotle, *Aristotle's Masterpiece: Or, the Secrets of Generation Displayed in All the Parts Thereof, etc* (London, 1694)

Ashelford, Jane, *The Art of Dress: Clothes and Society 1500–1914* (London, 1996)

Ashton, John, *The Fleet: Its River, Prison and Marriages* (London, 1888)

Ashton, John, *Social Life in the Reign of Queen Anne* (London, 1904)

Ashworth Underwood, E., ed., *A History of the Worshipful Society of Apothecaries of London*, vol.1, 1617–1815. Abstracted and arranged from the manuscript notes of the late Cecil Wall by the late Charles Cameron. Revised, annotated and edited by E. Ashworth Underwood (London, 1963)

Astell, Mary, *An Essay in Defence of the Female Sex* (London, 1696)

Astell, Mary, *A Serious Proposal to the Ladies for the Advancement of Their True and Greatest Interests … By a Lover of Her Sex*, Part 1 (London, 1696)

Astell, Mary, *Some Reflections Upon Marriage* (London, 1706)

Barbeau Gardiner, Anne, 'Elizabeth Cellier in 1688 on Envious Doctors and Heroic Midwives Ancient and Modern', *Eighteenth Century Life*, vol. 14 (1990)

Barbon, Nicolas, *An Apology for the Builder or a Discourse Shewing the Cause and Effects of the Increase of Building* (London, 1685)

Barbon, Nicolas, *A Discourse of Trade* (London, 1690)

Beattie, J.M., 'The Pattern of Crime in England 1660–1800', *Past and Present*, 72 (1974)

Beattie, J.M., *Crime and the Courts in England 1660–1800* (Oxford, 1986)

Beer, E.S. de, 'The Revocation of the Edict of Nantes and English Public Opinion', *Proceedings of the Huguenot Society of London*, henceforth HSP, xviii (1947–52)

Behn, Aphra (attributed to), *The Ten Pleasures of Marriage, and the Second Part, The Confession of the New Married Couple*. Reprinted with an introduction by John Harvey and the original plates re-engraved (London, 1922)

Beier, A.L. and Finlay, Roger, eds, *London 1500–1700: The Making of the Metropolis* (London, 1986)

Beloff, M., *Public Order and Popular Disturbances 1660–1714* (Oxford, 1938)

Beloff, Max, 'A London Apprentice's Notebook 1703–5', *History*, xxvii

Bernardi, John, *A Short History of the Life of Major John Bernardi, Written by Himself in Newgate* (London, 1729)

Blackstone, William, *Commentaries on the Laws of England* (London, 1765)

Booth, P., 'Speculative Housing and the Land Market in London 1660–1730', *Town Planning Review*, vol. 51, 4 (1980)

Boulton, Jeremy, 'London Widowhood Revisited: The Decline of Female Remarriage in the Seventeenth and Early Eighteenth Centuries', *Continuity and Change*, 5 (1990)

Boulton, Jeremy, 'Itching after Private Marryings? Marriage Customs in Seventeenth-Century London', *London Journal*, 16 (1991)

Bradley, Rose M., *The English Housewife in the Seventeenth and Eighteenth Centuries* (London, 1912)

Brewer, John, *The Pleasures of the Imagination: English Culture in the Eighteenth Century* (London, 1997)

Bristow, Edward J., *Vice and Vigilance: Purity Movements in Britain Since 1700* (Dublin, 1977)

Brown, Tom, *Amusements Serious and Comical for the Meridian of London & Letters from the Dead to the Living* (London, 1700; this edition edited with notes by A.L. Hayward, London, 1927)

Burford, E.J., *Wits, Wenchers and Wantons* (London, 1990)

Burford, E.J. and Wotton, Joy, *Private Vices – Public Virtues* (London, 1995)

Burn, John Southerden, *The Fleet Registers. Comprising the History of the Fleet Marriages, and Some Account of the Parsons and Marriage-House Keepers; With Extracts from the Registers* (London, 1833)

Calendar of State Papers, Colonial Series: America and West Indies, 15 May 1696–31 October 1697. Edited by the Honourable J.W.Fortescue (London, 1904)

Calendar of State Papers, Domestic Series: Of the Reign of William III, 1 January 1699–31 March 1700. Edited by Edward Bateson (London, 1937)

Campbell, Robert, *The London Tradesman* (London, 1747)

Cellier, Elizabeth, *To Dr — An Answer to His Queries, Concerning the Colledg* [sic] *of Midwives* (London, 1688)

Chamberlayne, Edward, *Angliae Notitia, or the Present State of England* (London, 1700)

Chancellor, E.B., *The Pleasure Haunts of Old London During Four Centuries* (London, 1925)

Chaytor, Miranda, 'Husband(ry): Narratives of Rape in the Seventeenth Century', *Gender and History*, vol. 7, no. 3 (1995)

Child, Sir Josiah, *A New Discourse of Trade* (London, 1694)

Clapham, Sir John, *The Bank of England, A History* (Cambridge, 1944)

Clark, Alice, *Working Life of Women in the Seventeenth Century* (London, 1919; this edition with a new introduction by Amy Louise Erickson, London, 1992)

Clarke, Peter, *The English Alehouse, A Social History 1200–1830* (London, 1983)

Cockburn, J.S. ed., *Crime in England, 1550–1800* (London, 1977)

Cook, Harold J., *The Decline of the Old Medical Regime in Stuart London* (Ithaca and London, 1986)

Cox, Margaret, *Life and Death in Spitalfields 1700 to 1850* (York, 1996)

Crawford, Patricia, 'Attitudes to Pregnancy from a Woman's Spiritual Diary', *Local Population Studies*, 21 (1978)

Crawford, Patricia, 'Attitudes to Menstruation in Seventeenth-Century England', *Past and Present*, 91 (1981)

Culpeper, Nicholas, *A Directory for Midwives: Or, a Guide for Women in Their Conception, Bearing and Suckling Their Children* (London, 1693)

Culpeper, Nicholas, *The English Physitian* [sic] *Enlarged* (London, 1695)

Cumming, Valerie, *A Visual History of Costume in the Seventeenth Century* (London, 1984)

Cunnington, Phillis and Lucas, Catherine, *Costume for Births, Marriages and Deaths* (London, 1981)

Curtis, Laura A., 'A Case Study of Defoe's Domestic Conduct Manuals Suggested by the Family, Sex and Marriage in England, 1500–1800', *Studies in Eighteenth Century Culture*, 10

Davidson, Caroline, *A Woman's Work Is Never Done, a History of Housework in the British Isles 1650–1950* (London, 1982)

Davis, Dorothy, *A History of Shopping* (London, 1966)

Davison, Lee, Hitchcock, Tim, Keirn, Tim and Shoemaker, Robert B., *Stilling the Grumbling Hive: The Response to Social and Economic Problems in England 1689–1750* (Stroud, 1992)

Defoe, Daniel, *Minor Single Works. An Essay Upon Projects* (London, 1697)

Defoe, Daniel, *The Poor Man's Plea to All the Proclamations, Declarations, Acts of Parliament, etc, Which Have Been, Or Shall Be Made, or Publish'd, and Suppressing Immorality in the Nation* (London, 1698)

Defoe, Daniel, *The True-Born Englishman: A Satyr* (London, 1700; this edition London, 1997)

Defoe, Daniel, *Minor Single Works. The Danger of the Protestant Religion Consider'd, From the Present Prospect of a Religious War in Europe* (London, 1701)

Defoe, Daniel, *Minor Single Works. The Villainy of Stock-Jobbers Detected, And the Causes of the Late Run upon the Bank and Bankers Discovered and Considered* (London, 1701)

Defoe, Daniel, *The Reformation of Manners: A Satyr* (London, 1702)

Defoe, Daniel, *The Levellers: A Dialogue Between Two Young Ladies, Concerning Matrimony* (London, 1703; Harleian Miscellany, vol. 5, 1944)

Defoe, Daniel, *Minor Single Works. A Hymn to the Pillory* (London, 1703)

Defoe, Daniel, *Minor Single Works. A Hymn to Tyburn. Being a Sequel of the Hymn to the Pillory* (London, 1703)

Defoe, Daniel, *Minor Single Works. The Shortest Way with the Dissenters: Or Proposals for the Establishment of the Church* (London, 1703)

Defoe, Daniel, *Minor Single Works. The Shortest Way to Peace and Union* (London, 1703)

Defoe, Daniel, *Giving Alms No Charity, And Employing the Poor* (London, 1704)

Defoe, Daniel, *Minor Single Works. An Enquiry into the Occasional Conformity Bill. Shewing that the Dissenters are No Way Concern'd in it. By the Author of the Preface to Mr Howe* (London, 1704; this edition 1929)

Defoe, Daniel, *Minor Single Works. More Short-Ways with the Dissenters* (London, 1704)

Defoe, Daniel, *Minor Single Works. The Anatomy of Exchange Alley; or, a System of Stockjobbing* (London, 1719)

Defoe, Daniel, *The Fortunes and Misfortunes of the Famous Moll Flanders* (1722; this edition edited with an introduction by Juliet Mitchell, London, 1978)

Defoe, Daniel, *Minor Single Works. Religious Courtship* (London, 1722)

Defoe, Daniel, *The Great Law of Subordination Consider'd; or, the Insolence and Unsufferable Behaviour of Servants* (London, 1724)

Defoe, Daniel, *Minor Single Works. General History of the Robberies and Murders of the Most Notorious Pyrates* (London, 1724)

Defoe, Daniel, *Roxana, the Fortunate Mistress* (1724; this edition edited by David Blewett, London, 1982)

Defoe, Daniel, *A Tour through the Whole Island of Great Britain* (1724–6; this edition London, 1971)

Defoe, Daniel, *Every-Body's Business Is Nobody's Business: or, Private Abuses, Publick Grievances* (London, 1725)

Defoe, Daniel, *Minor Single Works. Some Considerations upon Street-Walkers. With a Proposal for Lessening the Present Number of Them* (London, 1726)

Defoe, Daniel, *Conjugal Lewdness, or Matrimonial Whoredom* (London, 1727)

Defoe, Daniel, *A Proposal to Prevent Murder, Dishonour and Other Abuses, by Erecting an Hospital for Foundlings in Augusta Triumphans: or, the Way to Make London the Most Flourishing City in the Universe ... Concluding with an Effectual Method to Prevent Street Robberies* (London, 1728)

Defoe, Daniel, *Major Single Works. The Complete English Tradesman*, 2 vols (London, 1732)

Delaune, Thomas, *The Present State of London: or, Memorials Comprehending a Full and Succinct Account of the Ancient and Modern State* (London, 1681)

Dickson, P.G.M., *The Financial Revolution in England 1688–1756* (London, 1967)

Donnison, Jean, *Midwives and Medical Men, A History of Inter-Professional Rivalries and Women's Rights* (London, 1977)

Duffie, R.E., 'English Florists Societies and Feasts in the Seventeenth and First Half of the Eighteenth Century', *Garden History*, 10 (1982)

Dunlop, O.J. and Denman, Richard D., *English Apprenticeship and Child Labour: A History* (London, 1912)

Dunton, John, *The Athenian Mercury*, vols 14, 15, 16, 17 (London, 1692–94)

Earle, Peter, *The World of Defoe* (London, 1976)

Earle, Peter, *The Making of the English Middle Class, Business, Society and Family Life in London, 1660–1730* (London, 1989)

Earle, Peter, *A City Full of People, Men and Women of London, 1650–1750* (London, 1994)

Ellis, Aytoun, *The Penny Universities. A History of the Coffee-Houses* (London, 1956)

Bibliography

Evelyn, John, *Fumifugium: Or the Inconvenience of the Aer and Smoak of London Dissipated. Together with Some Remedies Humbly Proposed by J.E .Esq., to His Sacred Majestie, and to the Parliament Now Assembled* (London, 1661)

Evelyn, John, *Single Works. Acetaria; or a Discourse of Sallets* (London, 1699)

Evelyn, John, *The Diary of John Evelyn*. Edited from the original manuscript by William Bray. 2 vols (London, 1901)

Evelyn, Mary, with a preface by John Evelyn, *Mundus Muliebris: or, The Lady's Dressing Room Unlock'd, and Her Toilette Spread. Together with the Fop-Dictionary, Compiled for the Use of the Fair Sex* (London, 1690)

Evendon, Doreen, 'Mothers and their Midwives in Seventeenth-Century London' in Marland, Hilary, ed., *The Art of Midwifery: Early Modern Midwives in Europe* (London, 1933)

Faller, Lincoln B., 'In contrast to Defoe: The Reverend Paul Lorrain, Historian of Crime', *Huntington Library Quarterly*, vol. 40 (1976–7)

Faller, Lincoln B., *Turned to Account: The Forms and Functions of Criminal Biography in the Late Seventeenth and Early Eighteenth-Century England* (Cambridge, 1987)

Fielding, Henry, *An Enquiry into the Causes of the Late Increase of Robbers With Some Proposals for Remedying this Growing Evil, etc* (London, 1751)

Fiennes, Celia, *The Journeys of Celia Fiennes*. Edited and with an introduction by Christopher Morris (London, 1947)

Fildes, Valerie, ed., *Women as Mothers in Pre-Industrial England, Essays in Memory of Dorothy McLaren* (London, 1990)

Firmin, Thomas, *Some Proposals for the Imploying of the Poor, Especially in and about the City of London, and for the Prevention of Begging* (London, 1678)

Firmin, Thomas, *Some Proposals for the Imployment of the Poor, And for the Prevention of Idleness and the Consequence Thereof, Begging* (London, 1681)

Fisher, F.J., 'The Development of London as a Centre of Conspicuous Consumption', *Transactions of the Royal Historical Society*, 4th series, xxx (1948)

Fontaine, Jacques, *A Tale of the Huguenots; or, Memoirs of a French Refugee Family*. Translated and compiled from the original manuscripts of J.F. by one of his descendants. With an introduction by F.L. Hawkes (New York, 1838)

Forbes, T.R., 'By What Disease or Casualty: the Changing Face of Death in London', *Journal of Historical Medicine*, xxxi

Fox, Celina, *Londoners* (London, 1987)

Fox, George, *The Journal* (London, 1998)

Freke, Elizabeth, *Mrs Elizabeth Freke Her Diary 1671–1714*. Edited by Mary Carbery (Cork, 1913)

Fuller, William, *Mr William Fuller's Trip to Bridewell, With a True Account of His Barbarous Usage in the Pillory ... Written by His Own Hand* (London, 1703)

Gay, John, *Trivia; Or, the Art of Walking the Streets of London* (London, 1716)

George, M. Dorothy, *London Life in the Eighteenth Century* (1925; this edition London, 1992)

Gerard, John, *The Herball or General Historie of Plantes*. Enlarged and amended by Thomas Johnson, Citizen and Apothecary, 1633; this edition arranged by Marcu Woodward (London, 1931)

Gerzina, Gretchen, *Black England, Life Before Emancipation* (London, 1995)

Gillis, John, 'Married but not Churched: Plebian Sexual Relations and Marital Nonconfromity in Eighteenth-Century Britain', *Eighteenth Century Life*, 9

Ginsburg, Madeleine, 'The Secondhand Clothes Trade 1700–1978', *Costume*, 14 (1980)

Gittings, Clare, *Death, Burial and the Individual in Early Modern England* (London, 1984)

Glass, D.V., 'Notes on the Demography of London at the End of the Seventeenth Century', *Daedallus*, xcvii

Goodenough, Mary, *Fair Warning to the Murderers of Infants Being An Account of the Trial of Mary Goodenough* (London, 1692)

Graunt, John, *Natural and Political Observations Mentioned in a Following Index, and Made Upon the Bills of Mortality ... With Reference to the Government, Religion, Trade, Growth, Ayre, and Diseases of the Said City* (London, 1676)

Green, David, *Queen Anne* (London, 1970)

Greenberg, J., 'The Legal Status of the English Woman in Early Eighteenth-Century Common Law and Equity', *Studies in Eighteenth-Century Culture*, 4 (1975)

Griffiths, Arthur, *The Chronicles of Newgate* (London, 1884)

Gwillim, John, *The London Bawd: with her Character and Life etc* (London, 1711)

Gwynn, Robin, 'The Arrival of the Huguenot Refugees in England 1680–1705', *HSP*, xxi (1965–70)

Gwynn, Robin D., *Huguenot Heritage: The History and Contribution of the Huguenots in Britain* (London, 1985)

Gwynn, Robin D., *Minutes of the Consistory of the French Church of London, Threadneedle Street, 1679–1692* (London, 1994)

Hall, John, *Memoirs of the Right Villanous* [sic] *John Hall, the Late Famous and Notorious Robber, Penn'd from His Mouth Some Time Before His Death* (London, 1708)

Harding, V., 'Locations of Burials in Early Modern London', *The London Journal*, vol. 14 (1989–91)

Harrison, Henry, *The Last Words of a Dying Penitent* (London, 1692)

Harvey, Gideon, *The Family Physician and the House Apothecary* (London, 1678)

Hatton, Edward, *A New View of London* (London, 1708)

Hay, D., Linebaugh, P. and Thompson, E.P., eds, *Albion's Fatal Tree: Crime and Society in Eighteenth-Century England* (London, 1975)

Heal, Ambrose, *Signboards of Old London Shops* (London, 1947)

Hibbert, Christopher, *The Roots of Evil: A Social History of Crime and Punishment* (London, 1963)

Hill, Bridget, *Eighteenth-Century Women, an Anthology* (London, 1984)

Hill, Bridget, *Women, Work, and Sexual Politics in Eighteenth-Century England* (Oxford, 1989)

Hitchcock, Tim, 'Paupers and Preachers: the SPCK and the Parochial Workhouse Movement' in *Chronicling Poverty*, ed. Tim Hitchcock et al. (Basingstoke, 1997)

Hitchcock, Tim, King, Peter and Sharpe, Pamela, eds, *Chronicling Poverty; The Voices and Strategies of the English Poor, 1640–1840* (Basingstoke, 1997)

Hole, Christina, *English Home Life, 1500–1800* (London, 1947)

Hole, Christina, *The English Housewife in the Seventeenth Century* (London, 1953)

Hooke, Nathaniel, *An Account of the Conduct of the Dowager Duchess of Marlborough, etc.* (London, 1742)

Houblon, Lady Alice Archer, *The Houblon Family*, vol.1 (London, 1907)

Houlbrooke, Ralph, *English Family Life 1576–1716* (Oxford, 1988)

Houlbrooke, Ralph, ed., *Death, Ritual and Bereavement* (London, 1989)

Howson, G., *Thief-Taker General: The Rise and Fall of Jonathan Wild* (London, 1970)

Huguenot Society of London, *Estat d'Assistance reglées par le comité aux Protestants françois réfugiés, 3 fevrier 1701*, ms. 15

Huguenot Society of London, Quarto Series 2, *The Registers of the French Church, Threadneedle Street, London*, vol. III, 1686–1714. Edited by T.C. Colyer-Fergusson (Aberdeen, 1906)

Huguenot Society of London, *The Registers of La Patente de Soho*, 1689–1782, Quarto Series, vol. 45. Edited by Susan Minet (Frome, 1956)

Hunt, Margaret, 'Wife Beating, Domesticity and Women's Independence in Eighteenth-Century London', *Gender and History*, vol. 4, no. 1 (spring 1992)

Inwood, Stephen, *A History of London* (London, 1998)

Jackson, Francis (alias Dixie), *Jackson's Recantation; or, the Life and Death of the Notorious Highwayman now Hanging in Chains at Hampstead* (London, 1674)

Jeaffreson, John Cordy, *Brides and Bridals* (London, 1872)

Jenkins, Simon, *The Selling of Mary Davies and Other Writings* (London, 1993)

Joceline, Elizabeth, *The Mother's Legacy to Her Unborn Child* (London, 1894)

Johnson, Charles (pseudonym of Daniel Defoe), *A General History of the Robberies and Murders of the Most Notorious Pirates* (London, 1724)

Josselin, Ralph, *The Diary of Ralph Josselin 1616–1683*. Edited by Alan Macfarlane (London, 1976)

King, Gregory, *Natural and Political Observations and Conclusions Upon the State of England, 1696*. Edited by George E. Barnett (London, 1936)

Kiple, Kenneth F., ed., *Plague, Pox and Pestilence* (London, 1997)

Kramer, F.J.L., ed., *Archives ou correspondance inedité de la maison d'Orange-Nassau*, 3rd series 1689–1702, 3 vols (Leiden, 1907–9)

Landers, J., 'Mortality and the Metropolis: the case of London 1675–1825', *Population Studies*, 41 (1987)

Landers, J., *Death and the Metropolis, Studies in the Demographic History of London, 1670–1830* (Cambridge, 1993)

Landers, J. and Mouzas, A., 'Burial Seasonality and the Causes of Death in London 1670–1819', *Population Studies*, 42 (1988)

Laurence, Anne, 'Godly Grief: Individual Responses to Death in Seventeenth-Century Britain' in Houlbrooke, R., ed., *Death, Ritual and Bereavement* (London, 1989)

Laurence, John, *A History of Capital Punishment* (London, 1935)

Lemire, Beverly, 'Consumerism in Pre-industrial and Early Industrial England: the Trade in Second-hand Clothes', *Journal of British Studies*, 27 (1988)

Lemire, Beverly, 'The Theft of Clothes and Popular Consumerism in Early Modern England', *Journal of Social History*, vol. 24, no. 2 (1990)

Lillywhite, Bryant, *London Coffee Houses* (London, 1963)

Lindsay, Jack, *The Monster City, Defoe's London, 1688–1730* (London, 1978)

Linebaugh, Peter, 'The Tyburn Riot Against the Surgeons' in May, D., Linebaugh, P. and Thompson, E.P., eds, *Albion's Fatal Tree* (London, 1975)

Linebaugh, Peter, *The London Hanged, Crime and Civil Society in the Eighteenth Century* (London, 1991)

Litten, Julian, *The English Way of Death, the Common Funeral Since 1450* (London, 1991)

Llewellyn, Nigel, *The Art of Death, Visual Culture in the English Death Ritual c.1500–c.1800* (London, 1991)

Locke, John, *A Letter Concerning Toleration* (Oxford, 1691)

Locke, John, *Two Treatises of Government* (London, 1821)

Locke, John, *How to Bring Up Your Children, Being Some Thoughts on Education* (1693; this edition London, 1902)

London, II, Civic and Municipal Institutions, Sessions, *The Complete Proceedings of the King's Commission of the Sessions of the Peace, of Oyer and Terminer, and of Gaol Delivery* (London, 1684–1710)

London. Appendix, Miscellaneous, *The Petition of Widows, in and about London and Westminster for a Redress of Their Grievances* (London, 1693)

London. Appendix, Miscellaneous, *The Petition of the Ladies of London and Westminster to the Honourable House for Husbands* (London, 1693)

London, III, Miscellaneous Institutions, Societies, and Other Bodies, Royal College of Physicians. *Pharmacopoea Londinensis, Or, the New London Dispensatory.* Fifth edition corrected and amended by William Salmon (London, 1696)

London, III, Miscellaneous Institutions, Societies, and Other Bodies, Societies for the Reformation of Manners. *A Sixth Black List of the names ... of ... persons, who by the endeavours of a Society for promoting a Reformation of Manners in the City of London ... have been ... prosecuted and convicted, etc.* (London, 1700)

London. Appendix, Miscellaneous, *Proclamations Relating to the City of London* (London, 1700)

London, II, Civic and Municipal Institutions, Sessions, Abney, Mayor. *Order of the Court of Quarter Sessions as to the hours at which Vintners and others keeping Public Houses within the City of London and its Liberties shall close the same: dated January 10, 1700* (London, 1700)

London, III, Miscellaneous Institutions, Societies, and Other Bodies, Charity Schools, *An Account of the Methods Whereby the Charity Schools Have Been Erected and Managed, and of the Encouragement Given to Them* (London, 1705)

London, II. Civic and Municipal Institutions, Governors for the Poor, *An Account of the Corporation of the Poor of London; Shewing the Nature, Usefulness and Management of the Work-house in Bishopsgate Street* (London, 1713)

London. Appendix, Miscellaneous, *A View of London and Westminster: or, the Town Spy ... Containing an Account of the Customs ... of the People in the Several Most Noted Parishes. By a German Gentleman* (London, 1725)

The London Gazette

The London Post With Intelligence Foreign and Domestic

Lorrain, Paul, The Ordinary of Newgate, *Accounts of the Behaviour, Confessions, and Dying Speeches of the Condemn'd Criminals* (otherwise referred to as *Malefactors) that Were Executed at Tyburn*. Various accounts, 1700/01–1718. Catalogued in British Library under Cup.645.e.1. etc., 515.1.2 etc and 1852.d.4.

Lorrain, Paul, *The Ordinary of Newgate, His Account of the Behaviour, Confessions, and Dying-words of Captain W. Kidd, and other Pirates, that were executed ... May 23, 1701* (London, 1701)

Lorrain, Paul, *The Ordinary of Newgate His Account of the Life, Birth, Death and Parentage of John Hall, Richard Low, Stephen Bunch, William Davis and Joseph Monifano, Five Notorious Thieves and Housebreakers, etc* (London, 1707)

Lorrain, Paul, *The Whole Life and Conversation, Birth, Parentage and Education of Deborah Churchill* (London, 1708)

Lorrain, Paul, *The Ordinary of Newgate His account of the Behaviour, Confession, and Last Dying Speech of G. Skelthorp ... executed ... 23 March, 1708/9* (London, 1708/9)

Lorrain, Paul, The Ordinary of Newgate, *The Case of Paul Lorrain ... Humbly Offer'd to the House of Commons* (London, 1712)

Luttrell, Narcissus, *A Brief Historical Relation of State Affairs from September 1678 to April 1714* (Oxford, 1857)

MacDonald, Michael, *Mystical Bedlam, Madness, Anxiety and Healing in Seventeenth-Century England* (Cambridge, 1981)

MacDonald, M. and Murphy, T., *Sleepless Souls: Suicide in Early Modern England* (Oxford, 1990)

Macfarlane, Alan, *The Family Life of Ralph Josselin a Seventeenth Century Clergyman* (Cambridge, 1970)

Macfarlane, Alan, *Marriage and Love in England: Modes of Reproduction 1300–1840* (Oxford, 1986)

Malcolm, J.P., *Anecdotes of the Manners and Customs of London during the Eighteenth Century* (London, 1808)

Mandeville, Bernard de, *The Fable of the Bees: Or, Private Vices, Publick Benefits* (London, 1714)

Mandeville, Bernard de, *A Modest Defence of Publick Stews* (1724; this edition with an introduction by Richard I. Cook, Los Angeles, 1973)

Mandeville, Bernard de, *The Virgin Unmask'd: or Female Dialogues Betwixt an Elderly Maiden Lady and Her Niece ... on Love, Marriage, Morals, etc of the Times* (London, 1724)

Mandeville, Bernard de, *An Enquiry into the Causes of the Frequent Executions at Tyburn; and a Proposal for Some Regulations Concerning Felons in Prison* (London, 1725)

Markham, G., *The English House-Wife, Containing the Inward and Outward Vertues Which Ought to Be in a Compleat Woman, etc* (London, 1664)

Marly, Diana de, 'Some aristocratic clothing accounts of the Restoration Period in England', *Waffen und Kostumkünde*, vol 1976

Marly, Diana de, 'Fashionable Suppliers 1660–1700: Leading Tailors and Clothing Tradesmen of the Restoration Period', *The Antiquaries Journal*, vol. LVIII (1979)

Masters, Betty R., *The Public Markets of the City of London Surveyed by William Leybourne in 1677* (London, 1974)

Mauriceau, François, *The Accomplisht Midwife, Treating of the Diseases of Women With Child, and in Child-bed*. Translated, and enlarged with notes by H. Chamberlen (London, 1675)

Mauriceau, François, *The Diseases of Women with Child, and in Child-bed*. Translated by Hugh Chamberlen (London, 1697)

McCray Beier, Lucinda, *Sufferers and Healers: The Experience of Illness in Seventeenth-Century England* (London, 1987)

McKendrick, N., Brewer, J., and Plumb, J.H., *The Birth of a Consumer Society; the Commercialization of Eighteenth-Century England* (London, 1982)

McLaren, Dorothy, 'Marital Fertility and Lactation 1570–1720' in Prior, Mary, ed., *Women in English Society 1500–1800* (London, 1985)

Meldrum, T., 'A Woman's Court in London. Defamation at the Bishop of London's Consistory Court 1700–1745', *London Journal*, 19 (1) (1994)

Meneffe, Samuel Pyeatt, *Wives for Sale, an Ethnographical Study of British Popular Divorce* (Oxford, 1981)

Merryman, Tom, *The Matchless Rogue: Or, an Account of the Contrivances, Cheats, Stratagems and Amours of Tom Merryman, Commonly Called Newgate Tom* (London, 1725)

Miege, Guy, *The New State of England under our Present Monarch, King William III* (London, 1701)

Misson, Henri, *Memoirs and Observations in His Travels Over England* (1698; translated by Mr Ozell, London, 1719)

Mordaunt, Colonel Harry (also attributed to Bernard de Mandeville), *A Modest Defence of Public Stews; Or, an Essay upon Whoring, As It Is Now Practis'd in these Kingdoms* (Glasgow, 1730)

Morley, Henry, *Memoirs of Bartholomew Fair* (London, 1880)

Morris, Christopher, ed., *The Journeys of Celia Fiennes* (London, 1947)

Muralt, Beat Louis de, *Letters Describing the Character and Customs of the English and French Nations* (London, 1726)

Newcome, Henry, *The Compleat Mother: Or an Earnest Perswasive to All Mothers (Especially Those of Rank and Quality) to Nurse Their Own Children* (London, 1695)

N.H., *The Compleat Tradesman: or the Exact Dealer's Daily Companion ... Composed by N.H., Merchant in the City of London* (London, 1684)

N.H., *The Ladies Dictionary, Being a General Entertainment for the Fair Sex* (London, 1694)

O'Day, R., *Education in Society 1500–1800: Social Foundations of Education in Early Modern Britain* (London, 1982)

Orne, J., ed. (possibly written by John Dunton), *The Nightwalker or Evening Rambles in Search of Lewd Women with the Conference Held with Them* (London, 1696)

Outhwaite, R.B., 'Age at Marriage in England from the Late Seventeenth to the Nineteenth Century', *Transactions of the Royal Historical Society*, 23 (1973)

Outhwaite, R.B., ed., *Marriage and Society, Studies in the Social History of Marriage* (London, 1981)

Papali, George Francis, *Jacob Tonson, Publisher: His Life and Work (1656–1736)* (Auckland, 1968)

Payne, William L., ed., *The Best of Defoe's Review, An Anthology* (New York, 1951)

Pechey, John, *A General Treatise of the Diseases of Maids, Bigbellied Women, Child-bed Women, and Widows, Together with the Best Methods of Preventing or Curing the Same* (London, 1696)

Pechey, John, *The Compleat Midwife's Practice Enlarged* (London, 1698)

Peltzer, J. and Peltzer, L., 'The Coffee Houses of Augustan London', *History Today* (October 1982)

Pepys, Samuel, *The Shorter Pepys*. Selected and edited by Robert Latham (London, 1990)

Plumb, J.H., 'The New World of Children in Eighteenth-Century England', *Past and Present*, 67

Pollock, Linda A., *Forgotten Children: Parent-Child Relations from 1500–1900* (Cambridge, 1983)

Porter, Roy, *Disease, Medicine and Society in England, 1550–1860* (Basingstoke, 1987)

Porter, Roy, London, *A Social History* (London, 1994)

Porter, Roy and Hall, Lesley, *The Facts of Life; The Creation of Sexual Knowledge in Britain, 1650–1950* (New Haven and London, 1995)

Porter, Stephen, 'Death and Burial in a London Parish; St Mary Woolnoth 1653–99', *London Journal*, vol. 8, no. 1 (1982)

The Post Boy

The Post Man and the Historical Account

Prideaux, Humphrey, *The Case of Clandestine Marriages Stated, Wherein Are Shown the Causes from whence this Corruption Ariseth, and the True Methods Whereby It May Be Remedied* (1691, Harleian Miscellany, vol.1, 1944)

Prior, Mary, ed., *Women in English Society 1500–1800* (London, 1985)

Reddaway, Thomas Fiddian, *The Rebuilding of London after the Great Fire* (London, 1940)

Ritchie, Robert C., *Captain Kidd and the War Against the Pirates* (Cambridge, Mass. and London, 1986)

Rose, Craig, 'Evangelical Philanthropy and Anglican Revival: the Charity Schools of Augustan London 1698–1740', *London Journal*, vol. 16, no. 1 (1991)

Rumbelow, Donald, *The Triple Tree: Newgate, Tyburn and the Old Bailey* (London, 1982)

Salmon, William, *The Compleat English Physician: Or the Druggist's Shop Opened* (London, 1693)

Saussure, César de, *A Foreign View of England in the Reigns of George I and George II. The Letters of Monsieur César de Saussure to his Family.* Translated and edited by Madame van Myden (London, 1902)

Schofield, Roger, 'Did the Mothers Really Die?' in Bonfield, L., Smith, R. and Wrightson, K.,. eds, *The World We Have Gained* (Oxford, 1986)

Schorrenberg, Barbara Brandon, 'Is Childbirth any Place for a Woman? The Decline of Midwifery in Eighteenth-Century England', *Studies in Eighteenth Century Culture*, 10 (1981)

Scott Thomson, Gladys, *Life in a Noble Household 1641–1700* (London, 1937)

Sermon, William, *The Ladies Companion, or the English Midwife* (London, 1671)

Sharp, Jane, *The Midwives Book, Or the Whole Art of Midwifery Discovered* (London, 1671)

Sharpe, J.A., *Crime in Early Modern England, 1550–1750* (London, 1984)

Sharpe, J.A., 'Last Dying Speeches: Religion, Ideology, and Public Execution in Seventeenth-Century England', *Past and Present*, 107 (1985)

Sheehan, W.J., 'Finding Solace in Eighteenth-Century Newgate' in J. S. Cockburn, ed., *Crime in England 1500–1800* (London, 1977)

Sheppard, F.H.W., 'The Huguenots in Spitalfields and Soho', *HSP*, xxi (1965–70)

Sherlock. William, Dean of St Paul's, *A Practical Discourse Concerning Death* (London, 1699)

Shesgreen, Sean, *The Cries and Hawkers of London* (London, 1990)

Shirren, A.J., *Daniel Defoe in Stoke Newington* (London, 1960)

Shyllon, Folarin, *Black People in Britain, 1555–1833* (London, 1977)

Singleton, Robert R., 'Defoe, Moll Flanders and the Ordinary of Newgate', *Harvard Library Bulletin*, 24 (1976)

Slack, P., 'The Disappearance of Plague; an Alternative View', *Economic History Review*, 2nd series, 34 (1981)

Sloan, A.W., *English Medicine in the Seventeenth Century* (Durham, 1996)

Smith, Captain Alexander, *The Complete History of the Lives and Robberies of the Most Notorious Highwaymen, Footpads, Shoplifts, and Cheats of Both Sexes, 1714–19* (London, 1719; this edition with a foreword by A.L. Hayward, London, 1933)

Smith, Steven R., 'The London Apprentices as Seventeenth Century Adolescents', *Past and Present*, 61 (November 1973)

Speck, W., 'The Societies for the Reformation of Manners: a Case Study in the Theory and Practice of Moral Reform', *Literature and History*, 3 (1976)

Stone, Lawrence, *The Family, Sex and Marriage in England 1500–1800* (London, 1990)

Stone, Lawrence, *Uncertain Unions and Broken Lives: Marriage and Divorce in England 1660–1857* (Oxford, 1995)

Stone, Lawrence, *The Road to Divorce: A History of the Making and Breaking of Marriage in England* (Oxford, 1995)

Stow, John, *A Survey of the Cities of London and Westminster ... Brought Down from the Year 1633 ... to the Present Time by John Strype* (London, 1720)

Styles, J. and Brewer, S., *An Ungovernable People: The English and Their Law* (London, 1980)

Swift, Jonathan, Dean of St Patrick's, *Directions to Servants* (London, 1745)

Swift, Jonathan, Dean of St Patrick's, *Gulliver's Travels and Selected Writings in Prose and Verse*. Edited by John Hayward (London, 1990)

Tanner, Dr Anodyne, *The Life of the Late Celebrated Mrs Elizabeth Wisebourn,Vulgarly Call'd Mother Whybourn ... Together with her Last Will and Testament* (London, 1721)

Thomas, Keith, *Religion and the Decline of Magic* (London, 1973)

Thornton, P., *Seventeenth-Century Interior Decoration in England, France and Holland* (London and New Haven, 1978)

Thornton, P. and Rothstein, N., 'The Importance of the Huguenots in the London Silk Industry', *HSP*, xx (1958–64)

Thorold, Peter, *The London Rich: The Creation of a Great City from 1666 to the Present* (London, 1999)

Thorp, M.R., 'The Anti-Huguenot Undercurrent in Late Seventeenth Century England', *HSP*, xxii (1970–76)

Timbs, John, *Clubs and Club Life in London* (London, 1908)

Trenchfield, Caleb, *The Father's Counsel to His Son, An Apprentice in London* (London, 1678)

Ukawsaw Gronniosaw, James Albert, *A Narrative of the Most Remarkable Particulars in the Life of James Albert Ukawsaw Gronniosaw, An African Prince, as Related by Himself*. With a Preface by W. Shirley (Bath, 1770)

Verney, Margaret M., *Memoirs of the Verney Family from the Restoration to the Revolution 1660 to 1696* (London, 1899)

Verney, Margaret Maria, Lady, ed., *Verney Letters of the Eighteenth Century from the Mss. at Claydon House*, vol. 1 (London, 1930)

Von Uffenbach, Zacharias Conrad, *London in 1710*. Translated and edited by W.H.

Quarrell and Margaret Mare (London, 1934)

Walker, R.B., 'Advertising in London Newspapers 1650–1750', *Business History*, 15, no. 2 (1973)

Waller, W.C., 'Early Huguenot Friendly Societies', *HSP*, vi (1898–1901)

Waller, W.C., ed., 'Extracts from the Court Books of the Weavers Company of London, 1610–1730', Huguenot Society of London Quarto Series Publications, henceforth HSQS, vol. 33 (1931)

Ward, Ned, *The London Spy: The Vanities and Vices of the Town Exposed to View.* Edited with notes by Arthur L. Hayward (London, 1927)

Weatherill, Lorna, 'A Possession of One's Own: Women and Consumer Behaviour in England, 1660–1740', *Journal of British Studies*, 25 (1986)

Weatherill, Lorna, *Consumer Behaviour and Material Culture in Britain, 1660–1760* (London, 1988)

West, Richard, *The Life and Surprising Adventures of Daniel Defoe* (London, 1997)

Willis, Richard, successively Bishop of Gloucester, of Salisbury and of Winchester, *A Sermon Preach'd at the first meeting of the gentlemen concern'd in promoting the charity schools ... of London etc.* (London, 1704)

Wilson, Adrian, *The Making of Man-Midwifery, Childbirth in England 1660–1770* (London, 1995)

W.M., *The Queen's Closet Open'd* (London, 1696)

Woolley, Hannah, *The Cook's Guide: or Rare Receipts for Cookery* (London, 1664)

Woolley, Hannah, *The Ladies Delight: or a Rich Closet of Choice Experiments and Curiosities* (London, 1672)

Woolley, Hannah, *The Gentlewoman's Companion; or, a Guide to the Female Sex: Containing Directions of Behaviour in All Places* (London, 1682)

Woolley, Hannah, *The Queen-like Closet; or, Rich Cabinet* (London, 1684)

Woolley, Hannah, *The Accomplish'd Ladies Delight in Preserving, Physick, Beautifying, and Cookery, etc* (London, 1686)

Wrigley, E.A., 'A Simple Model of London's Importance 1650–1750', *Past and Present*, 37 (1967)

Zee, Van der, Henri and Barbara, *William and Mary* (London, 1973)

Zell, Michael, 'Suicide in Pre-Industrial England', *Social History*, 11 (1986)

Notes

Foreword

1 the chiefest emporium. Edward Chamberlayne, *Angliae Notitia, or the Present State of England* (London, 1700).

1 As slow as a Paul's workman. Ned Ward, *The London Spy: the Vanities and Vices of the Town Exposed to View* (London, 1927).

1 like a floating forest. This is Nicolas Barbon's description of the river traffic in *A Discourse of Trade* (London, 1690).

4 a few fishermen's houses. Celia Fiennes, *The Journeys of Celia Fiennes* (London, 1947).

4 a large town. Ibid.

4 one of the greatest. Daniel Defoe, *A Tour through the Whole Island of Great Britain* (London, 1971).

6 people here are so little sensible. William III to Antonious Heinsius, 23 November 1700, *Archives ou correspondance inedité de la maison d'Orange-Nassau,* 3rd series 1689–1702, edited by F.J.L. Kramer, 3 vols (Leiden 1907–9) p. 249 .

1 Marriage

9 discarded guts and offal. See Jonathan Swift, Dean of St Patrick, *A Description of a City Shower in Gulliver's Travels and Selected Writings in Prose and Verse* (London, 1990), p. 754.

9 brawling concert of fishwives. Tom Brown, *Amusements Serious and Comical for the Meridian of London & Letters from the Dead to the Living* (London, 1927).

9 Marriages Perform'd Within. Quoted in Lawrence Stone, *The Family, Sex and Marriage in England 1500–1800* (London, 1990), p. 32.

9 Sir, will you be pleased. Quoted in John Ashton, *The Fleet: Its River, Prison and Marriages* (London, 1888), p. 340.

10 goes at large ... a very wicked man. Ashton, *The Fleet*, pp. 337, 338.

10 2,251 marriages. See Roger Brown, 'The Rise and Fall of the Fleet Marriages' in R.B.Outhwaite, ed., *Marriage and Society, Studies in the Social History of Marriage* (London, 1981) p. 123.

11 without loss of time. Quoted in Peter Earle, *The Making of the English Middle Class, Business, Society and Family Life in London, 1660–1730* (London, 1989) p. 178.

12 N.B. they had liv'd together. Quoted in John Southerden Burn, *The Fleet Registers, Comprising the History of the Fleet Marriages* (London, 1833), p. 46.

12 N.B. the woman was big with child. Ibid.

12 antidates as he pleases. Ashton, *The Fleet*, p. 338.

12 offered … a marriage certifycate. Ibid.

13 We're contracted. Quoted in Lawrence Stone, *The Road to Divorce, A History of the Making and Breaking of Marriage in England 1530–1987* (Oxford, 1995), p. 75.

13 the said Stephen. Lambeth Palace Library/Court of Arches/ Depositions.

16 On Tuesday last two persons. Quoted in Ashton, *The Fleet*, p. 371.

16 A woman when she marries. César de Saussure, *A Foreign View of England in the Reigns of George I and George II. The Letters of Monsieur César de Saussure to his Family* (London, 1902).

17 Hence, too, happen polygamies. Henri Misson, *Memoirs and Observations in His Travels Over England* (London, 1719).

17 Mary Stokes, alias Edwards. London, II, Civic and Municipal Institutions, Sessions, British Library, *The Complete Proceedings of the King's Commission of the Sessions of the Peace, of Oyer and Terminer, and of Gaol Delivery,* henceforth abbreviated to *Old Bailey Sessions,* December, 1693.

18 Hence comes the matches. Misson, op cit.

18 the arts and tricks made use of to trepan. Daniel Defoe, *Conjugal Lewdness, or Matrimonial Whoredom* (London, 1727).

18 decoyed away from her friends. The heiress was one Ann Leigh. Quoted in Burn, op. cit., p. 7.

18 To proclaim banns. Misson, op. cit.

19 Dean Humphrey Prideaux, *The Case of Clandestine Marriages Stated, Wherein Are Shown the Causes from whence this Corruption Ariseth, and the True Mehods Whereby It May Be Remedied* (London, 1691; Harleian Miscellany, vol. 1, 1944).

19 persons of quality. Misson, op. cit.

19 When those of a middling condition. Ibid.

20 it is no wonder. Aphra Behn, *The Ten Pleasures of Marriage, and the Second Part, The Confession of the New Married Couple* (London, 1922).

20 because it was impossible. Ibid.

20 The bridegroom, that is to say. Misson, op. cit.

21 If the drums and fiddles. Ibid.

21 and when bed time is come. Ibid.

22 get rid of the troublesome. Ibid.

22 Matrimony is, indeed. Daniel Defoe, *The Levellers: A Dialogue Between Two Young Ladies, Concerning Matrimony* (London, 1703).

22 The market is against. Daniel Defoe, *The Fortunes and Misfortunes of the Famous Moll Flanders* (London, 1978).

22 Ask the ladies. Defoe, *Conjugal Lewdness.*

22 that the state of things. Defoe, *Moll Flanders.*

23 as the custom now is. Daniel Defoe, *The Complete English Tradesman* (London, 1732).

23 cripples his fortune. Ibid.

23 whether my trade wou'd carry. Quoted in Earle, *The Making of the English Middle Class*, p. 183.

23 The age difference. For a discussion on age at marriage see Earle, *The Making of the English Middle Class*, p. 181.

23 The 14th of February. Saussure, op. cit.

24 I never saw my lady. Quoted in Bridget Hill, *Women, Work, and Sexual Politics in Eighteenth-Century England* (Oxford, 1989) p. 175.

24 For a man to make a whore. Defoe, *Conjugal Lewdness*.

25 I first met Abigail. Greater London Record Office, henceforth abbreviated to GLRO/Consistory Court of London/Depositions/February 1700/1–January 1702/3, DL/C/247.

25 And as to the father. Defoe, *Moll Flanders*.

25 One in ten English brides. Alan Macfarlane, *Marriage and Love in England: Modes of Reproduction 1300–1840* (Oxford, 1986) p. 305.

26 Thus was three. Elizabeth Freke, *Mrs Elizabeth Freke Her Diary 1671–1714.* (Cork, 1913).

26 endeavour as much as possible. Quoted in Earle, *The Making of the English Middle Class*, p. 185.

27 A woman indeed can't properly. Mary Astell, *Some Reflections Upon Marriage* (London, 1706).

27 will enjoin a child. Quoted in Macfarlane, *Marriage and Love in England*, p. 129.

27 parents offer to their children. Ibid.

27 the daughter of a citizen. Quoted in Earle, *The Making of the English Middle Class*, p. 187.

27 A sign that they. Saussure, op. cit.

28 What will she bring. Astell, *Some Reflections Upon Marriage.*

28 Q. Gentlemen, I desire. John Dunton, *The Athenian Mercury*, vol. 15, 11 September 1694.

28 an ill husband that uses. Defoe, *Conjugal Lewdness.*

29 Elizabeth Wildey. Quoted from Peter Earle, *A City Full of People, Men and Women of London, 1650–1750* (London, 1994) p. 231.

29 Ann and Charles Norvos. GLRO/Depositions/January 1697/8–March 1699/1700, DL/C/246.

29 To London, to receive. John Evelyn, *The Diary of John Evelyn* (London, 1901), 16 March 1680.

30 You know my father. Defoe, *The Levellers.*

31 Ann Norvos. GLRO/Depositions/January 1697/8–March 1699/1700, DL/C/246.

31 Separate purses between. Addison, *Selections from Addison's Papers Contributed to the Spectator* (Oxford, 1886), no. 295, p. 280.

31 *feme sole.* See Greenberg, 'The Legal Status of the English Woman in Early Eighteenth-Century Common Law and Equity', *Studies in Eighteenth-Century Culture*, 4 (1975).

31/2 By marriage, the husband. Quoted in Greenberg, op. cit.

32 The corrupting of a man's wife. Richard Allestree, *The Whole Duty of Man.* (London, 1658).

32 The very nature of the marriage. Daniel Defoe, *Roxana, the Fortunate Mistress* (London, 1982).

32 The argument's good. Quoted in

Stone, *The Family, Sex and Marriage in England*, p. 164.

32 If all men are born free. Ibid., p. 165.

32 She then who marrys. Astell, *Some Reflections Upon Marriage*.

33 This was not kind done. Freke, op. cit.

33 The barber and wig-maker. Quoted from Margaret Hunt, 'Wife Beating, Domesticity and Women's Independence in Eighteenth-Century London', *Gender and History*, vol. 4, no. 1 (spring, 1992).

33 Ann Ferrers complained. Lambeth Palace Library/Court of Arches/Depositions.

33 out of her own estate. Ibid.

34 fell into a great passion. GLRO/Depositions/January 1697/8 – March 1699/1700, DL/C/246.

34 Defoe remarked that London. Daniel Defoe, *The Great Law of Subordination Consider'd; or, the Insolence and Unsufferable Behaviour of Servants* (London, 1724).

34 as Elizabeth Powell. GLRO/Depositions, op. cit., DL/C/246.

35 their condition *de facto* is. Chamberlayne, op. cit.

35 I hate everything that Old England. Quoted from John Ashton, *Social Life in the Reign of Queen Anne* (London, 1904) p. 69.

35 Englishmen do not spoil. Saussure, op. cit.

35 If Englishmen are not jealous. Ibid.

35 Most of the husbands keep mistresses. Beat Louis de Muralt, *Letters Describing the Character and Customs of the English and French Nations* (London, 1726).

36 When a married couple. Aristotle, *Aristotle's Masterpiece: Or, the Secrets of Generation Displayed in All the Parts Thereof, etc* (London, 1694).

36 There is no vast difference. Ibid.

36 clitoris will stand. Jane Sharp, *The Midwives Book, Or the Whole Art of Midwifery Discovered* (London, 1671).

37 too much frequency of embraces. Quoted in Stone, *The Family, Sex and Marriage in England*, p. 313.

37 rottenness and other filthy. Ibid.

37 We that have had good. London. Appendix, Miscellaneous, *The Petition of the Widows, in and about London and Westminster for a Redress of Their Grievances* (London, 1693).

38 was in bed and asleep. GLRO/Depositions/January 1697/8 – March 1699/1700, DL/C/246.

38 ordered them to be silent. Ibid.

38 the said Margaret. Lambeth Palace Library/Court of Arches/Depositions.

38 swore she was going to gett. Ibid.

38 Costing at least £20. See Hunt, op. cit.

39 Whereas … it is affirmed. GLRO/Depositions, op. cit. DL/C/246.

39 Whereas Elizabeth Stephenson. Quoted in Ashton, *Social Life*, p. 31.

40 Whereas Isabella Goodyear. Ibid., p. 41.

40 The said John Combs. GLRO/Depositions/January 1697/8 – March 1699/1700, DL/C/246.

40 They continued drinking. Ibid.

41 unkindness of her husband. GLRO/Depositions op. cit. DL/C/246.

41 puts a halter about. Quoted in Stone, *The Road to Divorce*, p. 144.

41 put to bed. The Counsellor's Plea for the Divorce of Sir G.D. and Mrs. F., 1715, quoted from Ashton, *Social Life*, pp. 29–30.

42 threescore thousand hands. London. Appendix, Miscellaneous, *The Petition of the Ladies of London and Westminster to the Honourable House for Husbands* (London, 1693).

42 the graver sort exclaim. Ibid.

43 'Tis a burning shame. Ibid.

2 Childbirth

44 their shoes slipping. See John Gay, *Trivia; Or, the Art of Walking the Streets of London* (London, 1716).

44 Madame X. See 'A London Midwife's Account Book, 1694–1714', Bodleian Library, Oxford, Rawlinson Ms., D.1141. Also, Doreen Evendon's article, 'Mothers and their Midwives in Seventeenth-Century London' in Hilary Marland, ed., *The Art of Midwifery; Early Modern Midwives in Europe* (London, 1933).

44 for gossips to meet. For a description of the lying-in room and some of the customs of childbirth see Adrian Wilson, *The Making of Man-Midwifery, Childbirth in England 1660–1770* (London, 1995), p. 30.

46 For the midwife is not able. Behn, op. cit.

47 All the time their being. John Pechey, *A General Treatise of the Diseases of Maids, Bigbellied Women, Child-bed Women, and Widows, Together with the Best Methods of Preventing or Curing the Same* (London, 1696).

47 She must not ride on horse-back. Ibid.

48 there were 23.5 deaths per 1,000 baptisms. See Roger Schofield, 'Did the Mothers Really Die?' in L. Bonfield, R. Smith and K. Wrightson, eds, *The World We Have Gained* (Oxford, 1986), p. 233.

48 when she first felt her self quick. Elizabeth Joceline, *The Mother's Legacy to Her Unborn Child* (London, 1894).

48 As concerning their persons. Quoted in Jean Donnison, *Midwives and Medical Men, A History of Inter-Professional Rivalries and Women's Rights* (London, 1977), p. 16.

49 to thrust it up. Sharp, op. cit.

50 by a man's assistance. Hugh Chamberlen in François Mauriceau, *The Diseases of Women With Child, and in Child-bed* (London, 1697).

50 The Chamberlen family. Ibid.

50 It would no longer be an attractive career. See Barbara Brandon Schorrenberg, 'Is Childbirth Any Place for a Woman? The Decline of Midwifery in Eighteenth-Century England', *Studies in Eighteenth-Century Culture*, 10 (1981).

50 If the head come forward. Sharp, op. cit.

51 Any of these herbs. Ibid.

51 if a woman has had. Aristotle, op. cit.

52 My wife's month being now out. Nicholas Blundell in 1704, quoted in Wilson, op. cit., p. 27.

52 to store your cellar. Behn, op. cit.

52 I am provided for caudle. Lady Margaret Maria Verney, ed.,

Verney Lettters of the Eighteenth Century from the Mss. at Claydon House, vol. 1 (London, 1930), Sir Thomas Cave to Lord Fermanagh, 17 December 1700, p. 231.

52 The first fruits. Ward, op. cit.

52 At last I came. Ibid.

52 a bumper of Canary. Ibid.

54 a paper of sweetmeats. Ibid.

54 Some children grow lean. Sharp, op. cit.

54 What now remained. Ward, op. cit.

54 the great danger …pains of hell. *The Thanksgiving of Women after Child-birth, Commonly Called, The Churching of Women* in *The Book of Common Prayer.*

54 you won't be troubled. Behn, op. cit.

54 the first and principal. Mauriceau, op. cit.

54 because it agrees. Sharp, op. cit.

55 A lady that will condescend. Henry Newcome, *The Compleat Mother: Or an Earnest Perswasive to All Mothers (Especially Those of Rank and Quality) to Nurse Their Own Children* (London, 1695).

55 it is too common. Ibid.

55 In general, she must. Mauriceau, op. cit.

56 Take a quantity. W.M., *The Queen's Closet Open'd* (London, 1696).

56 From the onset of menstruation. See Patricia Crawford, 'Attitudes to Menstruation in Seventeenth-Century England', *Past and Present*, 91 (1981).

56 This hypocrass soe taken. Freke, op. cit.

56 A human cargo. See Dorothy McLaren, 'Marital Fertility and Lactation 1570–1720' in Mary Prior, ed., *Women in English Society 1500–1800* (London, 1985), p. 30.

56 Henry Newcome felt. Newcome, op. cit.

57 Nurses generally are so. Ibid.

57 That a worthy divine. Ibid.

57 Jane Watson. *Old Bailey Sessions*, December 1697.

58 'Tis but too common. Daniel Defoe, *A Proposal to Prevent Murder, Dishonour and Other Abuses, by Erecting an Hospital for Foundlings in Augusta Triumphans: or, the Way to Make London the Most Flourishing City in the Universe* (London, 1728).

58 Phebe Ward. Paul Lorrain, *Accounts of the Behaviour, Confessions, and Dying Speeches of the Condemn'd Criminals that Were Executed at Tyburn* (British Library reference, 1852.d.4).

59 Mary Goodenough. Mary Goodenough, *Fair Warning to the Murderers of Infants Being An Account of the Trial of Mary Goodenough* (London, 1692).

59 Whereas many lewd women. London. Appendix, Miscellaneous, *Proclamations Relating to the City of London.*

59 Christine Russell. *Old Bailey Sessions*, December 1701.

60 It is commonly imagined. Bernard de Mandeville, *The Fable of the Bees: Or, Private Vices, Publick Benefits* (London, 1714).

60 There was an alarming rise. See Valerie Fildes, 'Maternal Feelings Re-assessed: Child Abandonment and Neglect in London and Westminster 1550–1800' in Valerie Fildes, ed., *Women as*

Mothers in Pre-Industrial England, Essays in Memory of Dorothy McLaren (London, 1990).

61   I am not able to subsist. Ibid., p. 154.

61   This child was borne of unhappy. Ibid., p. 153.

61   Those who cannot be so hard-hearted. Defoe, *Augusta Triumphans.*

61   Poor, abandoned children. Fildes, op. cit.

3 Childhood

62   Children, when little. John Locke, *How to Bring Up Your Children, Being Some Thoughts on Education* (London, 1902).

62   to our extreme sorrow. Evelyn, *Diary*, 26 March 1664.

62   it was ye youngest. Ralph Josselin, *The Diary of Ralph Josselin 1616–1683* (London, 1976), 21 February 1647, p. 114.

62   our inexpressible grief. Evelyn, *Diary*, 27 January 1657–8.

62   This day a quarter past two. Quoted from Josselin, op. cit., 27 May 1650, p. 203.

63   the more frequent fornications. Gregory King, *Natural and Political Observations and Conclusions Upon the State of England* (London, 1936).

63   they have an extraordinary regard. Misson, op. cit.

63   and having made them ill. Locke, *How to Bring Up Your Children.*

63   Nor indeed should. Ibid.

64   For young children who by reason. Hannah Woolley, *The Gentlewoman's Companion; or, a Guide to the Female Sex: Containing*

Directions of Behaviour in All Places (London, 1682).

64   my son being cripled. Freke, op. cit.

64   If you happen to let the child. Jonathan Swift, *Directions to Servants* (London, 1745).

64   You ought to be of a gentle. Woolley, *The Gentlewoman's Companion.*

65   Take special care. Ibid.

65   The child has hardly. Locke, *How to Bring Up Your Children.*

65   Narrow breasts. Ibid.

65   A child is set longing. Ibid.

66   Miss is scarce. Mandeville, *The Fable of the Bees.*

66   sweet and clean. Woolley, *The Gentlewoman's Companion.*

66   as long as he is in coats. Locke, *How to Bring Up Your Children.*

66   But whatever advantage. Ibid.

66   breed their teeth. Ibid.

66   We English are often. Ibid.

66   I should think that a good. Ibid.

67   drinking too much wine. Woolley, *The Gentlewoman's Companion.*

67   drinks should be only small. Locke, *How to Bring Up Your Children.*

67   prevent the custom. Ibid.

67   But strawberries. Ibid.

67   after meals. Ibid.

67   Apples and pears. Ibid.

67   What will my dear. Ibid.

67   well-brought-up children. Saussure, op. cit.

67   Breed up your children. Woolley, *The Gentlewoman's Companion.*

67   I imagine every one. Locke, *How to Bring Up Your Children.*

68   In 1694 'J.G.'. See J.H. Plumb, 'The New World of Children in

Eighteenth-Century England',
Past and Present 67.

69 those children who have been
    most. Locke, *How to Bring Up Your
    Children*.

69 if the mind be curbed. Ibid.

69 Be loving and chearful. Woolley,
    The Gentlewoman's Companion.

69 The usual, lazy. Locke, *How to
    Bring Up Your Children*.

69 a base custom. Robert Campbell,
    The London Tradesman (London,
    1747).

69 be bred up in abhorrence. Locke,
    How to Bring Up Your Children.

70 was wont always. Ibid.

70 sure to keep them. Ibid.

70 by their flatteries. Ibid.

70 unbred or debauched. Ibid.

70 accustom them to civility. Ibid.

70 This teaches them betimes. Ibid.

70 A smooth pebble. Ibid.

70 If they have a top. Ibid.

70 I have known a young. Ibid.

71 Edward Tinker. *Old Bailey Sessions*,
    June 1698.

71 Robert Ingrum. *Old Bailey Sessions*,
    June 1698.

72 Henry Simpkins. *Old Bailey
    Sessions*, January 1697.

72 to love them with wisdom.
    Quoted in Stone, *The Family, Sex
    and Marriage in England*, p. 274.

72 to consult their own. Locke, *How
    to Bring Up Your Children*.

73 Children were now identified.
    Plumb, op. cit.

73 After an hour's. Samuel Pepys, *The
    Shorter Pepys* (London, 1990), 4
    July 1662.

73 In it there stood. Zacharias Conrad
    von Uffenbach, *London in 1710*
    (London, 1934).

74 Dear Nephew, You give your.

Lady Margaret Maria Verney, op.
cit. Ralph Palmer to M. Ralph
Verney, at Mrs Moreland's
Boarding School in Hackney with
a parcell, 27 January 1695.

74 I cannot but complain. Woolley,
    The Gentlewoman's Companion.

74 Hasten to school. Ibid.

75 Tomorrow I intend to carry my
    girle. Margaret M. Verney,
    *Memoirs of the Verney Family from the
    Restoration to the Revolution 1660 to
    1696* (London, 1899) p. 220.

76 I find you have a desire. Ibid., p.
    221.

76 How can you be content. Mary
    Astell, *A Serious Proposal to the
    Ladies for the Advancement of Their
    True and Greatest Interests*, Part 1
    (London, 1696).

76 habits of sloth. Quoted in Craig
    Rose, 'Evangelical Philanthropy
    and Anglican Revival: the Charity
    Schools of Augustan London,
    1698–1740', *London Journal*, vol.
    16, no. 1 (1991).

77 The children shall wear. Anon, *An
    Account of the Methods Whereby the
    Charity Schools Have Been Erected
    and Managed, and of the
    Encouragement Given to Them*
    (London, 1705).

77 wash'd and comb'd. Ibid.

77 knowledge and practice. Ibid.

77 the true spelling. Ibid.

77 to fit them for services. Ibid.

77 some to spinning of wool. Ibid.

78 by no means during Bartholomew.
    Ibid.

78 descended of very mean. Paul
    Lorrain, *The Ordinary of Newgate
    His Account of the Life, Birth, Death
    and Parentage of John Hall, Richard
    Low, Stephen Bunch, William Davis*

and Joseph Monifano, *Five Notorious Thieves and Housebreakers, etc* (London, 1707).

78 near the Horse-ferry. Ibid.

78 Why should such a metropolis. Defoe, *Augusta Triumphans.*

4 Disease

80 These gentlemen of the faculty. Brown, op. cit.

80 This is to certify. Quoted in E. Ashworth Underwood, ed., *A History of the Worshipful Society of Apothecaries of London*, vol.1, 1617–1815 (London, 1963).

82 When a sick man leaves all. Brown, op. cit.

82 The practice of physick in London. Anon, *The Necessity and Usefulness of the Dispensaries Lately Set Up by the College of Physicians in London for the Use of the Sick Poor* (London, 1702).

83 The College of Physicians, observing. Quoted in E. Ashworth Underwood, op. cit.

84 When any trade. Anon, *The Present Ill State of the Practice of Physick in this Nation Truly Represented, and Some Remedies Thereof Humbly Proposed to the Two Houses of Parliament by a Member of the College of Physicians* (London, 1702).

85 That the physicians might clear. Anon, *The Necessity and Usefulness.*

85 a vomit is 1s. 6d. Ibid.

85 they shall either of them. Ibid.

86 See a consult of 'em. Brown, op. cit.

86 And though they make no scruple. Anon, *The Present Ill State.*

86 An eminent London surgeon. See Lucinda McCray Beier, *Sufferers*

and Healers; *The Experience of Illness in Seventeenth-Century England* (London, 1987), pp. 51–96.

87 Upon this the operator. Ward, op. cit.

88 have just now heard. Lady Margaret Maria Verney, op. cit., Nancy Nicholas to Sir J.V., 21 November 1699, p. 51.

88 They are seldom free. Ward, op. cit.

88 the stone in the bladder. Evelyn, quoted in McCray Beier, op. cit., p. 148.

88 such exceeding torture. McCray Beier, op. cit., p. 149.

88 carried a stone as big. Ibid.

88 my poor aunt. Pepys, op. cit., 5 May 1665.

89 People are not competent. Anon, *The Necessity and Usefulness.*

89 save nineteen shillings. Gideon Harvey, *The Family Physician and the House Apothecary* (London, 1678).

89 The seed, which heats. William Salmon, *The Compleat English Physician: Or the Druggist's Shop Opened* (London, 1693).

90 On a little shelf. Ward, op. cit.

90 Within this place. Ibid.

90 The wainscot. Ibid.

90 Present Remedy after Misfortune. Advertisement in *The London Post With Intelligence Foreign and Domestic*, 22 April 1700.

91 business to cheat. Ward, op. cit.

91 Just as the squabble. Ibid

91 if you have twenty distempers. Ibid.

91 an excellent outward. Ibid.

93 unparalleled medicine. Ibid.

93 a pound of Suffolk. Ibid.

93 the most powerful. Ibid

93 it is also a most rare. Ibid.

93 This impudence. Ibid.

94 If the person you visit. Woolley, *The Gentlewoman's Companion*.

94 much discourageth and dejecteth. Ibid.

94 In Clerkenwell-Close, where the. Quoted in Ward, op. cit.

95 the outside is a perfect. Brown, op. cit.

95 Many inoffensive madmen. Saussure, op. cit.

95 I am perswaded, that the frequency. Evelyn, *Fumifugium: Or the Inconvenience of the Aer and Smoak of London Dissipated.* (London, 1661).

96 the brewers, diers, lime-burners. John Evelyn, ibid.

96 For is there under. Ibid.

98 London rats seem to. See Andrew B. Appleby, 'The Disappearance of Plague: a Continuing Puzzle', *Economic History Review*, 2nd series, 33 (1980).

98 Take a hard egg. W.M., op. cit.

98 Oftentimes children are extremely. John Pechey, *The Compleat Midwife's Practice Enlarged* (London, 1698).

99 For the falling-sickness. Hannah Woolley, *The Queen-like Closet; or, Rich Cabinet* (London, 1684).

99 The gout most commonly. Quoted in A.W. Sloan, *English Medicine in the Seventeenth Century* (Durham 1996), p. 55.

100 Take feverfew. Ibid., p. 147.

100 When a cold grows. Misson, op. cit.

101 About the end of April. Quoted in Kenneth F. Kiple, ed., *Plague, Pox and Pestilence* (London, 1997), p. 148.

101 seiz'd with the jayl-distemper. This was one John Cooper in John

Allen's *A Full and True Account of the Behaviour, Confessions, and Last Dying-Speeches of the Condemn'd Criminals, that Were Executed at Tyburn, on Friday the 24th May, 1700* (London, 1700).

102 Some of them having scabbed. Brown, op. cit.

102 Evelyn noted the propensity. Evelyn, *Fumifugium.*

102 For a consumption. Woolley, *The Queen-like Closet.*

103 Take sage, rue. G. Markham, *The English House-Wife, Containing the Inward and Outward Vertues Which Ought to Be in a Compleat Woman, etc* (London, 1664).

103 If you will keep. Woolley, *The Queen-like Closet.*

104 Take wormwood. Ibid.

104 pessaries of shorn. See Patricia Crawford, 'Attitudes to Menstruation' ... *Past and Present*, 91 (1981)

105 the mist of a cup. John Graunt, *Natural and Political Observations* (London, 1676) p. 34.

105 only *hated* persons. Ibid.

105 The patient is affected. Quoted from McCray Beier, op. cit., p. 87.

107 to my fresh hares foot. Pepys, op. cit., 21 January 1665.

107 I am sorry to find. Lady Margaret Maria Verney, op. cit., Margaret Adams, at Baddow Hall, to Sir J.V., 21 August 1697, p. 21.

5 Death

108 The searchers repair. Quoted in T.R. Forbes, 'By What Disease or Casualty: the Changing Face of Death in London', *Journal of Historical Medicine*, xxxi.

108 The beating of thy pulse. See
Clare Gittings, *Death, Burial and
the Individual in Early Modern
England* (London, 1984), p. 133.

108 in the midst of life. Service for the
burial of the dead in *The Book of
Common Prayer.*

109 fresh and immediate. See Ralph
Houlbrooke, ed., *Death, Ritual and
Bereavement* (London, 1989).

109 Our lives are very short. William
Sherlock, *A Practical Discourse
Concerning Death* (London, 1699).

109 We now call it death. Ibid.

109 lingering anxiety at the loss. See
Nigel Llewellyn, *The Art of Death,
Visual Culture in the English Death
Ritual c.1500–c.1800* (London,
1991).

111 Plague had been terrifying. See
Houlbrooke, *Death, Ritual and
Bereavement.*

111 When anyone dies. Quoted in
Forbes, op. cit.

112 If you shou'd, as I hope. Quoted in
Phillis Cunnington and Catherine
Lucas, *Costume for Births, Marriages
and Deaths* (London, 1981),
p. 161.

112 There is an act of Parliament.
Misson, op. cit.

112 After they have wash'd. Ibid.

113 The body being thus equipped.
Ibid.

113 I went to see the corpse. Evelyn,
Diary, 24 March 1682.

114 They let it lye. Misson, op. cit.

114 Come, you that are to be the
mourners. Quoted in Ashton,
Social Life, p. 47.

114 A little before the company.
Misson, op. cit.

115 Elizabeth Bird. *Old Bailey Sessions*,
15, 16 January, 1691.

115 for the encouragement. Quoted in
Ashton, *Social Life.*

115 there were distributed. Evelyn,
Diary, 16 March 1685.

115 Mr Pepys had been. Ibid., 26 May
1703.

116 These cloths. Misson, op. cit.

116 the parish has always. Ibid.

116 German Princess. Recounted in
Ashton, *Social Life*, p. 51.

116 Before they set out. Misson, op.
cit.

116 Everyone takes a sprig. Ibid.

117 Riots and robberies. Quoted in
Ashton, *Social Life.*

118 Every thing being ready. Misson,
op. cit.

118 By special clause. Evelyn, *Diary*,
12 February 1683.

118 The parish of St Martin-in-the-
Fields. See Forbes, op. cit.

119 How noisome the stench. Quoted
in Stone, *The Family, Sex and
Marriage in England*, p. 63.

119 a tun of red port. Misson, op. cit.

119 Such women in England. Ibid.

119 When John Dryden died. Quoted
in George Francis Papali, *Jacob
Tonson, Publisher: His Life and
Work (1656–1736)* (Auckland,
1968) p. 88.

120 Five pounds two shillings.
Lambeth Palace Library/Court of
Arches/ Personal Answers,
1699–1707.

120 very little was left. Earle, *The
Making of the English Middle Class*,
p. 319.

120 This is to give notice. Quoted in
Ashton, *Social Life*, p. 50.

121 You must know. Muralt, op. cit.

121 Had I been an Englishman.
Saussure, op. cit.

121 On Thursday last a maid servant.

The Post Boy, 12–15 February 1700.

122   On Monday a Welsh taylor. *The London Gazette*, 14–16 September 1699.

123   The corps of a person. *The London Post With Intelligence Foreign and Domestic*, 20–22 January 1701.

123   Yesterday morning a woman. Ibid., 6–9 September 1700.

123   On Tuesday last. *The London Gazette*, 5–7 December 1699.

6 *The Home*

124   When Sir Thomas Grosvenor. See Simon Jenkins, *The Selling of Mary Davies and Other Writings* (London, 1993).

124   New squares, and new streets. Daniel Defoe, *A Tour through the Whole Island of Great Britain*.

125   the middle sort of mankind. Ibid.

126   St James's in Westminster. Edward Hatton, *A New View of London* (London, 1708).

126   The citizens, nay the whole. Nicolas Barbon, *An Apology for the Builder or a Discourse Shewing the Cause and Effects of the Increase of Building* (London, 1685).

126   there are no more houses. Ibid.

127   New buildings. Ibid.

127   Houses are of more value. Ibid.

127   the inventor of this new method. Roger North quoted in Peter Thorold, *The London Rich* (London, 1999), p. 54

128   In Barbon's building. Lady Margaret Maria Verney, op. cit., 27 April 1704, p. 100.

128   Englishmen build their houses. Saussure, op. cit.

129   I think I have already. Ibid.

130   Smith Street. John Stow, *A Survey of the Cities of London and Westminster ... Brought Down from the Year 1633 ... to the Present Time by John Strype* (London, 1720).

130   I have taken lodgings. Lady Margaret Maria Verney, op. cit., 18 May 1700, p. 78.

131   I am now with. Ibid., 5 December 1700, p. 50.

131   When Elizabeth Bauer. GLRO/Consistory Court of London/Personal Answers Book/April 1695 – July 1703, DL/C/198.

131   The man's income. London. Appendix, Miscellaneous, *A View of London and Westminster; or, the Town Spy ... Containing an Account of the Customs ... of the People in the Several Most Noted Parishes. By a German Gentleman* (London, 1725).

132   took a house. GLRO/Consistory Court of London/Depositions/ February 1700/01 – January 1702/3, DL/C/247.

132   did quarrel. Ibid.

132   Madam, I may. Lady Margaret Maria Verney, op. cit., 24 October 1697, p. 22.

132   Sir John, I rit. Ibid., October 1697, p. 27.

133   My Aunt Adams. Ibid.

133   My mother continues. Ibid.

133   in company with a gentlewoman. GLRO/Depositions/January 1697/8 – March 1699/1700, DL/C/246.

133   When the above-mentioned Jane Leonard. GLRO/Depositions/ February 1700/01 – January 1702/3, DL/C/247.

134   Simon Betts. *Old Bailey Sessions*, February 1694.

134 It appeared, that. *Old Bailey Sessions*, May 1698.

134 When Thomas Plummer. GLRO/Depositions/January 1697/8 – March 1699/1700, DL/C/246.

134 There came a man. GLRO/Depositions/February 1700/01 – January 1702/03, DL/C/247.

135 Elisabeth Smith. Ibid.

135 a looking-glass. Pepys, op. cit., 16 December 1664.

136 Proceedings upon the petition. *Calendar of State Papers, Domestic Series, Of the Reign of William III. 1 January, 1699–31 March, 1700* (London, 1937).

137 lightsome stair-cases. Misson, op. cit.

137 set my plasterer. Pepys, op. cit., 5 August 1664.

137 Plastered ceilings. Guy Miege, *The New State of England under our Present Monarch, King William III* (London, 1701).

137 for so damp a country. Ibid.

137 This tradesman's genius. Campbell, op. cit.

138 When Martha Cole. GLRO/Personal Answers/April 1695 – July 1703, DL/C/198.

138 Foreign visitors noted. Saussure, op. cit.

138 Martha Cole had. Ibid.

138 Both Martha Cole. Ibid.

140 *Un sofa est une espèce.* Quoted in P. Thornton, *Seventeenth-Century Interior Decoration in England, France and Holland* (London and New Haven, 1978).

140 TheEnglish use no. Misson, op. cit.

140 The smell of the sulphur. Ibid.

140 When Elizabeth Bauer. GLRO/Personal Answers, DL/C/198.

141 if there happens. Miege, op. cit.

142 This night I begun. Pepys, op. cit., 15 December 1664.

142 Never let the candles. Jonathan Swift, *Directions to Servants* (London, 1745).

142 up betimes by the help. Pepys, op. cit., 14 July 1665.

142 In the afternoon. Von Uffenbach, op. cit.

143 To supply this city. Miege, op. cit.

143 his bath at the top. Pepys, op. cit., 29 May 1664.

143 The Duke and Duchess. Fiennes, op. cit., p. 100.

143 My wife being busy. Pepys, op. cit., 21 February 1665.

145 a closet that leads. Fiennes, op. cit.

145 The French nickname. The theory is propounded in Thornton, op. cit.

145 Never empty. Swift, *Directions to Servants*.

145 into a great heap. Pepys, op. cit., 20 October 1660.

146 went to Sir W. Batten. Ibid., 16 July 1663.

147 Last night, several bullies. *The London Post With Intelligence Foreign and Domestic*, 29–31 January 1701.

147 most in this depraved. Woolley, *The Gentlewoman's Companion*.

147 all things at the best times. Ibid.

147 And then rose and settled. Pepys, op. cit., 6 July 1662.

147 Be careful to manage. Woolley, *The Gentlewoman's Companion*.

147 Be careful to keep. Ibid.

147 the inconvenience that doth attend. Pepys, op. cit., 30 October 1661.

148 two servants now. Daniel Defoe, *Every-Body's Business Is Nobody's Business: or, Private Abuses, Publick Grievances* (London, 1725).

148 If you wash at home. Ibid.

148 Wash your plate. Woolley, *The Queen-like Closet.*

149 do not suffer any servant. Woolley, *The Gentlewoman's Companion.*

149 The amount of water. Saussure, op. cit.

149 Now Moll had whirl'd her mop. Swift, *A Description of the Morning* in *Gulliver's Travels*, p. 753.

149 dust and ordure. Evelyn, *Fumifugium.*

149 when you wash. Swift, *Directions to Servants.*

149 Observe due times. Woolley, *The Gentlewoman's Companion.*

149 This day the wench. Pepys, op. cit., 12 March 1660.

149 slept pretty well. Ibid., 6 October 1663.

150 I found my wife. Ibid., 16 January 1660.

150 All their linnen. Misson, op. cit.

150 Make a good strong ladder. Woolley, *The Gentlewoman's Companion.*

150 the clothes that are expos'd. Evelyn, *Fumifugium.*

150 forget not to darn. Woolley, *The Gentlewoman's Companion.*

150 the grand affairs. Swift, *Directions to Servants.*

150 In order to learn. Ibid.

151 When you step but. Ibid.

151 our sessions papers. Defoe, *Every-Body's Business Is Nobody's Business.*

151 constantly pilfering. Ibid.

151 The prosecutor declared. *Old Bailey Sessions*, January 1701.

151 It appeared, that Hays. *Old Bailey Sessions*, June 1698.

152 There are two societies. Misson, op. cit.

152 For insuring of houses. Miege, op. cit.

152 To supply the light. Ibid.

152 Our streets are so poorly. Defoe, *Augusta Triumphans.*

7 Fashion

153 The hangman arrested carrying the dead man's clothes was John Price in 1714.

153 English women are fond. Saussure, op. cit.

153 Tom Brown described the dazzling. Brown, op. cit.

153 women walk fast. Saussure, op. cit.

153 this is the case too. Ibid

153 How often do you go. Quoted in Ashton, *Social Life*, p. 90.

155 These gentlemen in English. Misson, op. cit.

155 the Englishmen dress. Ibid.

155 His glass is the oracle. Mary Astell, *An Essay in Defence of the Female Sex* (London, 1696).

155 There sits a beau. Brown, op. cit.

155 A very gaudy. Ward, op. cit.

155 strut and toss. Ibid.

156 Handsome apparel. Mandeville, *The Fable of the Bees.*

156 The women indeed. Miege, op. cit.

156 I have not learnt. Brown, op. cit.

156 and to my great sorrow. Pepys, op. cit., 31 October 1663.

157 my new silk camelott sute. Ibid., 1 June 1665.

157 Pride and luxury. Mandeville, *The Fable of the Bees.*

157 is impossible there should. Ibid.

157 The poorest labourer's wife. Ibid.

158 of the common profession. Brown, op. cit.

159 Without doubt there. Princess Anne to Sarah Churchill, quoted in David Green, *Queen Anne* (London, 1970), p. 70.

159 I heare Sir E.D. Lady Margaret Maria Verney, op. cit., Elizabeth Adams to Sir J.V., 4 November 1699.

160 The Earl of Bedford's. Quoted in Gladys Scott Thomson, *Life in a Noble Household 1641–1700* (London, 1937), p. 341.

161 Evelyn's lady. See Mary Evelyn, *Mundus Muliebris; or, The Lady's Dressing Room Unlock'd, and Her Toilette Spread. Together with the Fop-Dictionary, Compiled for the Use of the Fair Sex* (London, 1690).

161 Jonathan Hibbert's Bill. Quoted in Scott Thomson, op. cit., p. 343.

161 large and oriental. Mary Evelyn, op. cit.

161 garters adorned. Ibid.

161 diamond buckles. Ibid.

161 Dear Mr Verney. Lady Margaret Maria Verney, op. cit., Lady Fermanagh to Ralph Verney, 3 March 1704.

162 The Earl of Bedford's. Scott Thomson, op. cit., p. 342.

163 The Earl of Bedford. Ibid., p. 341.

163 perhaps a third part. Defoe, *The Complete English Tradesman.*

164 if he does not make a good show. Ibid.

164 begging of custom. Ward, op. cit.

164 driving from shop to shop. Mandeville, *The Fable of the Bees.*

165 She had patronised. Nathaniel Hooke, *An Account of the Conduct of the Dowager Duchess of Marlborough, from her first coming to court, to the year 1710* (London, 1742), pp. 222–4.

165 She had indulged to the full. See Henri and Barbara van der Zee, *William and Mary* (London, 1973), p. 380.

165 King William loved. Ibid., p. 381.

165 Her lingerie. Ibid., p. 380.

165 men's clothes. Von Uffenbach, op. cit.

165 My Dearest. Lady Margaret Maria Verney, op. cit., Catherine to Ralph Verney, 11 September 1709.

167 Silk velvet. See Earle, *The Making of the English Middle Class*, p. 286.

168 Bought of William Gostlin. Quote from Scott Thomson, op. cit., p. 337.

168 A lace-man. Campbell, op. cit.

169 a fine muslin cravat. Quote from Scott Thomson, op. cit., p. 339.

169 2 pair of fine muslin. Ibid.

169 Elizabeth, Duchess of. Quote from Diana de Marly, 'Some Aristocratic Clothing Accounts of the Restoration Period in England'. *Waffen und Kostumkünde*, vol. 1976, pp. 112–13.

170 Men's coats made of cloth. See Earle, *The Making of the English Middle Class*, p. 287.

170 It appeared that the prisoner came frequently. *Old Bailey Sessions*, June 1697.

170 It appeared that the prisoner took the head-dress. *Old Bailey Sessions*, February 1697.

170 It appeared there was nobody. *Old Bailey Sessions*, October 1699.

170 parcel of nimble-tongued. Ward, op. cit.

172 Now I, that am. Brown, op. cit.

172 A good wardrobe ... savings account. See Beverly Lemire, 'The Theft of Clothes and Popular Consumerism in Early Modern England', *Journal of Social History*, vol. 24, no. 2 (1990).

173 Isabella Dickens. *Old Bailey Sessions*, June 1698.

173 Judith Jones. *Old Bailey Sessions*, June 1698.

173 William Martin. *Old Bailey Sessions*, February 1697.

173 It appeared that the goods. *Old Bailey Sessions*, February 1697.

175 ten hats and ten hatbands. *Old Bailey Sessions*, October 1689 and January 1690.

175 a pick-pocket. Brown, op. cit.

175 Edward Short. *Old Bailey Sessions*, October 1699.

175 Thomas Giblet. *Old Bailey Sessions*, March 1703.

175 When John Matthews. Lorrain, *Accounts*.

175 Anne Hughes. *Old Bailey Sessions*, January 1690.

176 A highwayman. Mandeville, *Fable of the Bees*.

8 *Food and Drink*

177 The English eat. Misson, op. cit.

177 At six o'clock. See Dorothy Davis, *A History of Shopping* (London, 1966), p. 80.

177 For pleasure, or luxury. Miege, op. cit.

178 Nowhere can you see. Saussure, op. cit.

178 Besides these public. Ibid.

180 The 1st of May. Ibid.

180 the less time is lost. Miege, op. cit.

180 The generality of them. Ibid.

180 The English eat a great. Misson, op. cit.

180 English beef. Ibid.

180 I always heard. Ibid.

181 to feast as nobly. Ibid.

181 it is common practice ... to have. Ibid.

181 according to the number. Saussure, op. cit.

181 in extreme hot. Defoe, *Augusta Triumphans*.

181 Beef a-la-Mode. Woolley, *The Gentlewoman's Companion.*

181 Beef Carbonadoed. Ibid.

182 take a clean cloth. Ibid.

182 If it were not for this tyranny. Mandeville, *The Fable of the Bees.*

182 a supplement, or accessory. Saussure, op. cit.

182 To make boiled sallads. Woolley, *The Queen-like Closet.*

183 porcelaine or of the Holland. John Evelyn, *Acetaria; or a Discourse of Sallets* (London, 1699).

183 At each of the barber-surgeons. Original account books at the Worshipful Company of Barbers.

183 A leg of roast. Misson, op. cit.

183 my ordinary housekeeping. Pepys, op. cit., 23 December 1662.

183 So my poor wife. Ibid., 13 January 1663.

184 These original manuscripts are in the archives at the Worshipful Company of Barbers.

184 The statistician. King, op. cit.

184 In carving at your. Woolley, *The Gentlewoman's Companion.*

184 If chicken-broth. Ibid.

184 the dainty most approve. Ibid.

185 If you are left. Ibid.

185 baul out aloud. Ibid.

185 It is not civil. Ibid.

185 fill your mouth. Ibid.

185 gnaw no bones. Ibid.

185 Belching at table. Misson, op. cit.

185 it is uncivil. Woolley, *The Gentlewoman's Companion.*

185 when they have boil'd. Misson, op. cit.

185 If your potage. Woolley, *The Gentlewoman's Companion.*

186 dearer than any. Misson, op. cit.

186 Not only strumpets. Defoe, *Augusta Triumphans.*

186 Thomas West. Quoted in Ashton, *Social Life*, p. 191

186 Oyster pyes. Woolley, *The Gentlewoman's Companion.*

187 for fear of inflaming. Ibid.

187 very expedient for the expulsion. Ibid.

187 unstuff the pipes. Ibid.

187 the head, heart. Ibid.

187 Every family against. Misson, op. cit.

187 You must stew dried raisins. Saussure, op. cit.

187 The pudding is a dish. Misson, op. cit.

188 An Almond Pudding. Woolley, *The Gentlewoman's Companion.*

188 To Make the Orange Pudding. Woolley, *The Queen-like Closet.*

188 rot the teeth. Woolley, *The Gentlewoman's Companion.*

188 candying, conserving, and preserving. Ibid.

188 to be taken up at the point. Ibid.

188 The desert they. Misson, op. cit.

189 The conclusion of our dinner. Ward, op. cit.

189 when the meat. Woolley, *The Gentlewoman's Companion.*

189 A parcel of choice mangoes. *The London Post With Intelligence Foreign and Domestic*, 28–31 March 1701.

189 one or two dishes of cream. Woolley, *The Queen-like Closet.*

189 To Make a Whipt Sillibub. Ibid.

189 To Make Thick Cream. Ibid.

190 When everyone has done eating. Saussure, op. cit.

190 All our empty plates. Ward, op. cit.

190 To drink at table. Misson, op. cit.

190 I own, that to a stranger. Ibid.

191 As civility absolutely. Ibid.

191 The usual kick. Ibid.

191 This throwing down. Woolley, *The Gentlewoman's Companion.*

191 After these toasts. Saussure, op. cit.

191 Would you believe. Ibid.

192 It goes down gently. Miege, op. cit.

192 To make cock-ale. Rose M. Bradley, *The English Housewife in the Seventeenth and Eighteenth Centuries* (London, 1912), p. 238.

192 In the vaults under. *The London Post With Intelligence Foreign and Domestic*, 25–7 June 1700.

193 There is now published. *The Post Boy*, 29 January–1 February 1699.

193 Take one quart. Woolley, *The Queen-like Closet.*

193 But I must not omit. Miege, op. cit.

9 Coffee-houses, Clubs, Alehouses and Taverns

195 Debauch runs riot. Saussure, op. cit.

195 women suspected it. Anon, *The Women's Petition Against Coffee. Representing to Publick Consideration the Grand Inconveniences Accruing to their Sex from the Excessive Use of that Drying, Enfeebling Liquor. By a Well-willer* (London, 1674).

195 Never did men. Ibid.

195 excessive use of. Ibid.

195 nothing moist. Ibid.

195 lodges at home. Astell, *An Essay in Defence of the Female Sex.*

196 rather assists us. Anon, *The Men's Answer to the Women's Petition Against Coffee* (London, 1674).

196 You may well permit. Ibid.

196 the place where several. Brown, op. cit.

196 Some coffee-houses. Saussure, op. cit.

196 you are waited on. Ibid.

198 adjourned to the wits'. Ward, op. cit.

198 much company. Ibid.

198 well known to all gentlemen. Quoted in John and Linda Pelzer, 'The Coffee Houses of Augustan London', *History Today* (October 1982).

198 We squeezed through. Ward, op. cit.

199 Having sat all this while. Ibid.

200 The manner of managing. John Houghton, quoted in Stephen Inwood, *A History of London* (London, 1998), p. 350.

200 'tis a compleat system of knavery. Daniel Defoe, *The Anatomy of Exchange Alley; or, a System of Stockjobbing* (London, 1719).

200 Exchange Alley. Ibid.

200 that by daily resort. London, *Proclamations Relating to the City of London.*

201 On Tuesday the 17th. *The London Gazette*, 16–19 October 1699.

201 Tomorrow, the 10th. *The London Post With Intelligence Foreign and Domestic*, 9 April 1700.

201 On Thursday the 4th. *The Post Man and Historical Account*, 15–18 January 1700.

202 In the evening we drove. Von Uffenbach, op. cit.

202 All gentlemen, country. Miege, op. cit.

203 What attracts enormously. Saussure, op. cit.

204 A lady will offer. Ibid.

204 'Come,' continued my friend. Ward, op. cit.

205 'Money,' Ned Ward observed. Ibid.

205 They are men whose conditions. Ibid.

207 I knew two Middlesex sharpers. Brown, op. cit.

207 'Tis mere madness … to hazard ones fortune. Defoe, *Augusta Triumphans.*

207 To the charms of the coffee. Brown, op. cit.

207 Considering coffee. Ward, op. cit.

207 The coffee-house. Anon, *The Women's Petition.*

207 For when people. Ibid.

208 the thickness and dampness. Saussure, op. cit.

208 The economist Gregory King. King, op. cit.

208 At the 3 Golden. *The London Post With Intelligence Foreign and Domestic*, 17–20 January 1701.

209 Though no wine is made. Saussure, op. cit.

209 a great quantity of French. *The Post Man and Historical Account*, 18 March 1700.

209 the *Pool* frigate. Ibid.

210 Whereas many murders. London, *Proclamations Relating to the City of London.*

210 a tavern is a little. Brown, op. cit.

210 Thither sober knaves. Ibid.

211 He's acquainted. Ward, op. cit.

211 The clothes were left. *Old Bailey Sessions*, June 1698.

211 Lost on Thursday. *The Post Man and Historical Account*, September 1700.

211 On Friday night. *Account of the Barbarous Murther of Philip Parry, Esq, committed by Mr Thomas Bond, Near Covent Garden, on Friday night last, being the 15th March, 1700* (London, 1700).

213 Each jack-a-lanthorn. Ward, op. cit.

213 Time taking advantage. Ibid.

214 As we had been fellow. Ibid.

214 But who pray. Brown, op. cit.

215 little else to do. Ibid.

215 treats him. Ibid.

215 where it is very common. Misson, op. cit.

215 Generally four spits. Ibid.

215 the very women. Ibid.

215 They were a second time. *Old Bailey Sessions*, October 1699.

216 to shoot ourselves. Ward, op. cit.

216 old, mild, sweet-scented. Ibid.

216 They behaved themselves. Ibid.

10 Amusements

217 Anything that looks. Misson, op. cit.

217 monstrous cannibal giant. *The London Post With Intelligence Foreign and Domestic*, 5–7 February 1700.

217 At the corner of Hosier Lane. Quoted in Henry Morley, *Memoirs of Bartholomew Fair* (London, 1880), p. 254.

217 To be seen the next door. Ibid., p. 255.

219 idle, loose, vicious. London.

Appendix, Miscellaneous, *Proclamations Relating to the City of London.*

219 for interludes. Ibid.

219 At Mr Barnes's. *The Post Man and the Historical Account*, 15–17 August 1699.

219 flying coaches. Ward, op. cit.

219 The smell of roasting pig. See Ned Ward's description in *The London Spy*, p. 177.

219 for the noise and uproar. Saussure, op. cit.

220 The living alligator. *The Post Boy*, 7–9 September 1699.

220 At Painters Coffee-house. *The London Post With Intelligence Foreign and Domestic*, 8–11 November 1700.

220 Beyond these were a parcel. Ward, op. cit.

221 If two little boys. Misson, op. cit.

221 the lower populace. Saussure, op. cit.

221 The spectators sometimes. Ibid.

221 Would you believe. Ibid.

221 to watch the fights. Von Uffenbach, op. cit.

221 The place where the fight. Ibid.

222 had probably drunk. Ibid.

222 two years ago. Ibid.

222 When it is time. Ibid.

223 those who put their money. Ibid.

223 First a young ox. Ibid.

224 very troublesome and insolent. Muralt, op. cit.

224 In cold weather. Saussure, op. cit.

224 The English are very fond. Ibid.

224 men of quality. Misson, op. cit.

224 an enchanted island. Brown, op. cit.

224 The beau there is known. Ibid.

224 What are all their new plays. Ibid.

225 When the humour takes. Ibid.
225 a sort of plays. Roger North quote taken from the English National Opera programme for Henry Purcell's *The Fairy Queen*, 1997/8.
225 There was on Monday. *The Post Man and the Historical Account*, 4–6 July 1699.
225 This present Monday. *The London Post With Intelligence Foreign and Domestic*, 5–8 September 1701.
225 when the Court ladies. Ward, op. cit.
225 We could not possibly. Ibid.
226 very fine walks. Misson, op. cit.
226 Here we saw much to do. Brown, op. cit.
227 wooden rollers. Von Uffenbach, op. cit.
227 You cannot see anything more. Saussure, op. cit.
227 Scholars, scholars. Ward, op. cit.
228 one does not take it for a bridge. Von Uffenbach, op. cit.
228 With my wife. Pepys, op. cit., 29 May 1662.
229 Near it is a house. Von Uffenbach, op. cit.
229 This is the nearest medicinal. Ibid.
230 As soon as it began. Ibid.
230 These are to give notice. *The London Post With Intelligence Foreign and Domestic*, 25–7 April 1700.
230 do you neither good. Misson, op. cit.
230 holy days of Christmas. Miege, op. cit.
230 From Christmas-Day. Misson, op. cit.
230 a solemn day. Miege, op. cit.
231 where I thought. Ward, op. cit.

231 the morning was usher'd. *The London Gazette*, 13–15 February 1700.
233 Moreover no one. Von Uffenbach, op. cit.

11 The Working City.

234 John Coggs. See Max Beloff, 'A London Apprentice's Notebook 1703–5', *History*, xxvii.
235 'Tis very ordinary to give. Defoe, *The Great Law of Subordination Consider'd*.
236 An apprentice is a sort of slave. Misson, op. cit.
236 so far are they from being subjected. Defoe, *The Great Law of Subordination Consider'd*.
236 James Smith. Corporation of London Record Office, henceforth CLRO, Lord Mayor's Court, Equity, 1700–01, Box 87.
237 The case of Samuel Pearse. Lorrain, *Accounts.*
237 He must consider, he risks. Campbell, op. cit.
237 the beautiful little wench. Quoted in E.J. Burford, *Wits, Wenchers and Wantons* (London, 1990), p. 47.
237 Sarah Fifield was discharged. GLRO/ Middlesex County Records/Sessions Book 594–April 1702, p. 53.
237 any familiarity. Caleb Trenchfield, *The Father's Counsel to His Son, An Apprentice in London* (London, 1678).
237 An apprentice is never. Campbell, op. cit.
238 Edward Green was discharged. GRLO/Middlesex County Records/Sessions Book 525 – October 1695, p. 41.

238 John Knight, apprentice. Ibid, p. 48.

238 Elizabeth Barnes. GLRO/Middlesex County Records/Sessions Book 594 – April 1702, p. 49.

238 Whereas Simon Smith. CLRO, Sessions Book, SM67.

238 William Barrow. Lorrain, *Accounts.*

238 John Hart. Ibid.

239 When he was yet. Ibid.

239 Elizabeth Wigenton, a coat-maker. *Old Bailey Sessions,* January 1691.

239 Richard Tate. Ibid.

240 What news. Brown, op. cit.

241 ship bound from Barbadoes. *The London Post With Intelligence Foreign and Domestic*, 29 July 1700.

241 The collection. Ibid.,19–21 August 1700.

242 The likes of Sir Peter Vansittart. Vansittart was an immigrant from Danzig and worth £120,000. See Earle, *The Making of the English Middle Class,* p. 35.

242 endured sleepless nights. Pepys, op. cit., 30 January 1665.

243 Our banks are indeed. Daniel Defoe, *An Essay Upon Projects* (London, 1697).

243 There are those who tell. Defoe, *The Anatomy of Exchange Alley.*

244 Benjamin Jones, etc. Lorrain, *Accounts*, 28 January 1701.

245 Pattern-drawers. Campbell, op. cit.

245 The calico-printer. Ibid.

247 Nine out of ten. Ibid.

247 the ladies have not found. Ibid.

247 She is sister to the taylor. Ibid.

248 the spirit of writing. Ibid.

248 But their chief riches. Ibid.

250 the press is loaded. Ibid.

250 There is a fate. Ibid.

251 Women servants are now. Defoe, *Every-Body's Business Is Nobody's Business.*

252 Were her dress. Ibid.

252 No sooner had a country girl. Ibid.

252 If your lady forgets. Swift, *Directions to Servants.*

252 If you are employed. Ibid.

253 Another great abuse. Defoe, *Every-Body's Business Is Nobody's Business.*

253 according as he behaves himself. Swift, *Directions to Servants.*

253 If your master. Ibid.

253 When your master. Ibid.

253 Nothing calls for more redress. Defoe, *Every-Body's Business Is Nobody's Business.*

254 This morning, sending the boy. Pepys, op. cit., 18 April 1662.

254 Having from my wife. Ibid., 21 June 1662.

254 to the disturbance of the house. Ibid., 19 February 1665.

254 Yesterday Perry. Lady Margaret Maria Verney, op. cit., Sir J.V. to Wm Coleman, 18 March 1699.

255 Elizabeth Deacon. *Old Bailey Sessions,* February 1690.

255 Ann Harris. Lorrain, *Accounts.*

255 She said she never was guilty. Ibid.

255 Elizabeth Chivers. Ibid.

256 Elizabeth Price. Ibid.

12 The Poor

257 Seeing they have not work enough. Defoe, *The Great Law of Subordination Consider'd.*

257 In January 1700 the London. *The London Post With Intelligence Foreign and Domestic*, 9 January 1700/01.

257 a young crew. Ward, op. cit.

257 Give me not poverty. Quoted in William L. Payne, ed., *The Best of*

Defoe's Review, An Anthology (New York, 1951).

257 Eleanor Gravenoz. Lorrain, *Accounts*.

258 imployment of the poor. Thomas Firmin, *Some Proposals for the Imployment of the Poor, and for the Prevention of Idleness and the Consequence Thereof, Begging* (London, 1681).

258 The children of the poor. Ibid.

258 Is it not enough. Ibid.

260 taught to work. Ibid.

260 The estimated cost of a child. London, II, Civic and Municipal Institutions, Governors for the Poor, *An Account of the Corporation for the Poor of London; Shewing the Nature, Usefulness, and Management of the Work-House in Bishopsgate Street* (London, 1713).

260 if the poor are not taken into one side. Ibid.

260 vagabonds, sturdy beggars. Ibid.

260 and there being sick. Eleanor Gravenoz. Lorrain, *Accounts*.

260 Sir Josiah Child. Sir Josiah Child, *A New Discourse of Trade* (London, 1694).

261 leaving it to the care. Ibid.

261 shift the evil. Ibid.

261 Mary Raworth. CLRO, Sessions Book, SM67.

262 Ellinor Elliston. Quote from A.L. Beier and Roger Finlay, eds, *London 1500–1700: The Making of the Metropolis* (London, 1986) p. 256.

262 All should be set. Mandeville, *The Fable of the Bees.*

263 Joanna Garwood. GLRO/Depositions, DL/C/246.

263 among the craving beggars. Daniel Defoe, *Giving Alms No Charity, And Employing the Poor* (London, 1704).

263 Alms to the idle. Trenchfield, op. cit.

263 alms ill directed. Defoe, *Giving Alms No Charity.*

263 can live so well. Ibid.

263 Under a stop of trade. Defoe, *The Great Law of Subordination Consider'd.*

264 Want of consideration. Defoe, *An Essay Upon Projects.*

264 He envisaged a Pensions Office. Ibid.

264 so small a part of their earnings. Ibid.

13 Huguenots and Other Strangers

265 On a February day of gentle frost. See John Evelyn's *Diary*, 18 February 1700, in which he describes the weather.

265 Louis Goujon, silk weaver. The baptism is listed in the Huguenot Society of London, *The Registers of the French Church, Threadneedle Street, London*, vol. III, 1686–1714. Edited T.C. Colyer-Fergusson (Aberdeen, 1906).

265 canary's cheerful song. The Huguenots are said to have introduced the idea of keeping canaries in the home as company during the long hours spent at the loom, and also cut flowers – both novel concepts to the English.

265 so afflicted by the heat. Quoted in Robin D. Gwynn, *Minutes of the Consistory of the French Church of London, Threadneedle Street, 1679–1692* (London, 1994), 10 August 1687.

266 Pierre Laurent of Picardy. Ibid., 4 July 1688.

266 Martha Guisard. Hilary Reneu,

The Preface to the Second English Translation (1707) of Jean Claude's *Les Plaintes des Protestants Cruellement opprimées dans le Royaume de France*, reprinted in Edward Akber, ed., *The Torments of Protestant Slaves* (London, 1908) pp. 31–2.

268 honour their religion in their attire. Gwynn, *Minutes of the Consistory of the French Church of London*, 15 September 1689.

268 public feasting and dancing. Ibid., 8 February 1691.

268 reported that a Spitalfields constable. Ibid., 8 July 1688.

268 French frequenting taverns. Ibid., 29 April 1688.

269 Jean Boulay. Ibid., 7 October 1688.

269 Four quarrelsome young men. Ibid., 16 October 1687.

269 When Jean Faviere. Ibid., 21 August 1687.

269 When Jean Hebert enquired. Ibid., 7 October 1688.

269 And the widow of Jacques Benoit. Ibid., 22 March 1691.

269 Nicolas Hesse. Ibid., 13 November 1687.

269 Whereas when François Testu. Ibid., 9 June 1689.

270 as Tobie Le Maistre. Ibid., 25 January 1688.

270 The consistory came down heavily. Ibid., 18 December 1687.

270 Judith Godefroy. Ibid., 16 October 1692.

271 Others listed their occupations. The Huguenot Society of London, op. cit., and *The Registers of La Patente de Soho*, 1689–1782.

271 Addresses were given in French. Ibid.

271 John Larguier. Quote in Robin D. Gwynn, *Huguenot Heritage: The History and Contribution of the Huguenots in Britain* (London, 1985), p. 69.

274 Marguerite Morisset. Listed in the Huguenot Society of London, *Estats d'Assistance reglées par le comité aux Protestants François refugiés, 3 fevrier 1701*, ms. 15.

274 After dinner my wife. Pepys, op. cit., 14 October 1663.

275 The Jews of London. Misson, op. cit.

275 the Jews here are building. *The London Post With Intelligence Foreign and Domestic*, 19–21 August 1700.

275 From this amphibious. Daniel Defoe, *The True-Born Englishman: A Satyr* (London, 1700).

275 a subtil people. Child, op. cit.

275 a penurious people. Ibid.

276 they bring no estates. Ibid.

276 Mrs Lucy. Brown, op. cit.

276 So then, I find. Ibid.

277 African-born James. See James Albert Ukawsaw Gronniosaw, *A Narrative of the Most Remarkable Particulars in the Life of James Albert Ukawsaw Gronniosaw* (Bath, 1770), in which he describes his arrival in England and first impressions.

278 Foreign slaves. Chamberlayne, op. cit.

279 Upon the petition. Quoted in Folarin Shyllon, *Black People in Britain 1555–1833* (London, 1977), p. 19.

280 A Negro girl. *The Post Man and the Historical Account*, 27–9 June 1699.

280 A Negro named Quoshy. Ibid., 30 December–2 January 1700/01.

280 Whereas a Negro boy. *The London Gazette*, 7–9 December 1699.

280 A black boy, an Indian. Shyllon, op. cit., p. 11.

281 Mary Harris. *Old Bailey Sessions*, January 1701.

14 Religion and Superstition

282 No city in the spacious. Daniel Defoe, *The Reformation of Manners: A Satyr* (London, 1702).

282 The man in the pillory. For a vivid personal account of an experience in the pillory see *Mr William Fuller's Trip to Bridewell, With a True Account of His Barbarous Usage in the Pillory ... Written by His Own Hand* (London, 1703). Defoe almost certainly read it, which would have increased his dread of his own spell in the pillory.

283 You have butchered one king. Daniel Defoe, *The Shortest Way with the Dissenters: Or Proposals for the Establishment of the Church* (London, 1703).

283 huffed and bullied. Ibid.

283 If ever you will leave. Ibid.

283 If one severe law. Ibid.

283 Alas, the Church of England. Ibid.

284 the most sacred thing. Defoe, *The Reformation of Manners*.

284 To talk of five shillings. Defoe, *The Shortest Way with the Dissenters*.

285 no man can so far abandon. John Locke, *A Letter Concerning Toleration* (Oxford, 1691).

285 No private person. Ibid.

285 If a Roman Catholick. Ibid.

286 My wife and I to church. Pepys, op. cit., 30 March 1662.

286 an ordinary lazy sermon. Ibid., 8 November 1663.

286 a young simple fellow. Ibid., 17 April 1664.

288 February 8, 1700. Kensington. *Calendar of State Papers, Domestic Series, Of the Reign of William III*.

288 22 April, 1700. Ibid.

289 We hear several hundred. *The London Post With Intelligence Foreign and Domestic*, 1 May 1701.

289 The growth of popery. Daniel Defoe, *The Danger of the Protestant Religion Consider'd, From the Present Prospect of a Religious War in Europe* (London, 1701).

289 Popery and slavery. Ibid.

290 a solemn fast. John Evelyn, *Diary*, 2 August 1665.

290 This day was ordered a general Fast. Ibid., 10 October 1666.

291 Sarah Griffith. *A Full and True Account of the Discovering, Apprehending and Taking of a Notorious Witch* (London, 1704).

291 The young man and some companions. Ibid.

15 Prostitution and Vice

293 Some thousands of lewd persons. Quoted in Edward J. Bristow, *Vice and Vigilance, Purity Movements in Britain Since 1700* (Dublin, 1977), p. 23.

293 A maze of dark alleyways. The route is described in Gay, op. cit. Gay is said to have been a friend and client of Mrs Whybourn.

293 The image of the woman halting his progress and tugging at his sleeve comes from such a description by Daniel Defoe in *Some Considerations Upon Street-Walkers*.

293 tossing a corner. J. Orne (possibly

John Dunton) describes this gesture in soliciting in *The Nightwalker or Evening Rambles in Search of Lewd Women with the Conference Held with Them* (London, 1696).

293 Bible lying open. Burford, op. cit., p. 44.

295 parting with her maidenhead. See John Gwillim, *The London Bawd: With her Character and Life etc* (London, 1711).

295 sold to new customers. Ibid.

295 so conveniently plac'd. Ibid.

295 to see what youth and beauty. Ibid.

295 We'd take all opportunities. Ibid.

295 surgeons and apothecaries. Ibid.

295 She used to change her strumpets. Orne, op. cit.

296 by taking notice of all. Ibid.

296 the open and avowed practice of vice. *King William III's Royal Proclamation for Preventing and Punishing Immorality and Profaneness*, 1698. Quoted in Bristow, op. cit., pp. 12–13.

296 Blessed be God, tho' the debauchery. Orne, op. cit.

297 These are all cobweb laws. Daniel Defoe, *The Poor Man's Plea to All the Proclamations, Declarations, Acts of Parliament, etc, Which Have Been, Or Shall Be Made, or Publish'd, and Suppressing Immorality in the Nation* (London, 1698).

297 You are a whore and a hott. GLRO/DL/C/246 January 1697/8 – March 1699/1700.

297 Mary Dickenson … charged on oath. *Old Bailey Sessions.* January, 1701.

297 Some thousands of lewd. Quoted in Bristow, op. cit., p. 23.

300 under a greater necessity. Orne, op. cit.

300 A grave gentleman. Ward, op. cit.

300 Another accusation. Ibid.

300 We followed our noses. Ibid.

301 These are ladies. Ibid.

301 appear'd in a very. Paul Lorrain, *The Whole Life and Conversation, Birth, Parentage and Education of Deborah Churchill* (London, 1708).

301 did most frequent. Ibid.

302 The playhouse is their place. Quoted in Burford, op. cit., p. 15.

302 smuttiness of expression. Quoted in Bristow, op. cit., p. 27.

302 A girl quits a place. Defoe, *Augusta Triumphans.*

302 our streets will swarm. Ibid.

303 to clear the streets. Ibid.

303 poverty, and not knowing. Orne, op. cit.

303 made a perfect prey. Ibid.

303 when she grew up. Lorrain, *The Whole Life … Deborah Churchill.*

303 While we want servants. Defoe, *Augusta Triumphans.*

304 To His Grace the D——. Anodyne Tanner, *The Life of the Late Celebrated Mrs. Elizabeth Wisebourne, Vulgarly Call'd Mother Whybourn* (London, 1721).

304 instead of saying the French pox. Orne, op. cit.

304 Mary Hill. GLRO/DL/C/246 January 1697/8 – March 1699/1700.

304 Thomas Ashworth. GLRO/Consistory Court of London/Deposition Book/DL/C/247 February 1700/1 – January 1702/3.

305 your endeavours to suppress. Bernard de Mandeville, *A Modest Defence of Public Stews* (Los Angeles, 1973).

305 such privileges. Ibid.

305 turn the general stream. Ibid.
305 the maintenance of bastard. Ibid.
305 No woman that has been. Ibid.
305 There are a particular gang. Ward,
     op. cit.
305 That he knowing the time.
     Lorrain, Paul, *The Ordinary of
     Newgate his account of the
     behaviour, confession, and last speech
     of G. Skelthorpe ... executed ...
     23rd of March, 1708/9.* (London,
     1708/9)

16 Crime and Punishment

307 It is 20 January. This scene is
     reported in *The Post Man and the
     Historical Account*, 20 January
     1700.
307 A woman up for the common
     practice. Ibid.
308 A highwayman opts for. Ibid.
308 John Locke's philosophy. John
     Locke, *Two Treatises of Government*
     (London, 1821).
309 Thou instrument of fate. Daniel
     Defoe, *A Hymn to Tyburn* (London,
     1703).
309 a noisome vault. Anon (possibly
     Daniel Defoe), *The History of the
     Press-Yard Or, a Brief Account of the
     Customs and Occurrences that Are Put
     in Practice in that Ancient Repository
     of Living Bodies Called Newgate etc*
     (London, 1717).
309 a dismal prison. Captain
     Alexander Smith, *The Complete
     History of the Lives and Robberies of
     the Most Notorious Highwaymen,
     Footpads, Shoplifts and Cheats of
     Both Sexes, 1714–19* (London,
     1933), p. 153.
310 We do find that the prisoners.
     GLRO/Middlesex County

Records/Sessions Book 597, July
1702, pp. 42–5.
310 upon ragged blankets. John Hall,
     *Memoirs of the Right Villanous John
     Hall, the Late Famous Notorious
     Robber, Penn'd from His Mouth Some
     Time Before His Death* (London,
     1708).
311 who fetch their drink in tubs.
     Ibid.
311 lewd and common strumpets.
     Quoted in Donald Rumbelow,
     *The Triple Tree: Newgate, Tyburn
     and the Old Bailey* (London, 1982),
     p. 82.
311 he locked up a whore.
     GLRO/Middlesex County
     Records/Sessions Book 597, July
     1702, pp. 42–5.
311 Tom Merryman. Tom Merryman,
     *The Matchless Rogue: Or, an Account
     of the Contrivances, Cheats,
     Stratagems and Amours of Tom
     Merryman, Commonly Called
     Newgate Tom* (London, 1725).
311 It is an encouragement. Bernard
     de Mandeville, *An Enquiry into the
     Causes of the Frequent Executions at
     Tyburn; and a Proposal for Some
     Regulations Concerning Felons in
     Prison* (London, 1725).
313 are now known to be the
     sanctuaries. Anon, *Hanging Not
     Punishment Enough For Murtherers,
     Highwaymen, and House-Breakers*
     (London, 1812).
313 their most serious hours.
     Mandeville, *An Enquiry into the
     Causes of the Frequent Executions at
     Tyburn*.
313 In the boozing ken. Hall, op. cit.
313 there to be laid. Miege, op. cit.
314 persons of bad character. *Calendar
     of State Papers, Colonial Series:*

America and West Indies, 15 May 1696 – 31 October 1697 (London, 1904), pp. 540–43.

314 That night about 12. *The London Post*, 10–12 July 1700.

314 On Tuesday last. Ibid.

315 Six forraigners goeing for France. Lady Margaret Maria Verney, op. cit. Sir J.V. to Wm Coleman, 11 June 1698.

315 I could not be well enough. Ibid., 5 December 1699.

315 Executions are frequent. Saussure, op. cit.

315 frequent interruption. Anon, *Hanging Not Punishment Enough.*

316 if some remedy be not found. Ibid.

316 the great numbers of soldiers. Ibid.

316 that after so many thousands. Ibid.

316 they have ruined several. Ibid.

316 With one hand. De Saussure, op. cit.

316 Here lies Du Vall. Quote from Captain Alexander Smith, op. cit.

317 If a person is robbed. De Saussure, op. cit.

317 meet any well-dressed. Ibid.

317 Whereas, on yesterday morning. *The London Post With Intelligence Foreign and Domestic*, 3 September 1700.

317 On Sunday and Monday. *The Post Man and the Historical Account*, 11 April 1700.

317 Elizabeth Brown, alias Latham. *Old Bailey Sessions*, October 1689.

318 I am told the gentlemen of Hackney. *The London Post With Intelligence Foreign and Domestic*, 9 November 1700.

319 the decoyed fool. Quote from Captain Alexander Smith, op. cit.

319 Moll Hawkins. Ibid.

319 Nann Holland. Ibid.

319 pickpockets are legion. Saussure, op. cit.

320 The examples of Newgate and criminal cant in these pages are quoted from Captain Alexander Smith, op. cit.

320 So that one would take. Hall, op. cit.

321 He that is to be hanged. Misson, op. cit.

321 a particular habit. Henry Fielding, *An Enquiry into the Causes of the Late Increase of Robbers With Some Proposals for Remedying this Growing Evil, etc* (London, 1751).

321 Tho' these criminal proceedings. Muralt, op. cit.

322 speedily and sincerely. Anon (probably Paul Lorrain), *A Select and Impartial Account of the lives, behaviour, and dying-words of the most remarkable Convicts from the year 1700* (London, 1745).

323 to my unspeakable grief. Paul Lorrain, *The Ordinary of Newgate, His Account of the Behaviour, Confessions, and Dying-Words of Captain William Kidd, and Other Pirates, that Were Executed at the Execution Dock in Wapping, on Friday May 23, 1701* (London, 1701).

324 those devouring and destroying. Francis Jackson (alias Dixie), *Jackson's Recantation; or, the Life and Death of the Notorious Highwayman now Hanging in Chains at Hampstead* (London, 1674).

324 His life of late. John Allen, *A full and true account, of the behaviour, confessions, and last dying-speeches of the condemn'd criminals, that were*

executed at Tyburn, on Friday, the 24th May, 1700 (London, 1700).

324 The very morning before they were executed. Anon (probably Paul Lorrain), *A Select and Impartial Account of the Lives, Behaviour, and Dying-Words of the Most Remarkable Convicts, from the Year 1700* (2nd edition, London, 1745).

325 You would, perhaps. Muralt, op. cit.

325 these rascals. De Saussure, op. cit.

325 either drinking madly. Mandeville, *An Enquiry into the Causes of the Frequent Executions at Tyburn.*

326 The courage that strong liquors. Ibid.

327 more a holiday. Fielding, op. cit.

327 that would be more dreadful. Ibid.

327 most sturdy. Mandeville, *An Enquiry into the Causes of the Frequent Executions at Tyburn.*

327 so great a crowd. *The London Post With Intelligence Foreign and Domestic*, 19–22 July 1701.

328 The chaplain who accompanies. De Saussure, op. cit.

328 putting them into lots. Hall, op. cit.

328 The bodies and clothes. De Saussure, op. cit.

328 The hangman does not. Misson, op. cit.

329 The English are a people who laugh. Ibid.

329 it is thought that the taking. De Saussure, op. cit.

329 There is a stomach-churning. See Hall, op. cit.

329 the people who do not like the bodies. De Saussure, op. cit.

329 blows are given. Ibid.

330 The hangman's Christmas box. The accounts may be seen in manuscript in the archives of the Worshipful Company of Barbers.

330 Sensible of very great pain. Quoted in Rumbelow, op. cit., p. 183.

332 so terrified at the dismal sight. *The London Post With Intelligence Foreign and Domestic*, 19–22 July 1700.

332 a young woman. Quoted in Gittings, op. cit., p. 68.

Index